THE U.S.-MEXICO TRANSBORDER REGION

EDITED BY

CARLOS G. VÉLEZ-IBÁÑEZ
AND JOSIAH HEYMAN

THE U.S.-MEXICO TRANSBORDER REGION

Cultural Dynamics and Historical Interactions

THE UNIVERSITY OF
ARIZONA PRESS
TUCSON

The University of Arizona Press
www.uapress.arizona.edu

Printed in the United States of America

ISBN-13: 978-0-8165-3626-9 (cloth)
ISBN-13: 978-0-8165-3515-6 (paper)

Cover design by Leigh McDonald
Cover art: *Borrada* by Ana Teresa Fernandez; courtesy of the artist and Gallery Wendi Norris, San Francisco

Publication was made possible in part by funding from the Endowed Motorola Presidential Professorship in Neighborhood Revitalization, School of Transborder Studies, Arizona State University, and from the Endowed Professorship in Border Trade Issues, University of Texas at El Paso.

Library of Congress Cataloging-in-Publication Data
Names: Vélez-Ibáñez, Carlos G., 1936– editor. | Heyman, Josiah McC. (Josiah McConnell), 1958– editor.
Title: The U.S.-Mexico transborder region : cultural dynamics and historical interactions / edited by Carlos G. Vélez-Ibáñez and Josiah Heyman.
Description: Tucson : University of Arizona Press, 2017. | Includes bibliographical references and index.
Identifiers: LCCN 2016046796 | ISBN 9780816536269 (cloth : alk. paper) | ISBN 9780816535156 (pbk. : alk. paper)
Subjects: LCSH: Mexican-American Border Region. | LCGFT: Essays.
Classification: LCC F787 .U67 2017 | DDC 972/.1—dc23 LC record available at https://lccn.loc.gov/2016046796

♾ This paper meets the requirements of ANSI/NISO Z39.48-1992 (Permanence of Paper).

CONTENTS

THE U.S.-MEXICO TRANSBORDER REGION

To Glenn White
with deepest respect
and affection
8/27/19
[illegible signature]

INTRODUCTION

JOSIAH HEYMAN

THIS BOOK CENTERS on the Southwest North America (SWNA) region, comprised of northern Mexico and the southwest United States, although we sometimes expand our geographic range (e.g., to consider broad patterns of immigration policy). We are grounded in place but speak to important and wide-ranging issues. The border zone stimulates us to think about how people bump against each other, interact, exchange, cooperate, dominate, combine, and innovate. Carlos Vélez-Ibáñez (1996, 2010) has envisioned this region as combining diverse and unequal groups, in dynamic motion, for thousands of years. This historical interaction involves conflicts, resistance, slanting, displacements, and persistence. The U.S.-Mexico border is only the most recent, if massively unequal and powerful, manifestation of this history. Vélez-Ibáñez emphasizes dynamic motion around and across the border, its "transborder" quality, precisely to combine a critical awareness of inequality with a questioning perspective on centralized claims to bounded simplicity and perfection. The other authors share this vision, and indeed, this volume is a tribute to Vélez-Ibáñez's profound work.

Scholarship about the border region typically began by reproducing the arbitrary national boundary between the United States and Mexico. The southwest United States has long been an object of interest to cultural anthropologists, ethnohistorians, archeologists, and others, but with some exceptions, they truncated their inquiries at the modern border, which made little sense for archaeology and ethnohistory and failed to cover fully connections and flows across the contemporary border. Northern Mexico, in turn, was orphaned between the distinctive Mesoamerican culture region to the south and the artificially truncated Unitedstatesian Southwest. Of course, exceptions can be found, such as Edward Spicer's (1962) impressive (if factually dated) synthesis *Cycles of Conquest: The Impact of Spain, Mexico, and the United States on the Indians of the Southwest, 1533–1960*, which reached across the modern border to address political and ideological power projects. But generally, the culture region approach was static and descriptive and reproduced modern nationalistic claims, in which people had natural "places" and were problematic outsiders when they moved and exchanged (e.g., the acculturation approach, often applied to Mexican-origin people in the United States, and likewise the Mexican concern with the loss of national language and culture by its northern borderlanders).

The U.S.-Mexico border has been an important site in anthropology's break with static, bounded, and localistic notions of culture. An exemplary work, Renato Rosaldo's *Culture & Truth: The Remaking of Social Analysis*, used the U.S.-Mexico border together with his principal field site, the Philippines, to critique how we assume fixed societies and cultures and separate ethnographer from ethnographee. Borders came to represent conceptual innovations within anthropology and other intellectual fields. As a result, the border discourse became "unplaced," losing its roots in regional historical formations and sociocultural processes. This is not just a secondary concern for regional specialization. The unmooring of border theory from its original critical attention to U.S.-Mexico movements and relations meant that it lost touch with ecology, materiality, long historical time (change was seen as postmodern), power relations, and contestation, and above all, massive and profound inequalities.

In parallel with the emergence of conceptual border theory, indeed somewhat earlier, Eric Wolf (1982) rethought anthropology as the dynamic unfolding of power relations across historical time. In the U.S.-Mexico border region, this deeply influenced Vélez-Ibáñez (1996), converging with his own mobile experience as a borderlander. He synthesized a place-based but theory-building perspective on SWNA, identifying pathways of connection and change that cut across conventional borders on the ground and in scholarly frameworks. This transborder perspective attends to complex and fluid cultural and linguistic processes, going beyond the modernist anthropological vision of one people with one culture and one language. The perspective is social as well as cultural, recognizing how vertical relations of power put life projects at risk and how people cope through horizontal bonds of mutual trust and shared knowledge. It attends to regional human-environmental dimensions, economy, and politics, both in terms of ideas and material practices. Also, the Vélez-Ibáñez tradition—again, deeply responsive to the region—brings together scholarly with engaged and applied anthropology, arguing that from community engagement comes important concepts and ethnographic relationships and knowledge (e.g., Vélez-Ibáñez and Greenberg 1992). In the corpus of his life's work, Vélez-Ibáñez brought the term *border* back from conceptual plaything to speak to complicated, often-harsh lived regional experiences, while always characterized by conceptual creativity. This synthesis is characteristic of all that is best in anthropology.

The book's first section speaks to how the SWNA informs the general concerns of anthropology and other social sciences, from methodology to social theory. In "Continuity and Contiguity of the Southwest North American Region: The Dynamics of a Common Political Ecology," Vélez-Ibáñez develops the historical, dynamic approach described above. Josiah Heyman follows by proposing that relationships that combine unequal and differentiated parts, dramatically displayed at borders, contributes to social theory as a whole. Margaret Dorsey and Miguel Díaz-Barriga critically examine the naturalized assumptions of nation-state sovereignty at borders, looking at their absolutist assumptions, imposed materializations, and regional resistance to them. Alejandro Lugo provides perceptive comments on this section, making the crucial point that border theory that is grounded in the region at the same time profoundly informs anthropology as a whole.

Building on these theoretical essays, the following chapters center on language. Jane Hill demonstrates that dynamic social and cultural movement, as inferred from linguistics and archeology, has characterized this region for millennia. Vélez-Ibáñez brings this history to the colonial period, examining Spanish-language imperialism over indigenous languages, noticing identities and sentiments subtly encoded in the documents. Heyman and Amado Alarcón move to the contemporary era, in which English and Spanish are institutionalized in nation-states, but attend to the transborder economy where processes of uneven and combined development often require bilingual brokerage. The distinguished border theorist and ethnographer Robert R. Álvarez provides comments.

Throughout the book, power relations, struggles, and political formations are fundamental, but the next section particularly concentrates on them. Anna Ochoa O'Leary provides an important case study of the transborder concept, showing how "householding" bonds of solidarity cut across and in some cases defy state borders and immigration laws. James Greenberg and Luminița Anda Mandache take note of divisive and impoverishing forces, examining partially contradictory neoliberal trends: liberalization of capital and commodities together with border and immigration enforcement escalation. Ruth Gomberg-Muñoz shows how U.S. immigration policies concentrated disproportionately on Mexican-origin people throughout the history of the last century but harshly intensified recently. Luis Plascencia explores the same point, meticulously demonstrating how U.S. legal interpretations reveal enhanced state power and racialized Mexican identifications. Álvarez synthesizes the important issues raised in this section.

Nationalistic and xenophobic politics imagine space as if it was a sheet of paper drawn with clear lines. Yet space and time are constantly flowing material processes, giving lie to abstracted political claims. Lucero Radonic and Thomas Sheridan examine the history of water in this arid region, subject to political claims and infrastructural rearrangements, yet always insufficient for top-down projects. Looked at from the enduring perspective of regional indigenous peoples, we come to understand that water and climate are far grander than human schemes. Kathleen Staudt exposes the workings of neoliberalism, parallel to Greenberg and Mandache, protecting a powerful transnational corporate polluter from accountability to a politically and socially marginal community. Sarah Horton examines how immigrant workers, especially farmworkers, have their Social Security and other tax payments and savings stolen under the cover of legal arrangements in the United States and Mexico, resulting in their impoverishment in old age. Guillermina Gina Núñez-Mchiri, Diana Riviera, and Corina Marrufo look at intersecting risks that bring about food insecurity in colonias, informal settlements in the U.S. borderlands, and also identify the bonds of mutual solidarity that help people cope with food shortage. Insightful comments are offered by the distinguished migration scholar Judith Freidenberg.

It is worth noting the challenge that this book faces in combining work in Mexico and the United States, despite its overall transborder orientation. First, the geopolitical border currently creates relatively differentiated geographic spaces of social and cultural life, although there are also important crossings and combinations. Any recent ethnographic site will require contextualization within a national economy and polity, retaining, however, strong awareness of transborder relations and processes. Our book has work from both sides of the border and cutting across the border, but more of it is from north of the border. Second, research and writing still tends to be done in national venues, languages, and academic systems, despite the obvious limitations entailed. We originally came together in Albuquerque, New Mexico, under the auspices of an organization based in the United States, the Society for Applied Anthropology, with mostly U.S.-based attendees.[1] We admit our challenge escaping the confines of the nation-state.

An important theme of this book is the ramifications of inequality, particularly within neoliberalism, for human agency and well-being, as Freidenberg points out. Radonic and Sheridan, O'Leary, Horton, Staudt, and Núñez-Mchiri, et al., show the consequences for the relatively powerless on both sides of the border of the dominating processes delineated by Gomberg-Muñoz, Plascencia, Dorsey and Díaz-Barriga, and Greenberg and Mandache, and more broadly Heyman and Vélez-Ibáñez. Yet creative responses are seen widely in these case studies also. All anthropologists, and especially applied and engaged anthropologists, are influenced by the political struggles and agendas of the dominant societies surrounding us, and we take pride in speaking out forthrightly about racism, xenophobia, strengthened state coercion, neoliberal policies, border-crossing capitalism (including criminal capitalism), and widening inequalities.

The U.S.-Mexico border region is large in population, it is a focus of economics, politics, and ideology, and it has given rise to interesting cultural expressions. It deserves our attention. Yet we propose that this book, and the individual chapters of which it is comprised, holds importance beyond the region. The book demonstrates, for anthropology as a whole, how we can develop concepts based on deep engagement with place and, relatedly, how we can understand place as unfolding over historical time through the interplay of differentiated peoples and ecologies. It demonstrates how a community of scholars goes about doing those place-understanding and conceptualizing tasks. And it is a demonstration that scholarly engagement with place can bring engagement with and for the peoples of that place. All the chapters share a core orientation to SWNA and its wider continental mutations as a complex web of unequal power, within which people struggle to live decent lives and fulfill their dreams, "an impossible living in a transborder world," as expressed memorably by Vélez-Ibáñez (2010).

NOTE

1. That organization has international aspirations and merits recognition for activities that do cross borders (e.g., the joint Mexico-U.S. issue of *Practicing Anthropology* edited by Friedenberg and Durand [2016]).

REFERENCES

Freidenberg, Judith, and Jorge Durand, eds. 2016. "How Do We Talk About Migration? Voices from the United States and Mexico." Edited issue of *Practicing Anthropology* 38(1): 3–57.

Rosaldo, Renato. 1989. *Culture & Truth: The Remaking of Social Analysis*. Boston: Beacon Press.

Spicer, Edward H. 1962. *Cycles of Conquest: The Impact of Spain, Mexico, and the United States on the Indians of the Southwest, 1533–1960*. Tucson: University of Arizona Press.

Vélez-Ibañez, Carlos G. 1996. *Border Visions: Mexican Cultures of the Southwest United States*. Tucson: University of Arizona Press.

———. 2010. *An Impossible Living in a Transborder World: Culture, Confianza, and Economy of Mexican-Origin Populations*. Tucson: University of Arizona Press.

Vélez-Ibáñez, Carlos G., and James B. Greenberg. 1992. "Formation and Transformation of Funds of Knowledge Among U.S.-Mexican Households." *Anthropology & Education Quarterly* 23:313–35.

Wolf, Eric R. 1982. *Europe and the People Without History*. Berkeley: University of California Press.

PART I

TRANSBORDER PROCESSES AND SITES

Theoretical and Methodological Innovations

1

CONTINUITY AND CONTIGUITY OF THE SOUTHWEST NORTH AMERICAN REGION

The Dynamics of a Common Political Ecology

CARLOS G. VÉLEZ-IBÁÑEZ

BIFURCATION: THE BRITTLE BORDER AND TRANSBORDER DYNAMICS OF THE REGION, CONTINUITIES, AND ASYMMETRIES OF THE SOUTHWEST NORTH AMERICAN REGION

THE BIFURCATION VIA the Mexican-American War of what I will term the "Southwest North American (SWNA) region"—a land mass larger than Germany, Italy, Spain, and Great Britain in circumference—dictated the imposition of the American capitalist narrative and its industrial mode of production. This consisted of processes of rapid urbanization, insertion of industrial forms of agriculture and corporate cattle raising, and the implementation of a transborder organization of mining, all coupled to a transcontinental and transborder railway system. It is at this early juncture of the post–Civil War United States that the interconnectivity and interdependence of transborder production and labor were initiated between the United States and Mexico. Nevertheless, these processes and bifurcation split a common regional ecology.

In the present, what I have termed the SWNA region (Vélez-Ibáñez 2010, 2, 5, 182) excludes Mesoamerica, which is roughly central Mexico and parts of Central America south from southern Sinaloa west to Leon, Guanajuato, and including Tampico, Tamaulipas. Therefore, Southwest North America in the present would include five U.S. states and six northern Mexican states, but more importantly, it shares a common ecology of deserts, valleys, rivers, mountain ranges, and flora and fauna. As a region it is coupled to an interdependent political economy albeit asymmetrical cultural populations (as elaborated in chapter 2), including indigenous populations as well as the offspring of European populations variously known as Españoles Mexicanos during the colonial era and Mexicanos during the national era and their historical offspring and, more recently, English-speaking populations made up of various penetrating and immigrant nationalities. With the imposition of English-speaking populations as the aftermath of the Mexican-American War to the present, and depending on which part of the region of reference, the SWNA region is an ecologically unique region that has given rise to diverse and complex modes of production and economy from the pre-Hispanic period to the present. Because of the bifurcation of the political line, the region after its establishment will be regarded as the "northern and southern regions" of the larger entity, which will be discussed more broadly. Such bifurcation created an important contradiction: first, it split the region into two seemingly separate ecologies when they are one; and second, it created two nations glued by nineteenth-century industrial capitalism and its present post-industrial version in the twenty-first century.

As I have said elsewhere (Vélez-Ibáñez 1996), after the Mexican-American War the economic structure of industrial capitalism penetrated both sides of the new border and created labor-intensive extractive modes of production and their accompanying urbanization and worker migration south to north and north to south both within each nation-state and between nation-states. This was the initiation of an integrated but asymmetrical regional political economy that in reality did not pay a great deal of attention to the political creation of the borderline but rather seemingly put their common ecology out of sight and out of mind. In the Sonora/Arizona area prior to 1882, Sonora had no permanent settlement in the area of the border so that "border settlements in Sonora developed as a direct consequence of economic exchange with the United States [and] new towns, such as Nogales, Sonora and Nogales, Arizona appeared along the once unpopulated border" (Tinker Salas 1992, 437). Copper mines in both Arizona and Sonora were owned and operated by Americans such as Colonel (self-promoted) William C. Green who owned the Cananea Consolidated Copper Company in the late nineteenth and early twentieth century.[1] Heyman (1991, 7) describes so well the process of the establishment of transborder copper mining from 1886 on: "Gigantic copper mines—Cananea and Pilares de Nacozari—were installed along with their associated complexes of mills and smelters, which provided thousands of wage-paying jobs. Railroads were built south through the vast desert expanses, and commerce turned to U.S. sources." The Greene Consolidated Copper Company owned over 10,000 acres in the Cananea Mountains of the then "free zone" of northern Sonora, twenty miles south of the Arizona border, and held another

486,000 acres of timber and grazing lands, leased by Greene's Cananea Cattle Company (Stevens and Weed 1910, 747–48).

Almost simultaneously, the copper mines of Arizona, basically owned by Phelps Dodge and others, as well as Sonoran mines controlled by Colonel Greene and later the Anaconda company (Cananea) and Phelps Dodge (Pilares de Nacozari) became a north to south copper belt of mineral extraction and milling and occupied very similar ecological environments interconnected by rail and capital. Labor movement in both directions became normative, and industrial forms of union organizing was extensive. When not suppressed by a combination of transborder police and military and the use of extralegal methods, transborder unions had a profound impact on wages, but this was differentially applied (Stevens and Weed 1910; Weber 2016). Mexicans born either in the United States or in Mexico could not join craft unions and were subjected to what was termed the lower "Mexican rate" in comparison to the higher laborer's rate for the same job (Stevens and Weed 1910).

The spread of American industrial agriculture in the remnants of the Mexican Republic by such companies as Anderson and Clayton in Sonora and especially Cuidad Obregón and the International Company of Mexico of Chihuahua was made possible particularly in Sonora by the Mexican railroad built by the Atchison, Topeka and Santa Fe Railway with mostly Chinese labor to link Guaymas to the Arizona border in the north. Thus in Sonora alone, by 1902, $37.5 million was invested in mining and agriculture, with social transformations mirroring those in Arizona during the same period because of intense capital formation (Tinker Salas 1992, 434).

King Copper and King Agriculture induced a viable labor force in the southern part of the SWNA region (to be developed in the next section) to migrate to its northern part as part of this important dynamic. However, as Tinker Salas (2007) describes, the Americanization of copper-created towns such as Cananea, Sonora, to serve especially American miners and engineers meant that for Sonora: "American culture dominated life in this booming Sonoran town. Cananea's newspapers served a bilingual readership, commonly publishing articles and advertisements in both English and Spanish. Stores sold the latest American products, including California wines, Milwaukee beer, Levi Strauss pants, and Stetson hats" (128). At the advent of the Mexican Revolution, American individuals and companies owned 78 percent of the mine production and its lands; 58 percent of the oil production (the rest divided among mostly British and other foreign investors) and ownership of the land and subsoil; 68 percent of plastic factories; 67 percent of railroad companies; and 72 percent of all other companies, including retail stores, hotels, theaters, and soap and textile factors (González Ramírez 1986, 679).

Such penetration during the Porfiriato Regime (1876–1880 and 1884–1910) had few political boundaries. The heavy dependence on irrigation, especially for cotton, induced the founding of a series of hydraulically oriented companies. In the Valley of Mexicali, the Colorado River Land Company was founded in 1901 by Harrison Gray Otis, publisher of the *Los Angeles Times*; his son-in-law, Harry Chandler, who was later publisher of the *Times*; and William Randolph Hearst, owner of a chain of twenty-eight newspapers (Garduño 2004, 24–25). By 1904, through their Mexican intermediaries, they were able to amass four hundred thousand hectares of the Valley of Mexicali to take advantage of the Alamo Canal. The canal had been developed by the California Development Company to divert Colorado River water to the Imperial Valley: the canal was constructed near Yuma then crossed into Mexico through the Rancho de Algodones and ran eighty kilometers to the west through Mexican territory to finally end in the United States where Calexico is now. The Colorado River Land Company by 1912 had been named "the largest cotton ranch in the world," having taken advantage of the transborder canal with its diverted Colorado River waters (Garduño 2004, 25; my translation). After the Mexican Revolution and with the active political activities of the *agraristas* (rural labor and land organizers), the Land Company's huge holdings were turned into ejidos, colonias, and small landholdings by 1939 with the advent of the Cárdenas presidency.

Bifurcated by imposed borders and the establishment of what I would suggest is at best and always has been a brittle border, what I have termed "the Southwest North American region" was cross-cut by subecologies, economy, migrations, interests, institutions, and the creations of cross-cutting kinship, multilayered cultural phenomena, and material expressions within which are contained the actual manifestations of contending and integrating cultural dynamics. In spite of such bifurcation, in a contradictory manner the region becomes even more closely associated economically especially during the Porfiriato, which made a policy of inviting unfettered foreign investment but was upended by the Mexican Revolution.

The Mexican Revolution did establish national sovereignty over what had been the foreign playground for profit in oil and land by nationalizing the former and protecting, especially, coastal land from foreign ownership. It established a series of protective tariffs designed to stimulate Mexican industry, particularly in metals, industrial production, and agriculture, together with large land distributions to poor peasants over a period of forty years until World War II, which furthered an intensive reintegration of American-owned capital ventures into the border region.

Two main labor and economic processes furthered this integration: the Bracero program between 1942 and 1964 (with some exceptions for large growers until 1968),[2] which contracted more than 4.2 million Mexican workers for agriculture, and the maquiladora assembly plants, which were established in 1965 along the two-thousand-mile-long border and played an important role in taking up the hundreds of thousands of returning workers after the end of the Bracero program. Both demanded the relatively open border mechanisms for people and assembled goods, and with the continued urbanization, especially of the northern side of the region, the need continued for Mexican skilled and unskilled labor, both documented and undocumented. The maquiladora contributed greatly to population concentrations in regional border cities because it always had a post-industrial modality in which little is manufactured, organized labor is mostly wanting, rapid turnover and replacement of workers are normative, "production is not fixed close to a natural resource" (Heyman 1991, 11), and wage labor is low, with benefits commensurate with wages. This results in the packing of populations in the region and close to border crossings where both documented and undocumented people could maximize their options by crossing the political border for better wages. Through these processes, SWNA, especially the border zone, has become central to neoliberal development on a continental and even global scale.

But the ecological impact of processes such as the development of maquiladoras accentuated the depletion of water resources and the assimilation of emissions and no doubt accentuated already existing ecological conditions such as in the Tijuana region, which is very vulnerable to erosion, floods, and landslides (Ojeda 2000). These interactive processes can be appreciated by recent findings of road-infrastructure impacts:

> Expansion of road-infrastructure, which is motivated by the maquila's transport demands, constitutes an indirect externality derived from the maquiladoras' choice of location. The corresponding environment impact is composed by the modification of the habitat for land and aquatic flora and fauna, of superficial water flows, as well as changes in land use. (Strömberg 2002, 20)

What is most pressing is that the impact of such interactive conditions is not localized and is regional and transborder. Strömberg (2002, 39), in his work concerning environmental issues of the maquiladoras, provides a simple conclusion: "structural factors encourage the maquilas to locate in the arid northern part of Mexico, and often close to residential areas . . . so that the most critical environmental issue is the maquila induced population growth and the subsequent pressure on long run water supply." For example, the interdependence of common water supplies in the Rio Grande–dependent aquifers of El Paso and Ciudad Juárez illustrate this, and the pollution of these water resources are directly associated with chemical spill-offs of the maquiladoras. These conditions are replicated throughout the region, and they impact agricultural production in both the north and south as well as attendant environmental pollution of air and environment. We need a broader heuristic to assist us in explaining these dynamics.

CONTINUITY AND CONTIGUITY OF THE SOUTHWEST NORTH AMERICAN REGION: DIFFERENT STROKES FOR DIFFERENT FOLKS

In trying to consider what heuristics are most beneficial to understand what we normally refer to as the "border" or the "border region" and their political ecology and how best to theorize our approaches, I often think our conjectures are too narrowly political or economic and not more broadly considered. Spicer (1962, viii) long ago expressed his dissatisfaction by preferring to hold off on a definitive label for the region until someone thought up a better name for the region as a whole. He thought that the complex cultural diversity needed a much broader definition. Léon Portilla (1972) incorporated the region as the "Mexican-American West" "made both to the geographical area and to the ancient cultural affinity between what in the United States is understood by 'Southwest' and in Mexico by 'Northwest,' with the somehow artificial exclusion of the Californias" (83). In explaining the region as involving complex and multidimensional historical processes, he states unequivocally: "In them (historical processes) as well as in its equally different physiographical, climatological and ecological characteristics, are found the antecedents without which it is impossible to understand the contemporary multicultural reality" (83).

Such an approach was proposed long ago by Ellwyn Stoddard, who in this work is recognized for his groundbreaking research and innovative propositions that articulated his findings with public policy, often resulting in professional risk and avoidance by more conservative academics.[3] His regional insistence truly crossed borders as he (1975, 1982 et al., 1984, 1986, 1989, 1991) in no uncertain terms regarded the border region as an artificially bifurcated one, and he was attentive to the common ecological formations, which from my point of view "grounds" all other discussions referent to the region. He was fully cognizant of the long period of regional development from the pre-Hispanic period to his present and the ongoing conflictive and cooperative relations between populations. Stoddard was much ahead of his time by insisting that the border was basically a demarcation of a regional economy, integrated by multiple economic, social, linguistic, and cultural relations not the least of which was a glaring economic inequality of wages and income. Population growth was clearly attributed by him to the maquiladoras and certainly later by the North American Free Trade Agreement (NAFTA) as a driver for further integration and massive inequality. His unpopular policy suggestions, which were based on the reality of an integrated border, insisted that new conceptual solutions had to be entertained because "the maintenance of pre-boundary frontier systems (i.e., political, economic, cultural and social) is necessary for the survival of borderland society. For centrist policymakers, any unauthorized transborder activity is a threat to national sovereignty and must be eradicated" (2001, 99). Stoddard and his colleagues, such as Oscar Martínez, Richard L. Nostrand, and Paul Kutsche, created the basis for "borderlands" studies and advanced the discussion for broader concepts to develop what I have termed "Southwest North America."

There are of course many others since Stoddard who have taken up the work of "U.S. borderlands studies," but thanks to his work, he set the stage much past Bolton's nineteenth-century colonial "Spanish borderlands" idea, now very well recognized as a regional entity, as stated well by Stephen P. Mumme. He states this eloquently by recognizing the enormous changes in the twentieth century, and certainly more so to the present time, as will be discussed: "It is today a regional locale within North America that is linking up the complex processes of regional economic and cultural integration and may thus properly be taken as a barometer of transformations well underway deep in the interiors of the contiguous polities and their societies" (1999–2000, 102).

Unfortunately Mumme's insights did not become the operating principles by which to understand the region by policymakers, and unless we take up much broader approaches, we will be doomed to contribute to the ongoing "border" narrative of trade, immigration, commerce, economy, and its human populations based mostly on the dual national entities comprising each side, each with its own interpretive narrative. One is based on an East Coast U.S. prism in which single-culture citizenship, cultural space, and place are homogeneous, unilineal, and ahistorical, with the borderline as its central determining feature. The other is the complex Mexican mosaic of nationalistic and transborder dependency filled with contradictions of revolutionary rhetoric long unfulfilled and an economy marked by extreme maldistribution of wealth rationalized by the impunity of legal and extralegal power, which relies on the exportation of part of its population for its maintenance. I would like to explore a different narrative, perhaps to set forth the construct of "Southwest North America region." A version of this had been raised by Américo Paredes (Saldívar 2007, 59) when he puzzled about "Greater Mexico." He thought it rather peculiar that he traversed both cultural regions with sometimes opposite expectations of culture and language even though the region was one of both peoples and environment, which he recognized as the borderlands.[4] Therefore, I would like to visit this peculiarity to provide a theoretical and empirical vantage point that might give us some clues to more fruitful directions and perhaps transborder policies. This approach very much is in contradistinction, for example, to James Byrkit's long essay "Land, Sky, and People" (1992)[5] which, although very rich in its geographical and topographical representations, seems to be stuck at the bifurcated borderline and seems not be able to budge conceptually in his rendition of the "Southwest."

Most recently a call for expanding our theoretical understanding of the "border" has been proposed by Ismael Aguilar Barajas et al. (2014, 22). They differentiate between "border strip," "border area," and "transborder region." While each category deals with specific assumptions, mostly political and economic, they neither historicize nor contextualize them within ecological frames, both of which from the point of view presented here are necessary. I would prefer a political ecology approach to the border region, which requires our attention to much more inclusive material, ecological, and cultural as well as economic and political factors.

Miguel Tinker Salas (1997) provides this direction in his discussion of the economic integration of Sonora and Arizona as well as more regionally. He pays well-deserved attention to the geographical and ecological constraints and limits of late nineteenth-century regional integration and the manner in which hemispheric changes of "modernity" emerged. Spanish anthropologist Alfredo Jiménez's concept of "El Gran Norte de México," also the title of his fine book published in 2006, provides two important directions that give us a historicized process as well as important ecological characteristics to define his broader construct. We are of course familiar with the broad swaths of often-problematic and oppositional archaeological frameworks of the Southwest/Greater Southwest and Oasisamérica/Aridamérica concepts, the former of which was based on precolonial peoples north of the U.S.-Mexico border with great emphasis on Pueblo-centric assumptions of, especially, New Mexico. These frameworks avoided important complexes like Casas Grandes in Chihuahua until Ralph Beals initiated the idea of the "Greater Southwest," which included the U.S. states, north-central and northwest Mexico, Southern California, and large parts of Texas, as Levin Rojo has so carefully described (2014, 50–54). To different degrees, these constructs are very much part of the "culture area" premises pertinent to early anthropological definitions for pre-Hispanic geographies; from the colonial period to the present these are important historic references, but they are problematic for the last three centuries especially.

Yet within a discussion of the colonial and early North American periods, Jiménez (2003) states: "I usually speak of the Great North for the sake of brevity, and to leave open the door to extend beyond the Spanish colonial period" although he suggests that the "Great Hispanic North for the 500 years of Spanish control is appropriate" (5). But there are two salient historical processes that Jiménez and that this author have emphasized since the 1990s: the emergence of the region as the aftermath of south–north migration and colonization. From the point of view of Vélez-Ibáñez (1996), perhaps these processes antedate the European entrance of the sixteenth century.[6] This south to north movement and its intended and unintended consequences continue to plague our thinking when not part of the calculus in considering a theoretical advance in our considerations of the thing called the "border" and topics of immigration, economy, and polity. From language to institutions, from extractive methods of production to political organization, from economic exploitive practices to the arrangement of methods of agricultural and animal production, and from the prisms of ideology and valuing of the worth of humans, this south to north expansion set the stage for continuous and contiguous processes of conflict and cooperation that are distinctly different in the region. These contrast to the fundamental understanding of the east to west movement of the recent Anglo-American expansion into the same regions.

Thus with broader treatments, how the "border" is considered becomes significant theoretically. Their omission propagates, rationalizes, and naturalizes an eastern prism in which the "American" version of expansion has become the major megascript that overwhelms all others. It is as if this prominent narrative, promulgated and emphasized in schools from New England to California, and its English-only patina commands and directs scholarship and policy in both subtle and unsubtle ways. For example, "immigration is done the right way" when the Presidio of Tucson is founded by Hugo O'Connor, an Irish mercenary of the Spanish Imperial Army in 1776. This misdirection and disregard of the south to north movement has often been corrected by scholars, but general public understandings, policy directives, and political discourse are often found wanting and continue to be the prism by which the region is perceived embossed an imprint by a border only as old as the lifetimes of two grandmothers.

The second and crucial process hinted at by Jiménez, but primarily only extending to the end of the Spanish colony, is the relations of conflict and cooperation between indigenous and Spanish Mexican peoples, which were continuous and contiguous ones, as will be seen, and then were bifurcated by the creation and imposition of what we now know as the U.S.-Mexico border. The conquest of these peoples on the now-northern end of the region introduced one more hegemonic population to the already established relationship between Spanish Mexican and indigenous peoples. It replaced Spanish Mexican hegemony with an Anglo-American version. The southern end of the regional process between Spanish Mexicans and indigenous groups continue their often-contentious dynamic to this day, influenced by the hegemony of the American presence in the region and its handmaiden: global capitalism.[7]

Even the genetic history of the region exemplifies these interactive processes and characterizes the region. This author's DNA mapping in shown in table 1.1.[8] His ancestors are primarily from Sonora and Sinaloa and to varying degrees are representative of the region according to Martínez-Cortés et al. (2012), who state that for Mexico "in the total population sample, paternal ancestry was predominately European (64.9 percent), followed by Native American (30.8 percent) and African (4.2 percent). However, the European ancestry was prevalent in the north and west

TABLE 1.1. DNA Breakdown of Ethnicity, the Author

ETHNICITY	PERCENT
Africa	4%
America	23%
Asia	<1%
Europe	70%
West Asia	2%
Africa	
North Africa	3%
Senegal	1%
America	
Native American	23%
Europe	
Italy/Greece	28%
Iberian Peninsula	26%
European Jewish	7%
Trace Regions	9%

Source: "DNA Tests for Ethnicity & Genealogical DNA testing at Ancestry DNA." http://dna.ancestry.com/#/tests[11/25/2014 1:08:49 PM].

(66.7–95 percent) and, conversely, Native American ancestry increased in the center and southeast (37–50 percent), whereas the African ancestry was low and relatively homogeneous (0–8.8 percent)."[9]

Thus such genetic distributions provide a shorthand script that reveals the transborder demographic characteristics of the region and characterizes the relations between those represented populations. They provide glimpses into the special foundations for the basis of the concept of the Southwest Border Region.

A SYNCRETIC HEURISTIC: A POLITICAL ECOLOGY OF THE SOUTHWEST NORTH AMERICAN REGION

What is obvious from the regional representation in figure 1.1 is that demarcating such a region using only political categories such as states or municipalities as the defining constructs is insufficient to establish some efficacy to the concept. Rather, from an ecological basis the region transcuts the borderlines and extends both north and south and includes shared coastal regions east to west, the grand Sonoran desert

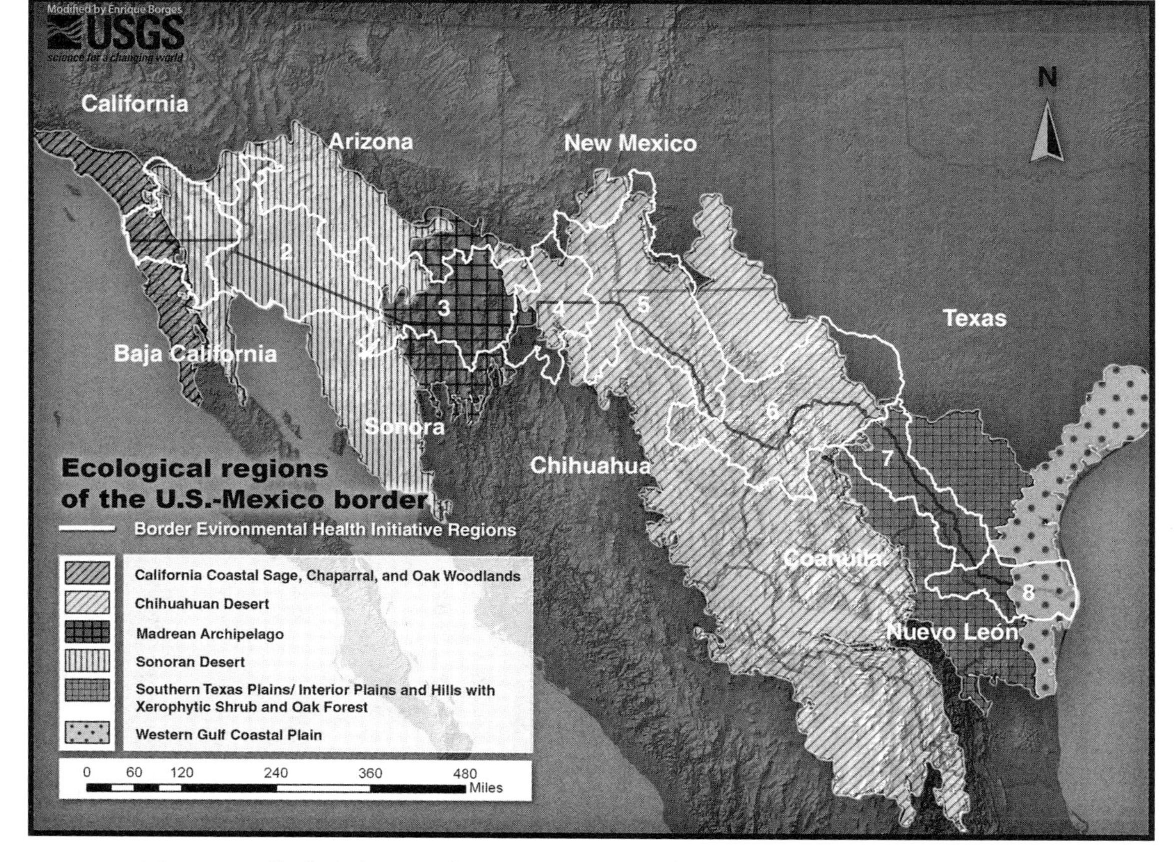

FIGURE 1.1. Ecological regions. Source: U.S.-Mexico Border Environmental Health Initiative (2015).

encompassing almost 311,000 square kilometers, the Madrean Archipelago formed by the convergence of the Rocky Mountains to the north and the Sierra Occidental to the south with the Chihuahuan desert to the east and the Sonoran desert to the west (Ruhlman, Gass, and Middleton 2014), the Chihuahuan desert with an area of 455,000 square kilometers (MBG.net. 2002), and the Southern Texas Plains/Interior Plains and Hills subregion. In fact, these subecologies together form a region larger than Germany, Italy, Spain, and Great Britain combined.[10]

For illustrative purposes, the desert commonalities in figure 1.2 provide us with a representation of the two largest cross-cutting deserts, each with its own particular fauna and flora but each characterized by low rainfall and scorching daylight temperatures and dissected by major riverine systems such as the Colorado and Rio Grande, both of which are also part of the regional transborder system. Each also contains its subecologies so that the Sonoran Desert's coastal boundaries with the Sea of Cortez made possible pre-Hispanic fisheries that today are exploited by large-scale shrimp industries mostly for export and for the development of shrimp farms and ponds in the fragile lagoons and mangroves. These introduced modes of production have changed these subsystems to their detriment as well as having impacts on such coastal tourist-oriented ports as Mazatlán and Ensenada and their attending fisheries.[11]

Among the most prominent of ecological features are the northern end of the Sierra Madre Occidental that extends into New Mexico and then is joined by the Southern Rockies, both stretching for thousands of miles from south to north and intersecting the regions. Both of their runoffs and rivers are crucial for the entire ecosystem of the region and its highly diverse ecosystem. These cordilleras are the key to the entire ecology of the region and key to understanding the myriad adaptive economic, social, political, linguistic, and cultural urban centers, townships, and settlements as well as transhumant spaces that arose and developed east and west of both from the pre-Hispanic period to the present.

Emerging from the northern end of the Rocky Mountains, the Colorado (to the left) and the Rio Grande Rivers (to the right) in figure 1.3 interconnect the region. These are the most important sources of water to other rivers such as the Gila and San Juan and for agriculture for the entire region. The marine biomasses for the Gulf of California and the Gulf of Mexico are dependent in part on these great rivers and are crucial to the maintenance of myriad basins and aquifers. The Colorado is known especially for its serpentine movement through the Grand Canyon and the Rio Grande as a major boundary marker between the two countries; however, in the present, human exploitation and damming has led to endangered species, invasive plants, contaminated lagoons, and a trickle to both the Gulf of Mexico and the Sea of Cortez from their point of origin in the southern Rockies.

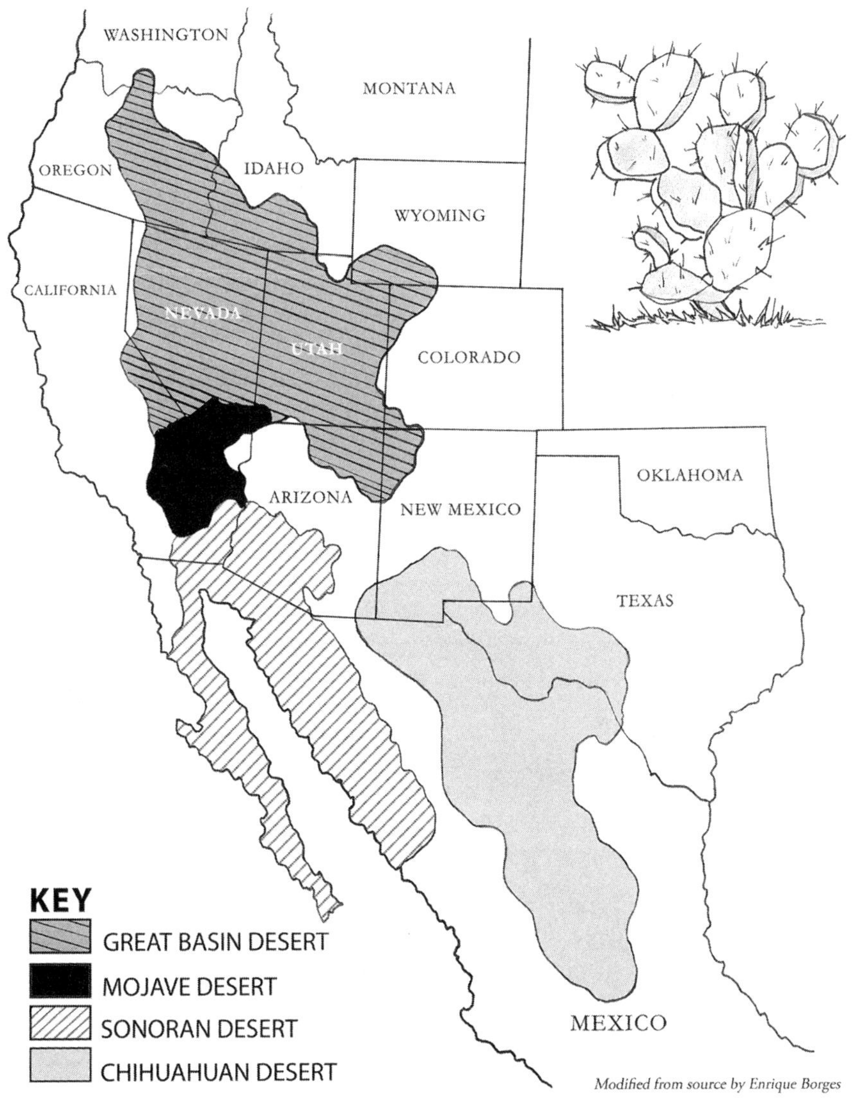

FIGURE 1.2. Desert commonalities. Source: Texas Parks and Wildlife (2015).

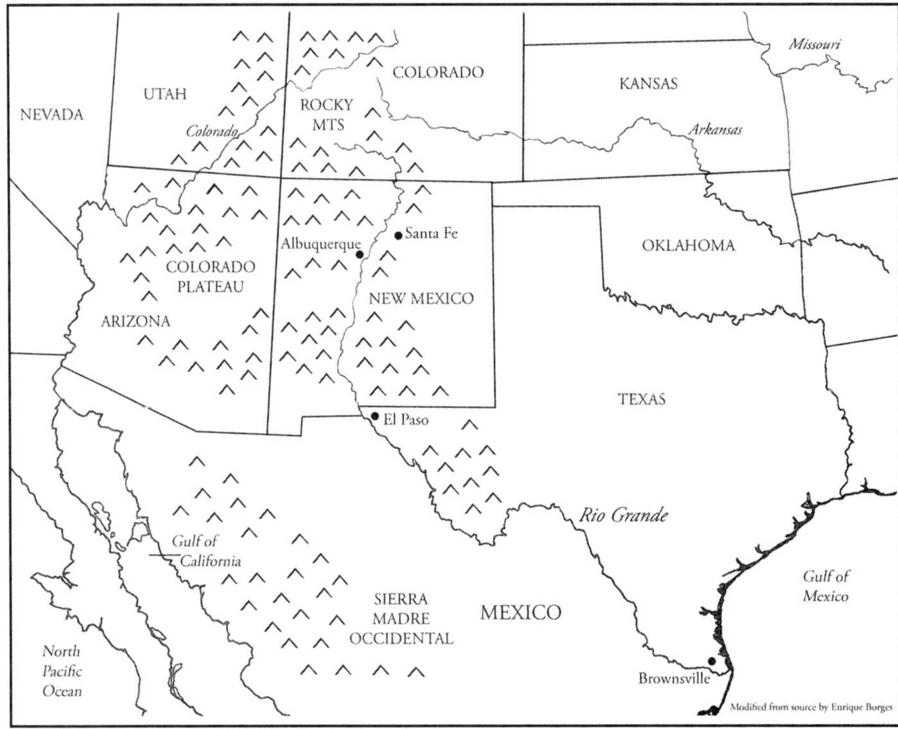

FIGURE 1.3. Colorado and Rio Grande Rivers. Source: "Rio Grande River" (2015).

This more ecologically oriented premise provides not only a sense of the expanse, diversity, and sheer volume of the region but also a material means of suggesting a regional identification of Southwest North America that cross-cuts political boundaries created by conquest, war, and annexation.[12] This allows us to place more attention on the impact of human invention and economy and their transborder political-ecological implications (as in chapter 14) than does narrowly using less encompassing and more convenient constructs. This parallels Alfredo Jiménez's (2006) concept in discussing the sixteenth through the nineteenth centuries and their expanding empires. He states: "A combination of demographic, economic, and international factors—mostly derived from geography—marks the history of the old Spanish North as well as the present U.S. Southwest. That is why I stress that the physical environment is the all-important foundation of the process of 'continuing frontiers'" (2) (which he defines "as a place or land where peoples from different cultures meet and interact," akin to this author's "cultural bumping" [Vélez-Ibáñez 1996]). And it is here where not only does Jiménez emphasize the ecological contexts for recognizing the "El Norte" as regionally specific but also accentuates the differences between Anglo expansion from east to west and its mythic premises and those of the Spanish Mexicans who had little pretentions of "Manifest Destiny" but who, especially after the Pueblo Revolt of 1680, developed a mutual interdependence between most indigenous populations and themselves though a system of military alliances against common indigenous enemies and highly elaborated religious syncretisms as well as intermarriage and other forms of group mixing and interactions. Such interdependence lasted until the Mexican-American War and the introduction of nineteenth-century industrial forms of production throughout the region, which tied together the now-bifurcated regions.

As well, this concept would more closely follow Miguel Tinker Salas's representation detailing the radical changes in the structure of production and labor and its establishment beginning shortly after the Mexican-American War, as illustrated in figure 1.4. This representation is not only inclusive of the various communities of the versions illustrated here but also attentive to the cross-cutting riverine and mountainous systems discussed here (Tinker Salas 1997).

As was introduced earlier in this chapter, the most recent rendition, which is inclusive of economic dynamics but does not include important ecological considerations, is that most recently designed by Mexican colleagues to denote what they term the "transborder region," which is very much in line with my notion and corresponds to Tinker Salas in figure 1.5. As has been stated, their representation features three definitions of the border region (border strip, border area, and transborder region): the first basically identified by the adjoining sixty-four municipalities; the second, by three hundred kilometers of Mexican territory south of the border and one hundred kilometers of U.S. territory north of the border; and the third, and from my point of view most pertinent to this discussion, as that area including the ten border states and their ninety-one million inhabitants (figure 1.5).

The border strip category is important for more localized relations between municipalities such as Nogales, Sonora, and Nogales, Arizona, which since their creation had often cooperated in many areas such as common charities, sharing of fire suppression equipment, cross-border commercial associations, and a long-held practice of Nogales, Sonora, children attending public schools in Nogales, Arizona, and Nogales, Arizona, children attending school in the other during summers.[13] The border area designation is important to recognize "important cross-border processes, for example economic corridors connecting urban markets such as Hermosillo-Tucson and Saltillo-Monterrey-Laredo" (Aguilar Barajas et al. 2014, 6). This corridor has long been an avenue not only for commercial goods but also for Mexican students from Hermosillo and other parts of Sonora attending the University of Arizona's College of Agriculture, who were largely responsible for the introduction of agricultural

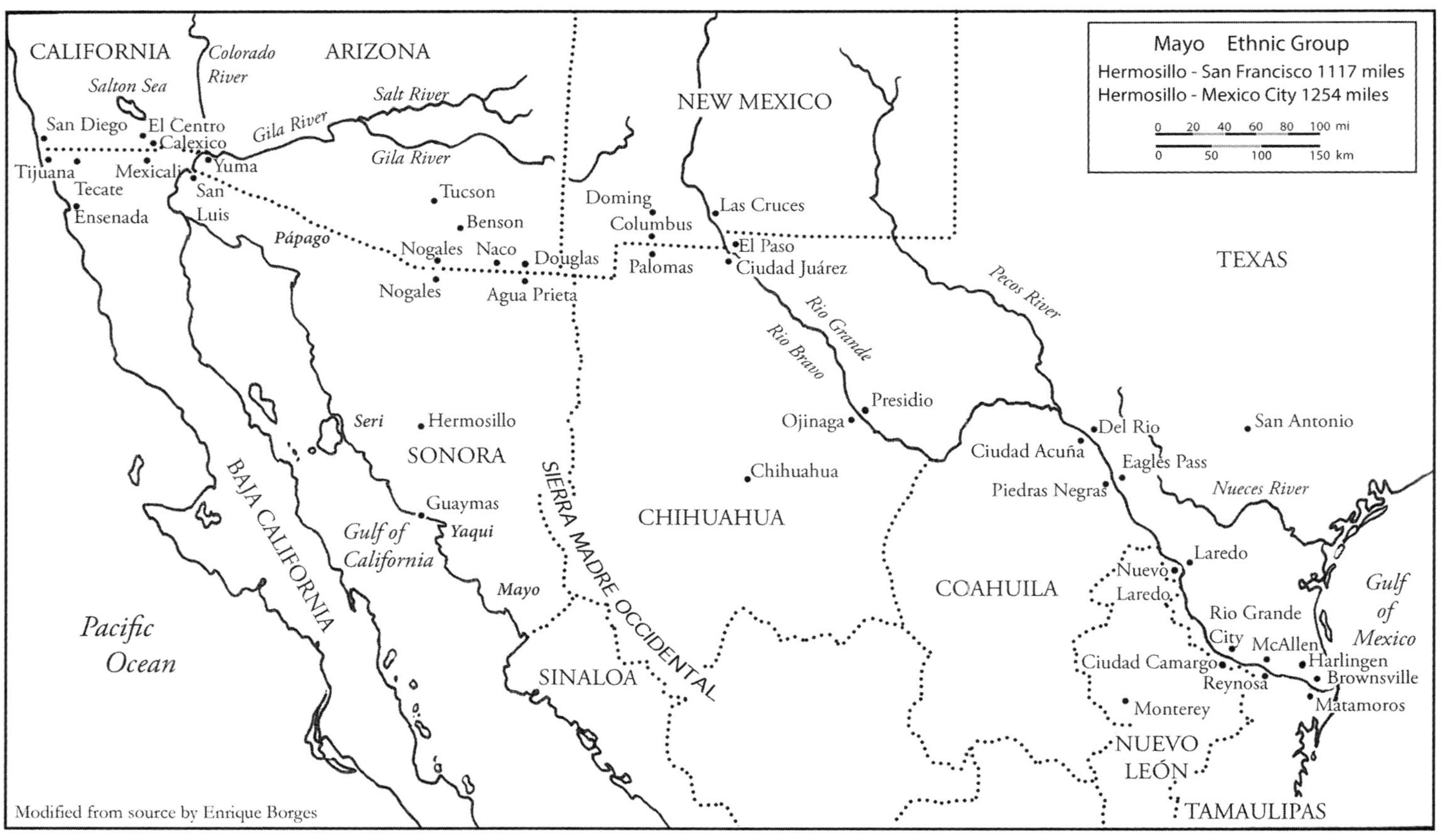

FIGURE 1.4. Northwest Mexico and Southwest United States. Source: Tinker Salas (1997).

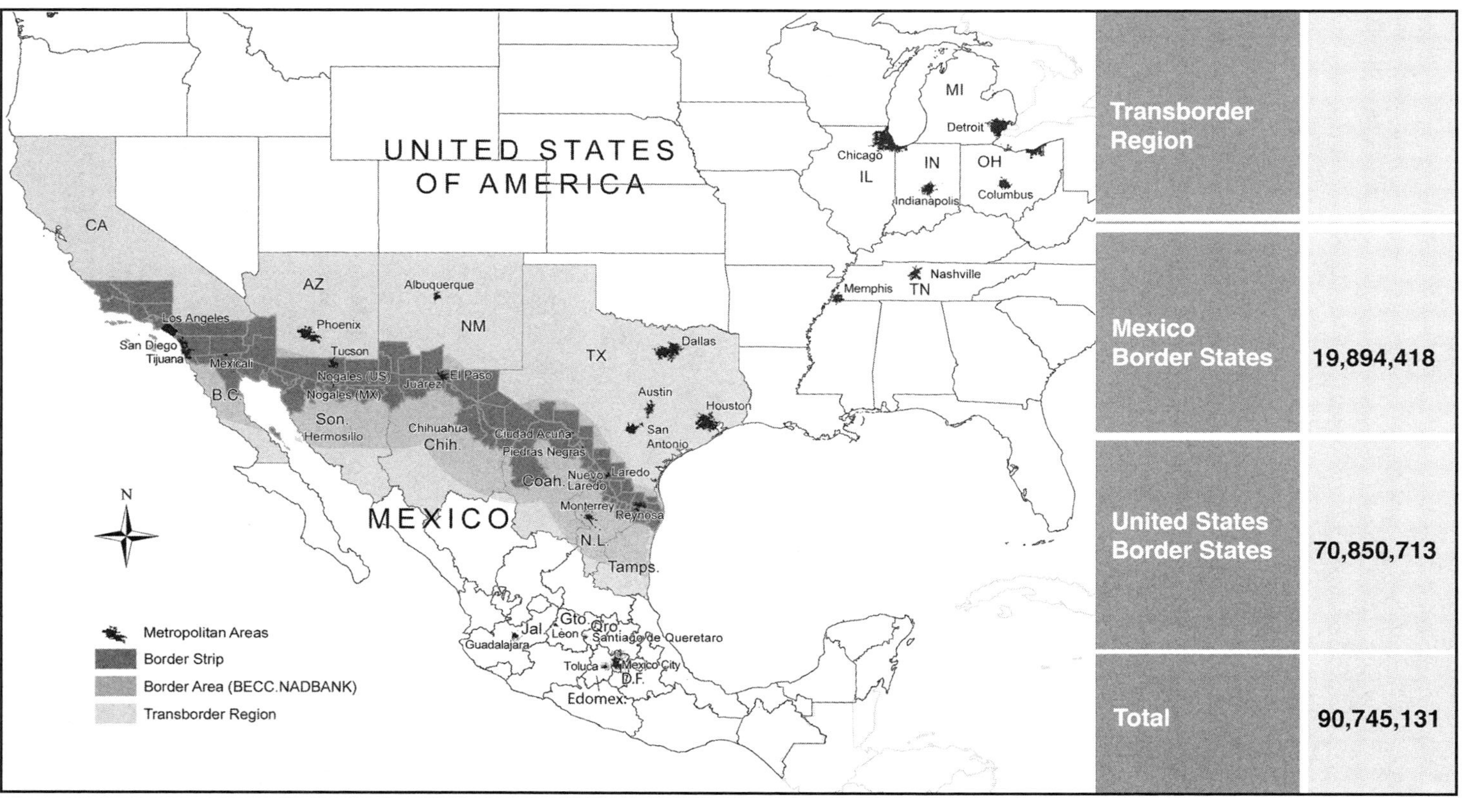

FIGURE 1.5. Transborder region. Source: Aguilar Barajas et al. (2014).

innovations during the 1950s into crop technology of Sonora.[14] The "transborder region" concept encapsulates the two other categories by expanding demographic growth and the interstices between trade, population, and manufacturing closely tied to regionally integrated asymmetrical economies and labor movements. I insist on integrating "ecology" as one of the central limitations and potentials within this mix. The map also identifies some specific non-border states in the United States as well as in Mexico. Some non-border states have accounted for a significant share of overall U.S.-Mexico trade. Finally, the map also reports the location of major urban areas within the transborder region and the aforementioned non-border states (Aguilar Barajas et al. 2014, 22).

What is important is that they have managed to move away from much narrower considerations. The categories discussed provide a direction for analysis in comparison to some of the more accepted renditions such as those provided by the United States-Mexico Border Health Commission (figure 1.6) and others that much more narrowly define the "border region" as basically that space one hundred kilometers south and north of the border and extending east and west for two thousand miles.[15]

THE POST-INDUSTRIAL PROCESS OF THE ASYMMETRICAL INTEGRATION OF THE SOUTHWEST NORTH AMERICAN REGION

But this common ecology, as has been discussed, is not only one of environmental concerns that will not abate since the neoliberal process of asymmetrical regional integration of the SWNA region will continue to expand. In the present, as Wilson (2011, 1) points out: "Beyond the $393 billion in bilateral merchandise trade each year is another $35 billion in services trade and an accumulated total of $103 billion in foreign direct investment holdings," which indicate the intense economic integration of Mexican and American economies in a most asymmetrical shape. Wilson establishes that 40 percent of the content of U.S. imports from Mexico were made in the United States through the maquiladora system, and Mexican imports from the United States are devoid of Mexican content and mostly created with American materials and assembly (Wilson 2011, 2). This asymmetrical economically integrated production process then speaks to the further unequal but combined regionalization of both economies, as discussed in chapter 2. Figure 1.7 illustrates this, with Mexico's economic growth greatly expanding in the northern Mexican states, contrasting with economic growth in 1970 through 1985 and 1985 through 2001 (BEHI 2015).

This continued shift has enormous economic impacts on human populations and the growth and distribution of gross domestic product per capita (GDP), which is

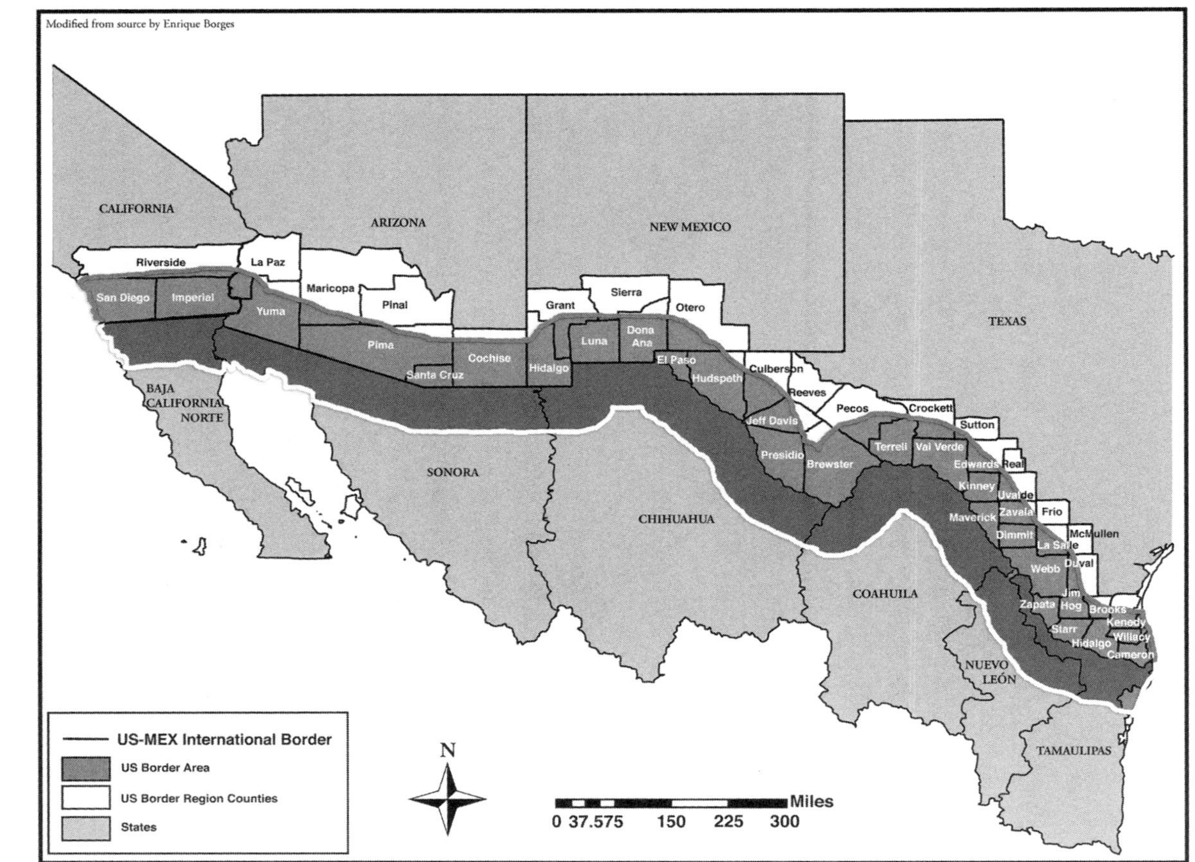

FIGURE 1.6. Border region. Source: United States–Mexico Border Health Commission (2002).

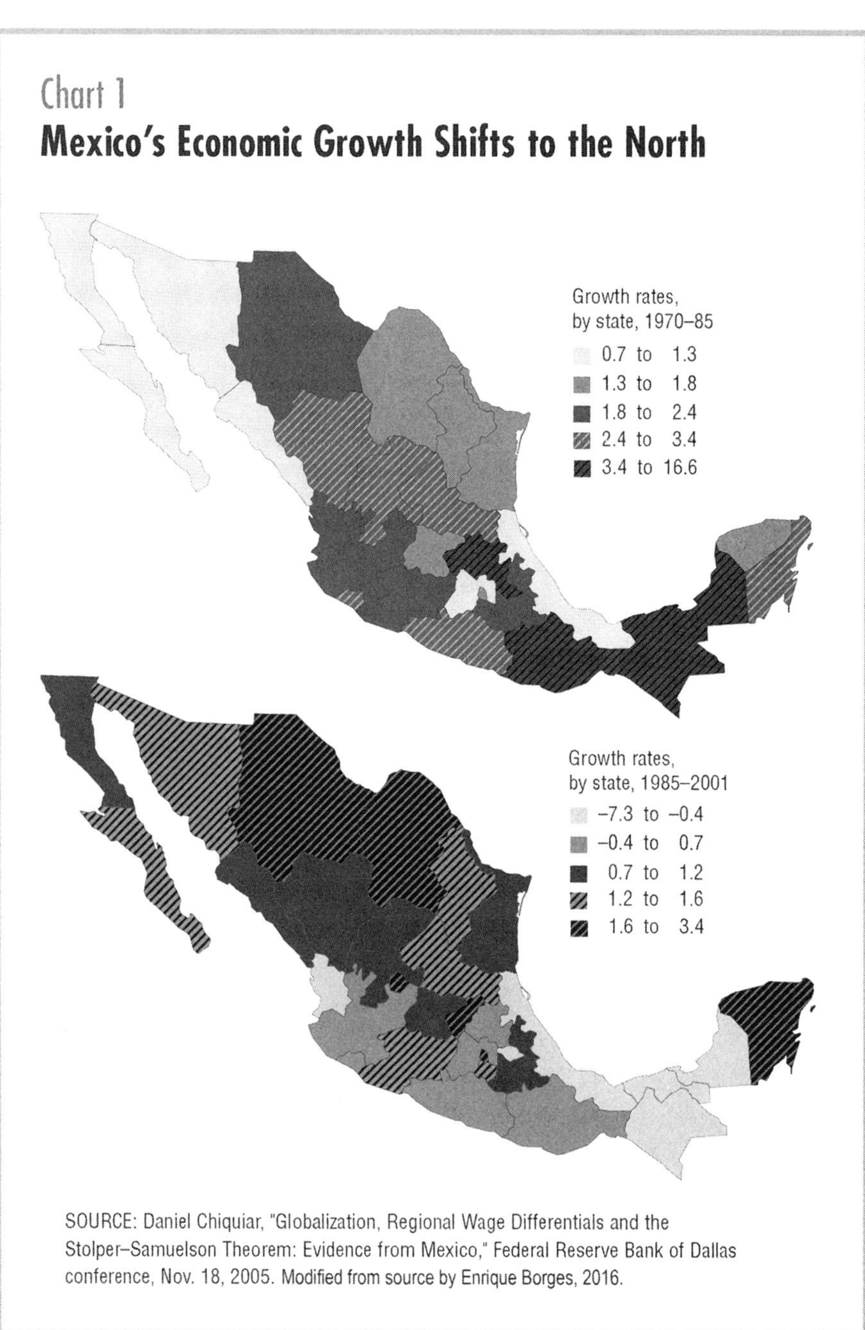

FIGURE 1.7. Mexico's economic growth shifts to the north. Source: Chiquiar (2008).

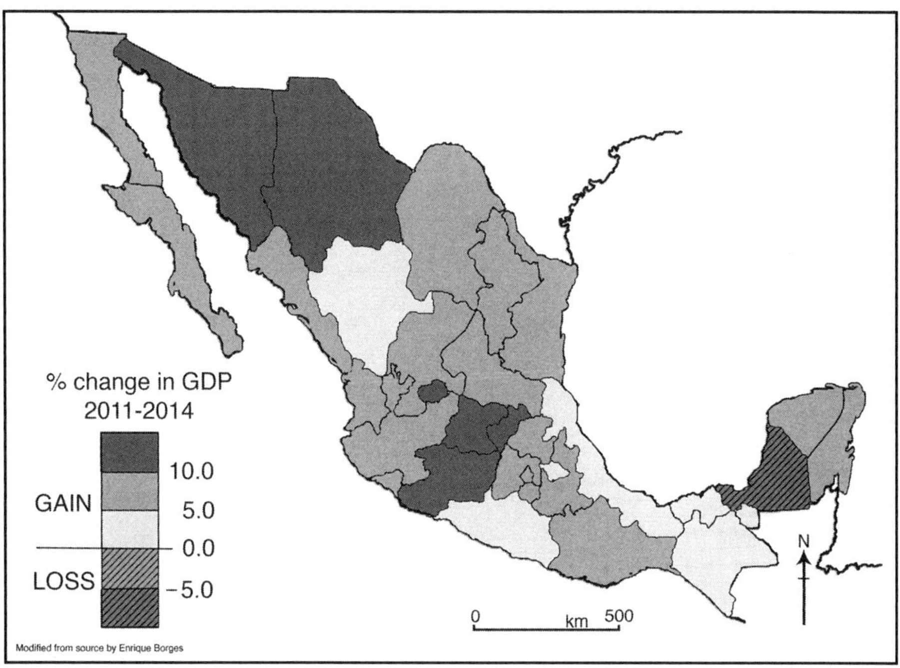

FIGURE 1.8. Change in GDP by state, 2011–2014: Which States are Growing Fastest? Source: "Which States Are Growing Fastest?" (2015).

a measure of such interdependency and integration of economies. As shown in figure 1.8, GDP increases of 5 to 10 percent are strong, especially in the southern regional areas of the six border states, and are an indication of the powerful commercial and post-industrial presence of the United States.[16]

This increase in GDP is also matched by the Human Development Index (HDI; figure 1.9) to indicate the economic and social well-being of populations, with the highest HDI grouped in dark green and the northern area again being the largest in Mexico. The HDI certainly is associated with an integrated and even asymmetrical political ecology and economy of the SWNA region.[17]

Nevertheless, such well-being does not translate into any sort of symmetry in terms of wages and income, and like the inequality of product content, so too the disparity in income is asymmetrical within the region so that the 2010 GDP per capita in the Mexican side is $9,522, approximately one-fifth the U.S. level (Wilson 2011, 18).

Such asymmetrical interdependence drives as well the search by populations to seek a balancing of such inequality farther north, with demographic and spatial impacts

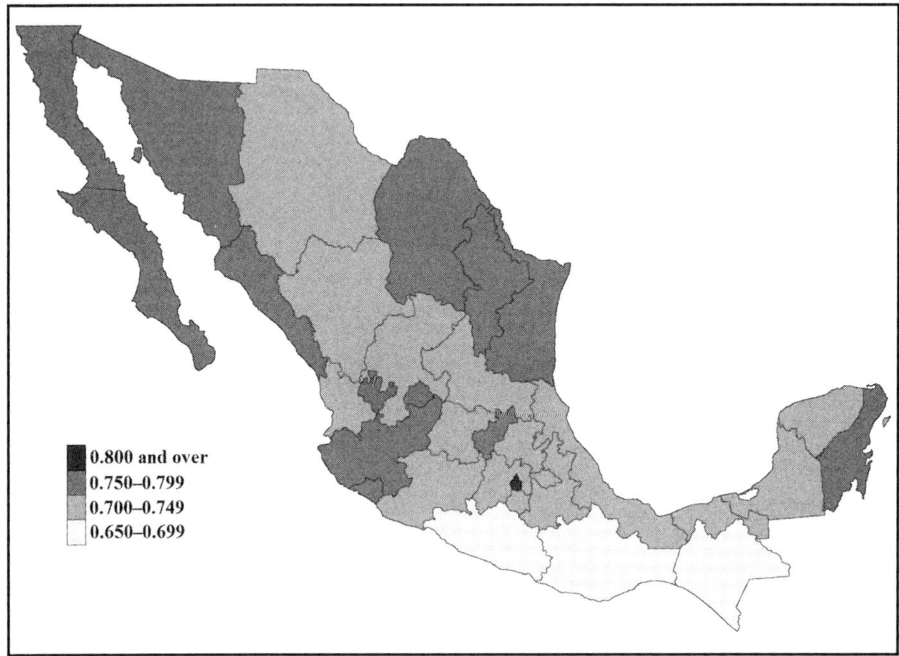

FIGURE 1.9. Human development index. Source: Wikimedia Commons (2015).

ensuing, as illustrated by the rise of "colonias." They also represent the inequality of economy north of the region of populations seeking a livelihood in subecologies characterized by a combination of fragile desert environments, unprepared areas for human habitation, large numbers of undocumented families, internal border enforcement, and communities formed by the purchase of aluminum trailers of limited adaptive capacities.

The rise of "colonias" on the northern end of the region developed in the past twenty years (figure 1.10), and they may number as many as one million persons distributed in 1,800 communities at various stages of arrival, political activity, and economic development (Vélez-Ibáñez, Núñez, and Rissolo 2002; also see chapters 15 and 17).

These are livable but difficult communities created from barren, ecologically unbalanced physical environments totally lacking in most amenities of community life including potable water, sewage, roads, schools, and centers for community life and subsidizing an agricultural labor system of regional importance as well as the migratory needs of other states in the northern region and beyond. Unlike their counterparts on the southern end of the region in which "land invasions" were responsible in part for the creation of urban areas of Mexico City, the northern colonias were

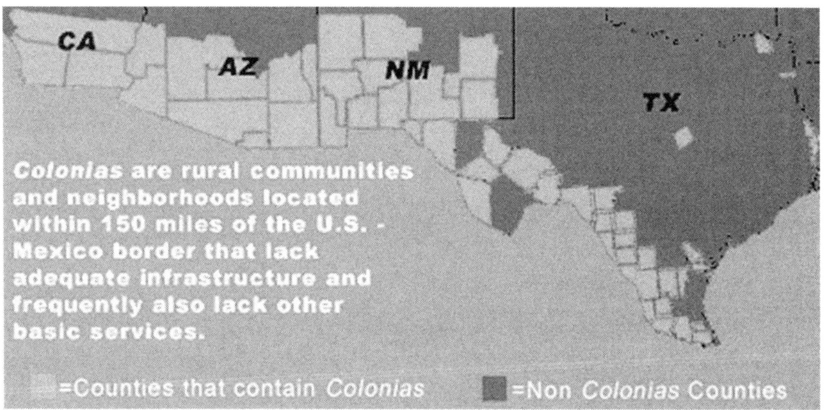

FIGURE 1.10. Colonias of Texas, New Mexico, Arizona, and California. Source: "The Forgotten Americans Focus: *Las colonias*" (2000).

inhabited largely by agricultural workers who purchased unoccupied lands built next to agricultural areas such as those of Doña Ana County, New Mexico, and border Texas, and in the case of California, rented trailers in Native American reservations next to agricultural fields such as those in the Coachella Valley. Most are marked by lack of sewage and potable water, contaminated soils from the overabundance of pesticides in the areas, and precarious and largely unhealthful living conditions. Most purchased lots used legal titles based on automobile-like purchase papers without collateral with occupancy based on monthly payments and not-infrequent repossessions. Yet many of the populations manage to use a modular housing approach by combining used trailers and brick or stucco housing to create one household such as that shown in "El Recuerdo," a small colonia west of Hatch, New Mexico (figure 1.11).

For twenty years these populations have also suffered the pangs of the agricultural employment and unemployment cycles, frequent migratory travel to other parts of the United States, and in the case of New Mexico colonias specifically, being watched, observed, and arrested by internal border patrol checkpoints eight-five miles north of the border. The presence and importance of such internal borders can be appreciated by a recent representation in figure 1.12, which details the number of arrests due to unauthorized border crossings coupled to the value of drugs intercepted. In this manner a narrative of unauthorized human crossings becomes conflated with illegal drugs. The aftermath of such presence and the occasional raids conducted is that many children stay away from school, persons are afraid to go to available health clinics, and elaborate escape and back road routes through the desert areas are developed, with a consequence of adding to environmental damage as well.

FIGURE 1.11. Modular housing in El Recuerdo, New Mexico. Photo by author.

FIGURE 1.12. Internal border checkpoint eighty-five miles north of the U.S.-Mexico border. Photo by author.

CROSS-BORDER PROCESSES AND STRUCTURAL INTEGRATIONS

Further amplifying the regional economic integrations are the immense cross-border movements of human populations. The sheer volume of human traffic crisscrossing the political border throughout the region reflects the modes of production imposed on the region. Pedestrian travel throughout the southern ports of the United States and Mexico vary according to both economy and political policy, especially by the United States. Nevertheless, this movement accounted for more than 40 million pedestrians traveling back and forth in 2013 with a high of almost 50 million in 2007.[18] Each crossing represents persons working on one side and living on the other, going to school in one and living in the other, having a business on one and living in the other, buying cheaper gasoline in one and driving in the other, buying groceries in one and eating in the other, and attending coming of age and birthday parties, weddings, baptisms, and funerals while living on one side or the other. Such pedestrian traffic accounts for billions in expenditures and earnings and the development of transborder cultural capital based on a transborder experience of handling language, institutional complexities, legal systems, economic strategies and calculi, and transportation and provisioning demands for home and hearth that are quite associated with daily experiences of the region. These figures, however, are augmented by the almost 15 million Mexicans who visited the United States for numerous reasons in 2013 and who together with the pedestrians total more than 50 million persons annually.[19]

Such volume, however, does not cease with foot traffic: automobiles flowing through the border have ranged from a high of over ninety-one million in 2004 to a lower number of over sixty-six million in 2013. While this reduction is significant, nevertheless when coupled to pedestrians and visitors, the actual number of persons crisscrossing the border region is immense. Each car is also a conveyer of commerce since gasoline is purchased on both sides of the border, foodstuffs, fresh or packaged, are transported in both directions, and informal trade such as the trafficking in perfumes from north to south are parts of the formula as well.[20] When such numbers are augmented by truck, train, automobile and bus passengers, and truckers, then the combination of all must easily number at least 150 million annual crossings of persons by these various means and conveyances.

Yet such dynamic movement is but a reflection of broader economic production processes, so we need to understand that regionally we have a phenomenologically very different circumstance from all other areas of either country, which is expressed by important interdependent but asymmetrical realities. First, as already indicated, U.S. imports from Mexico contain 40 percent U.S. content, according to Wilson

(2011, 17). Second, again according to Wilson: "The Southwest Border states are especially integrated with Mexico, and the Mexican market accounts for a quarter to more than a third of all exports for Texas, New Mexico, and Arizona. However, states throughout the country trade intensely with their southern neighbor. Mexico is the top export destination for five states: California, Arizona, New Mexico, Texas and New Hampshire" (2). Third, Mexican imports account for 42 percent of all the U.S. content, or value added and imported back into the country. Fourth, intra-industry trade, according to Wilson, indicates production sharing, which represents over 40 percent of all U.S.-Mexico trade and which occurs when two or more countries share in the manufacturing of a specific material (17). Fifth, and again according to Wilson, "U.S.-sourced materials made up 51% of the value in Mexico's processing exports" (18).[21] Lastly, such a process has developed a system of systems of "co-production" in which goods are not just traded with their attending asymmetries but rather are manufactured or assembled together so that "productivity and competitiveness of communities on both sides of the border are tighly linked" (Lee and Wilson 2015).

There can be no doubt that when all of this traffic of peoples, materials, commerce, and trade is coupled and attached to a two-thousand-mile-long ecology of intersectionality, then we can state that a more regional approach to guide our theories and methods needs to be applied from this perspective rather than from a "border" perspective.

Finally, beyond these actualities that also support this position is the work recently articulated by Aguilar Barajas et al. (2014). They have developed a business cycle synchronization model which measures correlations through time between GDP growth rates for Texas and northeastern Mexico.[22] According to this work, the model predicts the vector auto-regressive (VAR) model coefficients estimates and reveals a significant level of business cycle synchronization between Texas and northeastern Mexico, as well as between Texas and the rest of Mexico. They state that "in both cases, the estimated 'δi' are highly significant statistically. However, for the former pair the relationship is almost twice as strong as for the latter (0.90 vs 0.55). Moreover, the effect of NAFTA although significant in both cases (with statistically significant estimated 'θi') is stronger for northeastern Mexico (0.65) than for the Rest of Mexico (0.43)" (Aguilar Barajas et al. 2014, 27). These findings assert that more regional trade has increased cross-border economic integration for Northeastern Mexico.

CONCLUDING REMARKS

What can be stated unequivocally is that this synchrony of the business cycle is the continuing result of an integrating and asymmetrical regional integration of the

SWNA region begun in the nineteenth century and closely tied to the demographics of both sides of the border and explains the rise of Mexican-origin populations in the northern region of mostly legal Mexican immigrants and the increased population growth of the southern region.

It would seem that the bifurcation of the region "naturalized" the division of the region as if common ecologies never existed and none of the above had occurred. The concentration of post-industrial processes has led to the regional degradation of the environment while also sustaining the populations moving to take up the jobs and spaces necessary for their survival. Culture is not the mediator of such processes as thousands of indigenous Mexican Native peoples such as the Purépechas from Michoacán work in Tijuana in the maquiladoras and in the San Quintín Valley outside of Ensenada in vineyards and agricultural fields. They mirror their tribal brother and sister Purépechas who inhabit four hundred house trailers in the Coachella Valley of Southern California who work in lettuce and tomato fields. Theirs is a commonality not of culture but of economic necessity in which they are divided by a borderline but serve integrated regional and transnational interests and capital.[23] These mirrors are little different from those of millions of other Mexican-origin populations who work in the maquiladoras in the south and the Mexican-origin labor in the colonias of the north. Theirs is only a difference of the specificity of the organization of production; these are mirrors for the region, which has undergone such profound drastic changes in the last five hundred years, changes that can only become even more intense as those integrative and asymmetrical regional process also expand, despite the Trumpian rhetoric in the 2016 presidential elections.

NOTES

1. Wikipedia. "Cananea Strike." http://en.wikipedia.org/wiki/Cananea_strike.
2. Personal communication, Luis Plascencia, March 16, 2016.
3. Stoddard, from this writer's position, is among the most unappreciated scholars of the twentieth century. His far-ranging work spans two centuries, and his careful documentation and an early development of interdisciplinary social science is a model of what needs to be done for those interested in historically and economically based interdisciplinary social science that is always tinged with an uncommon humanity. His is truly a most instructive model of how to maintain continuously superior scholarship in the face of mostly traditional unimaginative academic criticism.
4. Saldívar (2007, 59) states that Paredes's "Greater Mexico represents an early, direct challenge to the traditional language of citizenship and liberal democratic notions that tie it indissolubly to state membership."

5. Byrkit's (1992) important essay is a discussion that seems to end a regional approach at the borderline created two grandmothers ago.
6. In this discussion, Leblanc (2008) lays out the major lines of argument for a Uto-Aztecan migration into the northern areas of what is termed the "Southwest." He states unequivocally that the linguistic evidence "provide a fairly good case for a Uto-Aztecan-speaking farmer spread resulting in the wide distribution of a language family" (130); patterns of genetic data, although limited, support Uto-Aztecan migration (124); and the archaeological evidence "provide a fairly good case for a Uto-Aztecan farmer migration into the Southwest" (130).
7. Tinker Salas (1992) states that "economic developments taking place in Sonora (in the late 19th and early 20th centuries) cannot be separated from the pattern of change occurring throughout Latin America during the turn of the century. Neither can be isolated from similar transformations taking place elsewhere in the Mexican north. American investments in mining and railroads significantly transformed states such as Chihuahua, Coahuila, and Nuevo León. The Mexican north shared similar forms of economic development and American customs also penetrated these regions" (430).
8. "DNA Tests for Ethnicity & Genealogical DNA testing at Ancestry DNA." http://dna.ancestry.com/#/tests[11/25/2014 1:08:49 PM].
9. Genetic admixture of Mexican-origin populations varies in general but seems to clump regionally, as has been stated, but that said, this study also shows that in examining maternal ancestry they "confirm a strong gender-biased admixture history between European males and Native American females that gave rise to Mexican mestizos" (Martínez-Cortés et al. 2014). An earlier study by Long et al. (1991) suggested a similar percentage for Arizona as that of the Mexican north with the following estimates: Amerindian, 0.29 +/− 0.04; Spaniard, 0.68 +/− 0.05; and African, 0.03 +/− 0.02. The interpretation of these results with respect to Amerindian and Spanish ancestry is straightforward. African ancestry is strongly supported by the presence of a marker of African descent, Fy. A very sophisticated analysis of Mexico and Sonora by Silva-Zolezzi et al. (2009) stated that Sonora had the highest estimates of mean European ancestry, 0.616 to 0.085 for Sonora, and the lowest of American Indian contribution, .0362 to 0.089 (8612).
10. "Ecological Regions of the U.S.-Mexico Border." http://geog7webb.blogspot.com/2009/10/ecological-regions-of-us-mexico-border.html.
11. http://www.tpwd.state.tx.us/learning/webcasts/urban/images/122_desert_map.jpg. Great Basin—Northwest Nevada (not the largest desert due to its encompassing parts of several deserts); Mohave—Southeast California (hottest); Chihuahuan—Southwest United States and Northern Mexico; and Sonoran—Southwest United States and Northwest Mexico. http://video.ecb.org/badger/download/vlc/images/VLC186_North_American_deserts.jpg.

12. The Spanish conquest from exploration to colonization lasted from 1540 through 1821, followed by the Mexican period of the establishment of the Republic of Mexico and partially disrupted by the loss of half of its territory through the Texas Separation of 1835, the Mexican-American War of 1846, and the further removal of forty-five thousand acres of land including southern New Mexico and what is now southern Arizona.
13. This practice of cross-border education was experienced by the author himself, and during his elementary school period, he learned to expand his home-learned literacy and writing knowledge with more formal instruction in Magdalena, Sonora—a town fifty-five miles south of Nogales. The Nogales towns did not differentiate students according to citizenship, and this cross-border educational process continued until the advent of restrictive immigration enforcement and conservative educational processes promulgated by state educational authorities ignorant of transborder practices and dynamics.
14. The numerous students from Sonora graduating from the University of Arizona prior to the restructuring of the border by more militarized formats were especially present in agriculture, engineering, and business. From the author's extended kin network in Sonora, three agronomers and two agricultural botonists attended the University of Arizona.
15. The U.S.-Mexico Border Region is defined "as the area of land being 100 kilometers (62.5) miles north and south of the international boundary (La Paz Agreement). It stretches approximately 2000 miles from the southern tip of Texas to California" (United States-Mexico Border Health Commission 2002).
16. "Which States Are Growing Fastest?" http://geo-mexico.com/?p=12070.
17. http://en.wikipedia.org/wiki/Economy_of_Mexico#mediaviewer/File:Mexico_HDI_states.svg.
18. The data show the range of southern border pedestrian crossings from a high of 49,538,963 in 2007 to 41,198,935 in 2013. http://transborder.bts.gov/programs/international/transborder/TBDR_BC/TBDR_BCQ.html.
19. http://travel.trade.gov/view/m-2013-I-001/index.html.
20. The tariffs in perfumes to Mexico are circumvented by women who mask the odor of the product by placing day-old burritos on the dashboard of the car. This works well if the same Mexican customs official is not present more than once. Observation by author crossing from Tecate, United States, to Tecate, Mexico, in 2004.
21. In 2008, according to Wilson (2011), 5.96 million U.S. jobs were dependent on trade with Mexico. "This statistic was estimated using a computable multi-sector model of the U.S. economy and includes the direct and indirect employment effects of exports and imports of both goods and services. This figure was estimated using the Global Trade Analysis Project computable general equilibrium (CGE) model, as updated for 2008 by Laura Baughman and Joseph Francois of the Trade Partnership Worldwide. California and

Texas are home to the most, with 692,000 and 463,000 trade-related jobs, respectively" (Wilson 2011, 12)

22. The model is by Aguilar Barajas et al. 2014. The analysis is carried out with a Vector Auto-Regressive model (VAR) that also includes growth rates for the rest of Mexico as well as the United States. It is presented as follows:

$$\begin{bmatrix}\Delta y_{Nt}\\ \Delta y_{Rt}\end{bmatrix} =$$
$$\begin{bmatrix}\alpha_{10}\\ \alpha_{20}\end{bmatrix} + \begin{bmatrix}\alpha_{11}(1) & \alpha_{12}(1)\\ \alpha_{21}(1) & \alpha_{22}(1)\end{bmatrix}\begin{bmatrix}\Delta y_{Nt-1}\\ \Delta y_{Rt-1}\end{bmatrix} + \cdots + \begin{bmatrix}\alpha_{11}(k) & \alpha_{12}(k)\\ \alpha_{21}(k) & \alpha_{22}(k)\end{bmatrix}\begin{bmatrix}\Delta y_{Nt-k}\\ \Delta y_{Rt-k}\end{bmatrix} +$$
$$\begin{bmatrix}\beta_1\\ \beta_2\end{bmatrix}\Delta y_{U.t} + \begin{bmatrix}\delta_1\\ \delta_2\end{bmatrix}\Delta y_{T.t} + \begin{bmatrix}\theta_1\\ \theta_2\end{bmatrix}(D_{nt}\Delta y_{Tt}) + \begin{bmatrix}\varepsilon_{1t}\\ \varepsilon_{2t}\end{bmatrix}$$

23. Observations made by the author in the San Quintín Valley, Baja California, in 2014, and in the Coachella Valley, California, in 1995.

REFERENCES

Aguilar Barajas, Ismael, Nicholas P. Sisto, Edgardo Ayala Gaytan, Joana Chapa Cantu, and Benjamin Hidalgo López. 2014. "Trade Flows Between the United States and Mexico: NAFTA and the Border Region." *Articulo-Journal of Urban Research* 10:4.

BEHI (U.S.-Mexico Border Environmental Health Initiative). 2015. "Ecological Regions of the U.S. Mexico Border." http://borderhealth.cr.usgs.gov/staticmaplib.html.

Brooks, James E. 2003. *Captives and Cousins Slavery, Kinship, and Community in the Southwest Borderlands*. Chapel Hill: University of North Carolina Press.

Byrkit, James. 1992. "Land, Sky, and People: The Southwest Defined." *Journal of the Southwest* 34(3): 257–387.

Chiquiar, Daniel. 2008. "Globalization, Regional Wage Differentials and the Stolper-Samuelson Theorem: Evidence from Mexico." *Journal of International Economics* 74(1): 70–93.

Ebright, Malcom. 2014. *Advocates for the Oppressed: Hispanos, Indians, Genízaros, and Their Land in New Mexico*. Albuquerque: University of New Mexico Press.

"The Forgotten Americans Focus: *Las colonias*." 2000. PBS. January 1. http://www.pbs.org/klru/forgottenamericans/focus.htm.

Garduño, Everardo. 2004. *La disputa por la tierra . . . La disputa por la voz: Historia oral del movimiento agrario en el valle de Mexicali*. Mexicali: Universidad Autónoma de Baja California.

González Ramírez, Manuel. 1986. *La revolución social de México*. Vol. 1, *Las idea–la violencia*. México, DF: Fondo de Cultura Económica.

Heyman, Josiah. 1991. *Life and Labor on the Border: Working People of Northeastern Sonora, Mexico, 1886–1986*. Tucson: University of Arizona Press.

Jiménez, Alfredo. 2003. "Space, Time, Peoples: Continuities in the Great Spanish North from Its Beginnings to the Present." In *Provincias Internas: Continuing Frontiers. Proceedings of a Symposium Held at Phoenix College, March 28, 2003*, edited by Pete Dimas, 1–24. Tucson: Arizona Historical Society.

———. 2006. *El Gran Norte de México: Una frontera imperial en la Nueva España (1540–1820)*. Madrid: Editorial Tebar.

Leblanc, Steven A. 2008. "The Case for an Early Farmer Migration into the Greater American Southwest." In *Archaeology Without Borders: Contact, Commerce, and Change in the U.S. Southwest and Northwestern Mexico*, edited by Laurie D. Webster and Maxine E. McBrinn, 10–42. Boulder: University Press of Colorado.

Lee, Eric, and Christopher Wilson. 2015. "The US-Mexico Border Economy in Transition." *Site Selection Magazine*, July. http://siteselection.com/issues/2015/jul/us-mexico-border-coridor.cfm.

Léon Portilla, Miguel. 1972. "The Norteño Variety of Mexican Culture: An Ethnohistorical Approach." In *Plural Society in the Southwest*, edited by Edward H. Spicer and Raymond H. Thompson, 77–114. Albuquerque: University of New Mexico Press. Published in cooperation with the Weatherhead Foundation, New York.

Levin Rojo, Danna. 2014. *Return to Aztlán: Indians, Spaniards, and the Invention of Nuevo México*. Norman: University of Oklahoma Press.

Long, J. C., R. C. Williams, J. E. McAuley, R. Medis, R. Partel, W. M. Tregellas, S. F. South, A. E. Rea, S. B. McCormick, and U. Iwaniec. 1991. "Genetic Variation in Arizona Mexican Americans: Estimation and Interpretation of Admixture Proportions." *American Journal of Physical Anthropolology* 84(2): 141–57.

Martínez-Cortés, Gabriela, Joel Salazar-Flores, Laura Gabriela Fernández-Rodríguez, Rodrigo Rubi-Castellanos, Carmen Rodríguez-Loya, Jesús Salvador Velarde-Félix, José Franciso Muñoz-Valle, Isela Parra-Rojas, and Héctor Rangel-Villalobos. 2012. "Admixture and Population Structure in Mexican-Mestizos Based on Paternal Lineages." *Journal of Human Genetics* 57:568–74.

MBG.net. 2002. "Deserts of the World." http://www.mbgnet.net/sets/desert/ofworld.htm.

Mumme, Stephen P. 1999–2000. "US-Mexico Borderlands Studies at the Millennium." *IBRU Boundary and Security Bulletin*, Winter, 102–5.

Ojeda, Lina. 2000. "Land Use and the Conservation of Natural Resources in the Tijuana River Basin." In *Shared Spaces: Mexico–United States Environmental Future*, edited by Laurence Herzog, 211–32. Mexico City: Colegio de la Frontera Norte/Center for United States–Mexican Studies at University of California.

"Rio Grande River." 2015. http://3rd-grade-rivers-mountains.wikispaces.com/.

Ruhlman, Jana, Leila Gass, and Barry Middleton. 2014. "Contemporary Land-Cover Change from 1973 to 2000 in the Madrean Archipelago Ecoregion." http://landcovertrends.usgs.gov/west/eco79Report.html.

Saldívar, Ramón. 2007. *The Borderlands of Culture: Américo Paredes and the Transnational Imaginary*. Durham, NC: Duke University Press.

Silva-Zolezzi, Irma, Alfredo Hidalgo-Mirandal, Jesus Estrada-Gill, Juan Carlos Fernandez-López, Laura Uribe-Figueroa, Alejandra Contreras, Eros Balam-Ortiz, Laura del Bosque-Plata, David Velazquez-Fernandez, Cesar Lara, Rodrigo Goya, Enrique Hernandez-Lemus, Carlos Davila, Eduardo Barrientos, Santiago March, and Gerardo Jiménez-Sanchez. 2009. "Analysis of Genomic Diversity in Mexican Mestizo Populations to Develop Genomic Medicine in Mexico." *Proceedings of the National Academy of Sciences* 106(21): 8611–16.

Spicer, Edward H. 1962[1970]. *Cycles of Conquest: The Impact of Spain, Mexico and the United States on the Indians of the Southwest, 1533–1960*. Tucson: University of Arizona Press.

Stevens, Horace J., and Walter H. Weed. 1910. *The Copper Handbook*. Houghton, MI: Horace J. Stevens.

Stoddard, Ellwyn R. 1975. "The Status of Border-Land Studies: Sociology and Anthropology." *Social Sciences Journal* 12(3)/13(1): 29–54.

———. 1984. "Functional Dimensions of Informal Border Networks." Center for Inter-American and Border Studies. Border Perspectives 8. El Paso: University of Texas Press.

———. 1986. "Border Studies as an Emergent Field of Scientific Inquiry: Scholarly Contributions of U.S.-Mexico Borderlands Studies." *Journal of Borderlands Studies* 1(1):1–33.

———. 1989. "Developmental Stages of U.S.-Mexico Borderlands Studies." In *A Multidisciplinary and Comparative Focus in Nigeria and West Africa: Borderlands in Africa*, edited by A. I. Asiwaju and P. O. Adenyl, 403–24. Lagos: University of Lagos Press.

———. 1991. "Frontiers, Borders and Border Segmentation: Toward a Conceptual Clarification." *Journal of Borderlands Studies* 6(1): 1–22.

Stoddard, Ellwyn R., Richard L., Nostrand, and Jonathan P. West, eds. 1982. *Borderlands Sourcebook: A Guide to the Literature on Northern Mexico and the American Southwest*. Norman: University of Oklahoma Press.

Strömberg, Per. 2002. "The Mexican Maquila Industry and the Environment: An Overview of the Issues." Mexico City: Industrial Development Unit, Naciones Unidas CEPAL/ECLAC.

Texas Parks and Wildlife. 2015. "Desert Map." http://tpwd.texas.gov/education/webcasts/urban/images/122_desert_map.jpg.

Tinker Salas, Miguel. 1992. "Sonora: The Making of a Border Society, 1880–1910." *Journal of the Southwest* 34(4): 429–56.

———. 1997. *In the Shadow of the Eagles: Sonora and the Transformation of the Border During the Porfiriato*. Berkley: University of California Press.

United States-Mexico Border Health Commission. 2002. "Border Region." http://www.borderhealth.org/border_region.php.

U.S. Department of Transportation, Bureau of Transportation Statistics. 2013. "BTS | Border Crossing/Entry Data: Query Detailed Statistics." http://transborder.bts.gov/programs/international/transborder/TBDR_BC/TBDR_BCQ.html.

Vélez-Ibáñez, Carlos G. 1996. *Border Visions: Mexican Cultures of the Southwest*. Tucson: University of Arizona Press.

———. 2014. "DNA Tests for Ethnicity & Genealogical DNA Testing at AncestryDNA." DNA Tests for Ethnicity & Genealogical DNA Testing at AncestryDNA. http://dna.ancestry.com/#/tests.

Vélez-Ibáñez, Carlos G., Guillermina Núñez, and Dominic Rissolo. 2002. "'Off the Backs of Others': The Political Ecology of Credit, Debt, and Class Formation and Transformation Among the Colonias of New Mexico and Elsewhere." In *Both Sides of the Borders: Transboundary Environmental Management Issues Facing Mexico and the United States*, edited by Linda Fernandez and Richard T. Carson, 97–116. Dordrecht: Kluwer Academic Publishers.

Weber, Devra. 2016. "Wobblies of the Partido Liberal Mexicano: Reenvisioning Internationalist and Transnational Movements Through Mexican Lenses. *Pacific Historical Review* 85(2): 188–226.

"Which States Are Growing Fastest?" 2015. http://geo-mexico.com/?p=12070.

Wikimedia Commons. 2015. http://commons.wikimedia.org/wiki/File:Mexico_StatesHDI_2015.png#filehistory.

Wilson, Christopher E. 2011. "*Working Together: Economic Ties Between the United States and Mexico*." Washington, DC: Mexico Institute, Woodrow Wilson International Center for Scholars.

2

CONTRIBUTIONS OF U.S.-MEXICO BORDER STUDIES TO SOCIAL SCIENCE THEORY

JOSIAH HEYMAN

THE STUDY OF BORDERS[1] draws on, and is a significant contributor to, important theoretical developments in the social sciences. We have moved away from envisioning societies and cultures as pure, bounded units, for which we identified inner essences (cultural patterns, social structures), toward envisioning them as internally and externally varied webs of relations, for which we trace connections and changes over time (Wolf 1982). Borders present precisely such mixtures and interactions. The agenda of this chapter, then, is to draw out theoretical lessons from work done on the U.S.-Mexico border. While grounded in a review of the literature on this region, the theoretical lessons are clear and transportable, both to other borders and to complex social and cultural situations generally. My approach derives from place-based science, which rejects abstract, timeless, and placeless theorizing in favor of building theory upward from particular places and times via nested generalizations; those generalizations can be transported and recontextualized for other places and times (Kates et al. 2001). I likewise draw on non-dogmatic Marxian theory, attending to the constitutive role of unequal relationships unfolding across historical time (Wolf 1982). No one border can do justice to all borders, and different lessons would be drawn from other sites; the point is not to hold this region as quintessential but to ask if ideas suggested here are informative and helpful as we range about the social world.

The relational perspective on borders begins with the seminal work of Fredrik Barth (1969), who proposes that identity contrasts between interacting groups define ethnicity rather than the preexisting content of their cultures. He thus takes an oppositional-relational view of ethnic boundaries. Following Barth, anthropologists think of social-cultural entities as being mutually constituted, precisely when they are in contrast.

Barth's work on interethnic boundaries concerned sites with weak state presence. The recent break with "methodological nationalism" brings his insight to bear on geopolitical borders between relatively thick states. Methodological nationalism is the assumption that societies with cultures are whole units coterminous with nation-states (Wimmer and Glick Schiller 2002; also see Gupta and Ferguson 1992 and Malkki 1992). Assuming methodological nationalism, borders are barely interesting containers for the more interesting inner societies and cultures, and flows across borders are external intrusions (e.g., immigrants to be assimilated). Relationship and connection are accidental, circumstantial, not essential. The conceptual break with methodological nationalism does not mean, however, a complete shift to borders, flows, and transnationalism. Rather, it involves stepping back from our presentist assumptions to ask about the historical construction of borders and flows and social containers of various sorts and what these assembling and bounding processes imply for contemporary social and cultural processes.

Let us examine, for example, asymmetry (inequality) at the U.S.-Mexico border, and relationships that connect across it, as demonstrated in chapter 1. Revealingly, emphasis on asymmetric interaction and continuing differentiation is the Mexican perspective on the U.S.-Mexico border (Bustamante 1991), the view from the historically robbed and exploited side.[2] This asymmetry began deep in the history of European colonization of the Americas, in the emerging capitalist world system. In the core of New Spain, subsequently Mexico, the Spanish reworked indigenous landlord-peasant societies into colonial ones that supported commodity production (above all, silver) for the world market. English North America, subsequently the United States and much of Canada, contained two main regions: a slave plantation zone and a dominant core of capital accumulation and free labor. Each dispossessing Native Americans, these power regimes eventually met in the zone of the U.S.-Mexico border. On arrival in the region, they were quite different, not because of some inner essence but rather as products of distinctive histories involving characteristic forms of social inequality and cultural codes.

The current boundary came about through warfare and—at least as important—legal dispossession of land, waters, and rights of Native Americans and Mexican frontier people (chapter 14 discusses the continuing relevance, and also complexity, of this process). After this, the region as a distinctive locale for unequal relationships emerged from a dual process of bordering, those separating legally Mexico and the United States and those building connections across these lines: railroads and highways, ports of entry, legal means for investment capital and commodities to flow, migration paths, and so forth (a comprehensive historical review goes beyond the agenda of this chapter, but among many works, see Montejano 1987; Heyman 1991; Sheridan 1995; Salas 1997; Gordon 1999; Mora-Torres 2001; and, though dated in details, the overall approach in Fernandez 1977 remains vital). Infrastructure and production site development were particularly important. Casey Walsh's (2009, 2013) expanded concept of infrastructure in the U.S.-Mexico border region is historically illuminating, with particular reference to water engineering for capitalist agriculture and later for industry and state-enforcement driven urbanization (as well as contributing significantly to political ecology theory [Greenberg and Park 1994]). In Walsh's view, infrastructure combines biophysical stocks and flows, material constructions, social-political institutions, and kinds of knowledge; in this rich definition, it makes sense to analyze infrastructure as a "base" for uneven and combined development at the border (also see chapter 14 here). Alejandro Lugo (2008) usefully summarizes this long border history as dual colonialisms, the deeper colonialisms of each core region, and the proximate colonialism of the United States over Mexico. Sometimes it is a helpful shorthand to think of the U.S.-Mexico border as a place where two distinctive social-cultural containers meet, but this is not because we assume they inherently differ but rather that we take a historical, constructionist approach that traces the encounter, coordination, and growth of an unequal border synthesis.

Some interactions (debordering processes) have weakened distinctions between the two national containers over time, and others (rebordering processes) have strengthened their separation (Staudt and Spener 1998). Debordering and rebordering are relatively easy to understand. But uneven and combined differences are conceptually more challenging, though crucial to the historical development of the modern borderlands. In uneven and combined development (Smith 1984),[3] intensive interactions between socially and economically unequal positions produce or reproduce political and cultural boundaries and economic inequalities, while in some ways debordering interpersonal/intercultural relations (Heyman 2010a, 2012b). To understand the border, we need to acknowledge the inequalities at its core, inequalities that involve relational flows and spatial divisions, via a broadly Marxist dialectic without doctrinaire predetermination.

In the uneven and combined junction of two postcolonial power formations, the articulation of Mexican peasants with North American wage labor capitalism was crucial. This theme, explored in the work of Michael Kearney (1986, 1991; Zabin et al. 1993) and Juan-Vicente Palerm and José Ignacio Urquiola (1993), as well as in chapters 11 and 16 in this book, undergirds Carlos Vélez-Ibáñez's (1996, 70–87) description of a United Statesian treatment of Mexican-origin people as "commodity Mexicans"—that is, a not-altogether human (as it were) unit of exploitable and disposable labor.

In addition to long-distance labor migration through the border, other features of the contemporary border (industrialization in Mexico, trade of various kinds, massive urbanization, etc.) have their roots in the marked inequality in wages and social benefits, political systems and legal regimes, and cultural codes that emerged over time in this peasant-worker with capitalist linkage. Key is not just the inequalities but the ways that such inequalities are coordinated into exploitative combinations. While some Mexican cultural elements and social identities are stigmatized in the commodity framing process, as described here, others are legitimized as means of access and control, often with the "diversity" label.

A straightforward and important example is the maquiladora export manufacturing industry in Mexico, clustered along the northern border, that under the coordination of international capital combines low-wage, high-productivity Mexican labor with North American and other international prosperous consumers. Another key component is management and engineering staff in both countries, a fair proportion of whom commute across the border every day to enact this uneven combination (the literature on maquiladoras is vast, but key works include Fernández-Kelly 1983; Kopinak 1996, 2004; Iglesias Prieto 1997; Peña 1997; Wright 2006; Lugo 2008; Tuttle 2012). The key idea of uneven and combined relations is that apparently separate entities or apparent opposites are brought into being and reproduced jointly, using limited shared elements (e.g., corporate bilingualism, as discussed in chapter 7), without full integration, shared citizenship, and equitable redistribution of resources. This is a core constitutive feature of the border.

The combinations of unequal endpoints enacted via the border are diverse and complex. I will indicate a number of them as I proceed through my analysis. I build on the observation of the historical merger of peasant Mexico and capital-accumulating North America, such as the inexpensive labor pools that supply the maquiladoras and unauthorized labor migrants. To analyze this combination, I use the concept of "global apartheid," which has two features. One is the political and ideological dividing role of the border. Peasant-worker Mexicans to a substantial extent do not have the legal right to move across the border, to follow the logic of labor markets, to go to places where their work is more highly rewarded (this is broadly true, but there are some Mexican working people and many upper- and middle-class Mexicans who can cross this border legally). The border keeps a lower social wage formation separate from a higher one. Thus, unauthorized migration can be considered—in this one dimension—resistance to inequality (Spener 2009).

At the same time, the word "apartheid" also indicates the actual presence of racialized, legally subordinated workers inside the high-wage and high-consumption space on the U.S. side of the border, a simultaneous there and not there, a presence yet denial of full human rights and societal recognition (Heyman 2012b; Nevins 2010;

and chapters 11, 12, and 16). It also points to their role in Mexico as trapped, devalued labor for transnational businesses who freely crisscross the border with investments, components, and products. In both the labor migration and assembly plant cases, this interpretation of global apartheid fits Vélez-Ibáñez's (1996) critical term, "commodity Mexican." In this regard, Mexican internal migration to the border and unauthorized migration to the United States is the opposite of resistance, the self-supply of super-exploitable labor to employers and indirectly prosperous consumers, a fundamental value transfer in capitalism (Heyman 2012b). In an uneven and combined perspective, of course, both views of global apartheid can be valid at the same time. These unequal relationships are, it merits emphasizing, not just silent and economic but painfully symbolized,[4] such as racist views of Mexican-origin people as entirely illegal outsiders (see chapter 12), the walled border as a perfect womb protecting against all dangers (Heyman 2012c), and the squalor of Mexican border cities as "out of sight, out of mind" (that is, in another country). Combined inequalities are coordinated through material and symbolic bordering practices.

It is not intuitively obvious, but in fact is crucial, that the apartheid-like division yet coexistence characteristic of the U.S.-Mexico border—put in simpler terms, its profound inequality—has given rise to its massive urban development from the late nineteenth century through the present (Fuentes and Peña 2010b). One might imagine that integration would favor development, but in fact, integration would erase much of the economy of the border, which depends on brokerage of a wide variety of disparities, many involving socioeconomic inequality. The maquiladoras, already mentioned, support immense workforces in northern Mexican border cities; the triangular illegalized guns-drugs-money and migrant-smuggling economies likewise pour money and work into both sides; the logistics and brokerage of legal trade likewise; the U.S. government has huge workforces dedicated to maintaining apartheid along the border; and so forth. Tito Alegría Olazábal (2009) has demonstrated that the economy, social structure, and urban structure in Tijuana and San Diego differ precisely because of their joined asymmetry, rather than being mixed border hybrids (also see Fuentes and Peña 2010a on Ciudad Juárez–El Paso–Sunland Park, New Mexico).

Hence, mediation between inequalities (accompanied by symbolic differences) is crucial in understanding border economics, politics, society, and culture. The most important segmentation is between the two countries, but there are other important segmentations, such as class and race within each country. To understand the region, it is crucial to identify key inequalities and their representations, and the people and processes combining them—recognizing that simultaneously there are intersecting, sometimes contradictory phenomena (e.g., the mobility of people and goods needed for the global assembly plant system side by side with anti-Mexican border exclusion practices). It is likewise important to understand this region's recent trajectory: across the twentieth century, and especially since 1965, capitalist and state processes have intensified enormously, whether in infrastructure, trade, industrialization, mobility, contraband, or state practices (for example, see chapter 10). As a result, it has become an influential site in the social sciences for the study of neoliberal capitalism and intensive state coercion.

The border region, then, is still in the midst of emergence, requiring analyses of struggles over possible paths and arrangements, rather than a static portrait of structure. While the boundary may seem to be a given fact, a territorial line, it is more illuminating to adopt a processual "bordering" approach that attends to power projects. There are, for example, projects of assembling masses of displaced peasants into northern Mexican border cities, ensuring that they are relatively vulnerable by rendering border crossing sufficiently risky and difficult that most do not access wages in the United States and thus will settle for lower wage and benefit packages in Mexican-side maquiladoras. For example, the Taiwanese electronics manufacturing company Foxxconn recently placed a computer assembly complex in the bare desert west of Ciudad Juárez that will eventually have upward of forty thousand workers (Robinson-Avila 2013). This new site includes a city of company houses for these workers. Most workers do not have visas to go to the United States (some do, based on kinship and other lines of access), but managers and technical personnel either have residential rights to live in the United States or have local border-crossing visas to travel there. At the same time, globally sourced preassembly parts and globally distributed final products cross the boundary on container trucks through a port of entry and local highway built by the state of New Mexico and can be transferred at a nearby multi-model facility onto railroad trains to be carried across the continent. The U.S.-side rail yards, one of the largest hubs in the continent, explicitly linked to the enormous maritime port of Los Angeles–Long Beach, was a recent joint government-private capital venture. This certainly merits the analytical label "power project."

These legal economic power projects occur alongside illegalized economic power projects, such as the recent Mexican organized criminal manufacture and export of illegalized drugs (I argue below that the coercive apparatuses of the two states actually are in a relation of mutual constitution and dependence with such illegalities). The border region on both sides is a key site for the transfer back and forth of guns, drugs, and money (Heyman 2011). Mexican scholars are now tracing the history of these criminal economies as constituted by and constitutive of Mexican authoritarian politics, nationally and in the border region (Flores Pérez 2013), while North American scholars examine the U.S. role in this same authoritarian construction process (Boyce, Banister, and Slack 2015). Rich oral histories and ethnographies document life in the drug trade (Campbell 2009; Velasco Ortiz and Contreras 2011; Muehlmann 2014). Furthermore, recent work has explored the complicated relationships between drug-based criminal organizations and human smuggling (Slack and Campbell 2016).

Cross-border human mobility is a complicated topic in this perspective: partially legal and favored, and partially illegalized and persecuted. For example, note the vocabulary involved: migration for the poor and legitimate movement or travel for privileged people (see Heyman 2012b, 2012d on differentiated cross-border mobilities). In a synoptic view, Efren Sandoval (2012) terms the entire flux of tourists, shoppers, traders, managers, and laborers as border "itineraries." Mobile people unquestionably have agency and diversity, but the classifications on which people act are power projects emanating from state and capitalist actors (Heyman 2001, 2012b). Above, I discussed how border apartheid enables value transfer in labor migration. In parallel, a key political project is border "security" performed as an ideological justification of the U.S. state during a period of economic and political decline (Heyman 1999a, 2012c).

Border studies in the 1970s and 1980s emphasized, to some extent, the capitalist economy (e.g., Fernandez 1977), while recent border research and theorization has turned markedly toward political concerns (e.g., Doty 2009; and chapter 3). This parallels the shift from Marxist to Foucauldian, Agambenian, and other such theories. Yet the sovereignty/governmentality perspective and the capitalist value perspective capture processes that co-occur and affect one another, even if they are not fully unified and coherent. What are the relationships of multiple interacting power projects? I have argued for a complicated coupling, in which U.S. border policy has global apartheid functions for capitalism discussed above but in performing separation, interdiction, punishment, and deterrence goes beyond functional labor control toward labor obstruction; I suggest this symbolic performance has grown because of surplus U.S. racism (aimed at "commodity Mexicans") in an era of declining hegemony, anxiety, and scapegoating (Heyman 2012b, 2012c). But others can reasonably disagree with me, viewing these arrangements as more tightly systematic, assisting with the labor exploitation of a fearful, stigmatized subproletariat, as well as excluding the larger group of surplus poor remaining in Mexico (see the review in Heyman 2014; and note the recent theoretical statement by Mezzadro and Neilson 2013). Indeed, this is a key topic for working out intersectional theories that identify key relationships but that avoid oversimplification and reductionism. In such complex analyses, the border is a crucial geographic site in attempted realizations of inequality. That such power projects are both enormously capable and inevitably flawed, incomplete, and unstable should be kept in mind.

Thinking about these combinations has inspired my efforts to view official, formal, legal states and unofficial, informal, illegal practices in one synoptic view (Heyman 1999b). Viewing states and illegal practices as opposed but also mutually constitutive processes is a promising way to grapple with the unity of opposites. Not only are states sometimes directly implicated in illegal activities, and often tolerate or encourage them, but also apparent opponents, states and criminals, feed each other. There is considerable evidence that repressive agencies of the U.S. state and its weaker client, the Mexican state, have been in a mutually reinforcing relationship with criminal organizations, where criminal organizations assist state agencies in building workforces, budgets, and legal powers, while prohibitionist law enforcement provides criminal organizations large increments of profit, as can be seen in price changes of contraband crossing the border in each direction (Heyman and Campbell 2011). States and illegal networks feed each other, to the detriment of more vulnerable people around these dealers of coercion and death.

These complicated and uneven relations help us understand the geography of the border region. Vélez-Ibáñez (1996, 2010, and chapter 1) has demonstrated the long historical presence of the transborder Southwest North American (SWNA) region. Routes, mobilities, and relationships constitute a spider's web of connections across this region (Sandoval 2012). It is precisely this connectivity that emerges from and enacts various border relations. The geopolitical border is a recent, highly artificial political project imposed across the region, though undeniably important as a barrier, bottleneck, time cost, incomplete imposition of rules, and symbol. Álvarez (2012, and also chapter 13) usefully captures these various views of the border as bridges and lines, with the former as key relationships (and literal movements and infrastructure) that cross the barrier presented by the latter.

Hence, mobilities are crucial to understanding relational processes (Adey 2010). Clearly, border crossing itself has complex mobility regimes and practices (Boehmer and Peña 2012), depending on citizenship, race, class, age, and gender (Chavez 2016; also see Heyman 2012d). Heyman (2004) and Kearney (2004) theorize how differential mobilities enter processes of unequal relationality and value transformation. Some of my ethnographic work has also explored socially unequal mobility on the U.S. side of the borderlands with Mexico (Pallitto and Heyman 2008; Núñez and Heyman 2007; Heyman 2009, 2010a). Mobility inequalities are crucial to unequal connections; I have explored how mobility inequalities produce and reproduce class-race patterns in the U.S.-Mexico borderlands. Furthermore, mobility approaches that emerge from the borderlands can be extended more widely in social theory and analysis (Greenberg and Heyman 2012; Heyman and Campbell 2009).

Velasco Ortiz and Contreras (2011), however, point to people who live on either side of the border but never cross, which makes up a large proportion of borderlanders, especially in Mexico. As they point out convincingly, many of these people are actually deeply enmeshed in border relationships, such as maquiladora workers, vendors of tourist goods, commercial sex workers, and so forth. Although Oscar Martínez

(1994) provides important insights by identifying actual border crossers (binationals) and people with multiple cultural repertoires (biculturalists), the prioritization of literal border crossing misses the important indirect effects of border mobilities and relationality as identified by Velasco Ortiz and Contreras (also see chapter 9).

Ironically, the border—because of law enforcement and illegalized economies, as well as trade, manufacturing, local binational commerce, binational commuter work, and so forth—is a site of marked inequalities but also of opportunity: employment, income, freedom, and escape (Staudt 1998; Ortiz 2004; Chavez 2016). Often, the stereotype is unrelenting suffering (e.g., Bowden 1998). This is misleading, not because the region actually has a good quality of life (for most people, it does not [Anderson and Gerber 2008]) but because that image does not capture the contradictory processes that draw people into this maelstrom and shape their lives. Mexican scholars Laura Velasco Ortiz and Oscar Contreras (2011) offer a more effective formulation, combining opportunity with risk in the analysis of life histories. A woman escapes abusive relationships with her husband and mother in interior Mexico through commercial sex work in Tijuana, facing constant threats of violence from men but also earning an income that funds her daughters' educational trajectories. Comparable analyses are offered of unauthorized migrants, migrant guides and smugglers, drug smugglers, maquiladora workers, border officers, and so forth. In a situation of value and power accumulation based on unequal exchange, it stands to reason that growth, opportunity, mobility, and so forth are accompanied by risk, exploitation, vulnerability, violence, harm, etc., distributed in highly unequal ways (Ruiz 2001; Slack and Whiteford 2011; Slack 2015; Slack et al. 2016; and chapters 9, 11, and 16). Likewise, unequal production and exchange concentrated in the border region generate uneven human-environmental risks, hazards, degradation, privileges, and protections (Heyman 2007; Grineski and Collins 2010; Collins and Jimenez 2012; and also chapters 1 and 15). And, these paradoxical combinations are not only economic or material but also manifest in culture, in the creativity and tragedy found together in border life (Campbell 2009; Muehlmann 2014). Vélez-Ibáñez (2010) powerfully expresses these experiences as an "impossible living in a transborder world."

Gender vulnerability, exploitation in workplaces and domestic economies, sexualization, and violence are not unique to the border; they may actually be worse in the Mexican interior, and they of course continue to mark the U.S. interior. However, gender power is a key vulnerability used in uneven and combined relations in the border setting, classically analyzed for the maquiladoras, with predominantly female workforces in most cases and male management (Fernández-Kelly 1983; Wright 2006). The gendered and sexualized violence at the border (Staudt 2008; Staudt and Méndez 2015) thus forms part of a wider pattern of boom economies and suffering in the region. Similar points can be made about the reworking of indigeneity at the border (Velasco Ortiz 2005, 2008) in the context of labor migration to and settlement in capitalist, export agro-industrial zones in Mexico's north (Velasco Ortiz, Zlolniski, and Coubès 2014).

The diverse uneven exchanges spanning multiple inequalities require social-cultural coordination of intricate kinds (Heyman 2010b, 2012a). For example, the fragmented interaction of a mostly English-monolingual householder and a mostly Spanish-monolingual gardener or cleaner, against an unspoken backdrop of legal-national boundaries, differs from the vertical Spanish command language of a Border Patrol officer arresting a Central American family, perhaps in front of a U.S. television camera crew, that in turn differs from slang and nickname encoded speech, communicating mixed trust and fear, when delivering drugs, cash, or weapons to a stash house. In each case, forging exchanges across inequality and difference is complex and subtle, and sometimes fragile. Observation and analysis of such exchange practices constitute a vital part of border studies.

This theoretical perspective, then, should help inform ethnographies of lived and expressed culture and social relations. Vélez-Ibáñez has provided important leads in this task, especially in his work (2010) on rotating savings and credit associations (ROSCAs). In his analysis, the specific ROSCA form and the more general learning of bonds of mutual trust (*confianza*) takes place in intimate lifeworlds twisted by inequality-based rapid development in the region. He finds some instances of resistance, especially to the dehumanizing "commodity Mexican" slot described above, but more often a mixture of striving to succeed in the dominant terms of social mobility and consumerism, which he memorably terms ideological "macroscripts," combined with creative and autonomous "slantwise" actions that ignore both resistance and domination in favor of goals and means emerging from everyday lifeworlds (a concept introduced by Campbell and Heyman 2007). A number of borderlands (or border/Mexican) cultural phenomena can be examined usefully in these terms, including *coyotaje* (migration facilitation and human smuggling, and brokerage more generally; Spener 2009); *movidas rasquaches* (tactics of improvised resourcefulness; Spener 2010); the morality of risk (Núñez and Heyman 2007); networks of family, *paisanos* (people from the same hometown), and *conocidos* (acquaintances; Álvarez 1987; Runsten and Kearney 1994; Vélez-Ibáñez 1996; chapter 17); border balance and other cross-border family forms (Heyman 1991; chapter 9); funds of knowledge (Vélez-Ibáñez and Greenberg 1992); hybridity (García Canclini 1995); the carnivalesque (Limón 1989); and Spanish-English borrowing and code-switching, discussed in chapter 7. A deep ethnography of binational, bicultural coordination is Robert Álvarez's (2005) participant-observation in the legal cross-border fruit and vegetable trade. More theoretically, a thread of my work has looked at border culture as emerging from and producing uneven and combined relations (Heyman 2010b, 2012a; and also see chapter 13).

Yet, as Vélez-Ibáñez takes pains to point out in his work on ROSCAs, this impressive cultural creativity should not be treated romantically. It is often coopted by macroscripts. Such dominating ideologies have an important presence in the region, which should not be surprising for a regional system emerging from intensive relations of power and inequality. These dominating ideologies include the overarching positive status of the United States and its association with modernity and purity, the converse stigma of "all poverty is Mexican" (Vila 2000) and "workers are Mexican" (Vélez-Ibáñez 1996). Relatedly, U.S. citizenship is a material and symbolic item of immense power in the region, and even legal access to visit the United States (such as a non-immigrant border-crossing card) is a status and identity symbol in Mexico (Yeh 2009, 2016). There also is the prestige position of the English language, and below that of educated Mexican Spanish, with working-class Spanish and mixed codes being stigmatized. Both the United States and Mexico harbor harsh classism and racism, though in different specific forms, which in each place humiliate working-class Mexicans (Lugo 2008; Rosas 2012). Lugo's expanded concept of border inspections is particularly revealing. Both countries' borderlands, in their own ways, have contested terrains of cultural valuation and affiliation, with highly positive feelings about Mexican-origin cultural creativity posed against hierarchical rankings of value in the wider political economy. People debate these options constantly (e.g., language choice and speech style) and choose personal affiliations in complex ways. Pablo Vila (2000, 2005) provides a rich ethnography of debates among these positional identities. While I listed first horizontal and then vertical cultural idioms and practices, as if they were separate, actually we expect to find complicated syntheses of them in a situation built on unequal relations and exchanges. We might expect, for example, horizontal exchanges among dominant people and organizations, then chains of vertical exchanges, with mediations of difference at each step, and finally more horizontal exchanges among subordinate groups. Those complex arrangements of inequality and difference require specific cultural codes, especially about how to conduct and interpret social relations. There are fairly few ethnographic studies of these mediations, although see Wright (2006, 123–50) on how a Mexican supervisor used her bicultural skills to mediate production control and optimization on behalf of maquiladora management, who did not understand what they had in her. The study of border culture would benefit from exploring this more (see Heyman 2012a). If the advanced study of culture and social relations has, in the past, focused on capturing deep and pure essences of bounded containers, border studies have the possibility of contributing new theories and cases from a perspective of uneven and combined relations.

The borderlands in both Mexico and the United States are key sites of social struggle. Broadly, the border region is perceived on the left as a symbol of social injustice and human rights violations and on the right as a symbol of insecurity and disorder—which holds broadly true in both countries. There are, of course, numerous actual lines of struggle and change, and differences of scale at which such politics take place: the national politics (in both countries) over border policies and much more variegated and subtle politics within the region. This complexity set to the side, however, I have proposed a triangular model of struggle over border projects, admittedly more with the United States in mind (Heyman 2012c). Elites seek managerialist approaches to the border, centered on investment and commodity projects such as the maquiladoras, taking advantage of low wages and high quality and productivity in Mexico; they also seek controlled but substantial labor mobility, permanent-legal, temporary-legal, or tolerated but illegalized. Elitist border approaches at times address social and environmental reforms but in most instances are locked into an agenda of uneven and combined development that favors growth with risk and suffering. In alliance but also tension with managerialist elites are populist right-wing movements, which reject mass immigration and focus on symbolic borders and militarized policing as imagined protections against external threat. The populist right wing makes border governance heavy-handed and contradictory but provides an important electoral resource for cynical elites. In open struggle with the populist right, and in alternating struggles and alliance with managerialist elites, human rights–social justice–labor coalitions seek the possibilities for well-being immanent in uneven and combined border relations, such as seeking legal and open migration (e.g., Nagengast, Stavenhagen, and Kearney 1992). This side of the struggle is currently politically the weakest, if also the most future looking.[5]

The social values involved in the sovereignty side are relatively simple, though worthy of study and analysis because of their political significance (e.g., Correa-Cabrera and Garrett 2014). The other two sides of the triangle, however, are more ambiguous because uneven and combined relations mean contradictory positions and tactics (also see chapter 3). For example, both managerialist elites and social justice advocates may favor reduction of security burdens in everyday border crossing (visiting, shopping, commerce, etc.). Yet they may disagree on labor justice for migrant workers involving increasing minimum wages in either or both countries. They may ally on some issues and diverge on others. Yet more paradoxically, their own values may contain important internal contradictions and ambivalences, due to the effects of uneven combinations. For example, the advocacy of more open, less vulnerable forms of international migration, unquestionably justified in terms of human rights and reduction of risk, is at the same time aligned with the liberalization of factors of production in neoliberal capitalism. The border analysis, attending to relationships of opposites, is a valuable starting point for thinking about hard issues in societal values.

This complex border situation likewise has important implications for research methods and ethics, which are intelligently explored in O'Leary, Deeds, and Whiteford

(2013). The research environment is shaped by the combination of opportunity and risk, exacerbated by a heavy presence of state security. Researchers must select topics thoughtfully in terms of societal values, use methods that protect the well-being of the researched, recognize complexity and ambiguity in their analyses, and negotiate relationships with communities, funders, and state agencies (for example, see chapter 15). An evident example is research with undocumented people, who are at risk of exposure and deportation, especially in this heavily policed region; they may also face risks from criminal organizations. Furthermore, undocumented people are mixed with citizen and legal immigrant household and community members and have connections to people at home in Mexico and Central America, so many people may be put at risk through research. Risk pervades both research ethics and relationship building. Yet for reasons of both public issues and social analysis, migration and enforcement processes should be the subject of research. Unauthorized migration is, perhaps, the starkest issue of research ethics and methods but hardly the only one presented by the disparities and contradictions that emerge from uneven and combined development.

Many points made here apply far from borders, forming the U.S.-Mexico border's contribution to social theory. Examining the border region helps us break with methodological nationalism, with the assumption of contained, uniform units, where the goal is the best possible characterization of deep essences. It brings us to ask how people, places, and environments that are apparently distinguished—most obviously by geopolitical borders but also by other social boundaries (Fassin 2011)—are brought together in uneven and combined relationships. This is crucial: societies are not uniform masses with homogenous cultures but rather relational webs of differentiated social actors mediated by complicated symbolic activities. Coordination across unequal difference is not functionally or structurally inherent but rather is the result of specific power projects, which could be otherwise arranged. Such coordination often is unstable and contradictory and also may harm human well-being (Wolf 1990).

Power-laden inequalities and processes of combination are highly visible at geopolitical borders, in symbolism and material practices, but many social situations upon close analysis are similarly uneven and combined. Borders, then, are condensed and valuable places to identify and tackle key issues in social-cultural theory. Keeping in mind the unity of apparent opposites—not just as coexisting, paradoxical contrasts but nexuses of dialectical relationships—is both difficult and necessary. When we identify a given analytical construct, we always need to ask what its relational inverse on the other side of the boundary is, the original and enduring insight of Barth (1969). Our task is not just to narrate one kind of ethnographic tale but also to think about such tales as arising within connections in a dynamic field. Such relational understandings are needed to analyze the emergence and transformation of specific arrangements (as opposed to possible other ones) and to address fundamental questions of humane values and struggles for them.

NOTES

1. I focus on geopolitical borders and the social-cultural milieu that emerge around them. I relate my analysis to social boundaries more widely (Fassin 2011) but do not aspire to cover that vast subject.
2. Vila (2003) and Kun and Montemezolo (2012) likewise contrast the Mexican emphasis on relational inequality with the U.S. fascination with liberation from convention and structure.
3. The concept of uneven and combined development began in the work of Leon Trotsky to account for apparently disparate or contradictory features of countries (especially in their politics) as capitalist transformations take hold. Smith (1984) extended this to spatial disparities and connections, building on David Harvey's (1982) notion of the spatial fix. Such spatial thinking speaks particularly well to borders.
4. Such symbolism is more common in the U.S. national interior and less so at the border.
5. Valuable work has been done on the possibilities and complexities of cross-border cooperation (from above) and activism (from below) (Staudt and Coronado 2002; Staudt and Méndez 2015). Suzanne Simon's (2014) perceptive ethnography of working-class northern border Mexicans involved in labor and environmental justice activism shows clearly the gaps, contradictions, and translations stemming from uneven and combined relationships inside and across the border.

REFERENCES

Adey, Peter. 2010. *Mobility*. London and New York: Routledge.

Alegría Olazábal, Tito. 2009. *Metrópolis transfronteriza: Revisión de la hipótesis y evidencias de Tijuana, México y San Diego, Estados Unidos*. Tijuana, Mexico: Colegio de la Frontera Norte; Mexico City: Miguel Ángel Porrúa.

Álvarez, Robert R. 1987. *Familia: Migration and Adaptation in Baja and Alta California, 1800–1975*. Berkeley: University of California Press.

———. 2005. *Mangos, Chiles, and Truckers: The Business of Transnationalism*. Minneapolis: University of Minnesota Press.

———. 2012. "Borders and Bridges: Exploring a New Conceptual Architecture for (U.S.–Mexico) Border Studies." *Journal of Latin American and Caribbean Anthropology* 17:24–40.

Anderson, Joan B., and James Gerber. 2008. *Fifty Years of Change on the U.S.-Mexico Border: Growth, Development, and Quality of Life*. Austin: University of Texas Press.

Barth, Fredrik. 1969. "Introduction." In *Ethnic Groups and Boundaries: The Social Organization of Culture Difference*, edited by Fredrik Barth, 9–38. Boston: Little, Brown.

Boehmer, Charles R., and Sergio Peña. 2012. "The Determinants of Open and Closed Borders" *Journal of Borderlands Studies* 27:273–85.

Bowden, Charles. 1998. *Juárez: The Laboratory of Our Future*. New York: Aperture.

Boyce, Geoffrey A., Jeffrey M. Banister, and Jeremy Slack. 2015. "You and What Army? Violence, the State, and Mexico's War on Drugs." *Territory, Politics, Governance* 3:446–68.

Bustamante, Jorge A. 1991. "Frontera México-Estados Unidos: Reflexiones para un marco teorico." *Estudios sobre las Culturas Contemporáneas* 4(11): 11–35. http://www.redalyc.org/articulo.oa?id=31641102.

Campbell, Howard. 2009. *Drug War Zone: Frontline Dispatches from the Streets of El Paso and Juárez*. Austin: University of Texas Press.

Campbell, Howard, and Josiah McC. Heyman. 2007. "Slantwise: Beyond Domination and Resistance on the Border." *Journal of Contemporary Ethnography* 36:3–30.

Chavez, Sergio. 2016. *Border Lives: Fronterizos, Transnational Migrants, and Commuters in Tijuana*. New York: Oxford University Press.

Collins, Timothy W., and Anthony M. Jimenez. 2012. "The Neoliberal Production of Vulnerability and Unequal Risk." In *Cities, Nature and Development: The Politics and Production of Urban Vulnerabilities*, edited by Sarah Dooling and Gregory Simon, 49–68. Surrey, UK: Ashgate.

Correa-Cabrera, Guadalupe, and Terence M. Garrett. 2014. "The Phenomenology of Perception and Fear: Security and the Reality of the US-Mexico Border." *Journal of Borderlands Studies* 29:243–55.

Doty, Roxanne Lynn. 2009. *The Law into Their Own Hands: Immigration and the Politics of Exceptionalism*. Tucson: University of Arizona Press.

Fassin, Didier. 2011. "Policing Borders, Producing Boundaries: The Governmentality of Immigration in Dark Times." *Annual Review of Anthropology* 40:213–26.

Fernandez, Raul A. 1977. *The United States-Mexico Border: A Politico-Economic Profile*. Notre Dame, IN: University of Notre Dame Press.

Fernández-Kelly, María Patricia. 1983. *For We Are Sold, I and My People: Women and Industry in Mexico's Frontier*. Albany: State University of New York Press.

Flores Pérez, Carlos Antonio. 2013. *Historias de polvo y sangre: Génesis y evolución del tráfico de drogas en el estado de Tamaulipas*. Mexico City: Centro de Investigaciones y Estudios Superiores en Antropología Social.

Fuentes, César M., and Sergio Peña. 2010a. "Globalization and Its Effects on the Urban Socio-Spatial Structure of a Transfrontier Metropolis: El Paso, TX-Ciudad Juárez,

Chih.-Sunland Park, NM." In *Cities and Citizenship at the U.S.-Mexico Border: The Paso del Norte Metropolitan Region*, edited by Kathleen Staudt, César M. Fuentes, and Julia E. Monárrez Fragoso, 93–118. New York: Palgrave Macmillan.

———. 2010b. "Globalization, Transborder Networks, and U.S.-Mexico Border Cities." In *Cities and Citizenship at the U.S.-Mexico Border: The Paso del Norte Metropolitan Region*, edited by Kathleen Staudt, César M. Fuentes, and Julia E. Monárrez Fragoso, 1–19. New York: Palgrave Macmillan.

García Canclini, Néstor. 1995. *Hybrid Cultures: Strategies for Entering and Leaving Modernity*. Minneapolis: University of Minnesota Press.

Gordon, Linda. 1999. *The Great Arizona Orphan Abduction*. Cambridge, MA: Harvard University Press.

Greenberg, James B., and Josiah McC. Heyman. 2012. "Neoliberal Capital and the Mobility Approach in Anthropology." In *Neoliberalism and Commodity Production in Mexico*, edited by James B. Greenberg, Thomas Weaver, Anne Browning-Aiken, and William L. Alexander, 241–68. Boulder: University Press of Colorado.

Greenberg, James B., and Thomas K. Park. 1994. "Political Ecology." *Journal of Political Ecology* 1:1–12.

Grineski, Sara E., and Timothy W. Collins. 2010. "Environmental Injustices in Transnational Context: Urbanization and Industrial Hazards in El Paso/Ciudad Juárez." *Environment and Planning A* 42:1308–27.

Gupta, Akhil, and James Ferguson. 1992. "Beyond 'Culture': Space, Identity, and the Politics of Difference." *Cultural Anthropology* 7:6–23.

Harvey, David. 1982. *The Limits to Capital*. Chicago: University of Chicago Press.

Heyman, Josiah McC. 1991. *Life and Labor on the Border: Working People of Northeastern Sonora, Mexico, 1886–1986*. Tucson: University of Arizona Press.

———. 1999a. "State Escalation of Force: A Vietnam/US-Mexico Border Analogy." In *States and Illegal Practices*, edited by Josiah McC. Heyman, 285–314. Oxford: Berg.

———, ed. 1999b. *States and Illegal Practices*. Oxford: Berg.

———. 2001. "Class and Classification at the U.S.-Mexico Border." *Human Organization* 60: 128–40.

———. 2004. "Ports of Entry as Nodes in the World System." *Identities: Global Studies in Culture and Power* 11:303–27.

———. 2007. "Environmental Issues at the U.S.-Mexico Border and the Unequal Territorialization of Value." In *Rethinking Environmental History: World-System History and Global Environmental Change*, edited by Alf Hornborg, J. R. McNeill, and Joan Martinez-Alier, 327–44. Walnut Creek, CA: AltaMira Press.

———. 2009. "Trust, Privilege, and Discretion in the Governance of the US Borderlands with Mexico." *Canadian Journal of Law and Society/Revue Canadienne Droit et Société* 24:367–90.

———. 2010a. "The State and Mobile People at the U.S.-Mexico Border." In *Class, Contention, and a World in Motion*, edited by Winnie Lem and Pauline Gardiner Barber, 58–78. Oxford: Berghahn Press.

———. 2010b. "US-Mexico Border Cultures and the Challenge of Asymmetrical Interpenetration." In *Borderlands: Ethnographic Approaches to Security, Power, and Identity*, edited by Hastings Donnan and Thomas M. Wilson, 21–34. Lanham, MD: University Press of America.

———. 2011. *Guns, Drugs, and Money: Tackling the Real Threats to Border Security*. Washington, DC: Immigration Policy Center.

———. 2012a. "Culture Theory and the US–Mexico Border." In *A Companion to Border Studies*, edited by Hastings Donnan and Thomas Wilson, 48–65. Malden, MA: Wiley-Blackwell.

———. 2012b. "Capitalism and US Policy at the Mexican Border." *Dialectical Anthropology* 36:263–77.

———. 2012c. "Constructing a 'Perfect' Wall: Race, Class, and Citizenship in US-Mexico Border Policing." In *Migration in the 21st Century: Political Economy and Ethnography*, edited by Pauline Gardiner Barber and Winnie Lem, 153–74. New York: Routledge.

———. 2012d. "Construcción y uso de tipologías: Movilidad geográfica desigual en la frontera México-Estados Unidos." In *Métodos cualitativos y su aplicación empírica: Por los caminos de la investigación sobre migración internacional*, edited by Marina Ariza and Laura Velasco Ortiz, 419–54. Mexico City: Instituto de Investigaciones Sociales, UNAM, y El Colegio de la Frontera Norte.

———. 2014. "'Illegality' and the U.S.-Mexico Border: How It Is Produced and Resisted." In *Constructing Illegality in America: Immigrant Experiences, Critiques, and Responses*, edited by Cecilia Menjívar and Daniel Kanstroom, 111–35. New York: Cambridge University Press.

Heyman, Josiah McC., and Howard Campbell. 2009. "The Anthropology of Global Flows: A Critical Reading of Appadurai's 'Disjuncture and Difference in the Global Cultural Economy.'" *Anthropological Theory* 9:131–48.

———. 2011. "Afterword: Crime on and Across Borders." In *Smugglers, Brothels, and Twine: Historical Perspectives on Contraband and Vice in North America's Borderlands*, edited by Elaine Carey and Andrae M. Marak, 177–90. Tucson: University of Arizona Press.

Iglesias Prieto, Norma. 1997. *Beautiful Flowers of the Maquiladora: Life Histories of Women Workers in Tijuana*. Austin: University of Texas Press.

Kates, Robert W., William C. Clark, Robert Corell, J. Michael Hall, Carlo C. Jaeger, Ian Lowe, James J. McCarthy, Hans Joachim Schellnhuber, Bert Bolin, Nancy M. Dickson, Sylvie Faucheux, Gilberto C. Gallopin, Arnulf Grübler, Brian Huntley, Jill Jäger, Narpat S. Jodha, Roger E. Kasperson, Akin Mabogunje, Pamela Matson, Harold Mooney, Berrien Moore III, Timothy O'Riordan, and Uno Svedin. 2001. "Sustainability Science." *Science* 292(5517): 641–42.

Kearney, Michael. 1986. "Integration of the Mixteca and the Western U.S.-Mexican Border Region via Migratory Wage Labor." In *Regional Impacts of U.S.-Mexican Relations*, edited by Ina Rosenthal Urey, 71–102. Center for U.S.-Mexican Studies Monograph Series 16. San Diego: University of California, San Diego.

———. 1991. "Borders and Boundaries of the State and Self at the End of Empire." *Journal of Historical Sociology* 4:52–74.

———. 2004. "The Classifying and Value-Filtering Missions of Borders." *Anthropological Theory* 4:131–56.

Kopinak, Kathryn. 1996. *Desert Capitalism: Maquiladoras in North America's Western Industrial Corridor*. Tucson: University of Arizona Press.

———, ed. 2004. *The Social Costs of Industrial Growth in Northern Mexico*. La Jolla: Center for U.S.-Mexican Studies, University of California, San Diego.

Kun, Josh, and Fiamma Montezemolo. 2012. "The Factory of Dreams." In *Tijuana Dreaming: Life and Art at the Global Border*, edited by Josh Kun and Fiamma Montezemolo, 1–20. Durham, NC: Duke University Press.

Limón, José E. 1989. "Carne, Carnales, and the Carnivalesque: Bakhtinian Batos, Disorder, and Narrative Discourses." *American Ethnologist* 16:471–86.

Lugo, Alejandro. 2008. *Fragmented Lives, Assembled Parts: Culture, Capitalism, and Conquest at the U.S.-Mexico Border*. Austin: University of Texas Press.

Malkki, Liisa. 1992. "National Geographic: The Rooting of Peoples and the Territorialization of National Identity Among Scholars and Refugees." *Cultural Anthropology* 7:24–44.

Martínez, Oscar J. 1994. *Border People: Life and Society in the U.S.-Mexico Borderlands*. Tucson: University of Arizona Press.

Mezzadra, Sandro, and Brett Neilson. 2013. *Border as Method, or, the Multiplication of Labor*. Durham, NC: Duke University Press.

Montejano, David. 1987. *Anglos and Mexicans in the Making of Texas, 1836–1986*. Austin: University of Texas Press.

Mora-Torres, Juan. 2001. *The Making of the Mexican Border: The State, Capitalism, and Society in Nuevo León, 1848–1910*. Austin: University of Texas Press.

Muehlmann, Shaylih. 2014. *When I Wear My Alligator Boots: Narco-culture in the U.S.-Mexico Borderlands*. Berkeley: University of California Press.

Nagengast, Carole, Rodolfo Stavenhagen, and Michael Kearney. 1992. *Human Rights and Indigenous Workers: The Mixtecs in Mexico and the United States*. San Diego: Center for U.S.-Mexican Studies, University of California, San Diego.

Nevins, Joseph. 2010. *Operation Gatekeeper and Beyond: The War on "Illegals" and the Remaking of the U.S.-Mexico Boundary*. New York: Routledge.

Núñez, Guillermina Gina, and Josiah McC. Heyman. 2007. "Entrapment Processes and Immigrant Communities in a Time of Heightened Border Vigilance." *Human Organization* 66:354–65.

O'Leary, Anna Ochoa, Colin M. Deeds, and Scott Whiteford, eds. 2013. *Uncharted Terrains: New Directions in Border Research Methodology, Ethics, and Practice*. Tucson: University of Arizona Press.

Ortiz, Victor. 2004. *El Paso: Local Frontiers at a Global Crossroads*. Minneapolis: University of Minnesota Press.

Palerm, Juan-Vicente, and José Ignacio Urquiola. 1993. "A Binational System of Agricultural Production: The Case of the Mexican Bajio and California." In *Mexico and the United States: Neighbors in Crisis*, edited by Daniel G. Aldrich Jr. and Lorenzo Meyer, 311–67. San Bernardino, CA: Borgo Press.

Pallitto, Robert, and Josiah McC. Heyman. 2008. "Theorizing Cross-Border Mobility: Surveillance, Security and Identity." *Surveillance & Society* 5(3): 315–33. http://www.surveillance-and-society.org/articles5(3)/mobility.pdf.

Peña, Devon G. 1997. *The Terror of the Machine: Technology, Work, Gender, and Ecology on the U.S.-Mexico Border*. Austin: Center for Mexican American Studies, University of Texas at Austin.

Robinson-Avila, Kevin. 2013. "Expansion Plans for Taiwanese Electronics *Maquila* Could Intensify Zone's Rapid Growth." *Albuquerque Journal*, May 20. https://www.abqjournal.com/200914/expansion-plans-for-taiwanese-electronics-maquila-could-intensify-zones-rapid-growth.html.

Rosas, Gilberto. 2012. *Barrio Libre: Criminalizing States and Delinquent Refusals of the New Frontier*. Durham, NC: Duke University Press.

Ruiz, Olivia. 2001. "Riesgo, migración y espacios fronterizos: una reflexión." *Estudios Demográficos y Urbanos* 47:257–84.

Runsten, David, and Michael Kearney. 1994. *A Survey of Oaxacan Village Networks in California Agriculture*. Davis: California Institute for Rural Studies.

Salas, Miguel Tinker. 1997. *In the Shadow of the Eagles: Sonora and the Transformation of the Border During the Porfiriato*. Berkeley: University of California Press.

Sandoval, Efrén. 2012. *Infraestructuras transfronterizas: Etnografía de itinerarios en el espacio social Monterrey-San Antonio*. Mexico City: Centro de Investigaciones y Estudios Superiores en Antropología Social; Tijuana: El Colegio de la Frontera Norte.

Sheridan, Thomas E. 1995. *Arizona: A History*. Tucson: University of Arizona Press.

Simon, Suzanne. 2014. *Sustaining the Borderlands in the Age of NAFTA: Development, Politics, and Participation on the US-Mexico Border*. Nashville, TN: Vanderbilt University Press.

Slack, Jeremy. 2015. "Captive Bodies: Migrant Kidnapping and Deportation in Mexico." *Area* 48(3): 271–77. doi:10.1111/area.12151.

Slack, Jeremy, and Howard Campbell. 2016. "On Narco-coyotaje: Illicit Regimes and Their Impacts on the US-Mexico Border." *Antipode* 48(5): 1380–99. doi:10.1111/anti.12242.

Slack, Jeremy, Daniel E. Martínez, Alison Elizabeth Lee, and Scott Whiteford. 2016. "The Geography of Border Militarization: Violence, Death and Health in Mexico and the United States." *Journal of Latin American Geography* 15:7–32.

Slack, Jeremy, and Scott Whiteford. 2011. "Violence and Migration on the Arizona-Sonora Border." *Human Organization* 70:11–21.

Smith, Neil. 1984. *Uneven Development: Nature, Capital, and the Production of Space*. New York: Blackwell.

Spener, David. 2009. *Clandestine Crossings: Migrants and Coyotes on the Texas-Mexico Border*. Ithaca, NY: Cornell University Press.

———. 2010. "*Movidas Rascuaches*: Strategies of Migrant Resistance at the Mexico-U.S. Border." *Aztlán: A Journal of Chicano Studies* 35(2): 9–36.

Staudt, Kathleen A. 1998. *Free Trade? Informal Economies at the U.S.-Mexico Border*. Philadelphia: Temple University Press.

———. 2008. *Violence and Activism at the Border: Gender, Fear, and Everyday Life in Ciudad Juárez*. Austin: University of Texas Press.

Staudt, Kathleen A., and Irasema Coronado. 2002. *Fronteras no más: Toward Social Justice at the U.S.-Mexico Border*. New York: Palgrave Macmillan.

Staudt, Kathleen A., and Zulma Y. Méndez. 2015. *Courage, Resistance, and Women in Ciudad Juárez: Challenges to Militarization*. Austin: University of Texas Press.

Staudt, Kathleen A., and David Spener. 1998. "The View from the Frontier: Theoretical Perspectives Undisciplined." In *The U.S.-Mexico Border: Transcending Divisions, Contesting Identities*, edited by David Spener and Kathleen A. Staudt, 3–34. Boulder, CO: Lynne Rienner Publishers.

Tuttle, Carolyn. 2012. *Mexican Women in American Factories: Free Trade and Exploitation on the Border*. Austin: University of Texas Press.

Velasco Ortiz, Laura. 2005. *Mixtec Transnational Identity*. Tucson: University of Arizona Press.

———. 2008. "Introducción: Migración, fronteras estatales y étnicas." In *Migración, fronteras e identidades étnicas transnacionales*, edited by Laura Velasco Ortiz, 5–32. Tijuana, Mexico: El Colegio de la Frontera Norte; Mexico City: Miguel Ángel Porrúa.

Velasco Ortiz, Laura, and Oscar F. Contreras. 2011. *Mexican Voices of the Border Region*. Philadelphia: Temple University Press.

Velasco Ortiz, Laura, Christian Zlolniski, and Marie-Laure Coubès. 2014. *De jornaleros a colonos: Residencia, trabajo e identidaden el Valle de San Quintín*. Tijuana, Mexico: El Colegio de la Frontera Norte.

Vélez-Ibáñez, Carlos G. 1996. *Border Visions: Mexican Cultures of the Southwest United States*. Tucson: University of Arizona Press.

———. 2010. *An Impossible Living in a Transborder World: Culture, Confianza, and Economy of Mexican-Origin Populations*. Tucson: University of Arizona Press.

Vélez-Ibáñez, Carlos G., and James B. Greenberg. 1992. "Formation and Transformation of Funds of Knowledge Among U.S.-Mexican Households." *Anthropology & Education Quarterly* 23:313–35.

Vila, Pablo. 2000. *Crossing Borders, Reinforcing Borders: Social Categories, Metaphors, and Narrative Identities on the U.S.-Mexico Frontier*. Austin: University of Texas Press.

———. 2003. "Conclusion: The Limits of American Border Theory." In *Ethnography at the Border*, edited by Pablo Vila, 306–41. Minneapolis: University of Minnesota Press.

———. 2005. *Border Identifications: Narratives of Religion, Gender, and Class on the U.S.-Mexico Border*. Austin: University of Texas Press.

Walsh, Casey. 2009. "'To Come of Age in a Dry Place': Infrastructures of Irrigated Agriculture in the Mexico-U.S. Borderlands." *Southern Rural Sociology* 24:21–43.

———. 2013. "Water Infrastructures in the U.S./Mexico Borderlands." *Ecosphere* 4(1): 8. http://dx.doi.org/10.1890/ES12-00268.1.

Wimmer, Andreas, and Nina Glick Schiller. 2002. "Methodological Nationalism and Beyond: Nation-State Building, Migration and the Social Sciences." *Global Networks* 2:301–34.

Wolf, Eric R. 1982. *Europe and the People Without History*. Berkeley: University of California Press.

———. 1990. "Distinguished Lecture: Facing Power—Old Insights, New Questions." *American Anthropologist* 92:586–96.

Wright, Melissa W. 2006. *Disposable Women and Other Myths of Global Capitalism*. New York: Routledge.

Yeh, Rihan. 2009. "Passing: An Ethnography of Status, Self and the Public in a Mexican Border City." PhD dissertation, Department of Anthropology, University of Chicago.

———. 2016. "Commensuration in a Mexican Border City: Currencies, Consumer Goods, and Languages." *Anthropological Quarterly* 89:63–92.

Zabin, Carol, Michael Kearney, Anna Garcia, David Runsten, and Carole Nagengast. 1993. *Mixtec Migrants in California Agriculture: A New Cycle of Poverty*. Davis: California Institute for Rural Studies.

3

EXCEPTIONAL STATES AND INSIPID BORDER WALLS

MARGARET E. DORSEY AND MIGUEL DÍAZ-BARRIGA

WE ARE FAMILIAR with the contradictions and stresses that define contemporary borders and place the forces of globalization, including economic and cultural flows, on one side and state sovereignty, both in protecting local economies and national identity, on the other. In this framework, theorists such as Wendy Brown (2014) and Peter Andreas (2009) view border wall construction as a desperate and theatrical attempt by "weakened" nation-states to exert their sovereignty in the face of strong transnational economic institutions and high levels of cross-border migration, trade, and cultural exchange. Anthropologists Donnan and Wilson (2010) agree with the "waning sovereignty" model but emphasize that states are reasserting sovereign power through rebordering international boundaries. Such rebordering processes are uneven, preserving some aspects of "national identity and national territory and sovereignty" while allowing others to "change drastically," as seen in accords that allow for freer flows of goods and people (Donnan and Wilson 2010, 6). In this formulation, it is the job of anthropologists, through fine-grained ethnographic analysis, to elucidate the contours of rebordering and debordering processes—both in terms of physically fortifying and economically opening borders—as it occurs on the ground. We agree with Donnan and Wilson's call for refined ethnographic analysis, and at the same time, we want to suggest that their rebordering concept would benefit from a more fully theorized understanding of sovereignty (the concept is often undefined), which includes identifying specific transformations in sovereign practices. Anthropology of borders is limited to Westphalian and post-Westphalian visions of sovereignty and borders as reflected in the application of concepts that focus on borders as "closed" or "open," such as "borders" and "bridges," "blockades" and "flows," or "enclosures" and "mobilities." Yet, it seems as though sovereign practices do not solely revolve around control of territory and maintaining the cultural integrity of the nation.

In this chapter, we theorize rebordering in relation to a global reconfiguration of sovereignty, examining its physical manifestations as it alters border landscapes, through an analysis of the construction and architecture of the U.S.-Mexico border wall.[1] We argue that the logic of rebordering, in the U.S.-Mexico border region and beyond, responds to a reconstitution of sovereignty based on generating states of exception and practices associated with necropower. As ethnographers, however, we do not view these exercises of state power as seamless and universal but rather as asymmetrical and contested (also see chapters 1 and 2). We therefore analyze the architectures of border walls both as conduits of sovereignties and as sites of local, national, and international challenges to specific iterations of state power. In drawing your attention to sovereign practices in the borderlands, we add a strand to Vélez-Ibáñez's (2010) helices (color, class, gender, and commodity) of the Southwest North American (SWNA) region, that of militarism and its attendant violence as it forms and reforms the SWNA region, in the process altering its ecologies and economies.

Anthropological approaches to architecture examine the ways in which states incorporate their agendas for development and governance in designing planned cities and urban centers (Holston 1989; Buchli 2013). Going against the grain of the state's development policies, anthropologists have shown how architecture and planning in fact reinscribe inequality and marginalization. In the case of border walls with their rusty poles, concertina wire, chain link fences, and concrete façades, the state does not engage innovative architectural designs to reference a wider vision of development and governance. Rather, military engineers and private contractors, not architects, play a primary role in the design of border walls both globally and within the United States. In response to this militarized approach to international boundaries, groups of architects have called for designing border barriers around principles of "productive infrastructure" (Rael 2012) and "social exchange" (J. Brown 2012). More specifically, in our field site, border residents in South Texas resisted the militarized approach that sees their homes, universities, and parks as sites for "tactical infrastructure." In some cases, in response to citizens' protests, the Department of Homeland Security (DHS) negotiated with elected officials and, in fact, changed the architecture of the wall.

BORDER WALLS: STATES OF EXCEPTION AND NECROPOWER

With the fall of the Berlin Wall in 1989, pundits rejoiced in the dawn of a new era, a world without walls. Instead, walls now permeate our world. Since 1989, thirty-three nation-states have constructed, or are in the process of constructing, border walls.[2] A few examples of border walls' surge in global popularity include the following: in Africa, fortifications between the Spanish exclave of Melilla and Morocco and Botswana's electrified fence on its border with Zimbabwe; in Asia, heavily patrolled border fences on the Indo-Bangladeshi border with a "shoot-on-sight" policy; in the Middle East, the Saudi Arabian state built a barrier dividing itself from Yemen; and in North America, the United States constructed the border fence along sections of its border with Mexico that is a combination of walls and barriers, sometimes including concertina wire and CBP (Customs and Border Protection) agents armed with M-16 assault rifles. In their rush to reborder, these nation-states (Spain, Botswana, India, Saudi Arabia, and the United States) either "waived" or ignored laws in order to expedite construction and/or unleashed border enforcement policies that contradict the laws of those very nation-states. For example, Spanish border agents at Melilla do not officially register migrants apprehended at its border fence, as is required by Spanish law. Instead, they often turn migrants over to Moroccan authorities, who then leave them in the desert to perish. In India, Border Security Forces (BSF) are the law—any order given by a BSF officer to maintain India's security constitutes a lawful command (Jones 2009, 887). The Ministry of Law's "Acts and Rules" for border security provides the legal basis for the BSF to act outside the law to maintain the law.[3]

The United States twisted its own laws in the process of rebordering. The Italian political philosopher Giorgio Agamben (2005) argues that sovereignty is exercised through the state's ability to create states of exception through which the state acts outside of the normal operation of the law to maintain the law (Clarno 2013, 446). Nation-states increasingly rely on states of exception to strengthen executive power at times of crisis and to justify waiving laws. The U.S.-Mexico border wall is a product of such a state of exception: it is a reaction to unauthorized immigration and security concerns that intensified after 9-11. Through the 2005 Real ID Act, which had as its aim the security and authentication of driver's licenses and personal identification cards, the U.S. Congress granted the Secretary of the DHS the power to waive any and all laws for the construction of barriers and roads between the United States and Mexico. The Real ID Act also limited court review of waiver decisions to cases that allege a violation of the Constitution of the United States. Congress followed the Real ID Act with the Secure Fence Act of 2006, which mandated the construction of 670 miles of border fence. The 2008 Consolidated Appropriations Act gave the DHS Secretary sole discretion in deciding construction locations. In erecting the wall, Secretary Chertoff "waived" over thirty laws, including the National Environmental Policy Act, the Endangered Species Act, and the American Indian Religious Freedom Act. Through the power to act outside the law, Secretary Chertoff stripped environmental, Native American, and other groups of the power to challenge border wall manufacture in court.

Border walls have multiple effects: state practices of exclusion intensify and migration patterns shift into more dangerous areas, such as seas and deserts, that cause increased harm and death. We characterize such sovereign (and petty sovereign) practices of organizing exclusion and death, following postcolonial theorist Achille Mbembe (2003), as exercises of necropower. Mbembe understands sovereignty as the state's capacity to decide who may live and who may die, who is disposable and who is not. This format of sovereignty is contingent on the development of states of exception, for example, colonial rule as a suspension of law. Mbembe's arguments correspond with the U.S.-Mexico borderlands, particularly when one considers the region's history through the prism of conquest where state agents break the law to maintain it (Lugo 2008; Rosas 2012). Here we only need remind ourselves of Américo Paredes's analysis of the Texas Rangers' application of violence against people of Mexican descent to "uphold" the law (Paredes 1970). As Paredes points out, this violence only makes sense if one starts with the assumption that a Mexican's life is not worth anything—a clear example of state actors deciding which lives are worth living.

In the United States, the DHS built the border wall to funnel unauthorized migrants into remote and desolate areas where state agents could more easily apprehend them. Since 1995, the DHS's strategy of deterrence has led to over five thousand migrant deaths, mainly due to dehydration and exposure (Doty 2011). CPB agents themselves are increasing playing a proactive role in killing unauthorized migrants. A 2013 report by the Police Executive Research Forum notes an escalation in the use of deadly force by the CBP that includes agents creating scenarios, such as standing in front of and firing at vehicles, that justify the use of such force. From January 2010 to October 2012, the CBP reported sixty-seven shooting incidents, which resulted in nineteen deaths (Bennett 2014). The account notes that the CBP demonstrates a "lack of diligence" in investigating these incidents.[4] Closing the circular logic of their deterrence strategy, CBP officials used the landscape to justify their actions: they noted that because their agents work in remote and harsh terrain they need more flexibility than other law enforcement agents.[5] The exceptional border thus allows for an intensification of necropower based on a rendering of "ecology" that makes death and violence a natural part of the hegemonic landscape—border walls funnel migrants into deserts and law enforcement has greater leeway in applying deadly force because of the border's remoteness and desolation (Dorsey and Díaz-Barriga 2015).

We find that the conditions—sovereign power based on states of exception and necropower—for the construction of the U.S.-Mexico border wall are not unique to our field site. In fact, one can find border walls as manifestations of sovereignty based on necropower more globally.[6] The border wall at Melilla serves as an example. At the wall, both Spanish and Moroccan security forces act as petty sovereigns wielding power over life. A report by Doctors Without Borders documents the dismal living conditions that sub-Saharan migrants face in camps near the Melilla border wall as they seek entry into Spain and Europe. The report describes increased violence against migrants by Spanish and Moroccan security forces, including severe beatings and rape, emphasizing that "migrants are caught in a sinister game of ping-pong between two sets of security forces" (Doctors Without Borders 2013). The report also highlights increases in death not only in skirmishes at the border wall but also due to drowning as migrants attempt to circumvent the wall by sea. In India, reports of the BSF killing, wounding, or abducting Bangladeshis crossing the border fence, many under questionable circumstances, are a routine part of border life (Jones 2009). This use of force, as mentioned above, both stands outside and within the law.

BORDER WALL ARCHITECTURE

While the edges do cut, cutting-edge design is not a priority for the expression of sovereign power at borders. Under the waning sovereignty model for interpreting rebordering, one might expect states to erect monumental border wall projects that embody the state's power infused with a positive vision for development and government largess. Nation-states do not invest their global aspirations into architecture as they do in other monumental projects, yet border walls are monumental government projects. The U.S.-Mexico border wall is the largest domestic building project of the twenty-first century—eight hundred miles of fortification that cost up to $16 million per mile. The wall has incurred $4.4 million in repairs, and the construction and maintenance costs are expected to exceed over $49 billion over the next twenty-five years (Rael 2012). The Secretary of the DHS exercised his power to waive laws, and the DHS constructed the border wall with minimal public input about its design and function.[7] From the DHS's perspective, the wall is simply a fortification. More specifically, in his book on border security, Secretary Chertoff described the wall as a "tool" whose function is to slow the crossing of unauthorized persons, smugglers, and terrorists and provide the CBP with an advantage (Chertoff 2009). Thus the "Bollard Wall and Ladder," as shown in figure 3.1, exemplifies its utility as a tool for more than one side.

We encountered the DHS's tool paradigm firsthand at a conference organized by the Lower Rio Grande Valley chapter of the American Institute of Architects (AIA) at the South Padre Island Convention Center. The AIA invited us to lead a continuing education class, and our seminar on aesthetics at the conference contrasted with the rest of the classes, which focused on practical issues such as building codes. To our surprise, those courses appeared moderately populated, and our room was standing room only. There were at least one hundred architects and builders in the audience. Our intention was to discuss (1) border wall architectures and their effects in South

FIGURE 3.1. Bollard wall and ladders. Photo by Margaret E. Dorsey and Miguel Díaz-Barriga.

Texas; (2) how various interest groups negotiated the design of the various border wall architectures in South Texas; and (3) alternative models of the U.S.-Mexico border wall and to conclude with innovative design proposals published by professional architects in a variety of venues, including the *New York Times* (Hamilton 2006), architecture journals, and blogs (Rael San Fratello Architects 2014).

In hindsight, our "seminar" turned out to be a slightly comedic lesson in the unexpected. Five minutes into our presentation an elderly gentleman interrupted to tell stories, which continued for the entire class. About two-thirds of the way through our presentation, an engineer from a prominent engineering company, one of the construction companies that built the border wall, vehemently objected to our slides, stating multiple times that we were misrepresenting the construction sites and that the border wall was well constructed following environmental and safety standards *and*, by the way, had a positive economic impact on the region. At one point, everyone in the room seemed to turn and stare at his boss, the owner of the company, who finally chimed in. His engineer continued and openly called our presentation biased. When we asked who had designed the border wall, they stated that they followed plans given to them by the U.S. Army Corp of Engineers. Several architects intervened in this heated exchange (two of them were professors at other universities in

Texas) either by stating their opposition to the border wall or by attempting to clarify our point about the lack of public discussion and legal recourse for borderland residents. After our formal presentation, the engineer chatted with us at length and told us the opposite; in fact, the plans for the levee wall, discussed below, were drawn up quickly—on a napkin.[8] In a published summary of the conference, a writer wistfully noted with relief that our class did not end in "fist-a-cuffs."

Because of constant interruption and this spirited exchange, we did not have time to engage the audience in a discussion about innovative design options for border infrastructure. Architects have developed plans for creating border security infrastructure that is multifunctional—fostering binational cooperation and generating green energy. In a detailed proposal for Friendship Park on the San Diego–Tijuana border, the architect James Brown planned a mobile border fence that fosters the park's role as a binational gathering place (J. Brown 2012). The architect Ronald Rael designed a U.S.-Mexico border wall that is green—producing solar energy for both sides of the border while fostering communications and trade (Rael 2012). Our visual presentation featured a sketch of Rael's border barrier. The engineer categorically dismissed it and shifted the discussion back to the border wall's effectiveness at reducing unauthorized immigration. It did not surprise us that his response to alternative strategies mimicked that of the state, shifting focus away from aesthetics and environmental and social productivity to detention and exclusion.

Necropower, as it emerges through border wall design, continues its march toward militarization in spite of alternative imaginaries proposed by anthropologists and architects as well as opposition from local constituents and international organizations. In both Africa and North America, states are installing more concertina wire. The Spanish government at the end of 2013 refitted its border fencing in Melilla with razor wire despite widespread criticism from opposition political parties, human rights groups, and members of the European Union.[9] Spain installed the razor wire in response to several attempts by waves of migrants to scale the fence. The Spanish government emphasized that concertina wire only causes minor wounds and has resisted calls from human rights groups, Spain's attorney general, and the Catholic Church to remove it (Cué 2013). Historically, the Spanish government has bowed to such pressure. On the San Diego–Tijuana border, the DHS initially did not install concertina wire, but in 2008, ignoring criticism from community and human rights groups, the DHS persisted and added razor wire. In a similar pattern five years later, the DHS proposed mounting concertina wire on the border fence in Nogales, Arizona (Prendergast 2013). The mayor of Nogales, in an effort to hinder the DHS, noted that razor wire is unacceptable to the city due to the costs associated with rescuing trapped people and providing them with medical treatment. A sharply worded editorial in the *Nogales International* rhetorically asks why Border Patrol limits itself to razor wire when it can electrify the fence (Coppola 2013). In the face of local opposition, the DHS halted. Is it only a matter of time before concertina wire becomes a normal part of border fencing across the United States[10] and the next protest is against electrifying the fence, following Botswana's model?

The architecture of the U.S. border wall, with its military referents, keys the state's seemingly inexorable drive to fabricate the SWNA region as a war zone. The wall requires constant maintenance and expansion. Arguments that draw attention to the ease of cutting through landing mats (now being replaced), the ease of placing ramps over Normandy barriers, and the rapidity that people scale bollard fences should not be misread as an indictment of the wall's effectiveness but as a call for more: augmenting concertina wire, adding more sensors, and heightening surveillance. The wall, as part of a wider "assemblage" of discourses, practices, infrastructure, and corporate profit that make up a growing border security apparatus, is a centerpiece for exhortations for increased funding, better technologies, and more surveillance (Harris 2012). Researchers at the University of Arizona's Science and Technology Park, for example, are part of a synergy between academia and industry aimed at making Arizona a leader in designing and manufacturing border security technologies (a state whose neoliberal policies are contextualized in chapter 10). The Science and Technology Park, according to border correspondent Todd Miller (2013), includes an eighteen-thousand-foot mockup of the border wall around which academic and industry-based researchers test surveillance and "interdiction" technologies.[11]

EXCLUSION AND BISECTIONS

The architecture of the border wall notifies the mainly Mexican-descent population of the borderlands that they, not only migrants and smugglers, are potential subjects of exclusion (comparable to chapters 11 and 12). In South Texas, as in many other areas of the Southwest, eighteen-foot rusty metal pylons wind through low-income urban neighborhoods in plain sight of and close proximity to people's homes. In its original border wall plans, the DHS called for demolishing homes in the town of Granjeno, Texas. The DHS altered its plans only after massive protests and much attention from local, regional, national, and international press outlets (Bustillo 2007; Cable News Network 2007). U.S. representative Thomas Tancredo characterized opposition to the border wall in South Texas as "multiculturalist" and "pro-open borders" and threatened, in front of an audience of civic leaders and activists in the border town of Brownsville, that the DHS might consider constructing the wall north of their city.[12] The wall, and its attendant threat of more walling, thus increasingly excludes and cuts communities not only at the international boundary but also within the United States, enveloping local development projects into a militarized state.

Approximately forty thousand acres of U.S. land now sit in an ambiguous state south of the wall (Rael 2012). The DHS built the border wall in South Texas up to two miles north of the international boundary, the Rio Grande/Río Bravo, slashing through private property, state and local parks, and communities. The DHS created a "no-man's-land" that disrupts border civic leaders' and environmental organizations' programs for fostering environmental stewardship, generating economic development, and intensifying binational cooperation. Consider the following:

1. Since 1979, the U.S. Department of Fish and Wildlife along with The Nature Conservancy and Audubon purchased land along the Rio Grande/Río Bravo to create an ecological corridor. Much of this land is now south of the border wall. The plans for the wildlife corridor are now on hold.
2. Cities along the Rio Grande/Río Bravo forged economic development plans to revitalize their riverfront property. Brownsville, for example, planned to construct a binational river walk along the Rio Grande/Río Bravo (following the example of San Antonio's River Walk), and Hidalgo developed a museum and World Birding Center with hike and bike trails leading to the river. Portions of Brownsville's and Hidalgo's development sites are now south of the border wall. Brownsville is no longer pursuing the binational river walk. Dozens of bicycles Hidalgo purchased for tourists to use sit mothballed in their museum as a consequence of border wall construction.

Under the state of exception granted to the DHS, city governments, environmental groups, and private landowners failed to challenge the state with success, even though many lawsuits were filed: some were dismissed and some were settled. Local groups forced the DHS to change the design of the border wall in a few cases. These instances are instructive for us because they demonstrate how local groups altered the wall, making it productive to local needs while melding its design into the landscape. These partial victories, however, came at a price (literally and metaphorically). We discuss two instances below.

THE UNIVERSITY OF TEXAS AT BROWNSVILLE

In October 2007, CBP agents sought entry onto the University of Texas Brownsville–Texas Southmost College (UTB-TSC) campus in order to survey land for the construction of the border wall. The UTB-TSC website states: "The request sought access to survey university land for 18 months for the possible construction of the fence, to store equipment and supplies, take samples and to do any other work they found necessary for the proposed construction of the fence" (UTB-TSC 2009).

UTB-TSC president Julieta Garcia refused to grant permission. After a series of protests, negotiations, and lawsuits, the DHS and the UTB-TSC agreed to a modified ten-foot-high fence—as opposed to the DHS's original plan for an eighteen-foot-high fence—that would complement the campus's landscape (Sieff 2008). The campus is scenic, located along a series of canals with meandering walkways and pedestrian bridges. Its buildings are new in a Spanish Mediterranean architectural style with arched walkways, tiled roofs, azulejos, porticos, and intimate courtyards. The DHS completed the border fence in early 2009. It is a green chain link fence located on the southern part of the campus. In March of that year a team of volunteers, with funding from a local businessman, planted three hundred budding jasmine vines along the border fence. The border wall melds into the campus to such an extent that it appears to be one of the outfield fences for the UTB-TSC baseball stadium. While they did not stop border wall construction, the UTB-TSC through a hard-fought campaign managed to force the DHS to change its location and design from rusty eighteen-feet-high pylons to a green ten-foot-high chain link fence. This fence is an aesthetic improvement over the brown pylon wall that meanders through other parts of Brownsville and Cameron County. In its negotiations, the UTB-TSC granted permission to the DHS to place high-tech sensors and other surveillance equipment on campus. The UTB-TSC also agreed to create a center for border security.

HIDALGO COUNTY: THE INFAMOUS LEVEE WALL

In 2007, the DHS sought to survey property in Hidalgo County to plan construction of the border wall. As the DHS continued surveying the area, environmental organizations, business leaders, and politicians across the Texas-Mexican border formed the Texas Border Coalition and joined forces to oppose the construction of the border wall. On December 11, 2007, in Hidalgo County, local "no border wall" protests culminated in a rally held at the same time and place as a DHS-sponsored forum on the border fence at the McAllen Convention Center. McAllen's Chamber of Commerce organized the rally, and more than two thousand protestors arrived at the DHS forum—including mayors, college students, Sierra Club representatives, citrus growers, farmworker activists, and residents of Granjeno and other towns affected by the proposed border wall (Osborne 2007). As protests continued, many of them coordinated by the newly formed No Border Wall group, Hidalgo County officials began negotiations with the DHS, and this move seems to have marked a shift in the conversation.

Instead of negotiating a border wall, Hidalgo County leaders came to an agreement with the DHS to build a combined levee-wall structure. In February 2008, claiming to make "lemonade out of lemons," Hidalgo County judge J. D. Salinas and other officials signed an agreement with the DHS that would allow border wall construction on existing levees in Hidalgo County. The county would gain by having its levee system reinforced, and the DHS would have the land it needed to build "tactical infrastructure." In towns such as Granjeno, the DHS would avoid demolishing homes. According to the agreement, the Hidalgo County Drainage District ($48.2 million) and the DHS ($65.7 million) would share the costs of the levee-wall construction, and local contractors and construction companies would be hired to build part of the wall (Leatherman and Roebuck 2008). While protests against the wall continued, the agreement effectively divided Hidalgo County's opposition to the border wall, with Hidalgo County paying a high price, over $40 million, for this compromise. In addition, it is unknown if the concrete facades constructed in Hidalgo County will protect from flooding. As an element of flood control, then it is perhaps ironic that the northern face of the border wall is landscaped to obscure the eighteen-foot drop behind it. When looking from the United States toward Mexico, on the one hand, the border wall melds into the landscape—a façade of belonging. When looking from south to north, on the other hand, the border wall is conspicuous—a smooth white concrete embankment winding through grassland and passing underneath an international bridge before abruptly ending.

CONCLUSION

We interpret borderlanders' protests—including not only opposition to the border wall itself but also criticism of the installation of razor wire and rusty bollard poles—as a reaction to sovereign practices based on legal exception, exclusion, and death. For the anthropology of borders, this wider theoretical consideration of sovereign practices can serve as a starting point for critically engaging the normalization and proliferation of border militarization as they impact the everyday lives of border residents. As such, we suggest incorporating an additional strand, militarism, to Vélez-Ibáñez's hermeneutic of the "Transborder Southwest North American Region" as it emerges and reemerges in the challenges of daily life (encounters at international boundaries, checkpoints, and border walls) and more monumental tussles with nation-state formation (Vélez-Ibáñez 2010, 123).

The militarized architecture of the border wall marks both the state's engagement with necropower and its marginalization. The rusted fences, concertina wire, and concrete façades represent the border wall as distinct from the center, like the border region itself, even though managing borders is central to the state's survival. The architecture of the wall thus manifests the border region as militarized but distant, in a state of exception to the rest of the nation yet key to its sovereignty. Architects have proposed innovative designs for border barriers that foster local economic development and binational cooperation while meeting security needs. These proposals, while having little impact on border wall construction, reveal how despite its large expenditures on border security the state views border infrastructure as a "tool." The DHS has not considered wider goals, such as meeting local needs, including environmental stewardship and fostering binational cooperation, as part of its infrastructure planning. In the few cases where local protests have had an impact, the DHS charged a heavy price both monetarily and by co-opting academia into its vision of border security and the privatization of the security apparatus. An ethnographic approach to rebordering demonstrates how local actors navigate and transform the state's agenda for border security within the context of sovereign power in the twenty-first century.

NOTES

1. This article derives from two years of National Science Foundation–funded ethnographic field research, including participant observation, video and photographic documentation, formal and open-ended interviews, focus groups, and a random survey.
2. A list of border walls and fences includes Botswana/Zimbabwe (2003), Brazil/Paraguay (2007), Brunei/Limbang (2005), China/North Korea (2006), Costa Rica/Nicaragua (2010), Egypt/Gaza (2009), Greece/Turkey (2013), India/Bangladesh (2005), India/Kashmir (2004), India/Pakistan, Iran/Afghanistan (announced in 2010), Iran/Pakistan (2011), Iran/Iraq (announced in 2010), Iran/Turkey (announced in 2010), Iraq/Syria (2010), Israel/West Bank (2003), Kazakh/Uzbekistan (2006), Kuwait/Iraq (1991), Morocco/Western Sahara (1980), North Korea/South Korea (1953), Pakistan/Afghanistan (2007), Pakistan/Iran (2007), Russia/Georgia/South Ossetia (2011), Saudi Arabia/Yemen (2004), South Africa/Mozambique (1975), Spain/Morocco (exclaves of Ceuta [2001] and Melilla [1998]), Thailand and Malaysia (joint project, 2016), Turkey/Syria (2013), Turkmenistan/Uzbekistan (2001), United Arab Emirates/Oman (2005), United Arab Emirates/Saudi Arabia (2005), United States/Mexico (1990–present), Uzbekistan/Afghanistan (2001), Uzbekistan/Kyrgyzstan (1999), and South Africa/Zimbabwe (1984). Internal border walls include Hong Kong/China (1962), Egypt/Sharm el-Sheikh (2005), Ireland/Belfast (1969), and Republic of Cyprus at Nicosia/Lefkosa (1974).
3. According to article 5 of the BSF Acts and Rules, "Any member of the force shall be liable to perform any duties in connection with the safeguarding of the security of the border

of India, the administration, discipline and welfare of the Force and such other duties as he may be called upon to perform in accordance with any law for the time being in force and any order given in this behalf by a superior officer shall be a lawful command for the purposes of the Act" (Border Security Force 2004, 75, cited in Jones 2009, 887).

4. This study does not include deaths caused by local and state-level law enforcement, not to mention the violence caused by vigilante groups working on private property. In October of 2012 in South Texas, for example, a sharpshooter in a helicopter working for the Texas Department of Public Safety shot at a pickup truck and killed two Guatemalan migrants. The FBI has been asked to investigate the shooting (Brezosky 2012).
5. As we discuss in another article, descriptions of the border as a "desolate" space are not accurate for regions such as the Rio Grande valley, which is verdant and populated (Dorsey and Díaz-Barriga 2010).
6. Border wall construction is a burgeoning global industry. Israeli-based companies, for example, drawing on their experience constructing the Israeli-Palestinian wall, consulted on the design of the U.S.-Mexico wall. In 2014, an Israeli company won a $145 million contract to build watchtowers in Arizona along the U.S.-Mexico border (see *Homeland Security News Wire* 2014; Lappin 2014).
7. In fact, we attended public input hearings on future border wall projects and found them vapid, including an anemic amount of energy and time allotted to public input. Our experience seemed to parallel stories of other hearings across the Rio Grande valley for the 2008 wall construction projects.
8. We later learned that our presentation generated a discussion beyond the walls and time frame of our lecture with a series of heated conversations in the convention center's exhibition hall.
9. In November 2013 the Spanish government ordered the placement of concertina wire in its border barrier, built primarily to prevent sub-Saharan Africans from entering Spain, with Morocco. The Interior Ministry justified the use of concertina wire because it is already used to enclose European summits and Spain uses it at prisons and nuclear plants.
10. Arizona's 2013 Border Security Expo featured razor wire along with high-tech surveillance technologies (see Miller 2013).
11. Some might argue that the dichotomy between academia and industry is false because public universities are rapidly privatizing and corporatizing themselves.
12. The House Natural Resources Committee, Subcommittee on National Parks, Forests and Public Lands, led by Rep. Raul Grijalva (D-Arizona), and Subcommittee on Fisheries, Wildlife and Oceans, led by Del. Madeleine Z. Bordallo (D-Guam), held a joint oversight field hearing on "Walls and Waivers: Expedited Construction of the Southern Border Wall and the Collateral Impacts on Communities and the Environment" at UT-Brownsville on April 28. Tom Tancredo was part of this committee.

REFERENCES

Agamben, Giorgio. 2005. *State of Exception*. Chicago: University of Chicago Press.

Andreas, Peter. 2009. *Border Games: Policing the U.S.-Mexico Divide*. 2nd ed. Cornell Studies in Political Economy. Ithaca, NY: Cornell University Press.

Bennett, Brian. 2014. "Border Patrol's Use of Force Criticized in Report." *Los Angeles Times*, February 28. http://www.latimes.com/nation/la-na-border-killings-20140227,0,2649003.story#axzz2uWugzp3V.

Border Security Force. 2004. *BSF Acts and Rules*. New Delhi, India: Ministry of Law.

Brezosky, Lynn. 2012. "Guatemala ID's Two Killed in DPS Shooting." *San Antonio Express News*, October 29. http://www.mysanantonio.com/news/article/Guatemala-ID-s-two-killed-in-DPS-shooting-3990662.php.

Brown, James. "Design Proposal." 2012. Friends of Friendship Park, San Diego, CA. http://friendshippark.org/html/Design.html#slideshow.

Brown, Wendy. 2014. *Walled States, Waning Sovereignty*. New York: Zone Books.

Buchli, Victor. 2013. *An Anthropology of Architecture*. London: Bloomsbury Academic.

Bustillo, Miguel. 2007. "A Town Against the Wall." *Los Angeles Times*, April 1. http://articles.latimes.com/2007/dec/17/nation/na-granjeno17/2.

Cable News Network. 2007. "Rick Sanchez, 'Out in the Open.'" April 1. http://transcript-s.cnn.com/TRANSCRIPTS/0712/14/oito.01.html.

Chertoff, Michael. 2009. *Homeland Security: Assessing the First Five Years*. Philadelphia: University of Pennsylvania.

Clarno, Andy. 2013. "The Constitution of State/Space and the Limits of 'Autonomy' in South Africa and Palestine/Israel." In *Sociology & Empire: The Imperial Entanglements of a Discipline*, edited by George Steinmetz, 436–64. Durham, NC: Duke University Press.

Coppola, Manuel C. 2013. "Ain't We Got Fun on the Border?" *Nogales International*, July 16. http://www.nogalesinternational.com/opinion/editorial/ain-t-we-got-fun-on-the-border/article_e0eee0ff8-ee32-11e2-9d05-0019bb2963f4.html.

Cué, Carlos E. 2013. "Government to Keep Wire on Melilla Fence." *El País*, February 25. http://elpais.com/elpais/2013/11/25/inenglish/1385391939_517074.html.

Doctors Without Borders. "Violence, Vulnerability and Migration: Trapped at the Gates of Europe." 2013. http://www.doctorswithoutborders.org/sites/usa/files/Trapped_at_the_Gates_of_Europe.pdf.

Donnan, Hastings, and Thomas M. Wilson. 2010. *Borderlands: Ethnographic Approaches to Security, Power, and Identity*. Lanham, MD: University Press of America.

Dorsey, Margaret, and Miguel Díaz-Barriga. 2010. "Beyond Surveillance and Moonscapes: An Alternative Imaginary of the U.S. Mexico Border Wall." *Visual Anthropology Review* 26(2): 128–35.

———. 2015. "The Constitution Free Zone in the United States: Law and Life in a State of Carcelment." *Political and Legal Anthropology Review*, part of Symposium on Punishment and the Sted, edited by Mieka Brand Polanco. 38(2): 204–25.

Doty, Roxanne Lynn. 2011. "Bare Life: Border-Crossing Deaths and Spaces of Moral Alibi." *Environment and Planning D: Society and Space* 29:599–612.

Hamilton, William L. 2006. "A Fence with More Beauty, Fewer Barbs." *New York Times*, March 3. http://www.nytimes.com/2006/06/18/weekinreview/18hamil-ton.html?_r=0.

Harris, Tina. 2012. "The Mobile and the Material on the Sino-Indian Border, for Border Architectures and Subjectivities: Global Reflections on Border Landscapes." Paper presented at the American Anthropological Association, San Francisco, November 17.

Holston, James. 1989. *The Modernist City: An Anthropological Critique of Brasilia*. Chicago: University of Chicago Press.

Homeland Security News Wire. 2014. "CBP Awards $145 Million Border Towers Contract to Elbit." March 6. http://www.homelandsecuritynewswire.com/dr20140306-cbp-awards-145-million-border-towers-contract-to-elbit.

Jones, Reece. 2009. "Agents of Exception: Border Security and the Marginalization of Muslims in India." *Environment and Planning D: Society and Space* 27:879–97.

Lappin, Yaakov. 2014. "Elbit to Build Surveillance Towers on Arizona's Border with Mexico." *The Jerusalem Post*, March 2. http://www.jpost.com/International/Elbit-to-build-surveillance-towers-on-Arizonas-border-with-Mexico-344005.

Leatherman, Jackie, and Jeremy Roebuck. 2008. "Local Border Wall to Cost $113.9 Million." *The Monitor*, May 5. http://www.themonitor.com/news/local/local-border-wall-to-cost-million/article_95976d82-9ec7-5f98-8001-65258fbc715f.html.

Lugo, Alejandro. 2008. *Fragmented Lives, Assembled Parts: Culture, Capitalism, and Conquest at the U.S.-Mexico Border*. Austin: University of Texas Press.

Mbembe, Achille. 2003. "Necropolitics." *Public Culture* 15(1): 11–40.

Miller, Todd. 2013. "Southern Arizona in the Crosshairs." *Tucson Weekly*, March 31. http://www.tucsonweekly.com/tucson/southern-arizona-in-the-crosshairs/Con-tent?oid=3668058.

Osborne, James. 2007. "Crowds Turn Out for Border Fence Rally." *The Monitor*, December 11. http://www.themonitor.com/news/security-7268-fence-homeland.html.

Paredes, Américo. 1970. *"With His Pistol in His Hand": A Border Ballad and Its Hero*. Austin: University of Texas Press.

Prendergast, Curt. 2013. "Border Patrol Considers Putting Razor Wire on Nogales Fence." *Nogales International*, July 12. http://www.nogalesinternational.com/news/border-patrol-considers-putting-razor-wire-on-nogales-fence/article_b5bba22c-eb04-11e2-995b-001a4bcf887a.html.

Rael, Ronald. 2012. "Boundary Line Infrastructure." *Thresholds* 40:75–82.

Rael San Fratello Architects. 2014. "Border Wall as Architecture." http://border-wallasarchitecture.blogspot.com.

Rosas, Gilberto. 2012. *Barrio Libre: Criminalizing States and Delinquent Refusals of the New Frontier*. Durham, NC: Duke University Press.

Sieff, Kevin. 2008. "UTB, DHS Accept Fence Compromise: Existing Campus Fence to Be Overhauled." *Brownsville Herald*, August 31. http://www.brownsvilleherald.com/news/fence-88825-campus-utb.html.

UTB-TSC (University of Texas Brownsville–Texas Southmost College). 2009. "Border Fence Information." http://www.utb.edu/newsinfo/archives/Pages/BorderFence/BorderFence.aspx.

Vélez-Ibáñez, Carlos G. 2010. *An Impossible Living in a Transborder World: Culture, Confianza, and Economy of Mexican-Origin Populations*. Tucson: University of Arizona Press.

4

OF BORDERS, BRIDGES, WALLS, AND OTHER RELATIONS, HISTORICAL AND CONTEMPORARY

A Commentary

ALEJANDRO LUGO

Las paredes
vueltas de lado
son puentes.

Walls
turned on their sides
are bridges.

—ANONYMOUS (IN RUTH BEHAR, 1995)

ANTHROPOLOGICAL VISIONS of the U.S.-Mexico border region in the first quarter of the twenty-first century do not happen in a vacuum. And border theory—that is, the social theory that emerged from the critical study of this particular region in the latter part of the twentieth century—is, first and foremost, a theory of society, just like Bourdieu's theory of practice (1977) or Ortner's practice theory (1984). In this sense, border theory should be applicable to any human society across time and across space—just like other anthropological theories (see Lugo 1997 and Lugo 2008, particularly chapter 9). Therefore, even though border theory was a historical product of complex social processes that emanated from the specific relationship between two nation-states, more specifically, the U.S.-Mexico border (see Paredes 1970[1958]; Anzaldúa 1987; Rosaldo 1989), it is not limited to that particular relationship or to such a specific geopolitical setting. It is, indeed, an academic tool that should help scholars, in this case, anthropologists and their interlocutors, to better explain human social life, past and present. This is the main point of reference from which I will briefly comment on the first three chapters of this important volume.

Within the halls of U.S.-based academia, and particularly with respect to theoretically informed, empirically grounded ethnography of the U.S.-Mexico border region—especially the rare ethnographic work that genuinely and thoroughly encompasses both sides of this particular international boundary—there is no better representative and precursor, and no other pioneer in American anthropology of border ethnography carried out on both sides of the border (and in between), than Carlos Vélez-Ibáñez. Vélez-Ibáñez's chapter 1 in this volume is a concrete example of the scope, breadth, and depth of the kind of border ethnography and its accompanying historically based analysis that all of us, including the new generations, should produce—particularly as we try to understand and document transnational, transcolonial, and transborder processes, past and present, in what he calls the Southwest North America (SWNA) region.

As a scholar trained at the beginning of the fourth quarter of the twentieth century, Vélez-Ibáñez's interweaving uses of political ecology and colonial and postcolonial histories, as well as Marxist critiques of capitalism and cultural ideologies, give new analytical life not only to Américo Paredes's notion of Greater Mexico but also to Julian Steward's cultural ecology and cultural area studies and Eric Wolf's political economy approaches by convincingly articulating such *long dureé* ecological, demographic, and historical approaches to politically relevant cases of archival and ethnographic voices and ethnographic sites—all well situated in specific geographies and ecologies, always in ways that clearly manifest the continuity and contiguity of the multiple border landscapes that constitute them, from the sixteenth century, the seventeenth century, and the eighteenth century to current twentieth- and twenty-first century empires. In the process, the Eastern Prism of the American empire of the nineteenth century and the Southern Prism of the Spanish and Mexican empires at the borderlands do not escape Vélez-Ibáñez's critical vision and exegesis, including the dialectical relation between the macro and micro, the individual and society, "the American" and "the Mexican," "the Spaniard" and "the indigenous," the local and the global—all without falling into simplistic dichotomies.

Vélez-Ibáñez's chapter is a tour de force, where the historical, the ecological, the demographic, the cultural, the political, the ethnographic, and even the deeply personal (Vélez-Ibáñez's DNA!) are and must be accounted for: methodologically, theoretically, and politically. Whether through the juxtaposition of the Colorado River with the Rio Grande (Río Bravo), or Northwest Mexico with the Southwest United States, or the working-class "colonias" of Texas, New Mexico, Arizona, and California, with the demographics of pedestrian and motor vehicle travels and traffic at specific border ports of entry across all these post-Mexican U.S. states, Carlos

Vélez-Ibáñez decisively locates border analysis, border theory, and border methodologies outside parochial positions that too often locate themselves on either side of the U.S.-Mexican border, without erasing the much-needed specificity of each border city, each border state, each border history, each border geography, and each border crossing and their always relevant border inspections (see Lugo 2000, 2008).

If the much-needed Marxist framework for a better understanding of colonial and postcolonial capitalisms at the borderlands is elegantly implied in Vélez-Ibáñez's highly encompassing essay, Josiah Heyman's chapter 2 suggestively and quite engagingly delves into theoretical shifts in the social science literature of the U.S.-Mexico border through what Heyman tends to do best: social analysis of everyday life and institutions, always in the complex contexts of webs of unequal social relations as manifested in what he calls "power projects." Being a student of Eric Wolf himself, Heyman's explicit articulation of Marxist dialectics serves as a much-needed reminder (similar to Vélez-Ibáñez, and Dorsey and Díaz-Barriga, and others in this volume) that "to understand the border, we need to acknowledge the inequalities at its core, inequalities that involve relational flows and spatial divisions, via a broadly Marxist dialectics without doctrinaire predetermination." This is a highly welcome contribution, particularly given the pervasive victories, across time and space, of capitalism in its many guises: industrial, monopolistic, post-industrial, late capitalist, global, and neoliberal—all in the context of Spanish and American forms of colonialisms at the U.S.-Mexico border (see Vélez-Ibáñez as well as Lugo 2008 for an elaboration of the latter colonial analysis).

Through a highly creative theoretical move, Heyman articulates his analytical lens of the border vis-à-vis a constructive unpacking of the ways in which "uneven and combined relations," more often than not, constitute "apparently separate or apparent opposites . . . brought into being and reproduced jointly . . . without full integration, shared citizenship, and equitable redistribution of resources." He correctly underscores that "the combinations of unequal endpoints enacted via the border are diverse and complex." In this process, Heyman effectively reinforces the call for the continuing analytical need to rigorously recapture the "uneven and combined relations" in society through border theory. Ultimately, he argues, "the border region, then, is still in the midst of emergence, requiring analyses of struggles over possible paths and arrangements, rather than a static portrait of structure."

Heyman's concrete analytical engagement with "the ethnographic" convincingly comes to fruition as he describes the multiple kinds of bordering as power projects: from his analysis of Foxconn, the Taiwanese multinational that has established its manufacturing plants at the Ciudad Juárez–New Mexico border in the San Jeronimo/Santa Teresa border crossing, to the complex border mobilities associated with the smuggling (north and south) of guns, drugs, and money, and particularly his analysis of legal/illegal yet interconnected performances of both state and non-state entities on both sides of the border. As he properly noted, "Not only are states sometimes directly implicated in illegal activities, and often tolerate and encourage them, but also apparent opponents . . . feed each other . . . States and illegal networks feed each other, to the detriment of more vulnerable people around these dealers of coercion and death."

Theoretically, one of Heyman's most important contributions, both within anthropology and across the social sciences, is his sharp yet eloquent analysis of the combinations of apparent opposites and their dialectical nature, always within a rich conceptual terrain that brings together both the specificity of the border region and the complex border relations that constitute broader social relations during the first decades of the twenty-first century. As he stated: "Routes, mobilities, and relationships constitute a spider's web of connections across this region. It is precisely this connectivity that emerges and enacts various border relations." For present and future ethnographers, and given that one of our ultimate goals as sociocultural anthropologists is to capture people's everyday life at the border and beyond, Heyman reminds his interlocutors that "such relational understandings are needed to analyze the emergence and transformation of specific arrangements . . . and to address fundamental questions of humane values and struggles for them."

It is precisely vis-à-vis the need to better understand border communities within a context in which the states' legal and the illegal activities depend on each other at the expense of the most vulnerable that Margaret Dorsey and Miguel Díaz-Barriga's chapter 3 critically and rigorously examines one of the major challenges we are confronting today: "border walls." At this historical moment in the second decade of the twenty-first century, regionally and globally, Dorsey and Díaz-Barriga's profound analysis of border walls as products of the deadly combination of "states of exception" and "necropower" is of vital importance for any student of contemporary society, culture, and state politics.

If in the history of American anthropology we have often depended on the theoretical proposals from such European sociologists and philosophers as Marx, Weber, Durkheim, de Saussure, Bourdieu, and Foucault as well as Gramsci, U.S.-Mexico border anthropology and border theory today also engage and, I would argue, enrich their theories and concepts as well with those by more recent thinkers as Giorgio Agamben and postcolonial scholar Achilles Mbembe—as Dorsey and Díaz-Barriga have compellingly shown in their application of Agamben's state of exception and Mbembe's necropower to their ethnographically rich materials of border wall construction and debate in the lower Rio Grande valley of Texas.[1] Their much-needed refined critique of Donnan and Wilson's (2010) analysis of sovereignty as it relates to the rebordering of international boundaries is more than welcome. Dorsey and

Díaz-Barriga's sophisticated cultural analysis of border militarism through their concept of the "exceptional border" as one that "allows for an intensification of necropower based on a rendering of 'ecology' that makes death and violence a natural part of the hegemonic landscape" takes border theory to a new ethnographically and politically relevant level—locally, regionally, and globally.

Dorsey and Díaz-Barriga, importantly, follow as their point of departure Américo Paredes's 1958 classic, *With His Pistol in His Hand*. They wrote: "Here we only need remind ourselves of Américo Paredes's analysis of the Texas Rangers' application of violence against people of Mexican descent to 'uphold' the law. As Paredes points out, this violence only makes sense if one starts with the assumption that a Mexican's life is not worth anything—a clear example of state actors deciding which lives are worth living."[2] In the process, Dorsey and Díaz-Barriga's contributions transcend their cogent and well-documented examination of the impact of the border wall in the local community of the Lower Rio Grande Valley, including the encroachment and invasion of private and public lands, and powerfully push forward their analysis of the border wall as one of the defining state strategies of containment around the world, at least since the 1989 fall of the Berlin Wall.

In a clear articulation of the utility of border theory beyond the U.S.-Mexico border, Dorsey and Díaz-Barriga accurately stated: "We find that the conditions—sovereign power based on states of exception and necropower—for the construction of the U.S.-Mexico border wall are not unique to our field site. In fact, one can find border walls as manifestations of sovereignty based on necropower more globally." Dorsey and Díaz-Barriga were able to document how border walls are mainly being used as "fortifications"—one of the main military strategies through which state-empires today, just like in the past, attempt to protect themselves with walls in the context of expectations of war, all while making war in the process. This imperial impulse to wall—or walling—is perhaps one of the most important challenges for border theorists or for anyone at the turn of the twenty-first century who cares about a better future for the new generations and their daily lives. In response to U.S. Representative Thomas Tancredo's threat that the Department of Homeland Security "might consider constructing a wall north" of Brownsville, Texas, Dorsey and Díaz-Barriga creatively and incisively argue that "*the wall, and its attendant threat of more walling*, thus increasingly excludes and cuts communities not only at the international boundary but within the United States, enveloping local development projects into a militarized state" [3] (my italics).

In the spirit of the brief poem by the anonymous Cuban author, who at the start of my commentary taught us that "walls, turned on their sides, are bridges," I would like to close this commentary with key relevant verses by the poet Robert Frost. In his 1914 poem, "Mending Wall," Robert Frost insisted, at the beginning of World War I, on the need to challenge the unnecessary existence of walls between human beings—whether in our individual lives or institutionally—a challenge that in 2016 turns Donald Trump into an embodiment of what his exclusionary narrative has become: a dangerous out-door game beyond the offence.

> Something there is that doesn't love a wall [. . .]
> Oh, just another kind of out-door game,
> One on a side. It comes to little more:
> There where it is we do not need the wall:
> He is all pine and I am apple orchard.
> My apple trees will never get across
> And eat the cones under the pines, I tell him.
> He only says, "Good fences make good neighbors."
> Spring is the mischief in me, and I wonder
> If I could put a notion in his head:
> "Why do they make good neighbors? Isn't it
> Where there are cows? But here there are no cows.
> *Before I built a wall I'd ask to know*
> *What I was walling in or walling out,*
> *And to whom I was like to give offence.*
> *Something there is that doesn't love a wall,*
> *That wants it down.*
> —Robert Frost (2015[1914]:1–2; my italics)

NOTES

1. In my 1997 essay on border theory, culture, and the nation, I juxtapose the theoretical work by Renato Rosaldo on cultural borderlands and cultural patterns with Benedict Anderson's analysis of the nation as a homogeneous imagined community, as well as the work by Foucault on relations of force with Gramsci's notion of force relations—all in relation to the complex articulation between theories of culture and the state vis-à-vis the previous historical moment of monarchy and its heterogeneity before the nineteenth century (Lugo 1997).
2. My own theorizing of borders, as well as Díaz-Barriga's, also follows from the genealogy of Américo Paredes, particularly vis-à-vis Renato Rosaldo's anthropological analysis of Gloria Anzaldúa, Ernesto Galarza, Sandra Cisneros, and Américo Paredes, especially through his chapters, "Border Crossings" and "Changing Chicano Narratives," in his groundbreaking book, *Culture & Truth: The Remaking of Social Analysis* (1989).

See Lugo 2012 for my review of the impact of Renato Rosaldo's border work in Latino ethnography beyond the U.S.-Mexico border; also see Díaz-Barriga 2012. Both my and Díaz-Barriga's essays form part of "Dossier: Celebrating and Engaging Renato Rosaldo's *Culture and Truth*" in the journal *Aztlán* 37 (2012).

3. I examine other imperial impulses at the border in the context of religiosity in Lugo 2015.

REFERENCES

Anzaldúa, Gloria. 1987. *La Frontera/Borderlands: The New Mestiza*. San Francisco: Spinsters/ Aunt Lute.

Behar, Ruth. 1995. "Introduction." In *Bridges to Cuba/Puentes a Cuba*, edited by Ruth Behar, 1–19. Ann Arbor: University of Michigan Press.

Bourdieu, Pierre. 1977. *Outline of a Theory of Practice*. Cambridge: Cambridge University Press.

Díaz-Barriga, Miguel. 2012. "Remaking Culture and Truth: Cultural and Necro-Citizenship in the Borderlands." *Aztlán* 37:191–204.

Donnan, Hastings, and Thomas M. Wilson. 2010. *Borderlands: Ethnographic Approaches to Security, Power, and Identity*. Lanham, MD: University Press of America.

Frost, Robert. 2105[1914]. *Robert Frost: Selected Poems*. New York: Fall River Press.

Lugo, Alejandro. 1997. "Reflections on Border Theory, Culture, and the Nation." In *Border Theory: The Limits of Cultural Politics*, edited by Scott Michaelsen and David E. Johnson, 43–67. Minneapolis: University of Minnesota Press.

———. 2000. "Theorizing Border Inspections." *Cultural Dynamic* 12:353–73.

———. 2008. *Fragmented Lives, Assembled Parts: Culture, Capitalism, and Conquest at the U.S.-Mexico Border*. Austin: University of Texas Press.

———. 2012. "Introduction: Renato Rosaldo's Border Travels." *Aztlán* 37:119–43.

———, ed. 2012. "Dossier: Celebrating and Engaging Renato Rosaldo's *Culture and Truth*." *Aztlán* 37 (1): 119–215.

———. 2015. "Occupation, Religion, and the Voidable Politics of Empire at the U.S.-Mexico Border." *Religion and Society: Advances in Research* 6(1): 98–126.

Ortner, B. Sherry. 1984. "Theory in Anthropology since the Sixties." *Comparative Studies in Society and History* 26:126–66.

Paredes, Américo. 1970[1958]. *With His Pistol in His Hand: A Border Ballad and Its Hero*. Austin: University of Texas Press.

Rosaldo, Renato. 1989. Culture & Truth: The Remaking of Social Analysis. Boston: Beacon Press.

PART II

SOUTHWEST NORTH AMERICAN LANGUAGE DYNAMICS AND THE CREATION OF BORDERING

5

PROTO-UTO-AZTECAN

A Community of Cultivators in Central Mexico?

JANE H. HILL

THE UTO-AZTECAN FAMILY of languages exhibits today an exceptionally large north–south geographical spread, from southern Idaho to El Salvador and Nicaragua. It is the only language family in North America with major extensions both inside and outside the tropics. The distribution of the family is shown on the map in figure 5.1. The family is also notable because of the range of cultural adaptations among communities of speakers, from Great Basin foragers like the Shoshone to urban state builders among Nahua speakers in Mesoamerica. The standard account of the origins of the family (cf. Hale and Harris 1979; Suárez 1979; Fowler 1983; Miller 1983; Campbell 1997) is that the Uto-Aztecans began their career as a foraging people in the U.S. Southwest and northwestern Mexico.

In recent work Bellwood (1997, 1999) argues that it is most likely that the Proto-Uto-Aztecan speech community was located in central Mexico and participated in the primary domestication of maize. Their northward expansion was driven by demographic pressure resulting from an increasing commitment to cultivation. New information is presented here that supports Bellwood's position. New data from the Hopi (Hill et al. 1998) permit us to reconstruct some vocabulary items for maize cultivation and processing for the Proto-Uto-Aztecan speech community. Furthermore, recent archaeological discoveries have pushed the dates on the earliest cultivation of maize in the U.S. Southwest back to a time that might reasonably correspond to

This chapter originally appeared in *American Anthropologist* 103(4): 913–34, 2001.

FIGURE 5.1. Distribution of the Uto-Aztecan languages (Miller 1983, 114).

the initial differentiation of the Uto-Aztecan languages. The first appearance of cultivated maize in central Mexico is placed at about 5600 BP.[1] In the Southwest, the oldest maize is dated to 3740 BP at Bat Cave in western New Mexico. Matson (1999) suggests that this relatively short time gap between the first maize in highland Mexico and the first maize in the Southwest means that it is likely that migration, instead of secondary adoption, was the primary cultural process that led to the establishment of maize agriculture in the U.S. Southwest. Many sites in Arizona and New Mexico now present well-established dates for maize remains prior to 3000 BP (cf. Gregory 1999, 8–9). Because the Uto-Aztecan language family is the only one that exhibits an unbroken chain of communities of cultivators from Mesoamerica to the U.S. Southwest, Uto-Aztecans are the most likely of several possible candidate groups to have been the migrants who brought cultivated maize north.

Based on Bellwood's proposals and the new data presented here, I propose the following model as an alternative to the Northern Origins hypothesis: The Proto-Uto-Aztecan (PUA) community formed in Mesoamerica between 5600 BP (the first evidence for maize domestication) and 4500 BP (the first evidence for settled villages [Matson 1999]). A northward expansion of Uto-Aztecan speakers, which included two processes—demic diffusion (Ammerman and Cavalli-Sforza 1973) and "leapfrogging" (Anthony 1990)—created a chain of dialects that developed roughly between 4500 and 3500 BP and was fully differentiated into at least five distinct languages by 2500 BP. These first-level daughter languages were Proto-Northern-Uto-Aztecan, Proto-Tepiman, Proto-Taracahitan, Proto-Tubar, and Proto-Corachol-Aztecan.

PRIMARY AGRICULTURE AND LANGUAGE SPREAD

During the last few years, dialogue between linguistics and archaeology has been enlivened by proposals about linguistic prehistory, advanced especially by Colin Renfrew (1987 and many subsequent papers) and Peter Bellwood (1985 and many subsequent papers).[2] The global distribution of linguistic diversity exhibits a contrast between geographically widespread and genetically multibranched language families—such as Afro-Asiatic, Austronesian, Indo-European, Niger-Congo, Sino-Tibetan, and Uto-Aztecan—and geographically compact, minimally branching language families and isolates—like Basque, Chinookan, Keresan, North Caucasian, and Zuni. Renfrew and Bellwood argue that this pattern is best explained by assuming that languages of the first type have spread at the expense of languages of the second type. The spreads were driven by technological innovations that gave a demographic advantage to members of the protolanguage communities ancestral to the first type. In the most significant cases, that technological innovation was cultivation, and spread was accomplished by what Ammerman and Cavalli-Sforza (1973) call "demic diffusion"[3] or, as Bellwood observes, "by some more dramatic process of emigration of the kind which we can read in the prehistories of many Pacific Islands" (1997, 124). Renfrew and Bellwood have argued that foraging peoples seldom accept agriculture but are instead usually exterminated or assimilated by cultivators.

These proposals have been challenged on several grounds: that they neglect evidence for forager language spreads (for instance, Athabaskan in North America); that they oversimplify complex historical processes, for instance, the interactions between

Austronesian and non-Austronesian peoples in western Oceania (cf. Terrell et al. 1997 or the recent review by Gibbons [2001]); and that they ignore strong counterevidence (for instance, the case of Indo-European). Linguists have especially have objected that Renfrew's argument that the spread of Indo-European was an expansion of primary cultivators into Europe exhibits a poor fit with well-established linguistic paleontological models.[4] These models hold that because words for ploughs, yokes, wheeled vehicles, wool, and, possibly, silver can be reconstructed for Proto-Indo-European, that speech community must still have been intact at the time of the earliest use of such items, which is not attested in the archaeological record before 5000–3000 BCE (Mallory 1989; Anthony 1995). This is too late for the spread of agriculture in Europe, which was under way by 7000 BCE. Furthermore, non-Indo-European speech communities that practiced agriculture are well attested in the Mediterranean region, including such examples as Etruscan and several non-Indo-European languages of the Iberian Peninsula. Linguists have tended to support the proposals about the spread of Indo-European speakers advanced by archaeologists such as Mallory (1989) and Anthony (1995), who favor a different model: expansion through elite domination made possible by new technologies that permitted the bitting and riding of horses and the use of horses to draw wheeled vehicles.[5] Finally, while Renfrew (1987) argues that the Indo-European speech community was probably located in Anatolia in the zone where the earliest cultivation is attested,[6] proposals by J. Nichols (1997) and Greenberg (1997) postulate an original Indo-European homeland in eastern Central Asia, well outside the zone of early agriculture.

Nor have Americanist linguists supported the Renfrew-Bellwood models. For instance, Campbell observes: "There is no evidence in Mesoamerica, highland South America, or the American Southwest for agriculturalists dispersing and replacing other languages along with the spread of agriculture" (1999, 221). Diamond (1997) even elevates this observation into a general principle, arguing that the dominant east–west axis of the Old World, which favored the rapid spread of domesticated plants and animals adapted to particular latitudes, provides one explanation for the early emergence of complex societies based on cultivation in that hemisphere. In contrast, the dominant north–south axis of the New World disfavored such a spread. However, the new linguistic data on Uto-Aztecan languages and new archaeological data on early agriculture in northern Mexico and the U.S. Southwest reviewed here suggest that we must question such statements. Indeed, the linguistic-paleontological case presented here for Uto-Aztecan as an example of the expansion of a community of primary cultivators is a strong one and suggests that linguists should take a second, more serious look at these new archaeological models as a source of hypotheses for work in linguistic paleontology.

UTO-AZTECAN PREHISTORY: TWO MODELS

THE NORTHERN ORIGIN MODEL

Linguists have agreed that the PUA speech community was located in the northern or central portion of the historically attested range of the family. Lamb (1958) and Romney (1957) argue for a homeland in the southern part of the Southwest, ranging from the Gila River Basin into northern Sonora and Chihuahua. Hopkins (1965) places the homeland on the Columbia Plateau, and M. Nichols (1981) argues for locating the PUA community in northeastern California or even Oregon. Fowler (1983) supports Lamb's and Romney's proposals with evidence from a reconstruction of the biogeography of the homeland. Fowler's map of the Uto-Aztecan homeland is shown in figure 5.2.

Fowler's proposed PUA homeland range is large; most Uto-Aztecanists have assumed that the protocommunity was linguistically internally diverse, forming a dialect chain.[7] Fowler (1983) suggests that the community might be visible archaeologically in the Oshara phase of the Desert Archaic. She estimates the age of this PUA community at around 5000 BP, based on glottochronological calculations, but states that a breakup date as late as 3000 BP for Northern Uto-Aztecan would fit her evidence (1983, 239). Fowler's work has received wide support among scholars working on the family and is probably the most detailed published version of the "Northern Origin" hypothesis.

The Northern Origin model assumes that agriculture spread north from Mesoamerica and was adopted in the Southwest by foraging peoples speaking not only Uto-Aztecan but other languages, including Yuman, Tanoan, Keresan, and Zuni. It assumes that speakers of the languages at the southern end of the Uto-Aztecan range, like Cora, Huichol, and Aztecan, were drawn south to the Mesoamerican frontier, perhaps attracted by opportunities for raiding more sedentary peoples, as suggested by Nahua historical traditions. The Aztecan peoples eventually became Mesoamericanized and came to dominate that region in the late prehistoric period. The most southerly extension of the family, the Aztecan-speaking groups found in southern Mexico (such as the Isthmus Nahuatl) and Central America (the Pipil), is the result of migration that took place during this period. The explanation for the foraging adaptation of all Northern Uto-Aztecan groups except the Hopi is that these groups (the Takic and Tübatülabal of California and the Numic of the Great Basin) retain the archaic Uto-Aztecan subsistence pattern.

Favoring the Northern Origin model was the widely accepted view that primary plant domestication and the development of the earliest complex societies

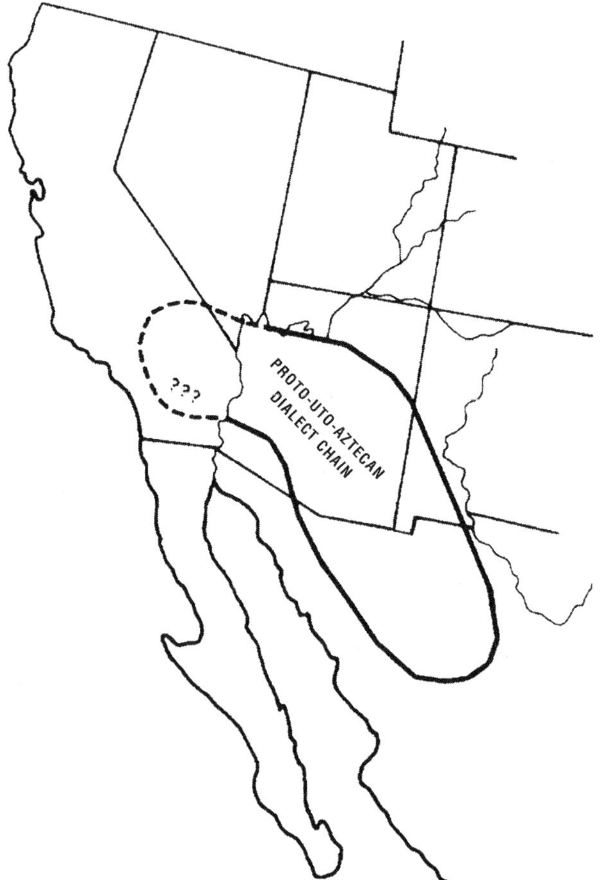

FIGURE 5.2. Location of the Proto-Uto-Aztecan dialect chain according to Fowler (1983).

in Mesoamerica were accomplished by a single group, probably speakers of Mixe-Zoquean, a language family today concentrated in Oaxaca and Veracruz in southern Mexico. This view was advanced especially by Campbell and Kaufman (1976), who argue that Mixe-Zoquean loan words in other Mesoamerican languages, including Aztecan, attest to the priority of the Mixe-Zoquean protocommunity not only in cultivation but in a wide range of other cultural developments associated with early civilization. Romney (1957) suggests that lexical items for cultivation could be reconstructed for Proto-Uto-Aztecan, but he published no cognate sets or reconstructions, so his proposal had little impact on the consensus in favor of a foraging adaptation.

THE SOUTHERN ORIGIN MODEL

Bellwood (1997, 1999) has proposed that the PUA community must have been located in the Mesoamerican zone where maize was first domesticated. He develops several lines of theoretical argumentation for this idea. First, he claims that where state-level social organization is absent, language shift over large areas is very unlikely and linguistic diversity is likely to be maintained. Prior to the emergence of contemporary bureaucratic technologies, the spread of a language meant the spread of a population of speakers. Second, a large-scale and rapid geographical spread (the rapidity indicated by "rake-like" multiple primary branching of the tree that models the genetic relationships internal to a language family, signifying a spread so rapid that subgroups became isolated from one another) requires a major technological innovation that yields both demographic pressure and the resources to overcome opponents to expansion. Cultivation is such an innovation. Third, there are few historically attested or archaeologically demonstrated cases in which foragers have adopted cultivation while maintaining their linguistic and ethnic integrity and differentiation from the donor community. Finally, primary cultivators are unlikely to replace or assimilate one another; thus, we should expect that sites where primary domestication took place will be linguistically complex. This is indeed the case with Mesoamerica, where four genetically distinct language families and several language isolates are identified (Suárez 1979).

If we adopt Bellwood's model, the distribution of Uto-Aztecan can be explained as follows: The PUA community included primary cultivators, located within the zone of maize domestication in central Mexico at around 5600 BP. These cultivators experienced rapid population growth but could not move to the south or east, the way being blocked by Oto-Manguean- and Tarascan-speaking peoples (and, farther east and south, by speakers of Mixe-Zoquean and Mayan), who presumably also became cultivators at a very early date. The only route open to expansion was thus north through western Mexico into the Southwest, where the expanding Uto-Aztecans encountered communities of foragers, not cultivators. On this model, the Corachol and Aztecan peoples are not newcomers to Mesoamerica but instead are the descendants of the original inhabitants of the northwestern quadrant of the region. The Uto-Aztecan peoples of northwest Mexico and the U.S. Southwest are not foragers who adopted agriculture but are, instead, primary cultivators who migrated into their present range. Nonagricultural Uto-Aztecan peoples in the extreme north, such as some Numic and Takic groups and the Tübatülabal, are foragers because they abandoned cultivation: because they entered regions inhabited by groups with well-established foraging techniques that were even more productive than cultivation (the acorn-collecting complex in California), because they moved into regions where their technologies did not permit cultivation (as in the northwestern regions of the Great

Basin or the deserts of eastern California), or because they abandoned maize agriculture when climatic change made it hopelessly unreliable and retreat from the newly arid zones was impossible (the southern and eastern regions of the Great Basin and most of the Colorado Plateau).

ARGUMENTS FOR THE SOUTHERN ORIGIN MODEL

I advance here the following arguments in support of Bellwood's model for the spread of Uto-Aztecan: (1) a reinterpretation of the biogeographic analysis conducted by Romney and Fowler; (2) evidence from the structure of subgrouping in the Uto-Aztecan language family; (3) presentation of a linguistic paleontological analysis that suggests members of the PUA community were maize cultivators; (4) evidence that the lexical items of the vocabulary of cultivation are not loan words from other Mesoamerican languages but, instead, have good etymologies internal to Uto-Aztecan; (5) evidence for the presence of Uto-Aztecan cultural practices in Mesoamerica at an early date; and (6) linguistic evidence for the use of irrigation at an early period among Uto-Aztecan speakers, correlating with new archaeological findings on the antiquity of irrigation among maize cultivators in the Southwest.

BIOGEOGRAPHIC DATA DO NOT RULE OUT A MESOAMERICAN HOMELAND

Fowler's (1983) rigorous reconstruction of the Proto-Uto-Aztecan biogeographic lexicon was primarily aimed at critiquing work like that of Hopkins (1965), who argues for a PUA homeland as far north as the Columbia Plateau. Fowler's data rule out such a northerly location. However, they do not preclude a Mesoamerican homeland. All the flora (e.g., pine, edible agave, edible prickly pear cactus) and fauna (e.g., cottontail rabbit, coyote, wild turkey, rattlesnake) for which she identified PUA lexical items are found in Mesoamerica, especially in montane regions. Fowler rules out a PUA homeland within the tropics because names for tropical species can be reconstructed only for Aztecan. However, the absence of lexical items for tropical species such as sapotes and avocados in the more northern languages can be understood as the result of lexical loss after thousands of years of life beyond the range of such species.

THE "RAKE-LIKE" STRUCTURE OF UTO-AZTECAN

Before turning to the details of the vocabulary of maize cultivation, we must explore the structure of the Uto-Aztecan family. I argue here for a primary division into five subgroups. These are Northern-Uto-Aztecan (NUA), Tepiman, Taracahitan, Tubar, and Corachol-Aztecan.[8] One component of this structure is quite important for my interpretation of the distribution of the maize vocabulary cognate sets in the various daughter languages. This is the recognition of Proto-Northern Uto-Aztecan (PNUA). Basically, the argument is as follows: if NUA is a valid genetic unit—that is, all of the NUA languages listed in note 8 are daughters of PNUA, which is a first-level branch of PUA—then the identification of cultivation vocabulary cognate to that in the southern languages in any NUA language attests to the presence of cultivation in PNUA and hence in PUA itself. In the discussion below, Hopi (the single language, with three major dialects, constitutes one branch of NUA) is almost always the only NUA source for cognate vocabulary with a meaning within the maize complex. While one cognate lexical item with a maize-cultivation-complex meaning (example 9 in table 5.1) is also found in Southern Paiute, a language of the Numic branch of NUA, and words meaning "to plant" are attested in all branches of Numic as well as in Hopi, my argument that the maize-cultivation vocabulary reconstructs to Proto-Uto-Aztecan would be considerably weakened if NUA is not in fact a genetic unit.

There has been extensive debate over the internal structure of the Uto-Aztecan family. Miller (1984) and Cortina-Borja and Valiñas (1989) approach the structure of the family from the perspective of wave theory, using statistical analyses of lexical similarities between the languages in the family to suggest that the relationships among the various daughter languages were fuzzy and meshlike, rather than clean splits among the daughter communities. This is the type of pattern we expect from a relatively slow and gradual breakup, not the pattern predicted by Bellwood's model for a language group undergoing rapid expansion.

When we look at Uto-Aztecan from the perspective of tree theory and emphasize the historical phonology, however, we can argue for a rather different picture, one that can be modeled as a set of splits defined by shared innovations. First, Heath (1977, 1985) and Manaster Ramer (1992) have proposed that innovations shared by a set of northern languages including Hopi, Numic, Tübatülabal, and the Takic languages of California—and only by those languages—require that we recognize NUA as a genetic subgroup branching directly from PUA. Heath's proposals, involving ablaut in certain verb themes, are too complex to be reviewed here. Manaster Ramer's proposal is a straightforward one for a classical diagnostic marker of "innovation-defined" (Ross 1997) subgrouping, a phonological innovation shared in all the northern languages: PUA **c (the symbol represents the affricate ts) became PNUA *y. The innovation is blocked, however, if the PUA context is **ʔc.

I believe that arguments for NUA developed by Heath (1977, 1985) and Manaster Ramer (1992), while restricted to a few phenomena, are rigorous and methodologically sound. I maintain that they are, in fact, stronger than the evidence (reviewed below) that has been presented in support of SUA, the only major first-level subgroup recognized by Miller (1983) in his review of Uto-Aztecan in the *Handbook of North American Indians*.[9] An additional point should be made: If we recognize SUA but not NUA, then evidence for cultivation vocabulary in Hopi constitutes an attestation in two branches of Uto-Aztecan, that of SUA and Hopi. No Uto-Aztecanist has proposed that SUA and Hopi share any exclusive innovations in common. That is, there is no higher-level node for a PSUA-Hopi. Thus the identification of UA maize-cultivation vocabulary in Hopi means that cultivation must have been present at least at a very early period of Uto-Aztecan prehistory. However, the confirmation of UA cultivation vocabulary in Hopi within a structure that recognizes SUA plus several independent northern branches would not preclude the possibility that the northern branches other than Hopi and perhaps Southern Numic have always been communities of foragers. In summary, continued development of arguments for the integrity of NUA are essential if the line of argumentation developed here for the presence of maize cultivation as a defining cultural adaptation of the PUA community is to be sustained.

Several authors have proposed the existence of a second major first-level branch, Southern Uto-Aztecan (SUA), parallel to NUA, which would include Tepiman, Taracahitan, Tubar, and Corachol-Aztecan. Miller, while generally favoring the conceptualization of PUA as a dialect chain and arguing that "any classification into distinct subgroups will distort the nature of the interrelationships to a greater or lesser extent" (1983, 117), does recognize a PSUA community, although not, at least in his *Handbook* essay, a PNUA one. Campbell and Langacker also support a PSUA but note that their evidence "consists of various cognate sets which allow reasonable Proto-Southern-Uto-Aztecan reconstruction but lack known cognates in the northern languages" (1978, 197), rather than the more highly valued evidence of shared phonological innovation. Kaufman (1981, cited in Campbell 1997:136–37) argues for a phonological innovation shared by all the SUA languages: PUA **ng ([ŋ]) became PSUA *n, and PUA **n became PSUA *r.[10] However, an equally plausible opposite case has been made by Langacker (1977), who reconstructs PUA **n and **r not as innovations but as the original state, with the innovation being to *ng and *n, respectively, and occurring in PNUA. Thus, in Langacker's argument, this is an addition to the list of shared innovations that define PNUA. While I follow Langacker's usage in the reconstructions below, it is probably not possible to resolve this dispute, for neither Kaufman's nor Langacker's proposed sound changes are more marked than the other's. This is in contrast to the shared innovation for NUA proposed by Manaster Ramer, where the change from PUA **c to PNUA *y is an unmarked consonantal lenition, while a change in the opposite direction, from PUA **y to PSUA *c, would be highly marked and therefore improbable. One possible shared innovation for PSUA that would satisfy the preference for a relatively unmarked and likely change is proposed by Kaufman (1981). This is the lenition of PUA **p to *w in word-initial position in the southern languages. Kaufman postulates *w as an intermediate stage in a lenition that led ultimately to /h/ in Cora and Huichol and zero in Aztecan (although Aztecan retains PUA **p in enough forms that Sapir [1913] believed that this was the regular reflex). The *w stage is attested in Tepiman and Tubar (in most varieties of Tepiman the sound is [v], not [w]; in Tubar we also find /b/). However, the lenition to /w/ is rare in the Taracahitan languages, where we usually find initial /p/ or /b/. Thus, the innovation does not in fact occur regularly in all the southern languages and should not be used to define them until the many exceptions can be explained. A possible shared innovation in the southern languages is discussed in the next section in connection with Lexical Set 5, but the historical phonology involved is complex and will require further research. In summary, our evidence for SUA is, in my opinion, weaker than that for NUA, and we should probably speak informally of "the southern languages" or the "non-NUA languages," rather than using the term *Southern Uto-Aztecan*, which suggests an innovation-defined subgroup comparable to NUA.

Among the southern languages, shared innovations have been identified that define some subgroups. For instance, Corachol-Aztecan can be defined by an innovative vowel shift whereby PUA u becomes /i/ (Campbell and Langacker 1978). Tepiman is defined by the presence of the shift of PUA **w, **y, and **k^w to *g, *d, and *b, respectively.

Figure 5.3 shows a structure for the Uto-Aztecan family that represents the earliest division as one into five subgroups: NUA, Tepiman, Taracahitan, Tubar, and Corachol-Aztecan. If this structure survives challenge, it will favor a component of Bellwood's model for innovation-driven language spreads: the formation of what Bellwood has called a "rake-like" structure. Bellwood observes that in such a rapid spread "there would be insufficient time during the expansion for a nested hierarchy of shared linguistic innovations to form. Many localised subgroups of equal time-depth would eventually form independently of each other, once the widespread mesh of mother-daughter community links encouraged by colonisation had begun to succumb to regionalisation" (1997:127). However, the demonstration of a "rake-like" structure for the early history of Uto-Aztecan is not essential to my arguments here and should probably be regarded as a minor component of Bellwood's model.[11]

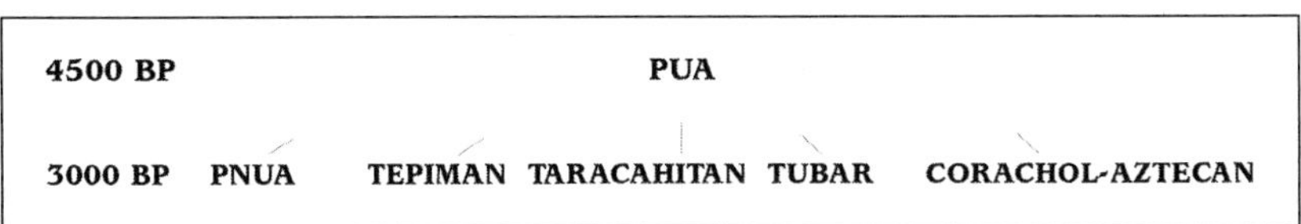

FIGURE 5.3. Internal structure and chronology of the early history of Uto-Aztecan.

THE VOCABULARY OF MAIZE CULTIVATION RECONSTRUCTS TO THE PROTO-UTO-AZTECAN PERIOD

It has long been recognized that the southern languages share many cognate items for maize parts, maize-cultivation implements and techniques, and maize processing. The linguistic paleontological exercise of examining the vocabulary of the maize complex in the Uto-Aztecan languages was given great impetus by the work of Wick Miller, who reviewed this southern system in detail and compared it with the maize vocabulary of Hopi, the only NUA language with a solidly attested prehistoric tradition of cultivation. At the time of his tragically premature death in 1994, Miller had presented his findings only in conference papers (see 1988b). These papers confirm the similarities among the southern languages and assert that Hopi was not a part of this complex. Miller found that the elaborate Hopi maize vocabulary was of obscure source, sharing no confirmed cognates with the southern Uto-Aztecan languages. Obviously Miller's proposal is consistent with the Northern Origin hypothesis in that it supports the idea that agriculture had diffused into the Hopi communities—probably not even directly from SUA but from some other, unknown source—replacing a foraging adaptation. Furthermore, because Miller supported the idea of PSUA, a single primary branch of PUA ancestral to the modern southern languages, in order to reconstruct maize cultivation for PUA it was methodologically necessary for him to identify cognate cultivation vocabulary in at least one northern language. Because Miller found no Hopi cognates, it meant that there was no linguistic support for the presence of maize cultivation in the PUA community, only in SUA after it had broken off from the remainder.

Since Miller's death, an important new source of lexical data has become available for Hopi. The *Hopi Dictionary* (Hill et al. 1998), a dictionary of Third Mesa Hopi, includes over twenty-four thousand base words. This wealth of lexical data reveals that while there are, of course, many words in the extensive Hopi vocabulary for maize cultivation that are not obviously related to forms in sister UA languages, several words in the Hopi lexicon for this domain, in fact, are shared with the southern languages. Most importantly, there are regular sound correspondences between the Hopi lexical items and items in the southern languages. The presence of such regular correspondences implies that this vocabulary dates to the PUA period. That is, this maize vocabulary was not loaned into Hopi but, in fact, was part of the vocabulary of ancestral speakers of Hopi before the separation of the PNUA speech community (from which Hopi is descended) from the remainder of PUA.

The evidence is given in table 5.1.[12] Each example in the table is a "cognate set": the forms given in the various languages are related to one another by regular sound correspondence (where I have departed from standard understandings, this is reviewed in the discussion). Words that are phonologically cognate but are not semantically within the maize complex are in square brackets. Where the words are present in both the southern languages and in Hopi or in some other northern language, the regular sound correspondence means that the words can be reconstructed for PUA. Where the meanings in both Hopi or some other northern language are related to maize cultivation, this means that a meaning within the maize complex can be reconstructed for PUA.

The reconstructed forms are given first in each list. The PUA forms have two asterisks. Reconstructions for forms found only in the southern languages have only one asterisk. Note, however, that on the model presented in the previous section, which holds that each of the southern language groups is an independent branch from PUA, a reconstruction based on the southern languages is, in fact, a reconstruction for PUA, with the form simply unattested in NUA because of actual lexical loss to variation in the protolanguage community or to gaps in our knowledge. In some cases, forms given in the cognate sets are reconstructions in their own turn; these are indicated with a superscript asterisk and the name of the subfamily. Examples are numbered consecutively throughout the six tables in this chapter, to permit ease of reference.

Set 1 includes a Hopi word that is a good phonological cognate but is not semantically within the maize complex. The Hopi word is for a type of reed-like grass that is used to weave mat containers that are rolled around the contained item (prototypically, a bride's robe). The tassels of the grass are worn by certain kachinas. The meaning of the word in most of the other languages (except Mayo) is "the mature ear of corn, with its kernels." However, given the general tendency of forms in the maize

TABLE 5.1. The Uto-Aztecan maize complex

1.	*sunu "corn ear, maize" (maíz, mazorca) (M su-5): [HO soŋowi "sand grass (*Calamovilfa gigantea*)"], Tepiman *hu:nu-i, EU sunú-t, GU sunú, TA sunú, MA súnnu "cornfield," NA *sin-tli/*sen-tli.
2.	**sono "maize byproducts such as cobs, leaves, cane" (M so-9): [Tümpisha Shoshone-soni "grass,"] HO sööŋö "corn cob" (mazorca), Taracahitan *sono "corn element," [EU sonó "corn leaf" (hoja de maíz), GU sonó, sonógola "corn crib" (troje para maíz)], TU [sonó "cane"], sonovoLi-t "straw storage bin" (troje), (but hona-Li-t "corn stubble" (rastrojo)).
3.	**paʔci "corn ear ('elote'), corn kernel, seed" (semilla de maíz) (M pa-3, C&L 313): HO pa:cama "hominy"; [GU pahcí "semilla (como de calabaza, mata silvestre, pero no de maíz, para sembrar)], hueso"; Taracahitan *paci "semilla, elote" (YA baci, MA bácia "semilla"); CR hací "elote," [NA a:č-tli "seed"].

continued

TABLE 5.1. *(continued)*

4.	*saki "popcorn, parched corn, to make parched corn or popcorn (esquite, preparar esquite)" (M sa-2, Manaster Ramer 1996): [TB a:-sagɨ: "to roast" (Manaster Ramer (1993)), possibly Numic words with *sa- meaning "to cook, melt," e.g., Northern Paiute sa: "cook," Shoshone saiG "to melt," Southern Paiute sa'a "to boil"]; Tepiman *ha:ki "parched grain," Taracahitan *sakɨ/saki "to toast, parch" (GU sagilá "comal," MA sá:ki "esquite," EU sakít "maiz tostado, esquite"), CR šačéh "popcorn," HU sak(:)kí "esquite," Aztecan *saki/ɨ (Manaster Ramer 1996).
5.	**wɨra "to shell corn, corn, cob (olote)" (desgranar maíz) (M o-19, o-20, Karen Dakin, personal communication): [Tümpisha Shoshone wɨppu'ah "winnow"??, CA wepin- "to winnow something, to sift something, to blow something (like husks) away from grain"], HO: wɨtaqa "corn gruel," wɨ hi-ta "be sifting (using wind), winnowing" (e.g., corn kernels); TOʔoḍ "to harvest" (reflecting Tepiman *'ora); EU hóran "desgranar maíz," TA orimea "desgranar," TA ohó "desgranar" (Stubbs 1995:402)??; HU 'oríyári, 'o:ríyá:ri "desgranado," NA tla-o:y(a) "to shell something (corn, peas, etc.)," tla-o:l-li "corn, shelled" (tla- is the indefinite inanimate-object prefix); Pipil ta-wiya-l "maíz (desgranado)."
6.	*oʔra/*oʔri "to shell corn, corn, cob (olote)" *desgranar maíz) (M 'o-19, 'o-20): [Kawaiisu ono-ci "hooked stick used to pull down pinyon cones," Tümpisha Shoshone onno-cci "pine cone harvesting hook"], HO qa:ʔö "dried ear of corn," ö:vi(-ʔat) "butt end of the corn cob, proximal end of cob" (probably from ö: "cob" + with combining form –vi from pi:hu "breast, teat"); TA oʔna/koʔná "olote," GU wohna "olote"; NA o:lo:-tl "corncob with kernels removed."
7.	**tɨma "tortilla, tamale" (M tɨ-8): [Serrano tɨ:ʔ "to roast, bake," Kawaiisu tɨʔma-, tuʔma-, "to roast, bake," Southern Paiute tɨʔma- "to roast under ashes"??], HO tɨma "griddle" (comal), TO čɨmait "tortilla," MP tɨmič "tortilla," ST tɨ-:mkal^y "tortilla," TA remé/rimé, GU remé/temai, CR tem^{w}á, NA tamal-li "tamale."
8.	**komal "griddle" (M ko-25): HO qöi "oblong cake of baked sweet corn, flour" (torta de masa, dulce), qöma "to make qömi"; Tepiman *komarika (cf. TO komal "flat and thin object, such as a tortilla griddle," komaḍ "flat," komalik "a flat place"); NA koma:l-li "griddle."
9.	**ku:mi/u "to nibble small pieces of food, especially corn on the cob or popcorn" (masticar comida que tiene la forma de migas o pedazos pequeños) (M ku-12): Southern Paiute qumia "old Indian name for corn, rarely used now" (Sapir 1931, 641), San Juan Paiute kumwi "Zea mays," kumut "Amaranthus caudatus" (Franklin and Bunte 1987:28); HO kokoma "dark red, almost purple corn," komo "Amaranthus cruentus"; TO ku:m "to eat, chew on something that comes in little pieces," ku:mi-kuḍ "corncob"; GU ku'mi-ná/-má "morderse una cosa dura y chiquita como esquite," TA gumí "corner cosas pequeñas, comer maíz) o elote," MA kú:me "masticar," CR má-h-ki-'i-ma-ka "they eat it," HU ki-mé "mascar a morditas," NA kimič-in "mouse" (ratoncito).

complex to shift around among leaves, stalks, and cobs, it seems highly likely that the Hopi word ultimately belongs to this metonymic complex.

Miller notes Hopi *söönö* 'corncob', which I place here in Set 2, but compared it only with Set 1, concluding (correctly) that it did not exhibit regular sound correspondence in that set. Miller suggested that Hopi *sööŋö* was related to a Paiute word meaning "lungs" and thus was an example of metaphoric extension. In focusing on the possibility of a relationship to Set 1 for this item, Miller failed to identify Set 2, even though the pertinent Taracahitan cognates are included in his own databases of Uto-Aztecan resemblant forms (Miller 1967, 1988a) and even though the Hopi form is an excellent cognate for the words in the Taracahitan languages. Miller may have rejected the Taracahitan cognate forms as semantically too distant from the Hopi word, but all forms fall into the general domain of "maize by-products" (cob, leaves, cane, stubble) or, with additional derivational material, storage structures for maize components. The Tümpisha (Panamint) Shoshone form (the language is spoken in Death Valley and nearby regions) has an aberrant second vowel that is otherwise a good phonological fit. Note that the Tümpisha meaning, "(a kind of) grass," is easily derived by metonymy from "maize by-products" including leaves and cane.[13]

Set 3 is newly proposed here. Given the presence of medial /c/ from PUA **c in the southern languages, we would expect Hopi, a NUA language, to exhibit /y/, according to the proposal for PNUA **c-lenition by Manaster Ramer (1992) discussed above. However, Manaster Ramer finds that the presence of an immediately preceding syllable-final laryngeal consonant will block the shift of PUA **c to PNUA *y. In this set, the /h/ in the Guarijio form *pahcí* directly attests to the presence of a laryngeal. The laryngeal is also reflected in the long vowel in the Nahuatl form; Dakin (1997, 64) observes that PUA **CVʔV yields Nahuatl CV: or CVh. Thus, Hopi *pa:cama*, with PUA **c appearing as /c/, can be interpreted as providing additional evidence for the presence of the laryngeal in PUA. We thus reconstruct the protoform as **paʔci. The etymological problems remaining involve resolving the presence of Hopi /a/ in the second syllable, instead of /i/, and the presence of an apparent increment *-ma* in Hopi. Semantically, the Hopi form is an excellent fit.

For Set 4, only the southern languages attest a meaning within the maize complex. Manaster Ramer (1993) has argued carefully for the cognacy of the Tübatülabal form. Its meaning, "to roast" (meat and other food), is appropriate to the set but is not related to maize processing. The Tepiman form, while not restricted to maize, is at least restricted to the parching of grain. I note the Numic forms, which include widely attested roots in *sa- with various increments meaning "to cook by boiling" or "to melt." These are interesting but are not as good as the Tübatülabal cognate in that only the first syllable is a match for the words in the southern languages. They are also more distant semantically from the southern forms.

Sets 5 and 6 require detailed discussion. The reconstruction in Set 5, **wɨra, is contributed by Karen Dakin (personal communication, 2001). Dakin points out that in some varieties of Huasteca Nahuatl and in Pipil the /o:/ element seen in most varieties of Nahua (*tla-o:ya* 'to shell something') appears as /wi/, compared with the Pipil *ta-wiya-l* 'maíz (desgranado)' (Campbell 1985, 733). If we take /wiya/ to be the conservative Aztecan verb root, this permits a simplification of our understanding of the structure of Aztecan verbs. /o:ya/ is the only exception to a general pattern in which the element /-ya/ appears only after the high vowels, /i/ or /u/. Internal reconstruction to /wiya/ would resolve this irregularity. If this Aztecan reconstruction is correct, then several northern languages exhibit potential cognates, including Hopi, Tümpisha Shoshone, and Cahuilla.[14]

The vowels in Set 5 do not exhibit regular sound correspondences. The Hopi, Tümpisha Shoshone, and Cahuilla words for "winnow" support a PUA **ɨ. The vowel of the first syllable is irregular in the southern languages. The /wi/ variants in Huasteca Nahuatl and Pipil should come from PUA **wu. However, such a syllable is unattested for PUA. Most daughter languages seem to avoid sequences of /wu/, /kʷu/ (for a detailed discussion, see Stubbs 1995). Miller (1988a) lists only two attestations for a possible *wu, both problematic Proto-Tepiman reconstructions given by Bascom (1965). There are two sources for /o/ or /o:/ in the other southern languages. One is the regular development of PUA **o. Dakin (1990) has shown another source for Aztecan /o:/: Proto-Aztecan VLV, where L is a labial (*p or *w), will yield Nahuatl /o:/. The southern language /o/ forms might all be from such a rule.

An additional problem with Set 5 is that in the northern languages only the first syllable is a match. We would expect the northern languages to show /wina/, with /n/ as the regular northern development of PUA **r. Finally, Stubbs (1995) cites the Tarahumara form *ohó* 'desgranar', which does not exhibit a regular development of PUA *r. In summary, there are problems with this set that require further research, but this etymology is a promising one.

An important implication of Dakin's reconstruction for this set would be that all of the southern languages except Huasteca Nahuatl and Pipil would share a development of **wɨ to *o:. This might constitute the hitherto elusive evidence of a shared innovation that defines Southern Uto-Aztecan and would contradict my proposal above for the structure of the family. Confirmation of this point requires not only a more secure etymological account of Set 5 but also the identification of additional sets with this development, work that is beyond the scope of this chapter.

Set 6 includes forms that have usually been taken to be part of the etymology of Set 5. The reason for this is that scholars have assumed that NA *tla-o:ya* 'to shell corn, peas', NA *tla-o:l-li* 'shelled corn', and NA *o:lo:-tl* 'corncob' were related by derivation. However, I propose that this apparent derivation is in fact the result of a coincidence that resulted when /o:/ in *tla-o:ya* from **wɨra fell together with /o:/ in *o:lo:-tl* from **oʔra. If we separate out the two sets as shown here, we can suggest solutions to some fascinating etymological problems, especially the resolution of the etymology of Hopi *qa:ʔö* 'dried corn ear', the prototypical "maize" word in Hopi. A crucial reflex here is the Tümpisha Shoshone form *onno-cci* 'pinecone-harvesting hook' with the predicted sounds in a meaning clearly related to the harvesting complex (*-cci* is a "classificatory absolutive suffix" [Dayley 1989, 240]). The geminate /nn/ reflects the presence of a geminating "final feature" closing the first syllable. Such features are analyzed by Manaster Ramer (1993) as reflexes of PUA syllable-final consonants. The final consonant is almost certainly a laryngeal, attested by the long vowel in the Nahuatl form and by the laryngeals in the Taracahitan (TA, GU) words for *olote* 'corncob'. For this reason I reconstruct a final laryngeal, PUA **ʔ, in the first syllable of the PUA form. Most importantly, the closed syllable predicts a long vowel in Hopi. Once we make this prediction, the cognate form is obvious: Hopi *ö:-vi(-ʔat)* 'butt end of corncob'. Here the *-vi* component is probably the combining form of *pi:hu* 'breast', a very common element in words referring to objects with blunt protrusions. The recognition of *ö:-vi(-ʔat)* permits the resolution of the *qa:ʔö* problem. Miller (1988a) tentatively—and, I believe, correctly—included this Hopi word in this set. The qa:- element should be from PUA **ka- 'hard' (Dakin and Wichmann 2000).[15] Indeed, this element also appears in Hopi *qaro(k)* 'to harden, as of damp earth or a fresh hide'. Given *ö:-vi(-'at)*, we can reconstruct *qa:ʔö* as underlying *qa:-ʔö:* 'hard corncob', with the vowel in the second element shortened by regular phonological rule in Hopi, which does not permit long vowels in unstressed syllables. On the evidence of the Tümpisha Shoshone form, having to do with pinecones, *ʔʔö:* may have originally meant simply something like "seed head" (Emory Sekaquaptewa [personal communication, 2001] states that the word for a very young green pinecone in Hopi is *qa:ʔö-at* 'its dried ear of corn').[16]

Miller (1988a) noted some elements of Sets 7 and 8 in the typescript version of his computerized database of Uto-Aztecan cognate sets. He included Hopi words with the notation (cognate?) after the Hopi form. While he noted the Serrano (Takic) word for "to roast," he did not identify it with Set 7. He did not mention the Southern Numic (Kawaiisu and Southern Paiute) words in Set 7 (or in any other set in the 1988a collection) or the Tepiman form in Set 8. The Hopi semantics are particularly interesting in these sets, where Hopi shows a clean semantic reversal, strongly suggesting that the forms are indeed cognate. It is also very interesting that the other NUA languages have glosses in the domain of the cooking process rather than the resulting food. The glottal stops in the Serrano and Southern Numic forms are problematic and may be what deterred Miller from including them.

Set 8 may seem to some readers to be unlikely, for the Tohono O'odham word *komal* looks so much like a recent loan from Nahuatl. Several Nahuatl loans are attested in Tohono O'odham. However, unlike *komal*, none of these recognized Nahuatl loan words is part of a derivational complex (I include the derivationally related words). Furthermore, Bascom (1965) gives the Proto-Tepiman reconstruction, glossing it as "thin," with attestations in all the Tepiman language. The Tohono O'odham word *komal* is a regular development of this set.

Note that the meanings of the PUA reconstructed words in Sets 7 and 8 in PUA are obscure. In the case of Set 7, tamales and tortillas depend on soaking maize kernels in a solution of water and ash. This process, which can be identified archaeologically by the presence of a lime residue in vessels used for soaking, does not appear in the U.S. Southwest until after 1300 CE (Snow 1990). In the case of Set 8, the use of the ceramic grill known as *comalli* in Nahuatl is attested archaeologically in central Mexico only from the first millenium BCE (Fournier 1998), too late to have been part of the material culture of the PUA community. The northern form of the *comal*, a thin stone slab supported by fire dogs on a rectangular hearth, is, like evidence for soaking maize in lime, very late (Snow 1990). Thus, the PUA gloss on these forms should be, strictly speaking, something like "preparation of ground maize, exact nature unknown" in the case of Set 7 and "hot surface used for cooking maize" in the case of Set 8. The Southern Paiute form in Set 7 may hint at the archaic meanings in this pair of related forms. However, I do not consider this to be a serious problem. There are many examples in which vocabulary of an older technology shifts in meaning to accommodate a new one. An excellent example is found within Uto-Aztecan:

> Set 10 **wata 'atlatl, spear-thrower' (M a-4; Manaster Ramer 1996): Numic *eti 'gun, bow'; Tübatülabal 'a:lit 'gun'; HO awta 'bow'; Tepiman *ga:toi 'bow, gun, rifle'; GU atÿ 'arma'; TA atá 'bow'; NA atla- 'spear-thrower'.

This etymon must originally have referred to the atlatl. With the arrival of bows and arrows, the item shifted its meaning to "bow" in most languages, except in Nahuatl, where the atlatl continued in use. In historic times, many of the languages used the word to designate guns.

Finally, in Set 9 the relevant forms permitting us to reconstruct the item to PUA are found not only in Hopi but in two dialects of Southern Paiute, a member of the Numic subfamily of NUA: Kaibab (Sapir 1930) and San Juan (Franklin and Bunte 1987). In Hopi one cognate refers to *Amaranthus crudentus*, a plant used for dye, not for food. I speculate that the amaranth word is derived from the Hopi word meaning "dark red, almost purple corn." The Hopi dictionary notes that this corn is boiled to make a dye that is added to white cornmeal to produce *palaviki*, red piki bread, so the extension to the amaranth, another source of a dark red dye, seems reasonable.

This last item is particularly important because it provides the most solid evidence for the presence of an element of PUA maize vocabulary with maize-related semantics in a northern language other than Hopi. If we found elements of the maize vocabulary present only in Hopi, the case for reconstruction to PUA would be weakened; we could argue that the items appear in Hopi because of early borrowing, prior to the sound changes that now distinguish Hopi from the other languages. However, the presence of cognates in Numic strengthens the case for maize cultivation at the PUA level. It has generally been assumed that the Southern Paiute borrowed agriculture from the Hopi. However, these words for "corn" in Set 9 are not loans from Hopi, for such a loan word would have the vowel /o/, not the attested /u/, which is the regular development in Numic of PUA **u.

Thus, in summary, we can identify seven members of the nine-member set for the maize lexicon shown in Figure 5.1 as components of the vocabulary of PUA because they have cognate forms with maize-related meanings not only in the southern languages but in either Hopi or Southern Paiute, both northern languages. Thus, it is highly likely that maize cultivation was present in the PUA community.

The PUA lexicon includes other forms that suggest the presence of cultivation in the protocommunity but have been traditionally associated with the cultural complex of intensive wild seed use. These include the forms in Table 5.2: Set 11 **wɨka 'digging stick, dibble' and Set 12 **ʔɨca 'to plant'. Set 12 is found throughout the Numic languages as well as in Hopi and the southern languages and, in light of the new information on the maize complex presented above, should probably be taken to constitute additional evidence for the presence of cultivation in the PUA community.

Set 12 is especially important because here Hopi and the other NUA languages show the distinctive reflex of PUA **c > y, a sound change that is shared throughout NUA and is attested in a number of other lexical items (Manaster Ramer 1992). That is, it is most unlikely that this is a borrowed word.

TABLE 5.2. Planting

11.	**wika "digging stick" (M wi-2): (TB wi:ginat/'iwi:gin "to stir"), HO wihkʸa "digging stick," Tepiman *gi:kai "dibble stick, plow," Taracahitan *wika "coa," HU wiká/wi:.ká "pichueca."
12.	**ɨca "to plant" (M'-l, Manaster Ramer 1993): Northern Paiute masta "plant," Tümpisha Shoshone ɨʔa "plant," Kawaiisu ɨʔa "to plant," Southern Paiute ɨa "to plant," HO i:ya "to plant"; Tepiman *ʔisa "to plant"; Taracahitan *e:ca "to plant," HU 'e- "sembrar colocando semillas en la tierra" (NA e-tl "bean" (??)).

Note that I do not consider the PUA cognate set for "metate" (PUA **mata), which has been known for a century, to be evidence for cultivation, in spite of Romney's (1957, 38) citation of it in this connection. Metates are found all over the Southwest from a very early date and clearly were used by foraging peoples prior to the arrival of cultivation.

SQUASH, BEANS, AND THE CHRONOLOGY OF THE BREAKUP OF PUA

Archaeologists have recently found evidence that the well-known Mesoamerican trio of cultivated plants, maize, squash/gourds, and beans, did not all arrive in the Southwest at the same time. Beans do not appear routinely in the archaeological record of the U.S. Southwest until about 2500 BP. Squash and cultivated gourds are not identified until 2900 BP in the Tucson Basin and 2800 BP on the Colorado Plateau. The comparative lexical materials for the cucurbits in Uto-Aztecan are consistent with this later date, for they suggest a more profound dialectal differentiation in the speech community than that displayed by the neatly cognate lexicon of the maize complex. The PUA forms for "squash" are shown in Table 5.3. I give also a set for "turtle," for reasons discussed below.

A semantic connection between Sets 13 and 14 is suggested by the presence of forms in both sets meaning "rattle." Particularly, the Hopi form, shown in square brackets in the "squash" set in 13, designates a gourd rattle. It is an excellent cognate with the "turtle" words in Set 14 except for its semantics. As noted above in the discussion of Set 5 in Table 5.1, Dakin (1997) suggests for the southern languages a complex dialectal breakup of PUA **r into /y/, /l/, and /'/. PUA **r is attested in the "squash" words in Set 13 in Tohono O'odham and Gaurijio, while variants in /y/ are seen in Mayo and Nahuatl. The Hopi "squash" word in 12, with a /y/ found also

TABLE 5.3. Squash

13.	**ari-(wɨ) "squash, pumpkin" (calabaza) (M 'a-2):, HO a:ya "hand rattle (made of dried *Cucurbita foetidissima* [Fowler 1994, 460])," TO ha:l "squash, pumpkin," GU aláwe "calabaza. *C. pepo* (Fowler 1994, 460)," MA a:yaw "calabaza." NA ayoh-tli "squash, calabash"; 'ayoh- "pumpkin" (Huasteca Nahuatl).
14.	**aya-(wɨ) "turtle, tortoise, rattle" (M 'a-14) LU pá:ʔaya-t "turtleshell rattle"; SE a:yt "rattle," yuʔa:ṯ "water turtle" (where yu- is from **yu "wet"), Cupan ayi- "desert tortoise, turtle, tortoise shell rattle," SN *aya "turtle," TU haya-wé-t "tortuga," HU ʔayé "tortuga," NA a:yo:-tl "turtle, tortoise"; a:yakač-tli "rattle."

in these latter two languages, could be a /y/ reflex from **r in this system. However, recall that the northern languages are defined by *n from PUA **r; thus we would expect Hopi /a:na/. Instead, however, Hopi shows *a:ya*. It is highly likely, then, that the Hopi word originally referred not to a rattle made from a dried gourd but to a rattle made from a tortoiseshell.

The historical process represented in Hopi *a:ya* 'gourd rattle' is probably linguistic convergence due to contact, with contact-induced semantic change in a reflex of an archaic etymon. Such a convergence, however, requires an appropriate stimulus. I believe that the Hopi word probably would not have changed its meaning from "rattle made of tortoiseshell" to "rattle made of a gourd" unless the Hopi were in contact with "y dialects" of Uto-Aztecan—that is, languages like Mayo or Nahuatl—at the time of the arrival of cultivated cucurbits. By "y dialects" I refer to languages where we see reflexes of PUA **r as /y/ before high vowels and thus a /y/in the word for "squash." This change resulted in a word for squash (and gourds and gourd rattles) that resembled the Hopi word for "tortoiseshell rattle." Had the Hopi only been in contact with "l/r dialects" (represented in Set 13 by Tohono O'odham and Guarijio), the parallelism between their word for "tortoiseshell rattle," with a /y/, and the word for a gourd (with /r/ or /l/) would not have been apparent. In such a case, the semantic convergence probably would not have occurred. (The Hopi continue to use tortoiseshell rattles; they are called *yöŋösona* [the same word is used for the tortoise itself].)

That Hopi does not share a cognate word for "squash" suggests that by 2900 BP, the Uto-Aztecan dialect continuum was already beginning to break up. However, the convergence discussed above reveals that contact within the emerging languages of the continuum was still present at this date.

Finally, the lexical items for "beans" are also consistent with archaeological data, which identify this cultigen in the Southwest no earlier than 2500 BP. There is a single exception, a bean dates to 2931 BP from the bottom of a bell-shaped storage pit at Las Capas in the Tucson Basin (Mabry 2001). It is possible that this single early bean is a trade item from farther south. It is also possible that more evidence for local cultivation of beans at this early date will be identified; beans (and squash) do not preserve as well as maize and are less likely to show up in the archaeological record. The pertinent set of lexical items is shown in table 5.4.

It has been clear for many years that these words for beans do not exhibit regular sound correspondences, not only among Numic, Hopi, and the southern languages but within the latter group as well. This can be easily seen in reference to the vowels by comparing this irregular set with the regular Set 1 in table 5.1 for **sunu* 'corn'. The medial consonant is also quite irregular. Note that there is no Aztecan cognate; the Aztecan word for *Phaseolus vulgaris*, seen in Nahuatl *e-tl*, is probably derived from the verb meaning "to plant." These words for beans unquestionably resemble one

TABLE 5.4. Beans

15.	**mu- "(kidney) beans, *Phaseolus vulgaris*" (frijoles) (M mu-3): SP mu:ti "beans" (given by Miller 1988b), mo:ri "beans" (from Sapir 1931). CH muri: "bean," muri:vɨ "bean plant, bean straw." HO mori "bean(s)," TO mu:ñ "beans"; Taracahitan *muni "frijol," CR múhme "beans," HU mó(:)me "frijoles" (and cf. Seri *mon*, Yavapai *merik*, and Siouan forms with roots in *wVrí*, *mVní* [Rankin 2000]).

another. However, their lack of regular sound correspondence suggests strongly that the ancestral form, whatever it was, was not part of the lexical stock of the PUA community but instead diffused through UA and its neighbors (as shown in the table, similar words appear in Seri, the Yuman languages, and in Siouan) after the breakup of the community. This permits us to state that the UA dialect continuum was already divided into distinct daughter languages by 2500 BP.

In summary, the results of analysis of the vocabulary for the main cultigens and their management in UA is consistent with the picture of the spread of agriculture that is beginning to emerge archaeologically: an initial expansion of maize cultivators from Mesoamerica into the U.S. Southwest between about 4000 and 3000 BP, followed by the spread of cultivated cucurbits by around 2900 BP, followed still later by the diffusion of beans through established agricultural communities by about 2500 BP. It is also consistent with Bellwood's model for the spread of the family.

UTO-AZTECAN WORDS FOR CULTIVATION ARE NOT LOAN WORDS

Campbell and Kaufman (1976) propose that many of the Uto-Aztecan etyma discussed above are loan words from Mesoamerican languages with a well-established connection to early agriculture, especially from Mixe-Zoquean. Recent works by Wichmann (1995, 1998) and Dakin and Wichmann (1995, 2000) have challenged these proposals. New work on the historical phonology of Aztecan (cf. Canger and Dakin 1985; Dakin 1999, 2000) and new comparative-linguistic research on Mixe-Zoquean (Wichmann 1995) permit us to make a case for the autochthonous Uto-Aztecan origin of much of the maize-cultivation vocabulary. For instance, a suggested Mesoamerican source for Set PUA *sunu does not hold up. Fowler (1994) cites Rensch's reconstruction of Proto-Otomanguean *sen- 'corn' but observes that this etymology has been questioned by Kaufman. Otomanguean *sen-, assuming it is a correct reconstruction, resembles only the innovative (Canger and Dakin 1985) Aztecan dialect variant *sen-tli* 'mazorca' rather than regular Aztecan *sin-tli* from PSUA *sunu;

so if this pair is evidence of contact, the direction of diffusion would have been from the innovative Aztecan dialects into Otomanguean, not vice versa. For Set 3, PUA **paʔci, Campbell and Langacker (1978) suggest that it is ultimately a loan word from Proto-Mixe-Zoquean (PMZ) **paci/pici 'leached corn'. Wichmann (1995, 1998:305) finds this proposal to be invalid; he reconstructs PMZ **pici and finds no cognates with /a/ in the first syllable in any daughter languages. For Set 13, PUA **ari-(wɨ) 'squash, gourd', Campbell and Kaufman (1976) give PMZ *awa 'gourd'. Wichmann (1995) does not concur with this reconstruction and suggests that the form, attested only in Chimalapa Zoque in his data, diffused into this language from Tequistlatec, a neighboring Otomanguean language. Wichmann (1995) reconstructs PMZ *ciʔwa 'squash' and **cima 'gourd'. For "squash," most of the daughter languages listed by Wichmann have only the ci- component of this form. In fact, the -wɨ element in the Guarijio and Mayo words for "squash" seems to be a derivational suffix, not the root, which is **ari/ayi, so the Campbell-Kaufman proposal is probably incorrect.

THE HOMELAND OF THE AZTECANS

An important—and politically charged—question has to do with the origins of the Aztecans. The traditional analysis of Uto-Aztecan prehistory sees the Aztecans, the most southerly Uto-Aztecan group, as marginal to Mesoamerica until a very late date, perhaps about 1000 BP. Nahua ideology in support of this marginality, best known from the Mexica Aztec origin account, included an account of a migration by their ancestors from a place northwest of Tenochtitlan, known as "Aztlan" (of uncertain meaning, sometimes translated as "Place of Herons") or Chicomoztoc ("At the Seven Caves"). The Nahua origin account has been interpreted by activists in the Chicano political movement in the United States as referring to a location in the U.S. Southwest. This interpretation implies that Chicanos, as cultural and biological descendants of Mexican Indians, have a special claim of priority in that region. However, a good deal of evidence argues against locating "Aztlan" in the U.S. Southwest or even in northwest Mexico outside Mesoamerica. Fowler (1983) has pointed out that Proto-Aztecan was almost certainly spoken within the tropics, given that many Proto-Aztecan etyma can be reconstructed for tropical plants and animals. Several recently developed lines of research suggest that Aztecan peoples were important in Mesoamerica throughout the Classic period. Research on Uto-Aztecan religious ideologies (Hill 1992; Hayes-Gilpin and Hill 1999) reconstructs for a very early stage of UA a "flower-world" complex, where flower metaphors and imagery were central symbols of the sacred. Clear expression of flower-world ideology is found in Classic period murals at Teotihuacan. Dakin and Wichmann (2000) and Wichmann (1998) present arguments for the presence or even dominance of Nahua speakers at

Teotihuacan in the Early Classic period. Macri (2000) has proposed a reading of a Classic period glyph for the Maya day name *ahau* that associates it with an origin in a Nahua-language calendar system.

WATER MANAGEMENT TECHNIQUES MAY HAVE PERMITTED THE RAPID SPREAD OF CULTIVATION INTO THE SOUTHWEST

The time lapse between the earliest sedentary villages in Mesoamerica, at about 4500 BP, and the earliest appearance of maize and settled villages in the Southwest, at about 3500 BP, is quite short. Ammerman and Cavalli-Sforza (1973), based on radiocarbon dates for the spread of grain cultivation from Anatolia into Europe, estimate the average speed of a "wave of advance" movement by primary agriculturalists undergoing demic diffusion at approximately one kilometer/year. The highway distance between Mexico City and Phoenix, Arizona, is 3,878 kilometers. Even if we use the earlier date of 5600 BP for the earliest cultivated maize in the Tehuacan Valley (rather than the date of sedentism at 4600 BP) and approximately 3500 BP for the earliest maize in the Southwest, then the spread of cultivation into the U.S. Southwest was almost twice as fast as the spread of domesticated grains into Europe! Thus, it is unlikely that demic diffusion was the only mechanism of the Uto-Aztecan expansion. One possibility is that a second mechanism, "leapfrogging" (Anthony 1990), hastened their arrival in the Southwest. The leapfrogging pattern was associated with the use of irrigation. The traditional view of the spread of agriculture from Mesoamerica to the Southwest admitted only rainfall cultivation. For this reason, Haury (1962) thought that the route of diffusion of cultivation must have been along the Sierra Madre Occidental, where at higher elevations summer rain was more reliable. However, some of the earliest dates for southwestern maize are in low river valleys, as at La Playa in northwestern Sonora (Carpenter et al. 1999) and in the Tucson Basin, where there are several dates from around 3300 BP (Gregory 1999). Mabry (1999) has excavated a canal at the site of Las Capas in the Tucson Basin that dates to 2800 BP. A model in which maize cultivators move up the west coast of Mexico, leapfrogging from one river valley to the next looking for environments where maize could be planted in damp alluvium and even irrigated would partly account for the rapidity of the spread of maize agriculture. The "leapfrog" model supplements the model of "demic diffusion." While "demic diffusion" would form one stage (from the initial move into a river basin up to the point of exhausting the supply of cultivable sites in the appropriate microenvironments of that basin), this would alternate with the "leapfrog" stage between rivers. Given the distances between such cultivable zones in northwest Mexican and the Southwest, such a "leapfrog" move would resemble what Bellwood calls a "more dramatic process of emigration" (1997, 124), as seen in the Pacific.

TABLE 5.5. Water Management Compounds: Phonologically Cognate and Semantically Similar

16.	NA a:-wa:ki "flooded"	HO pa:-laki "to die of overwatering"
	WATER-DRY	WATER-DRY
17.	NA a:-teko-ni "canal"	HO pa:tkiwɨn^{w}a "member of the Parted Water Clan"
		pa:-tɨki-wɨn^{w}a
	WATER-CUT?-AGENTIVE	WATER-CUT-CLAN MEMBER

Note: a:-pan-teka "hacer un acueducto" WATER-WALL-LAY

In addition to the archaeological evidence for irrigation, linguistic paleontological evidence suggests the use of irrigation at a very early period in Uto-Aztecan history. A suggestive set of vocabulary items for the management of water is similar in the two Uto-Aztecan languages for which we have the richest lexical resources: Nahuatl, the southernmost of the southern languages, and Hopi, an NUA language. Two sets of compound words show striking similarities between the two languages. The first two are shown in table 5.5.

The compounds in table 5.5 are good cognates in the two languages, with substantial semantic resemblance and regular sound correspondence. Especially striking is Set 16, where both languages have a form "WATER-DRY" to mean precisely an excess of water. This is an unusual rhetorical choice that is unlikely to have arisen independently in the two languages.

The case of Set 17 involves the suggestion that the source of *-teko-ni* in the Nahuatl form is *teki* 'to cut' and not *te:ka* 'to lay down'. The authoritative dictionaries of Classical Nahuatl give the perfective *teko* for *teki* and *te:ko* for *te:ka*; the two perfectives are indistinguishable in the Classical sources, where the long vowel is not indicated. I give *a:pan-te:ka* so that the reader can see that a source with *te:ka* is a possibility. However, this form speaks of a "water-wall" (*a:-pan*), perhaps formed by a course of adobe bricks, for which the *te:ka* 'to lay down' verb is appropriate. In *a:tekoni* we have only *a:-* 'water', incorporated before the verb form (which looks like it has an agentive suffix, *-ni*), making a source in *teki* 'to cut' more likely. In the Hopi case, I do not know the meaning behind the idea of "Parted (Cut) Water," a clan name. It may be that the clan origin legend is published somewhere. In summary, this is a speculative example.

A second set of compounds for water management that are not phonological cognates in Nahuatl and Hopi exhibits striking semantic parallelisms. These are shown in table 5.6. I have listed the compounds in table 5.6, beginning with those in which the

TABLE 5.6. Water Management Compounds: Semantically Similar Only

18.	NA a:-celwia "irrigate, moisten"	HO pa:-cayaya-toyna "to sift rain water" (in song)
	WATER-SIFT	WATER-SIFT-CAUSE
19.	NA a:-koyok-tli "canal"	HO pa-höva "ditch"
	WATER-MAKE HOLE-ABS	WATER-MAKE GROOVE
20.	NA a:-tla-k^{w}i-tiw "go to look for water"	HO pa:-hep-nɨma "to search around for springs"
	WATER-OBJ-GET-GO: FOR	WATER-SEARCH-GO: AROUND
21.	NA a:-cak^{w}a "to dam, close off water"	HO pa:-ʔɨ:ci "dam"
	WATER-CLOSE	WATER-CLOSED: THING

semantic parallelism between the two languages is striking, because the meaning of the form is unusual and thus unexpected, and ending with those where the semantics of the compound is not particularly unusual and where the parallelism could well have arisen as the result of independent innovation in the two languages.

The pair in Set 18 shows that both languages use the striking metaphor "WATER-SIFT" to designate irrigation. In Hopi the word is restricted to ceremonial contexts; the "water sifter," *paatsayànpi*, is a ceramic sifter used to sprinkle the beans being sprouted for the Powamɨytikive, Bean Dance, held in February (Patrick Lyons, personal communication, 2000). The term is also used for a bride's robe, said to be loosely woven so that it can serve as a "water sifter," "like a cloud."

In the case of Set 19, both languages have a word for "canal" or "ditch" that involves WATER compounded with a rather specialized word for "CUT": the Hopi form means "to make a groove," while the Nahuatl form involves "perforation." Both verbs involve the making of a hole with rounded edges, and I judge them to be interestingly similar in the context of the other expressions. Note that a number of other words for "canal" have been recorded for Classical Nahuatl; I give two of them here. The forms in Sets 20 and 21 might well have arisen independently in the two languages. Nonetheless, it is interesting that both languages have fully lexicalized compounds meaning "to search for water" and "close off water in a canal, dam."

In summary, the compounds shown in tables 5.5 and 5.6 suggest a common "way of speaking" about water management in two languages that are separated by over one thousand miles and are in two different branches of the Uto-Aztecan family. This way of speaking may, then, be inherited from a common ancestral community that began to use irrigation in the PUA period. This is consistent with archaeological evidence for canal irrigation in the U.S. Southwest and northwest Mexico at a very early date.

ARGUMENTS AGAINST THE SOUTHERN ORIGIN MODEL

There are at least four main lines of argument against Bellwood's proposal for the southern origin of Uto-Aztecan and the evidence for it that is presented above. The first is the probability (Lyle Campbell, personal communication, 2000) that the words in the maize complex are not, in fact, originally words involving maize at all but, rather, words that originated within a foraging adaptation and then underwent semantic shift to refer to maize and maize processing as the original foraging community adopted cultivation. Indeed, there is some evidence that many of these words once meant something different. In Set 1, the Hopi word refers not to maize but to a reed with a thick stalk. In Set 3, the Nahuatl and Guarijio words simply mean "seed," and in the Guarijio case the lexical entry in the dictionary specifically exclused "corn seed" as a meaning. In Set 4, the Tübatülabal form can refer to the roasting of meat, and the various Numic "cooking" words involve boiling, not parching. In Set 5 the Tohono O'odham word *'oḍ* 'to harvest' is not restricted to maize. The words in NUA languages for "winnowing" in Set 5 have to do with the processing of wild grass seeds, and the Tümpisha Shoshone word in Set 6 has to do with pine nut harvesting, not maize harvesting. In Set 7, the Serrano and Southern Numic forms attest to a meaning involving cooking that is not restricted to maize.

My answer to this argument is the standard one from parsimony: It is unlikely that, after the breakup of PUA, independent daughter communities would each, separately, have shifted the same lexical items for food collecting over to the same set of meanings for cultivation. It is much more likely that such a series of semantic shifts from foraging-associated to cultivation-associated meanings—which indeed may have occurred—all happened in a single protocommunity and were inherited by the daughter languages. The terms would probably have retained the original meanings as secondary alternatives,[17] and in some of the languages these original meanings outlasted the cultivation-related meanings, especially in communities that abandoned cultivation.

The second argument is that the late date offered here, between 3500 and 2900 BP, for the final breakup of PUA does not give sufficient time for the diversification of the northern languages. My reply to this argument is that in fact we know very little about the rates of diversification of languages. I have done firsthand fieldwork and publication on Takic languages, on Tohono O'odham, and on Nahuatl. While the informal claim has often been made that the Takic languages are the most diverse of the Uto-Aztecan subfamilies, it is not at all clear to me that Cupeño and Serrano in Takic are more different from one another than are Nahuatl and Huichol in Corachol-Aztecan—or, for that matter, more different from one another than French and Spanish, known to have diverged by about 1,500 years ago. The fact is that we have no standard replicable ways of measuring "linguistic diversity." While I believe that informal lexico-statistic comparisons are useful, the glottochronological constant, the only quantitative measure of linguistic diversity that has to my knowledge been proposed, has been repeatedly challenged (indeed, the evidence reviewed here presents yet another challenge to it). However, it should be noted that the glottochronological date for the breakup of Numic of between 1300 to 1900 BP suggested by Miller (1986) is in no way challenged by the present proposal. As noted above, Fowler (1983), an authority on the Numic languages, has proposed that PNUA began to break up around 3000 BP. This does not contradict my chronology that has PNUA separating from the other UA languages at about that date; it merely implies that PNUA did not last very long as a coherent unit. A breakup date for Takic on the order of 2500–2000 BP would make the dates for Takic comparable to the usual estimates for Germanic, which seems reasonable given the level of differentiation within Takic.

The third argument is that the Takic languages and Tübatülabal, the two California branches, do not seem to share the cultivation terminology found among other Uto-Aztecan groups, even in the form of cognates with a more general food-collecting or -processing reference. There are some exceptions. For instance, Manaster Ramer's (1993) proposal relating Tübatülabal *a:-sagi:* 'to roast' to PUA *saki was discussed in connection with Set 4 in table 5.1. Cahuilla *wepin-* 'winnow' is a possible member of Set 5. The Numic groups are also sparsely attested, with non-maize-related cognates in Sets 1, possibly 4, possibly 5 and 6, and 7. Only for Set 9 do we encounter a PUA maize-related meaning in Southern Numic. Set 12 for "plant" is found in all Numic subgroups. Additional research may identify some of the missing vocabulary. I would argue that the absence of cognate terms in the northern languages may simply reflect our very inadequate lexical resources. While for Nahuatl and Hopi we have tens of thousands of lexical items attested and several thousand words as well for Tohono O'odham, for the great majority of Uto-Aztecan languages our lexical database amounts to under two thousand items, sometimes even less, making it in fact rather remarkable that any cognate sets at all can be identified except for those in basic vocabulary. Our resources are especially poor for the California languages. Because hardly any primary speakers (that is, speakers who were fluent as children) of the California languages survive today, it is unlikely that these resources will ever improve. However, it is also possible that cultivation-related vocabulary was simply lost once speakers shifted completely to foraging. Vocabulary can be lost very quickly. Consider, for instance, the English-language lexicon of horsemanship. In the beginning of the twentieth century, every English speaker had a rich repertoire of words for breeds and colors of horses, for gaits, for equestrian technique, and for saddles, bridles, and the like. After only one hundred years of the shift to motor vehicles, the vast majority of this lexicon has been lost and is now known only to a few equestrian hobbyists. Bloomfield (1933:400) illustrates this phenomenon with the vocabulary of falconry, richly developed in English into the early modern period and now nearly extinct.

The fourth argument involves my claim that the foraging adaptation of most of the NUA groups is a result of devolution. The contemporary range of Uto-Aztecan extends far to the north and west of the area of North America where climatic regimes permit maize agriculture using archaic techniques. The traditional understanding of this distribution has been that the ancestral groups in the NUA community, established in this area beyond the limits of maize cultivation, were always foragers until a very late date. For instance, Sutton (2000) argues that the community originated in the Mojave Desert, west of the limits for maize cultivation. Some subgroups moved east along the Virgin and Colorado Rivers and adopted cultivation. However, very early maize agriculture has now been identified in many sites on the Colorado Plateau, in areas now occupied by Numic-speaking peoples. New radiocarbon dates in southeastern Utah range back to 3300 BP for maize and 2800 BP for squash (Smiley 2000).[18] It seems most likely that these early Colorado Plateau cultivators constituted the PNUA ancestral community. Shaul (1999a) argues that the Southern Numic languages (Kawaiisu, Chemehuevi, the various dialects of Southern Paiute, and Ute) are considerably more different from one another than are the different groups of the Central and Western Numic, suggesting a more ancient presence for Numic languages in the southern area, which was within the range of maize agriculture until quite recent times.

During the Archaic period the climatic regime in the Southwest and the Great Basin was wetter than it is today, permitting cultivation well beyond the range attested in the historic period. In the eastern Great Basin cultivation appears archaeologically as far north as northern Utah between about 2100 (at Steinaker Gap [Mabry 2001]) and 700 BP (the latest dates on Fremont sites [Aikens 1994]). Under the traditional model it has often been assumed that those Numic peoples for whom cultivation is ethnographically attested (which include every branch of Numic: the Owens Valley

Paiute in Western Numic; Tümpisha Shoshone and Comanche in Central Numic; and Chemehuevi, Southern Paiute, and some bands of the Ute in Southern Numic) borrowed the complex from the Puebloans or from Colorado River Yumans. The evidence presented here suggests that we should reevaluate this proposal and explore the possibility that the ancestral Numic groups were cultivators who, with the exception of those groups found cultivating in the historic period, shifted to foraging with climatic change or as they were forced into regions beyond the limits of cultivation.

Cultivation may have extended farther west than is usually supposed. Lawton and Bean (1968) (reprinted in Bean and Saubel 1972) and Bean and Lawton (1976) argue for prehistoric cultivation, probably only of cucurbits, in favorable locations on the western fringes of the Colorado Desert in regions inhabited historically by some bands of the Cahuilla, speakers of a language in the Takic subgroup of Uto-Aztecan who were primarily dependent on foraging (including the use of acorns in the mountains).[19] Thus, only for the Tübatülabal are there no claims for the possibility of prehistoric cultivation.

For a group of cultivators to abandon that adaptation is certainly unusual, but it is attested. A famous case is that of the South Island New Zealand Maori. Another example is the Austronesian-speaking Penang of Borneo. The so-called Sand Papago, noted below, are an undisputed case within Uto-Aztecan itself. An anonymous reviewer who in general objected that such a process is extremely unlikely noted another North American case, the shift to foraging of cultivators who moved onto the plains to become buffalo hunters. Nevertheless, in order to sustain this dimension of my argument, we require models of how such an abandonment might have occurred—that is, how such groups might have been pushed beyond the range of climatic regimes that permitted cultivation or failed to retreat into the appropriate zone once summer rainfall in their original area dropped below the critical level.

One model comes from Levy's (1992) recent restudy of the Hopi town of Oraibi. Levy argues that access to cultivable land was controlled by senior clans, which favored other senior clan groups and relegated low-ranking clans to marginal lands. A similar tradition, of a division between high-ranking people who control access to lands and commoners who do not, is also reported for Takic groups (Hill and Nolasquez 1973). Thus, social discrimination could have forced low-ranking marginalized lineages to emphasize foraging and eventually to abandon cultivation entirely. Given this kind of tradition, we can imagine that in a situation of a general retreat to the south off of the Colorado Plateau and out of the Basin, driven by a worsening climate (a process that is well attested archaeologically, especially on the Colorado Plateau, and is also attested in Hopi oral tradition), many groups might have found it impossible to gain access to scarce cultivable lands and would have been forced to remain as foragers outside the range of cultivation.

Another model can be seen among the Upper Pimans, where there is a stratification among River People, cultivating along permanent streams; Two-Village People, moving between winter water tanks and summer rainfall fields; and the so-called Hia c-eḍ O'odham or Sand Papago, who were foragers. These groups all spoke the same language, and Sand Papago and Two-Village people occasionally were coresident with River People, working for them in exchange for access to food and water (Hackenberg 1983). Peoples living in the remote parts of the Papaguería during the Hohokam period were evidently involved in the trade in shells from the Gulf of California; this Upper Piman system should probably be seen as a total adaptation, with foragers, semisedentary cultivators, and fully sedentary cultivators (some of whom were Yumans, not Upper Pimans [Shaul and Hill 1998]) all playing an important role.

The Takic case suggests yet another model; moving beyond the margins of cultivation into California, Takic peoples could turn to acorns, a highly dependable and high-yield resource that sustained quite complex cultural systems among California foragers (an elaborate acorn-complex vocabulary can be reconstructed for Proto-Takic). Thus, there are plausible ethnographic scenarios for the sort of devolution from cultivation to foraging that Bellwood has proposed.

CONCLUSION

I have reviewed new linguistic evidence that favors Bellwood's model of an origin for the Uto-Aztecan peoples as Mesoamerican cultivators.[20] Under this model, the Uto-Aztecan presence in California, the Great Basin, and the Southwest is the result of a migration northward, driven by the demographic consequences of an early commitment to cultivation. If these proposals hold up, the implications are substantial. First, they will require that we sharply shorten the chronology of the Uto-Aztecan languages, placing the initial breakup of the protolanguage into Northern Uto-Aztecan and the remaining southern languages closer to 3000 BP than to 5000 or 6000 BP—dates that were proposed based on glottochronology and lexico-statistics (e.g., Hale 1958–59; Hale and Harris 1979; Miller 1983; Swadesh 1955). Most authorities have used a date of 5000 BP.[21] For instance, Aikens (1994) assumes the 5000 BP date and gives a date of between 4000 and 3000 BP for the breakup of NUA. Based on the materials summarized here, these dates are all far too early. If the Uto-Aztecans were primary cultivators, it is unlikely that their expansion would have begun before about 4500 BP, when sedentism first appears in Mesoamerica. Maize does not appear in the Southwest until about 3700 BP. The archaeological evidence does not suggest a breakup immediately upon this arrival; for instance, Cordell observes that "there is really nothing to suggest social differentiation of local populations" (of early cultivators in the Southwest) (1997, 146). Evidence from the etymology for "squash" discussed here suggests that population elements ancestral to the Hopi were still in close contact with population elements ancestral to the Cahitan peoples as late as 2900 BP, the date for the earliest squash in the Southwest. Thus, the breakup of Uto-Aztecan into NUA and the various southern groups cannot have happened much earlier than that period, with subsequent differentiation among the northern languages necessarily even later. This chronological revision has implications for all of our assumptions about the dates of ancient linguistic communities in the Americas—if the glottochronological dating for Proto-Uto-Aztecan, a well-known family with relatively good lexical data, is so wildly off, the status of all such dating must be regarded as highly questionable, except for the most informal and preliminary purposes.

The evidence also has implications for the geographic distribution of the proto-communities for ancient macrofamilies. Most of the attempts to link Uto-Aztecan to other language groups have involved Tanoan.[22] The Southern Origin model of Uto-Aztecan prehistory suggests that we should turn our attention away from Tanoan to Otomanguean, Mixe-Zoquean, and other Mesoamerican languages.[23] Similarly, Bellwood's model motivates a search for relatives for Tanoan and the two language isolates spoken by Southwest cultivators—Keresan and Zuni—in Mesoamerica, not among families that are primarily found in North America. While these families show up today as linguistic isolates in the U.S. Southwest, it is quite possible that they were originally more widely distributed. Profound disturbances of the populations of northern Mexico in the immediate postconquest period could easily have eliminated communities of speakers of languages that could link these groups to Mesoamerican ancestors. Of course, Bellwood's hypothesis does not preclude the occasional case of adoption of cultivation by foragers, so one or more of these groups may be indigenous descendants of Southwest Archaic period populations.

The model presented here has other implications as well. Archaeologists may wish to test the model by seeking evidence for a devolution from cultivation to foraging on the Colorado Plateau and in the Great Basin. Linguists and ethnographers working in those communities in which fluent primary speakers of Uto-Aztecan languages remain may wish to push very hard for additional lexicons in areas such as water management and the use of plant resources, especially for cultivation-related lexicons.

In summary, in spite of their well-known problems, the proposals by Renfrew and Bellwood that large, multibranched language groups may represent the trace of human expansions driven by Neolithic technological innovations, especially cultivation, must be taken seriously. Rather than dismissing these hypotheses without further attention, we need to seek data that will permit us to test them, and we must subject old data and models to new testing in light of these ideas. In the case of Uto-Aztecan, such testing using historical-linguistic methods reveals important evidence in support of the hypothesis that speakers of the protolanguage were maize cultivators who spread from northwest-central Mexico into their present very large range. This evidence must now be answered by those who wish to defend the Northern Origin hypothesis.

ACKNOWLEDGMENTS

A project of this scope necessarily depends on the help of more people than can be enumerated in this space. But I would especially like to thank Lyle Campbell, Karen Dakin, Kenneth C. Hill, Jonathan Mabry, Alexis Manaster Ramer, Barbara Mills, José Luís Moctezuma, Emory Sekaquaptewa, David L. Shaul, Ofelia Zepeda, and the exceptionally conscientious anonymous reviewers for *American Anthropologist*.

NOTES

1. Compare Fritz (1994), who lists calibrated 3640–3360 BCE for an AMS date on a corncob from the Tehuacan Valley, at San Marcos Cave, zone F (cited in Long et al. 1989). On the gulf coast of Mexico in the delta of the Grijalva River, Pope et al. (2001) report maize pollen dated to 6200 BP. Dates are uncalibrated radiocarbon dates unless otherwise indicated.
2. Bellwood (1997) credits papers in Ehret and Posnanski (1982) with even earlier developments of these ideas.
3. By "demic diffusion" (sometimes called "demic expansion"), Ammerman and Cavalli-Sforza (1973) mean a process whereby demographic pressure causes a community to bud off descendant groups that found new communities, with the process being continually repeated until descendants of a single ancestral group may cover an enormous area.
4. *Linguistic paleontology* is a term commonly used for the exercise of reconstruction of the meaning of vocabulary in the lexicon of a protolanguage, in order to make suggestions about the culture of its speakers. A famous example involves the reconstruction of the proto-Indo-European name of the divinity known in Latin as Jupiter and in Greek as Zeus; the name reconstructs to a compound meaning "Sky-Father" (Thieme 1964).
5. New work on the genetics of domesticated horses shows that they were probably domesticated several times in different Eurasian sites. Thus, the Indo-European ancestral community probably was not the only domesticator of horses (Vilà et al. 2001). This does not, however, eliminate the likelihood that their use of horses and wheeled vehicles played a substantial role in their expansion.

6. Gamkrelidze and Ivanov (1994[1984]) also place the proto-Indo-European community in Anatolia. Anthony (1995) argues that it was probably on the trans-Pontic steppes, perhaps on the lower Volga, where the earliest evidence for the bitting of horses has been identified as part of the Sredny Stog archaeological culture, representing likely communities of Indo-European speakers.
7. In a "dialect chain," regional language varieties at opposite ends of the chain will be mutually unintelligible, but there is no clean break between any two segments of the chain.
8. Shaul (1999b) does not accept the unity of Taracahitan, arguing that Opatan (Ópata and Cahitan) should be distinguished from the Tarahumaran languages. If Shaul is correct then Uto-Aztecan has six primary branches. Valiñas (2000) includes a useful review of the various positions regarding the classification of the southern languages. For the information of readers who may not be familiar with the family, the major groups and their major member languages are listed here:

   NUA:
   - Hopi
   - Numic
     - Western Numic: Mono, Northern Paiute
     - Central Numic: Tümpisha (Panamint) Shoshone, Shoshone, Gosiute, Comanche
     - Southern Numic: Kawaiisu, Chemehuevi, Southern Paiute, Ute
   - Tübatülabal
   - Takic
     - Cupan: Cahuilla, Cupeño, Luiseño
     - Serrano, Gabrielino-Fernandeño

   Southern Languages (SUA?)
   - Tepiman
     - Pima-Tohono O'odham (Papago)
     - Lower Pima
     - Mountain Pima
     - Northern Tepehuan
     - Southern Tepehuan
     - Tepecano
   - Taracahitan
     - Ópata
     - Eudeve
     - Tarahumara
     - Guarijio
     - Yaqui-Mayo (Cahitan)
   - Tubar

Corachol-Aztecan
- Corachol
  - Cora
  - Huichol
- Aztecan
  - Nahua (several varieties)
  - Pochutec
  - Pipil

9. An anonymous referee objected, on the basis of personal communication with Miller, that he definitely did not accept PNUA. However, Manaster Ramer includes the following sentence on the first page of his article on the sound change PUA **c > PNUA *y, published two years before Miller's death: "The importance of this sound law, which I refer to as C-LENITION, lies not only in the numerous etymologies which it enables us to sort out but also in the fact that it gives us perhaps the clearest argument for the reality of NUA as a valid classificatory unit in the UA family tree (Wick Miller, personal communication)" (1992, 251).
10. I prefer **r instead of **l because this permits me to refer without confusion to Dakin's (1997) work on the dialectology of this segment, which she calls **r, in the southern languages. This is a minor point, and nothing in the present discussion turns on it.
11. An anonymous referee pointed out that most scholars reconstruct the structure of the Austronesian family as deeply nested, with considerable hierarchy even within the Oceanic branch, which is that part of the family that would have participated in a cultivation-driven expansion into Melanesia and the Pacific. The most "rake-like" part of Austronesian is constituted by the several first-level groups found on Taiwan, a fairly small area (for a useful nontechnical review of the structure of Austronesian, see Tryon 1995). Thus, the "rake-like" structure idea, while interesting, requires additional refinement.
12. Abbreviations in the table are as follows: CA, Cahuilla; C&L, reference number in Campbell and Langacker 1979 (e.g., C&L 313); CR, Cora; EU, Eudeve; GU, Guarijio; HO, Hopi; HU, Huichol; M, reference number in Miller 1967 (e.g., M su-5); MA, Mayo; MP, Mountain Pima (O'ob No'ok); NA, Nahuatl; SN, Southern Numic; TA, Tarahumara; TO, Tohono O'odham (Papago); TB, Tübatülabal; TU, Tubar; and YA, Yaqui.
13. Sets 1 and 2 are suspiciously alike, suggesting a possible dialect difference between /u/ and /o/ in the PUA community. This point requires further attention. A second point regarding sets like Set 2 was raised by an anonymous referee: The diversity of meanings of the lexical items in the cognate sets is counter to the admonition, advanced by, for instance, Johanna Nichols, that permitting considerable latitude in semantics increases the likelihood that chance resemblances will be misinterpreted as genuine cognates. Nichols was addressing the case in which scholars attempt to demonstrate genetic relationships between remotely related languages, as in the recent work of Joseph Greenberg

(cf. 1987). In the case of Uto-Aztecan, there is no serious challenge to the hypothesis that all the languages assigned to the family are part of a single genetic unit. In such a case, we can use the technique that I have adopted here, of searching dictionaries based on predicted phonological forms and then seeing whether a phonetically predicted form may be realistically assigned to a cognate set based on its meaning by invoking known processes of semantic change such as metaphor, metonymy, and reversal. This is not to claim that all the etymologies here will ultimately prove to be correct—only that they are grounded in appropriate method.

14. Karen Dakin (personal communication, 2001) proposes also the possibility that these forms are related to NUA words with **wɨ, meaning "acorn." Yet another proposal related to this set is that by Stubbs for the following: ***kwuh* 'grain coming off ears' (1995:402); CA *búh-te* 'espigarse (grain or seed to fall from ears)'; TA *ohó* 'desgranar'; and NA *kwi'kwi* 'chip off (wood or stone), clean up a surface, take something away, get ready, be prepared'. While Stubbs offers supporting correspondence sets, I find it difficult to prefer his NA form as a cognate for TA *ohó* 'desgranar' over NA *(tla-)o:(-ya)* 'desgranar'! There seem to be no northern language cognates for Stubbs's proposal.
15. The long /aa/ in Hopi *qa:'ö* is predicted by Dakin and Wichmann's (2000) proposal of a final feature for this component of the word.
16. One problem with this etymology is to account for why we do not see something like Hopi *qa:'öna, ö:navi* with the long vowel (the reflex of the lost final consonant) and the predicted consonant /n/ from PUA **r. It may be that the *ra component of PUA *o'ra is a verbal suffix. Note that Tarahumara *o'na* and Guarijio *wohna* (as well as the Tarahumara form *ohó* 'desgranar', cited by Stubbs [1995], included here in Set 6 on semantic grounds) also do not show the expected /r/, and that Nahuatl has *-ya* in the verb "desgranar," but *-l* as the final consonant in the noun, attested in *tlao:lli* 'shelled corn' and *o:lotl* 'corncob'.
17. Tohono O'odham *ga:t* 'bow, gun, rifle' in Set 9 is a good example; both the archaic meaning "bow" and the innovative "firearm" meanings are known to speakers (although I do not believe that speakers would be able to use this word for an atlatl, which must have been its original meaning). An English example suggested by Kenneth C. Hill is *menu*, with a new meaning referring to lists found on computer screens that permit access to various operations and an older meaning referring to the lists of dishes found in restaurants.
18. Smiley's dates are calibrated C14 dates. The date on squash is from squash seeds in looter back dirt in a rock shelter on the Comb Ridge.
19. Bean and Lawton (1976) and Lawton and Bean (1968) follow the lead of Barrows (1967[1900]) who was convinced that the Cahuilla cultivated aboriginally, probably borrowing their cultivation complex from neighboring Yuman peoples. The argument presented here would shift this argument to one that suggests that the Cahuilla simply continued a Uto-Aztecan cultivation complex that included water management techniques discussed in Bean and Saubel (1972). It should be noted, however, that the Cahuilla

vocabulary for the cultivated plants is not cognate with the Uto-Aztecan vocabulary discussed here. The relevant forms, given in Bean and Saubel (1972), are as follows: *Zea mays*: *pahavoshlum*; *Phaseolus vularis*: *tevinymalem* (glossed as "the old kind of beans"), *huul* 'frijoles, modern beans' (Bean and Saubel believe this to be a Spanish loan. Compare Cupeño *verxool* 'beans'—the Cahuilla form would presumably thus originate as the second syllable of *frijol*); *Cucurbita moschata*: *paxhushlam*, *estuish*. The word for "to plant" is *-wés-* (Seiler and Hioki 1979). The use of the planting stick is attested, but I can find no Cahuilla term for it in the literature. Note that the use of indigenous words for most of the cultigens in Cahuilla is in striking contrast with the tendency to use Spanish loan words elsewhere in Takic, Numic, and Tübatülabal.

20. Of course there is no reason to predict an association between any particular language family and any particular subsistence form. This Boasian presupposition (most recently supported in detail in, for instance, Welsch 1996) is not, in its essence, challenged by the Renfrew and Bellwood proposals. They argue, however, that historical forces may very well produce such an association.
21. Note that in the tree diagram of the Uto-Aztecan family in Miller (1983, 118) the breakup date is given as 6000 BCE! This is almost certainly a typographical error.
22. I do not support the case for the genetic unity of Uto-Aztecan-Tanoan. If there is such a connection, it is probably very remote, such that it is impossible to distinguish the few resemblances between the two groups from loan words or from items that resemble one another by chance.
23. Wichmann (1994) published some Mixe-Zoquean/Uto-Aztecan etymologies that seemed hopelessly far-fetched at the time, but that certainly deserve reevaluation in light of the material presented here.

REFERENCES

Aikens, C. Melvin. 1994. "Adaptive Strategies and Environmental Change in the Great Basin and Its Peripheries as Determinants in the Migrations of Numic-Speaking Peoples." In *Across the West: Human Population Movement and the Expansion of the Numa*, edited by David B. Madsen and David Rhode, 35–43. Salt Lake City: University of Utah Press.

Ammerman, Albert J., and L. L. Cavalli-Sforza. 1973. "A Population Model for the Diffusion of Early Farming in Europe." In *The Explanation of Culture Change: Models in Prehistory*, edited by Colin Renfrew, 335–58. London: Duckworth.

Anthony, David W. 1990. "Migration in Archaeology: The Baby and the Bathwater." *American Anthropologist* 92:895–914.

———. 1995. "Horse, Wagon, and Chariot: Indo-European Linguistics and Archaeology." *Antiquity* 69:554–65.

Barrows, David P. 1967[1900]. *The Ethnobotany of the Coahuilla Indians of Southern California*. Classics in California Anthropology 1. Banning, CA: Malki Museum Press.

Bascom, Burton W. 1965. "Proto-Tepiman." PhD dissertation, University of Washington.

Bean, Lowell, and Harry Lawton. 1976. "Some Explanations for the Rise of Cultural Complexity in Native California with Comments on Proto-Agriculture and Agriculture." In *Native Californians: A Theoretical Retrospective*, edited by Lowell J. Bean and Thomas C. Blackburn, 19–48. Ramona, CA: Ballena Press.

Bean, Lowell, and Katherine S. Saubel. 1972. *Temalpakh: Cahuilla Indian Knowledge and Usage of Plants*. Banning, CA: Malki Museum Press.

Bellwood, Peter. 1985. *Prehistory of the Indo-Malaysian Archipelago*. Sydney: Academic Press.

———. 1997. "Prehistoric Cultural Explanations for Widespread Linguistic Families." In *Archaeology and Linguistics: Aboriginal Australia in Global Perspective*, edited by Patrick McConvell and Nicholas Evans, 123–34. Melbourne: Oxford University Press.

———. 1999. "Austronesian Prehistory and Uto-Aztecan Prehistory: Similar Trajectories?" University of Arizona Department of Anthropology Lecture Series, Tucson, January 27.

Bloomfield, Leonard. 1933. *Language*. New York: Holt, Rinehart, and Winston.

Campbell, Lyle. 1985. *The Pipil Language of El Salvador*. Berlin: Mouton Publishers.

———. 1997. *American Indian Languages: The Historical Linguistics of Native America*. Oxford: Oxford University Press.

———. 1999. "Nostratic and Linguistic Paleontology in Methodological Perspective." In *Nostratic: Examining a Linguistic Macrofamily*, edited by Colin Renfrew and Daniel Nettle, 179–230. Papers in the Prehistory of Languages. Cambridge: The MacDonald Institute for Archaeological Research.

Campbell, Lyle, and Terrence Kaufman. 1976. "A Linguistic Look at the Olmecs." *American Antiquity* 41:80–89.

Campbell, Lyle, and Ronald A. Langacker. 1978. "Proto-Aztecan Vowels, Parts I–III." *International Journal of American Linguistics* 44:85–102, 197–210, 262–79.

Canger, Una, and Karen Dakin. 1985. "An Inconspicuous Basic Split in Nahuatl." *International Journal of American Linguistics* 51:358–436.

Carpenter, John P., Guadalupe Sanchez de Carpenter, and Elisa Villalpando C. 1999. "Preliminary Investigations at La Playa, Sonora, Mexico." *Archaeology Southwest (Center for Desert Archaeology)* 13:6.

Cordell, Linda. 1997. *Archaeology of the Southwest*. 2nd ed. New York: Academic Press.

Cortina-Borjas, Mario, and Leopoldo Valiñas C. 1989. "Some Remarks on Uto-Aztecan Classification." *International Journal of American Linguistics* 55:214–39.

Dakin, Karen. 1990. Irregular Vowel Correspondences in Nahuatl. Paper presented to the Friends of Uto-Aztecan, Mexico City, June 29.

———. 1997. "Long Vowels and Morpheme Boundaries in Nahuatl and Uto-Aztecans Comments on Historical Developments." *Amerindia* 21:55–76.

———. 1999. "*Isoglosas e innovaciones yutoaztecas.*" In *Avances y Balances de Lenguas Yutoaztecas, Homenaje a Wick R. Miller*, edited by José Luis Moctezuma and Jane H. Hill. Noroeste de México (número especial). CD-ROM. Hermosillo, Sonora: Centro de INAH Sonora.

———. 2000. "Proto-Uto-Aztecan *p and the e-/ye- Isogloss in Nahuatl Dialectology." In *Uto-Aztecan, Structural, Temporal, and Geographic Perspectives: Papers in Memory of Wick Miller by the Friends of Uto-Aztecan*, edited by Eugene Casad and Thomas Willett, 213–20. Hermosillo, Sonora: Division de Humanidades y Bellas Artes, Universidad de Sonora.

Dakin, Karen, and Søren Wichmann. 1995. "Cacao, chocolate, y los nahuas y mixezoques en el sur de Mesoamerica." In *Revista Latina de Pensamiento y Lenguaje (Estudios de filología y lingüística náhuatl* 2(28): 455–75.

———. 2000. "Cacao and Chocolate: A Uto-Aztecan Perspective." *Ancient Mesoamerica* 11:55–75.

Dayley, Jon P. 1989. *Tümpisa (Panamint) Shoshone Grammar*. University of California Publications in Linguistics 116. Berkeley: University of California Press.

Diamond, Jared. 1997. *Guns, Germs, and Steel: The Fates of Human Societies*. New York: W. W. Norton.

Ehret, Christopher, and Merrick Posnanski, eds. 1982. *The Archaeological and Linguistic Reconstruction of African History*. Berkeley: University of California Press.

Fournier, Patricia. 1998. "*El complejo nixtamal/comal/tortilla en Mesoamérica.*" *Boletín de Antropología Americana, Julio*. Mexico City: Instituto Panamericana de Geografía e Historia.

Fowler, Catherine. 1983. "Lexical Clues to Uto-Aztecan Prehistory." *International Journal of American Linguistics* 49:224–57.

———. 1994. "Corn, Beans, and Squash: Some Linguistic Perspectives from Uto-Aztecan." In *Corn and Culture in the Prehistoric New World*, edited by Sissel Johannessen and Christine A. Hastorf, 445–67. Boulder, CO: Westview Press.

Franklin, Robert J., and Pamela A. Bunte. 1987. *From the Sand to the Mountain: Change and Persistence in a Southern Paiute Community*. Lincoln: University of Nebraska Press.

Fritz, Gayle J. 1994. "Are the First American Farmers Getting Younger?" *Current Anthropology* 35:305–9.

Gamkrelidze, Thomas, and Vjaceslav Ivanov. 1994[1984]. *Indoeuropean and the Indoeuropeans*. Berlin: Mouton de Gruyter.

Gibbons, Ann. 2001. "The Peopling of the Pacific." *Science* 291:1735–37.

Greenberg, Joseph. 1987. *Language in the Americas*. Stanford: Stanford University Press.

———. 1997. "The Indo-European First- and Second-Person Pronouns in the Perspective of Eurasiatic, Especially Chukotian." *Anthropological Linguistics* 39:187–95.

Gregory, David, ed. 1999. "Early Maize in the Southwest." Theme issue, *Archaeology Southwest* 13(1).

Hackenberg, Robert A. 1983. "Pima and Papago Ecological Adaptations." In *Handbook of North American Indians*. Vol. 9, *Southwest*, edited by Alfonso Ortiz, 161–77. Washington, DC: Smithsonian Institution Press.

Hale, Kenneth L. 1958–59. "Internal Diversity in Uto-Aztecan, I–II." *International Journal of American Linguistics* 24–25:101–7, 114–21.

Hale, Kenneth L., and David Harris. 1979. "Historical Linguistics and Archaeology." In *Handbook of North American Indians*.Vol. 9, *Southwest*, edited by Alfonso Ortiz, 170–77. Washington, DC: Smithsonian Institution Press.

Haury, Emil. 1962. "The Greater American Southwest." In *Courses Toward Urban Life: Some Archaeological Considerations of Cultural Alternates*, edited by Robert J. Braidwood and Gordon R. Willey, 10–131. Viking Fund Publications in Anthropology. New York: Aldine.

Hayes-Gilpin, Kelley, and Jane H. Hill. 1999. "The Flower World in Southwest Material Culture." *Journal of Anthropological Research* 55:1–37.

Heath, Jeffrey. 1977. "Uto-Aztecan Morphophonemics." *International Journal of American Linguistics* 43:27–36.

———. 1985. "Proto-Northern Uto-Aztecan Participles." *International Journal of American Linguistics* 51:441–43.

Hill, Jane H. 1992. "The Flower World of Old Uto-Aztecan." *Journal of Anthropological Research* 48:117–44.

Hill, Jane H., and Rosinda Nolasquez. 1973. *Mulu'wetam: The First People*. Banning, CA: Malki Museum Press.

Hill, Kenneth C., Emory Sekaquaptewa, Mary Black, Ekkehart Malotki, and the Hopi Tribe. 1998. *Hopi Dictionary*. Tucson: University of Arizona Press.

Hopkins, Nicholas A. 1965. "Great Basin Prehistory and Uto-Aztecan." *American Antiquity* 31:48–60.

Kaufman, Terrence. 1981. "Comparative Uto-Aztecan Phonology." Unpublished manuscript, University of Pittsburgh.

Lamb, Sydney. 1958. "Linguistic Prehistory in the Great Basin." *International Journal of American Linguistics* 24:95–100.

Langacker, Ronald W. 1977. *An Overview of Uto-Aztecan Grammar. Studies in Uto-Aztecan Grammar 1*. Dallas: Summer Institute of Linguistics.

Lawton, Harry W., and Lowell J. Bean. 1968. "A Preliminary Reconstruction of Aboriginal Agricultural Technology Among the Cahuilla." *The Indian Historian* 1(5): 18–24, 29.

Levy, Jerrold. 1992. *Orayvi Revisited*. Santa Fe: School of American Research.

Long, Austin, B. Benz, J. Donahue, A. Jull, and L. Toolin. 1989. "First Direct AMS Dates on Early Maize from Tehuacán, Mexico." *Radiocarbon* 31:1035–40.

Mabry, Jonathan B. 1999. "Las Capas and Early Irrigation Farming." *Archaeology Southwest (Center for Desert Archaeology)* 13:14.

———. 2001. Early Irrigation in the Southwest. Paper presented at the Desert Archaeology Brown Bag, Tucson, February 10.

Macri, Martha. 2000. "T536 Xo from Nahuatl *Xochitl* 'Flower.'" *Glyphdwellers Report* 11. http://cougar.ucdavis.edu/na/Maya/glyphdwellers.html.

Mallory, J. P. 1989. *In Search of the Indo-Europeans*. London: Thames and Hudson.

Manaster Ramer, Alexis. 1992. "A Northern Uto-Aztecan Sound Law: *-c- → -y-." *International Journal of American Linguistics* 55:251–68.

———. 1993. "Blood, Tears, and Murder: The Evidence for Uto-Aztecan Syllable-Final Consonants." In *Historical Linguistics 1991: Papers from the 10th International Conference on Historical Linguistics*, edited by Jaap van Marle, 199–209. Amsterdam: John Benjamins.

———. 1996a. "Eudeve and Huichol Evidence for Proto-Uto-Aztecan Phonology." *Journal de la Société des américanistes*. 82:117–27.

———. 1996. "/ih/-, /ah/-: The Joys of Nahuatl Historical Phonology." Unpublished manuscript.

Matson, R. G. 1999. "The Spread of Maize to the Colorado Plateau." *Archaeology Southwest (Center for Desert Archaeology)* 13(1): 10–11.

Miller, Wick R. 1967. *Uto-Aztecan Cognate Sets*. University of California Publications in Linguistics 48. Berkeley: University of California Press.

———. 1983. "Uto-Aztecan Languages." In *Handbook of North American Indians*. Vol. 9, *Southwest*, edited by Alfonso Ortiz, 113–24. Washington, DC: Smithsonian Institution Press.

———. 1984. "The Classification of the Uto-Aztecan Languages Based on Lexical Evidence." *International Journal of American Linguistics* 50:1–24.

———. 1986. "Numic Languages." In *Handbook of North American Indians*. Vol. 11, *Great Basin*, edited by Warren L. d'Azevedo, 98–107. Washington, DC: Smithsonian Institution Press.

———. 1988a. "Computerized Data Base for Uto-Aztecan Cognate Sets." Unpublished manuscript, University of Utah.

———. 1988b. "Corn and Tortillas in the Greater Southwest." University of Arizona Department of Anthropology Lecture Series, Tucson, November. Paper presented at the 88th Annual Meeting of the American Anthropological Association, November.

Nichols, Johanna. 1997. "The Epicentre of the Indo-European Linguistic Spread." In *Archaeology and Language I: Theoretical and Methodological Orientations*, edited by Roger Blench and Matthew Spriggs, 122–48. London: Routledge.

Nichols, Michael J. P. 1981. "Old California Uto-Aztecan." In *Reports from the Survey of California and Other Indian Languages, Report I*, edited by Alice Schlichter, Wallace L. Chafe, and Leanne Hinton, 5–41. Berkeley: The Survey of California and Other Indian Languages.

Pope, Kevin O., Mary E. D., Pohl, John G. Jones, David L. Lentz, Christopher von Nagy, Francisco J. Vega, and Irvy R. Quitmeyer. 2001. "Origin and Environmental Setting of Ancient Agriculture in the Lowlands of Mesoamerica." *Science* 292:1370–73.

Rankin, Robert L. 2000. "On Siouan Chronology." Unpublished manuscript, University of Kansas and La Trobe University Research Centre for Linguistic Typology.

Renfrew, Colin. 1987. *Archaeology and Language: The Puzzle of Indo-European Origins*. London: Jonathan Cape.

Romney, A. Kimball. 1957. "The Genetic Model and Uto-Aztecan Time Perspective." *Davidson Journal of Anthropology* 3:35–41.

Ross, Malcolm. 1997. "Social Networks and Kinds of Speech-Community Event." *In Archaeology and Language I: Theoretical and Methodological Orientations*, edited by Roger Blench and Matthew Spriggs, 209–61. London: Routledge.

Sapir, Edward. 1930. "Southern Paiute, a Shoshonean Language, Parts 1–2." *Proceedings of the American Academy of Arts and Sciences* 65(1–2): 1–536.

———. 1931. "Southern Paiute Dictionary." *Proceedings of the American Academy of Arts and Sciences* 65(3): 537–730.

———. 1990[1913]. "Southern Paiute and Nahuatl: A Study in Uto-Aztecan." In *The Collected Works of Edward Sapir*. Vol. 5, *American Indian Languages*, edited by William Bright, 351–443. Berlin: Walter de Gruyter.

Seiler, Hansjakob, and Kojiro Hioki. 1979. *Cahuilla Dictionary*. Banning, CA: Malki Museum Press.

Shaul, David L. 1999a. "The Numic Unspread: Bad Linguistics, Convenient Archaeology." Unpublished manuscript.

———. 1999b. "The Opatan Languages, Plus Jova." In *Avances y Balances de Lenguas Yutoaztecas, Homenaje, a Wick R. Miller*, edited by José Luís Moctezuma and Jane H. Hill. Noroeste de México (número especial). CD-ROM. Hermosillo, Sonora: Centro INAH Sonora.

Shaul, David L., and Jane H. Hill. 1998. "Tepimans, Yumans, and Other Hohokam." *American Antiquity* 63:375–96.

Smiley, Francis E. 2000. "First Farmers: New Basketmaker II Research on the Colorado Plateau." Paper presented at the 65th Annual Meeting of the Society for American Archaeology, Philadelphia, April 8.

Snow, David. 1990. "'*Tener comal y metate*': Protohistoric Rio Grande Maize Use and Diet." In *Perspectives on Southwestern Prehistory*, edited by Paul E. Winnis and Charles L. Redman, 289–300. Boulder, CO: Westview Press.

Stubbs, Brian D. 1995. "The Lexical Labyrinth in Uto-Aztecan." *International Journal of American Linguistics* 61:396–422.

Suárez, Jorge. 1979. *The Mesoamerican Languages*. Cambridge: Cambridge University Press.

Sutton, Mark Q. 2000. "Prehistoric Movements of Northern Uto-Aztecan Peoples Along the Northwestern Edge of the Southwest: Impact on Southwestern Populations." In *The Archaeology of Regional Interaction: Religion, Warfare, and Exchange Across the American Southwest and Beyond. Proceedings of the 1996 Southwest Symposium*, edited by Michelle Hegmon, 295–316. Boulder: University Press of Colorado.

Swadesh, Morris. 1955. "Toward Greater Accuracy in Lexico-Statistic Dating." *International Journal of American Linguistics* 21(2): 121–37.

Terrell, John, Terry L. Hunt, and Chris Gosden. 1997. "The Dimensions of Social Life in the Pacific: Human Diversity and the Myth of the Primitive Isolate." *Current Anthropology* 38:155–96.

Thieme, Paul. 1964. "The Comparative Method for Reconstruction in Linguistics." In *Language in Culture and Society*, edited by Dell H. Hymes, 585–96. New York: Harper and Row.

Tryon, Darrell. 1995. "Proto-Austronesian and the Major Austronesian Subgroups." In *The Austronesians, Historical and Comparative Perspectives*, edited by Peter Bellwood, James J. Fox, and Darrell Tryon, 17–28. Canberra: Department of Anthropology, Research School of Pacific Studies, Australian National University.

Valiñas C., Leopoldo. 2000. "La que la lingüística yutoazteca podría aportar en la reconstrucción histórica del Norte de México." In *Nómadas y sedentarios en el Norte de México: Homenaje a Beatriz Braniff*, edited by Marie-Areti Hers, José Luis Mirafuentes, María de los Dolores Soto, and Miguel Vallebueno, 175–206. Mexico City: Universidad Nacional Autónoma de México.

Vilà, Carles, Jennifer A. Leonard, Anders Götherstrom, Stefan Marklund, Kaj Sandberg, Kirsten Lidén, Robert K. Wayne, and Hans Ellegren. 2001. "Widespread Origin of Domestic Horse Lineages." *Science* 291:474–77.

Welsch, Robert L. 1996. "Language, Culture, and Data on the North Coast of New Guinea." *Journal of Quantitative Anthropology* 6:209–34.

Wichmann, Søren. 1994. "On the Relationship Between Mixe-Zoquean and Uto-Aztecan." *Kansas Working Papers in Linguistics* 24(2): 101–13.

———. 1995. *The Relationships Among the Mixe-Zoquean Languages of Mexico*. Salt Lake City: University of Utah Press.

———. 1998. "A Conservative Look at Diffusion Involving Mixe-Zoquean Languages." In *Archaeology and Language II: Archaeological Data and Linguistic Hypotheses*, edited by Roger Blench and Matthew Spriggs, 297–323. London: Routledge.

6

THE HEGEMONY OF LANGUAGE AND ITS DISCONTENTS

Spanish Impositions from the Colonial to the Mexican Period

CARLOS G. VÉLEZ-IBÁÑEZ

INTRODUCTION: THEORY OF MIND AND PLACE

THIS WORK EXPLORES the manner in which the human populations of what I have termed the Southwest North American (SWNA) region and have discussed in chapter 1 of this work have faced multiple intruding colonial projects that sought to change and replace language, meaning, thought, and expected behaviors at a most profound level—the consciousness of self, others, surroundings, and almost every means of expression and communication. For this work we will only concentrate on the long Spanish colonial presence and briefly discuss the immediate post-Independence period to understand these processes, while a much more inclusive work in progress will take up the Mexican and American processes (Vélez-Ibáñez n.d.).

This process of attempted replacement and simultaneous substitution of the language of one population over the other we may regard as "language hegemony" or, as William Roseberry (1994, 360–61) states its parameters:

> I propose that we use the concept *not* [italics in original] to understand consent but to understand struggle; the ways in which the words, images, symbols, forms, organizations, institutions and movements used by subordinate populations to talk about, understand, confront, accommodate themselves to, or resist their domination are shaped by the process of domination itself.

But this struggle, as Roseberry would agree, and which undergirds the works by Gramcsi (1971, 1973) and is elaborated by Williams (1977) and deliberated by Derrida

(1974), is part of the daily interaction within and between different cultural populations from childhood through adulthood. These take place between the narratives told in households and the narratives told in schools and institutions, within and between contending rituals, between children and children and between adults and adults, and importantly between children and adults. These are articulated between major means of communication and populations who are being convinced or coerced to consent to the message givers, which has taken place from ancient empires through modern nation-states.

Hegemonic impositions are deeply and profoundly historical, ecological, economic, cultural, social, and psychological in that hegemonic processes seep into the very consciousness of that which makes us "us" and them "them" and the "theres" of absent spaces and places. And of course actual physical places and spaces become imbued with what they are called, termed, or categorized. For example, "El Río Grande" in Spanish is not the same as "the Rio Grand," as most Americans are prone to pronounce this both large and grand river; the English version is erased of meaning by its mispronunciation.

As Deacon (2012) suggests: "Like meanings and purposes, consciousness may not be something *there* in any typical sense of being materially or energetically embodied, and yet may still be materially causally relevant." The means of transferring the "not there" is another not "there" phenomena—language, whether written, spoken, heard, or imagined, is materially causally relevant, as Deacon would say. From my point of view, language, like consciousness, has an "unnoticed option" in that it too is defined by its absential character, yet it deeply impacts the material, social, emotive, and cultural worlds of our species, about which I have always tried to make sense in a material way. But the wringer is that language, like consciousness, is not also not there, and what is not there as well is "me," to paraphrase Deacon. This wonderful space and not space is among the great contradictions as well as possibilities for invention, innovation, and experimentation but also is perhaps a source of denial when their opposite occurs, such as imposition, oppression, and exploitation, and is justified by stints of elaborated ritualization and ideological convictions. From my point of view the "me" is probably in others and they in what I consider the "me" with all of their attending spaces/not spaces. So that for millennia this funny species has set up all sorts of parameters for those "me" and "not there" meanings and sounds and patterns that we call language. Therefore, language impositions and their myriad attending behaviors have profound possible shatterings and generative possibilities to the not-present "there," and in a way, that is what my "not there" "me" is interested in.

This work is one in development in which I am trying to understand how language imposition takes shape of the "me" and the others when peoples meet, collide, fight, resist, accommodate, and cooperate. The me of me is very much like everyone else, a complex of deeply pushed "not theres" emergent from an experimental imagining that I have termed the SWNA.

THE SOUTHWEST NORTH AMERICAN REGION

In chapter 1, I have laid out the essentials of what I have termed the SWNA, and I have insisted on a number of important elements to partially define its parameters: first, a complicated but persistent ecology formed by the various subecologies that transcend the present border and limit as well as make possible the human inventions long imposed in the region; second, the five-hundred-year-old struggle and accommodation of Spanish/Mexican and indigenous relationships that were endemic and embedded in the structure of the imperial Spanish mandate to explore, conquer, missionize, and colonize; third, the crucial and important bifurcation of the region into northern and southern regions as a consequence of the Mexican-American War and the Gadsden Purchase; fourth, the ongoing struggle and accommodation in the southern part between ascendant national Mexican mestizos and indigenous populations; and fifth, the ongoing struggle and accommodation in the northern part of the tripartite struggle between hegemonic American populations and Mexican-origin and Native peoples. Lastly, this bifurcation is cross-cut by the economic integration of an asymmetrical political economy and its large-scale population movements between regions.

Thus these elements that comprise the region contribute to the substance of relations between populations and make possible the manner in which language hegemony was attempted by at least two major populations during the colonial and national periods, and in the present. That said, however, pre-European language practices in the region will be explored briefly to gain a fundamental understanding of the impact of European impositions as well as the manner in which those so impacted articulated their responses and negotiations and attention, but only from the colonial period to Mexican independence. A broader work inclusive of English hegemony is to be treated in another book.

PRE-HISPANIC LANGUAGE COMMUNICATION OF THE REGION

David L. Shaul (2014, 14–15) has recently gauged the language repertoire of the SWNA, which he refers to as "western North America," as being made up of six language families and language stocks including Uto-Aztecan, Athabaskan, Hokan, Penutian, Algic, and Tanoan. *Families* and *language stocks* are linguistic terms that include many different languages that in fact share linguistic elements that are peculiar to a broader category such as those listed for the region. However, for example, Uto-Aztecan, which ranges from California to Central America, is composed of at least eight subfamilies, and some of these are composed of subfamilies. The subfamily Takic, for example, has two subfamilies: one of them, Cupan, has three languages, without considering attending dialects, and the other, Serran, is made up of two other subfamilies not including dialects (26). Thus for example, Hopi, which is spoken in twelve pueblo villages in northeastern Arizona and which is itself a subfamily of Uto-Aztecan, has three dialects distributed between three mesas (first, second, and third), but the variances between them are small (118). None of these languages can ever be considered as isolated; rather, as demonstrated in chapter 5, they are dynamic due to changes in ecology, raiding, exchange, and commerce from multiple directions and borrowing from others as well as elimination due to climatic or ecological necessities. The pre-Hispanic transborder region demanded linguistic and other means of communication between these various populations, who spoke one of many dialects and languages of the region.

The point of this exercise is that the region is linguistically made up of many languages—many mutually unintelligible. Given the enormous trade and exchange systems as well as south–north and north–south migrations of peoples of the region, communication must have been regularized by one or more communication modes. Thus ancient contact from Mesoamerican sources to and from the region was part and parcel, for example, of the turquoise trade during post-Classic periods from the northern region of the SWNA to Tula, passing through what are now the Mexican states of Zacatecas and Durango (Wiegand 1997, 28; 2008, 348–50). Equally, long-distance trade of the scarlet macaw from southern SWNA, such as from southern Tamaulipas to Pueblo Bonito, the largest Chaco site of the tenth century, traversed hundreds of miles and required linguistic or sign communication (Vélez-Ibáñez 1996, 31). Without delving into the enormous archaeological literature indicating the transfer of motifs, ideas, and practices between and among Native peoples west to east and back and south to north and back, we may conclude that many populations of the SWNA region did in fact interact directly in some cases or indirectly in others with complex systems farther into what is known as Mesoamerica [and that] there is sufficient evidence to conclude that for at least 1,696 years the pre-Hispanic [SWNA region] was part of a series of exchange systems made up of centers of production, trade, and redistribution (Vélez-Ibáñez, 34–35).

Such a complex of trade and exchange demanded and required linguistic and cultural accommodation and communication, so it is highly likely that one or more means of language use was prevalent including a lingua franca, bilingualism, and sign language.

Trade and war as well, especially in the form of raiding, were the basic dynamics of the pre-Hispanic era as Athabaskan and Uto-Aztecan and other speakers met in many regions of the SWNA such as in the Chama Valley of eastern New Mexico around the ancient pueblo of Abiquiú. Ebright and Hendricks (2006, 16) state that "Abiquiú was the center of *la tierra de Guerra* [land of war; my translation and italics], at the same time as it was the focus of trading networks among Pueblos, Apaches, and Navahos . . . and represented a middle ground before Spanish contact." But war was not a necessary condition, and neighboring tribes had speakers who were bilinguals, such as those reported by Father Eusebio Kino in Sonora, who in his long and intense missionary travels reported that the Ópas (Ópata) and Cocomaricopas spoke very different languages from that of the Pimas (living around present-day Phoenix). Kino stated, "Though it is very clear, and as there were some who knew both languages very well" (Bolton 1919, 128). From Kino as well we have an indication that Native leaders were also likely to be bilingual when he describes how the Yumans were asking that he visit them and that he spoke "leisurely with this governor, who knew very well both the Pima and Yuma languages" (250).

Carroll L. Riley (1971, 286) states that when Spanish explorers in the middle of the sixteenth century traveled up through Sinaloa—the area directly south of Sonora—they were in contact with "people who spoke varying dialects, some of which were related to Aztec . . . and with considerable use of Nahuatl as far north as the Piaxtla River," which is north of present-day Mazatlán. Given that these explorers traveled with bilingual Nahuatl-Spanish speakers from central Mexico, communication was made much easier, especially in learning about routes north, water availability, and food resources, whether from hunting or trading or extraction from indigenous villages.

As well, however, there seems to be also the circumstance in which one language was well-known over a wide area as a kind of lingua franca, such as Pima, which is indigenous to Sonora (including much of what is now Arizona) through Sinaloa (Riley 1971). Riley states the following in describing Cabeza de Vaca's description of the language used by his companions upon meeting Spanish slave raiders after almost eight years of walking throughout the SWNA region between 1528 and 1536:

> They were speaking a language called *Primahaitu* which, according of Cabeza de Vaca, had been in use by Indians for the last four hundred leagues. The statement is somewhat ambiguous, but it meant that over a long stretch of back trail, the Spaniards had been able to communicate in a trade jargon or a lingua franca. The four hundred leagues (ca. 1200 miles) probably should not be taken too literally. The language itself was most likely Pima. This does hint at widespread linguistic contact in that part of the world. (288)

However, the other form of communication was sign language, which was extensively used by Plains tribal groups, who covered a geographic area from Canada through southern Texas and northern Mexico (Davis and Supalla 1995, 80). More specifically, Foster (1995, 208–9) traced Fray Gaspar José de Solís's diaries of his inspection of the Franciscan missions in Texas in February of 1768 and his return seven months later to Zacatecas from where he had begun. Among his many observations of numerous Native peoples of Texas, Solis wrote that many different groups who together congregated near one of the major rivers (the Brazos) could not communicate with each other verbally but instead used sign language, which allowed them to communicate with each other for entire days. Foster states that according to Solis, one of the first responsibilities of new priests was to learn Native signs (208–9).

In fact, Plains Indians such as the Comanche who entered Texas and New Mexico interacted both violently and in trade with Pueblo Indians of New Mexico with linguistic, ritual, and sign forms of expression exchanged as well. With the intrusion of the Spaniards, raids by Comanches as well as slave raids by the Spanish combined so that each sold slaves in the annual trade fairs held in such places as Taos, New Mexico. Such interactions encouraged not only the capture of slaves and the trading of goods but also the capture of each other's modes of language and communicating by the use of sign. This interaction is recalled even to this day, when ritualized dances are held in various Spanish/Mexican and indigenous pueblos that enact the taking of their respective populations by Comanches (Brooks 2003).

SPANISH HEGEMONY OF THE SOUTHWEST NORTH AMERICAN REGION

Antonio de Nebrija, Bishop of Avila, in the fifteenth century stated to Queen Isabella that "Soon Your Majesty will have placed her yoke upon many barbarians who speak outlandish tongues" (Ferguson 2003). This statement, as a general principle, has been followed by all empires or imposing nations; however, such a process is not unilineal nor is it ever an easily accepted dictum. For the most part human populations upon which any type of hegemony is attempted usually accommodated to some degree or the other, resisted to a finite conclusion, or negotiated in the favor to some degree as well of the population "culturally bumped" by the other.

No hegemony—ideological, linguistic, cultural, economic, social, or economic—is ever complete. The most hegemonic empires can hope for is that the seeds of their controls take hold strategically rather than only by coercion so that those seemingly controlled accept their lot based on some legitimate claims such as religiosity or economic convenience, ideological parallels, and occasional breakthroughs and transformations such as by the use of middle-range brokers to interpret or ease various impositions. Strategically oriented empires and nations using methods to gain "legitimacy" rather than using only a coercive approach will achieve a more probable ease of control than by an egregious imposition by force of arms. As well, those upon which such impositions are impressed do not go gentle into the good night gladly. For one, such populations may choose to negotiate from "positions of strength" with the interlopers in strategically viewing themselves to be able to maneuver into much better positions. For example, the Yaqui nation of Sonora, who long resisted Spanish and Mexican political subjugation, were able to allow Jesuits into the Yaqui Valley of Sonora in the seventeenth century after they had soundly defeated Spanish forces and their Indian allies and negotiated an alliance with the Spaniards as respectful allies rather than as subordinated populations, as Brewster-Folsom (2014, 73–95) has noted. Their strategic decisions would allow them to have the advantage of allowing linguistic and cultural influences only through the hands of the Jesuits, until their expulsion in the eighteenth century, and without the presence of a civil or military authority. In fact, Yaquis, like the Pueblos in New Mexico, retained territorial autonomy, not unlike the Tarascans of central Mexico who served the Spanish well and often. The Yaquis in fact did not allow the Jesuits or later the Franciscans wholesale access to their environments although the eighteenth century saw enormous seesaw relations of conflict and accommodation between Yaquis and Spanish authorities and religious missions established in their territorial confines (Brewster-Folsom 2014).

As well, there were peoples like those of the Ópata who not only were amenable to Jesuit and imperial penetration but in fact became the poster examples of eventual strong acculturation, linguistic replacement by Spanish, the bearing of arms for the Spanish in the field of combat, and the forming of entire companies of presidial soldiers. They became highly hispanized in religion, dress, behaviors, social relations, language, religion, and economic and political institutions for a number of reasons including their dispersed spatial locations, disease and demographic reduction, encroachments of their territories, and absence from homelands by working in mines established by Spanish authorities nearby (Yetman 2010, 223–59).

Thus in general, linguistic hegemony for the Spanish colonial periods was a hydra-headed enterprise dependent in part on the measure of resistance, the use or misuse of the Spanish narrative by the indigenous populations themselves, the impact of schooling by the missionaries, and the capacity of indigenous populations to maintain their cultural and linguistic resources. On the other hand, the cross, the sword, and the pen demanded unyielding acceptance of the Spanish colonial narrative to one degree or the other, and Spanish-language policy and learning was entirely focused toward directing their Spanish colonial subjects, Native or not, to fall under the aegis of the

Crown and its agents by combining coercion and accommodation. These were the mechanisms of seeking to exchange the complex and diverse indigenous narratives of selves, "theres," spaces, and places with a seemingly homogeneous imperial version, itself beset with internal contradictions, imperative adjustments, and the reality of a dynamic, often violent, and exceedingly fragile Spanish/Mexican existence as mostly unwanted interlopers.

SPANISH COLONIAL LITERACY AND LANGUAGE AND ITS DISCONTENTS

Spanish colonial literacy was one of the main agents of transmitting the Spanish imperial narrative and the oral and written transmissions of that narrative. For some three hundred years, the empire established its cultural, linguistic, political, social, and economic fragile, but persistent, dominance through the continuous use of highly ritualized forms and presentations. As well, imperial language policies between missionaries and the court were at times both contradictory and oppositional, depending on the colonial period, but nevertheless were important in establishing linguistic hegemony as a standard for the acculturation of Native peoples, as will be discussed in a later part of this work.

Written Spanish during the colonial empire had myriad functions not the least of which was the central means of transatlantic communication to the Crown relating civic, religious, and military information as to the status of its various regions, political units, missions, and military forces. Literally thousands of letters, journals, reports, complaints, and accounts were written during the colonial period and later during the Mexican period. The Documentary Relations of the Southwest holdings of the Arizona State Museum of the University of Arizona number over one hundred thousand Spanish and Mexican colonial documents, largely in microfilm gleaned from multiple sources and collections. But contained within such a collection are the nuggets of persuasion, cognitive restructuring, spatial redefinition, and ultimately the attempt to negotiate and impress alternative identities and relationships as well as extract and exploit their physical and cultural contexts. Such a process in fact is an attempt, sometimes highly successful and sometimes not, to redefine the "mes" and the "theres" and the "mes" and the "not mes" and the "others" and the "not others."

From declarations of possession and obedience required of Native persons to religious scripts of various sorts including biblical, sacramental, and dogmatic treatises, and their performances in ritual or in public performances, besides the cross and the gun was the pen, which became the central means of establishing brittle but persistent Spanish hegemony over populations. From the manner in which presidial soldiers' service records were organized and the premises, categories, and concepts used to define their identities to petitions for redress by Native persons, the litany of imperial design was present and indefatigable.

UNPACKING THE NARRATIVE: THE ACTS OF POSSESSION AND OBEDIENCE AND OTHER PERFORMANCES OF IMPRESSION

The Act of Possession was a statement by the Spanish colonizing authorities as well as other European powers from the fifteen through the eighteenth centuries proclaiming complete control over an area of land for his sovereign (Servín 1978, 295). It ironically was based on "rights of discovery," i.e., that if the "discoverer" or his agent was present and had complete control of a section of the land, it was proclaimed for the monarch (295)—all this precluding the presence of thousand-year-old settlements among Native peoples. The act was in fact performed by a symbolic act of control or something equivalent from Columbus through Juan de Oñate in New Mexico in 1598 (303). In Oñate's case, which we will examine here, it was accompanied by a celebratory theater representation written by one of his lieutenants and the first theatrical piece written in the SWNA region.[1]

Thus upon crossing the Rio Grande ("Del Norte" according to Oñate) from what is now Ciudad Juárez into El Paso del Norte on April 30, 1598 (Hammond and Rey, 1953, 329–30), Oñate issued his proclamation. This was inscribed by his notary and secretary of the expedition, and in it contained highly rationalized statements of legitimacy based on a series of celestial calls. The proclamation included reference to the holy trinity, the omnipresent and omniscient power of a godhead, and its direct lineage to all forms of human endeavor. These included a plethora of political entities buttressed by a metaphor in which the godhead is the originator of all things, and invokes the Virgin Mary who herself is the apogee of kindness as an arm of God, and in a sort of chain of being introduces Saint Francis, as well as an extended treatise into the resurrection, the life of Jesus, and the direct connectivity to Saint Peter and all of his religious descendants and to the kings of Castile and all of their successors.

Finally, according to the notary, Governor don Juan de Oñate took possession "of these kingdoms and provinces" by tacking a cross on a tree and then uttering the following:

> I take and seize tenancy and possession, real and actual, civil and natural, one, two, and three times, one, two and three times, one, two and three times, and all the times that by right I can and should, at this said Rio del Norte, without excepting anything and

> without limitations, including the mountains, rivers, valleys, meadows, pastures, and waters. I in his name I also take possession of all the other lands, pueblos, cities, towns, castles, fortified and unfortified which are now established in the kingdoms of New Mexico, those neighboring and adjacent thereto, and those which may be established in the future. (Hammond and Rey, 1953, 335)

The litany continued so that all natural resources were included from mountains to rivers, all wildlife, and, of course, all minerals and, just as importantly, "together with the Native Indians in each and every one of the provinces, with civil and criminal jurisdiction, power of life and death, over high and low, and from the leaves of the trees to the stones and sands of the river" (335).

DISCUSSION

One wonders then what Native peoples could have possibly gleaned from such packed statements, symbolized by the nailed cross on a tree and accompanied by actual theater production. What major meanings and mappings were divulged, other than puzzlement from either not understanding the language or the ritualized performances by Oñate and Captain of the Guard Marcos Farfán de los Gados, who composed and produced the play. Yet from the point of view of Oñate, such an oration and reference was the lineal connection between himself, his sovereign, Christ, the Virgin Mary, and the godhead and created an unbroken rationalization for the hegemonic impression upon land, animals, minerals, rivers, and most importantly, the rationalization for judgment, evaluation, sentencing, and legal legitimacy for a kind of control probably unknown to the indigenous nations of the region. That Pueblo peoples, for example, also had developed hierarchical domains divided by privileges there is no doubt, but these were for the most part not associated with the control of other indigenous peoples but rather engaged in a combination of trade and exchange and war, as has been noted. Such a dynamic for the most part consisted of peace punctuated by fierce combat and enslavement of each other's peoples, but such enslavement also included the integration for the most part of such persons within the cultural milieu of the tribe. It was not in their best interests to engage in wars of annihilation since these would preclude the trading of goods and people with those no longer present, although there are examples of complete devastation by raiders of pre-Hispanic pueblos such as Riano in the Chama Valley (Ebright and Hendricks 2006, 12).

On the other hand, given the religious rationalizations noted in the Act of Possession, any opposition could be met with swift and uncompromising punishments and near-annihilation, as it was against the Acoma, who killed thirteen Spaniards when a soldier named Vivero stole two turkeys, a bird sacred to the Pueblos, and violated a Pueblo woman (Trujillo 2008, 95). Because of their celestially and judicially declared authority, as noted above, which included life and death judicial proceedings, these punishments ensued after Oñate declared a "war by blood and fire" against the people of Acoma. According to Trujillo (2008, 96), the result was that in 1599 eight hundred Acomas were killed while five hundred survived, were taken prisoner, tried, and found guilty by Oñate. He ruled that children under twelve were not guilty and dispersed the girls to a priest and the boys to the brother of one of the captains killed in the original conflict. Sixty of the girls were sent to convents in Mexico City, never to be seen again by the outside world.

Trujillo states:

> All women over twelve and young men between twelve and twenty-five were sentenced to twenty years of personal servitude. Two Hopis captured in the fight were sentenced to have their right hands cut off and were set free to take home news of their punishment. Finally, men over the age of twenty-five were sentenced to twenty years of servitude and to have a foot cut off and twenty-four people suffered this punishment. For maximum effect and as an example of the dangers of rebellion, this sentence was carried out over several days in nearby pueblos. (97)

Yet within two years, most had escaped from servitude and rebuilt the Pueblo of Acoma, which stands today, four hundred years later.

It would seem that whatever legitimacy declared by Oñate and his colonists was superseded by the willingness of the Acoma not only to resist the declarations of the empire but also to rebuild what had been destroyed regardless of the imposed narrative and its justifications. Ultimately the sword was mightier than the pen, but it was insufficient to establish the type of hegemony and defeat leading to either cultural or linguistic replacement.

PRESIDIAL SERVICE RECORDS: INSIGHT INTO THE IMPORTANCE AND ESTABLISHMENT OF CATEGORIES OF IDENTITY

The presidio system, the military arm of the imperial design of the cross and the sword, was the major mechanism of subjugation and control of indigenous populations throughout the Southwest North American region. Comprised mostly of ill-equipped mestizos, mulattos, and *claimed* criollos (my italics[2]; and see Moorehead 1975, 182–83[3]), they were often poorly armed, mostly underpaid, and often exploited by their own officers in tiny garrisons of no more than fifty and often much fewer due to frequent illnesses, death, and desertion. The presidial soldiers often faced overwhelming odds against skilled Native persons and were often far outnumbered during the three-hundred-year presence of the presidios in the region, with the earliest established in 1600, from Parral, Chihuahua, to Santa Fe, New Mexico, and later between east and west to Texas and Sonora and one in Baja California.

But these very hardy soldiers were for the most part persons, as will be shown, accustomed to hard conditions, and their service records indicate not only their points of origins and their means of livelihood but also, more importantly for our purposes, the categories of importance that identified each one and provide an insight into the cognitive mappings most important to their identity. These contrast to what Native persons might be likely to have used for their identity markers as warriors, and these differences provide an insight into the manner in which subtle but important linguistic and cultural hegemonic penetrations were established and were the "natural" categories probably used as daily masked discourses.

It is not possible to contrast these categories directly with their warrior counterparts for two important reasons: first, there was no comparable record for indigenous warriors kept by Native peoples; and second, the enormous heterogeneity of indigenous populations of the region precludes easy generalizations and comparisons. However, we know that warrior societies among the Pueblos and the Plains peoples were prevalent and cross-cut the divisions created by membership in other kin groupings such as lineages, clans, or moieties and in medicine societies and dancing groups. It is probable that, especially among Pueblo groups generally, they can be divided among the eastern and western groups, with the former emphasizing patrilineal lines of descent and the latter emphasizing matrilineal lines with ownership of housing and unmovable property in the hands of each (Eggan 1979, 227). Yet it is also the case that regardless of lineality, as Tracy L. Brown (2013, 60) has stated, authority was the hands of men in the precolonial period so that the most important political leaders were men; in such peoples as the Hopi, land and communal labor were provided to balance the time that men would invest in their political offices.

The point of this is that the groups of most importance are kin related, warrior related, and care related, and they, not the individual, are the primary principles of social organization and identity. Even the naming of children did not fall into the hands of the parents; for example, among the Tanoan Pueblos the child was baptized with corn water during the first solstice ceremony and named by the father's sister, emphasizing the patrilineal side of the group (Ellis 1979, 356–57). While obviously there is individual recognition of differences, such differences were strongly engaged in group identities and how well each individual carried out rights and obligations to the particular group event or activity. As well, as Brown (2013, 39) states, stratification among the Pueblos was evident in their political spheres during the colonial period and were "divided by class and gender differences . . . [i.e.,] a ranking of people based on gender and power, [and] prestige and authority" (Ellis 1979, 39). Nevertheless the general dictum was to render onto the group and not the individual.

PRESIDIAL SOLDIER'S SINGULAR IDENTITY

Thus one way in which we may understand the manner in which the group orientation was countered by the Spanish narrative and its focus on the individual is to follow the basic categories of identity for presidial soldiers. A document that followed a presidial soldier's career is known as a *filiación*, or origination of service and details, depending on the year being reported. Other important events of multiple types are noted, sometimes in the margins of the document, and these margins are sometimes covered by references to illnesses, death, place of demise, battles, and judicial proceedings. My research of 438 analyzed soldiers from a much larger unanalyzed sample spans the Southwest North American region, except for New Mexico, and dates mostly between 1772 and 1790, reveals that eighty-five did not finish their enlistments due to desertion, illness, death (either natural or at the hands of Natives in combat), discharge by permission, and removal in fifteen cases for being *inutil* (useless), with one released for being a minor.[4] Thus in examining *filiaciones*, we find that most consist of two paragraphs that provide an insight into the emphasis on individual identity within a single sort of social organization—the military presidial company—and, as importantly, the order of presentation itself gives an insight into the most important source of identities for the individual soldier.

They follow the standard format used in this type of document and are provided here in English (my translation) and in italics.[5] Variant spellings of words and names and surnames are original to the documents.

Filiación

3rd Company of the Second Platoon of Dragoons of San Carlos Squadron

Juan Francisco Villalobos, son of Francisco and of Junana Maria Aguirre, natural son of the Pueblo of San Pablo, Jurisdiction of San Jose de la Cienega bishopric of Durango, his occupation agricultural worker, his height 5 feet 2 inches 4 lineas (.0571348 per in), his age 31 years, his religion Apostolic Roman Catholic, his physical characteristics: light brown curly hair, light brown eyes, white color, broad nose, a scar close to the right eyebrow, close cropped beard.

Elected Sergeant of Militias on 9th of December of 1778 and will serve ten years counted since this day and the penalties were read to him that pertain to this order and he signed it and was warned of its justification and there will be no excuse of any sort [to not understand it] and witnessed by Bernardo Sanches and Juan Josef Portillo, Sergeant and Corporal of the Platoon.

He lives in the Pueblo of San Pablo

[Signature] Juan Francisco Villalobos [with rubric]

[Signature] Bustamante [with rubric]

DISCUSSION

Thus the document begins with the individual's "Christian" name, "Juan Francisco," and surname, "Villalobos," which rationalizes his individual identity and links him to a religious tradition of naming as well as his cultural and physical source of origin. This places him squarely in the Spanish tradition of surnames referring to physical places: "villa" and a specific characteristic pertinent to that place, "lobos" (wolves), although the origin of the surname is Italian: *villa lupos*.[6] This is immediately followed by his parents' names and surnames, with his father's first, "Francisco," which cements his descent to him, and then his mother's lineage, "Aguirre." Both define him as legitimate, which is a crucial referent defining his legal "place," while the reference to his being a "natural" of the Pueblo of San Pablo defines his identity by virtue of a physical space itself ensconced within the bishopric of Durango, the larger entity to the district of San José de la Cienega. Both provide the religious contextualization of the named places themselves and are coupled to his identity as a Roman Catholic. Thus by paying attention to only these categories, the overwhelming context for an individual is the legitimacy of the Church as the source of individual identity as well. His former occupation as a "campista" (camper) places him specifically within the most undesirable category of occupational statuses as well. This is in stark contrast to the sources of identity for pre-Columbian peoples.

The document outlines as well the importance of physical attributes classified by color of eyes, hair (even its state), skin, and height down to small increments, as well as the shape of the nose and any physical scars or marks.[7] The presence or absence of a beard was the culminating identity of the individual as well. In this manner, internal racialized categories are accentuated, especially in relation to color and composition of hair, nose, and skin tone, and subtly focuses on the most desired characteristics as well, as the next example illustrates also.

However, within the present document the second paragraph also provides insights into the most important categories concerning rank, chronology, and legal constraints and responsibilities. Villalobos's record shows that he was promoted to sergeant and reenlisted in 1778 for ten years. The presidial soldier was part of a system of recognition that was highly stratified, with rights, duties, and obligations that were prescribed and not ascribed per se, although mastery of arms, leadership, and the number of combat engagements in which they had participated would have also been of importance. In contrast to this, the indigenous populations were recognized for their individual prowess and entitled to some degree of differentiation as war captain or war leader because of proven capacities at war making. They did not follow a chronological system of promotion, and their participation as warriors was limited by age and health. They were recognized by the military society or medicine clan or tribal group without an institutionalized system of stratification. The admonitions and warnings of Villalobos's expected fulfillment of duties, witnessed by two presidial soldiers, were never part of either the nomenclature or expectations of Native persons but rather secular group expectations that were the basis of recognition of value and of their sustained efforts on the group's behalf. Finally, in this particular case, his signature completes his contract and also provides an insight into the formality of effort and the importance of the legal structure behind the document itself and modifies and accentuates the importance of the individual's identity. If the person was illiterate, he made the sign of the cross, as the next filiación will illustrate. Illiteracy was the case for the great majority of the cases analyzed in my research of 291 records: 208 could not sign their names except with a cross, 42 (20 percent) signed with their names, and some signed with a rubric. The balance of the records did not indicate whether they could or could not affix their signature. In general, this literacy rate was not quite as low for New Mexico, as shown in Bernardo P. Gallegos's work, but nevertheless he estimates one-third of his sample of 424 enlistees were illiterate (1992, 53).

Filiación

2nd Company of the 1st Squadron Platoon of Dragoons of the Province of San Carlos

Manuel Rodriguez de Leon, son of Dionicio and of Maria Rita Alvarez, natural son of the Valley of San Bartolomé, of the Jurisdiction of the Bishopric of Durango, neighborhood of the Hacienda of San Yldefonso, his occupation agricultural worker, his height 5 feet 2 inches, his age 27, Apostolic Roman Catholic, his physical characteristics: black hair, hazel eyes, dark color, narrow nose, pockmarked by smallpox, close cropped beard.

Elected militia member on 15th of August 1779, will serve ten years counted since this day and the penalties were read to him that pertain to this order and he could not sign it because he did not know how and made the sign of the cross, was warned of its justification and there will be no excuse of any sort [to not understand it] and witnessed by Sergeant Julian Verrar and Corporal Pioquinto.

He lives in the Hacienda of San Yldefonzo.

[No signatures in the original document.]

DISCUSSION

This filiación, like most, accentuates the individuation of the soldier, but like many cases revealed in this research, smallpox pockmarks play an important role in the individual's identity as well as giving an indication of its widespread character during the colonial period.[8] Since these were the survivors and possibly immune to further illness, it also indicates how deeply the disease impacted Spaniards but in particular Native peoples throughout the colonial period as early as 1593 and especially through 1625. Over hundred and fifty years before this filiación was written, the Jesuit missions of the SWNA early on suffered from smallpox and measles and epidemics of various sorts (Reff 1991, 162–68, 235). The diseases traveled north to Santa Fe from Zacatecas through mission and trade wagons on the Camino Real and from missionizing, mining, and town sources to the northern areas in general. Thus for Sinaloa and Sonora, among the Yaqui, Pima Bajo, and Ópata as well as New Mexico Pueblos, the Native population was reduced by 90 percent by the eighteenth century (Reff 1991, 325).

Thus the filiación as an instrument of individual identity of presidial soldiers, and its contrast to the group reference for most Native persons, also reveals it to be a tool that supports one of the most important sources of linguistic and cultural hegemony—the demographic reduction and tragedy embedded within a simple category of visual markings of pockmarks among the soldiery itself.[9]

SPANISH COLONIAL LANGUAGE POLICY AND PRACTICE: 1523–1821

While the filiación and the Acts of Obedience provide an "on the ground" glimpse of the characteristic use of Spanish and its contrast to Native persons' social and cultural premises to identity and sense of self, Spanish colonial language policy is an important area to understand to gauge policies over time and their impact on Native peoples in the region. For the Spanish colonial period between 1523 and 1821, the Mendicant orders focused on the recovery of Mexican indigenous languages from the early 1500s to about 1580 but were interrupted by changing imperial policy toward indigenous languages and the learning of Spanish (Hidalgo 2006, 358–59). Charles V's proclamation of 1550 stated specifically the official policy of the New Worlds would be "Spanish Only," but in fact Mendicant orders and especially the Jesuits embarked on learning the language of the Americas through the sixteenth and eighteenth centuries until they were expelled in 1767. Phillip II, who became king when Charles V abdicated in 1578, overturned the proclamation and emphasized the necessity for Nahuatl to be taught as the normative language because at the time it was the largest and most concentrated in New Spain. On the other hand, the same seemingly enlightened king confiscated the *Encyclopedia on Mexican Language and Civilization* in 1580 and interrupted the Crown's liberal policy on the Mexican language (Hidalgo 2006, 359–60).

Yet for the missionaries of central Mexico and the SWNA, in practice learning the Native language was crucial; in fact, they instituted a type of transitional bilingualism to spread their doctrines and the entire edifice of the mission complex. In the SWNA early language transmission was divided such that Franciscans worked mostly in Coahuila, Nuevo León, Nuevo Santander, New Mexico, and Texas and the Jesuits mostly in Sinaloa, Sonora (including present-day Arizona), Chihuahua, and Baja California, with their replacement in Baja California by Dominicans and in Alta California by the Franciscans (Kelly 1940, 349). The Jesuits especially used a stepped bilingual approach in which missionaries such as Eusebio Kino first learned one or more indigenous languages before embarking physically to Sonora and then used this knowledge to write local dictionaries to communicate indigenous versions of the Catholic doctrines to Native peoples. Thus in his *Memoir of Pimería Alta* previously cited in describing his interactions with the Ópas and Cocomaricopas, he stated that because of their common language, "I at once and with ease made a vocabulary of the said tongue, and also a map of those lands, measuring the sun with the astrolabe" (Bolton 1919, 128). Following Kino in 1756 in Sonora, Friar Ygnacio Pfefferkorn states that he found learning Pima was difficult because of the lack of dictionaries and grammars so he remained with another missionary who had learned the language: "I remained for a time with Father Gaspar Seiger . . . who had supposedly mastered their language [and] to learn . . . at least as much of the language as would be indispensable to me for the necessary offices when I took my post" (Pfefferkorn 1989, 230).

On the other hand, such practices, while acknowledging the necessity for missionaries to learn indigenous languages, were designed to Hispanicize Native persons. It was basically a transitional method of both communication and proselytizing and organizing indigenous populations around the mission. Yet it was also likely that the farther the mission or villa was from either central colonial authorities or from Spanish Mexican towns, the greater the probability of not only the retention of the Native language but also its necessity since obviously the demographics were such that there were greater numbers of Native speakers than Spanish speakers and this required bilingual skills on the part of the missionaries.

Given these circumstances, the Crown sought to formalize "Spanish Only" and announced its legal stricture, "La Real Cedula" (Royal Proclamation), on May 10, 1770, in which it sought to teach Spanish systematically to all indigenous children in schools and to adults to persuade them to send their children to school for instruction and to promote their learning of the language in order to replace the numerous indigenous languages to their extinction (Rospide 1995, 1416). Rospide states:

> The proclamation demanded that each town should have schools of Spanish with the provision that indigenous priests may fulfill the necessary sacraments but that finally Spanish would be the only and universal language in the colonial domains since it is the language of monarchs and conquistadores which together may lead to the extinction of the numerous indigenous vernaculars. . . . The underlying rationales were that Spanish was part of a superior culture and the sole and ideal instrument of communication to evangelize and civilize the "naturals." (1417–18, my translation)

On the other hand, the reality was that in practice the use of Spanish by Native peoples varied according to their needs, necessities, and objectives, which was certainly frustrating for missionaries such as Ygancio Pfefferkorn, who provided the following account of Sonoran Pimas negotiating their bilinguality on call:

> Sonorans do not at all like to speak the Spanish language even though they may have learned it quite well by constant association with Spaniards living among them. When they are questioned in Spanish, they reply in their own language. They may rarely be persuaded to given an answer in Spanish, even though they know that the person who is speaking with them understands not a word of their language. On the other hand, those who are raised in the houses of the missionaries prefer Spanish . . . [and] . . . which they generally like to display by answering in Spanish if they are addressed in Sonoran [but] they seem to forget every Spanish word the moment they come into confessional. (Pfefferkorn 1989, 229)

However, Native persons in the region, like those in all other parts of New Spain, were constantly inundated with legal documents as one of the main sources of linguistic hegemony. Yet they learned to use legal documentation for petitions, legal complaints, and claims of land or setting, as the *Genizaro* document illustrated in chapter 1 shows. As well, in New Mexico, there were Franciscan friars working in twenty-five missions among sixty thousand indigenous peoples in ninety pueblos each with a school in which the peoples to various degrees of success and continuity were taught reading, writing, manual arts, singing, and instrumental music (Spell 1927, 31).

As well, Native persons depending on the Spanish governor in power were subjected to proclamations of many sorts such as those issued to Pueblo communities "concerning marriage in the eighteenth century" and for illegal cohabitation (Brown 2013, 12). She states that the end point for all such communications and legal interventions was ultimately for "Spanish authorities—be they civil or religious—to remake Pueblo identities and communities" (12). How hegemonically successful Spanish was was very much also an artifact of how well and how often Native peoples declared their own autonomy and how well they managed to impress Spanish authorities that they were needed more by them than they were of the Spanish, especially so in relation to their defense against other indigenous populations. On the other hand, the Spanish also had to provide the legal means and space for their allied populations to have a degree of cultural and linguistic autonomy "on the ground," without which their own survival was in jeopardy.

Beyond the province of this discussion are the hundreds of literacy and language discourses from pageants to festivals, from sung masses and liturgies to performed calendric events such as Christmas and Saint's Days and to the synthesis of Spanish/Mexican forms within traditional conflict dance reenactments such as the *matachines*—a highly ritualized drama of dancers that was integrated within both indigenous and Spanish/Mexican Pueblos and spread from Chihuahua and Zacatecas to the Taos Pueblos and beyond (Rodríguez 1996). In this syncretic form, principal players include Moctezuma of Aztec origin, La Malinche, converted to a child virgin from her traditional translator and cultural broker roles, and ancient ones, bulls, clowns, and mayordomos (foremen) together with an array of dancers dressed in combinations of Spanish, indigenous, and original dress topped by bishopric miters.[10]

When all of these sources and the changes to language hegemony combine as a whole, then what is really understood is that language and cultural hegemony were never complete but rather tossed about by negotiations, compromises, resistances, and a tempered acceptance of a language of the empire that was the central mechanism for both severity and accommodation. In this manner, multiple "mes" and "theres" and "heres" and "the not theres" became situated among both indigenous and Spanish/Mexican populations so that with the exception of a few peoples such as the Ópata at least three-quarters of indigenous peoples of the region maintained their languages up to 1950, according to Spicer (1962, 448). As well, continuing the tradition of bilinguality and trilinguality was further layered with the addition of Spanish, as their forbearers had before Spanish colonialism.

For three hundred years, then to one degree or the other, "Spanish Only" was the policy focus but tittered by the reality of distance and ecology as well as determined indigenous resistance. This policy, however, became overturned in the nineteenth century by Mexico independence, and although Spanish became the de facto national language integrated with indigenous "Mexicanismos" and was supported by an early Mexican Academy of Language, the forced aspects of the imperial colony were removed (Hidalgo 2006, 361–62). For the next two hundred years, the southern part of the region struggled to adopt policies both detrimental and supportive of indigenous languages, some leading to erasure and others not. Linguistic struggles continue to this day but that is another narrative. But in 1847 in the northern region at almost the same time period a new hegemonic language described as "English" appeared. From the middle of the nineteenth century to this day, the struggle with this imposition continues, but that is another narrative and of the continued emergence of the multiple "mes" of a region that is so situated that guarantees their development.

NOTES

1. According to Texas Beyond History (2008), the act is known as "La Toma." It marked the beginning of over two hundred years of Spanish rule in Texas. The celebration was concluded with a play written by Captain Marcos Farfán de los Gados. Although copies of the play have not survived, it is likely the first theatrical piece written in what is now the United States.
2. I use the term "claim" because although the category of criollo indicated a person born of Iberian-born parents, it is the case that such a category was loosely constructed, and changes of identity were not only possible but also probable. Often such categories could be claimed without reference to records of authenticity of birth, with the most important indicator being control and ownership of land and Native peoples as slaves. Even in Spain the genitor of attention to bloodlines was open to negotiation, and as John Nieto-Phillips (2004, 19) writes in his work *The Language of Blood*: "For a fee, families of dubious origins could produce documents that, effectively, purified their bloodlines by the mere assertion of blood purity. This practice was rather commonplace among the nobility, who, despite claims to the contrary, 'had been impregnated with Jewish blood.'"
3. See Moorhead 1975. He states that "of the 911 officers and men of the sixteen garrisons . . . between 1773 and 1781, only . . . 49.6. percent were listed as . . . europeos, españoles, or criolles; . . . 37 percent as . . . mestizos, castizos, mulatos, moriscos, coyotes, lobos and less specifically castas . . . [and] . . . 13.3 percent were Indians" (182–83).
4. Arizona State Museum, Documentary Relations of the Southwest (DRSW) Archives: *Archivos General de la Nación*: Microfilm records of 302 presidial soldiers from the following, in order of appearance in the record: 1° Compañía del 7mo Escuadrón; 2nda Compañía De Volantes De La Colonia Del Nuevo Santander; 2nda Compañía Del 1° Escuadrón Del Cuerpo De Dragones Provinciales Del Presidio De San Carlos; 3rd Compañía De 1° Escuadrón; 3ra Compañía De 2ndo Escuadrón; 7ma Compañía De

Alternación; Compañía Presidial De Bexar; Compañía De Caballería Y Voluntarios De Monclava; 1° Compañía De Volantes De La Nueva Santander; 2nda Compañía Del Real Presidio De Aguave; Compañía De Caballería Del Real Presidio De Rio Grande. Microfilm references available for each upon request.

5. Arizona State Museum, Documentary Relations of the Southwest (DRSW) Archives: *Archivos General de la Nación*: Filiación de la 3ª Compañia del 2° Escuadrón, 1779. P1:1179B-G13 and Filiación de la 2a Compañia del 1° Escuadrón del cuerpo de Dragones Provinciales, 1782. P38:1782-G13.
6. "Meaning of "Villalobos." http://www.misapellidos.com/significado-de-Villalobos-20542.html.
7. The statistical and analytical discussion of physical categories will be part of a much larger work and illustrate the cognitive categories used to accentuate the racialized identity of each soldier (Vélez-Ibáñez n.d.).
8. Arizona State Museum Archives, DRSW: Microfilm records of 302 presidial soldiers. In this research, of 291 soldiers, 34 were described as having *pozos de viruelas* (pockmarks from smallpox), representing 12 percent of the sample.
9. Vélez-Ibáñez (n.d.). This work will elaborate the link between the decimation of the indigenous population and the establishment of political authority and with it language hegemony, as was the case of the depopulation in Nueva Vizcaya (present Texas and Nuevo León) where, according to Peter Gerhard (1981, 191, 353, 354), the population was reduced from 100,000 in 1540 to 1,000 in 1740 by a combination of disease and violence.
10. Personal observations of the Bernallio, New Mexico, matachine dances of the Festival of San Lorenzo on August 9–11, 2014, and the matachine dances at Picuris Pueblo on November 12, 2014.

REFERENCES

Bolton, Herbert Eugene. 1919. *Kino's Historical Memoir of Primeria Alta: 1683–1711*. Vol. 1. Cleveland: Arthur H. Clark Co.

Brewster-Folsom, Raphael. 2014. *The Yaquis and the Empire: Violence, Spanish Imperial Power, and Native Resilience in Colonial Mexico*. New Haven: Yale University Press.

Brooks, James E. 2003. *Captives and Cousins: Slavery, Kinship, and Community in the Southwest Borderlands*. Chapel Hill: University of North Carolina Press.

Brown, Tracy L. 2013. *Pueblo Indians and Spanish Colonial Authority in Eighteenth-Century New Mexico*. Tucson: University of Arizona Press.

Davis, Jeffrey, and Samuel Supalla. 1995. "A Sociolinguistic Analysis of Sign Language Use in a Navajo Family." In *Sociolinguistics in Deaf Communities*, edited by Ceil Lucas, 80. Washington, DC: Gallaudet University.

Deacon, Terrence W. 2012. *Incomplete Nature: How Mind Emerged from Matter*. New York: W. W. Norton.

Derrida, Jacques. 1974. *Of Grammatology*. Translated by G. C. Spivak. Baltimore: John Hopkins University Press.

Ebright, Malcom, and Rick Hendricks. 2006. *The Witches of Abiquiú: The Governor, the Priest, the Genizaro Indians, and the Devil*. Albuquerque: University of New Mexico Press.

Eggan, Fred. 1979. "Pueblos: Introduction." In *Handbook of North American Indians*. Vol. 9, *Southwest*, edited by Alfonso Ortiz, 224–35. Washington, DC: Smithsonian Institution.

Ellis, Florence Hawley. 1979. "Isleta Pueblo." In *Handbook of North American Indians*. Vol. 9, *Southwest*, edited by Alfonso Ortiz, 351–65. Washington, DC: Smithsonian Institution.

Ferguson, Margaret W. 2003. *Dido's Daughters: Literacy, Gender, and Empire in Early Modern England and France*. Chicago: University of Chicago Press.

Foster, William C. 1995. *Spanish Expeditions into Texas, 1689–1768*. Austin: University of Texas Press.

Gallegos, Bernardo P. 1992. *Literacy, Education, and Society in New Mexico, 1693–1821*. Albuquerque: University of New Mexico Press.

Gerhard, Peter. 1981. *The North Frontier of New Spain*. Rev. ed. Norman: University of Oklahoma Press.

Gramsci, Antonio. 1971. *Selections from the Prison Notebooks*. Edited and translated by Quintin Hoare and Geoffrey Nowell Smith. New York: International Publishers.

———. 1973. *Letters from Prison*. Edited and translated by Lynne Lawner. New York: Harper & Row.

Hammond, George Peter, and Agapito Rey. 1953. *Don Juan Oñate: Colonizer of New Mexico, 1595–1628*. Albuquerque: University of New Mexico Press.

Hidalgo, Margarita. 2006. "Language Policy: Past, Present, and Future." In *Mexican Indigenous Languages at the Dawn of the Twenty-First Century*, edited by Margarita Hidalgo, 357–69. Berlin: Druyter.

Kelly, Henry W. 1940. "Franciscan Missions of New Mexico, 1740–1760." *New Mexico Historical Review* 15(4): 345–68.

Kino, Eusebio Francisco. 1919[1708]. *Spain in the West: Kino's Historical Memoir of Pimería Alta: A Contemporary Account of the Beginnings of California, Sonora and Arizona, 1682–1711*. Translated and annotated by Herbert Eugene Bolton. Cleveland: Arthur H. Clark Co.

Moorhead, Max L. 1975. *The Presidio: Bastion of the Spanish Borderlands*. Norman: University of Oklahoma Press.

Nieto-Phillips, John. 2004. *The Language of Blood: The Making of Spanish-American Identity in New Mexico: 1880s–1930s*. Albuquerque: University of New Mexico Press.

Pfefferkorn, Ignatz [Ignaz, Ignaico]. 1989. *Sonora: A Description of the Province*. Translated by Theodore E. Treutlein. Tucson: University of Arizona Press. Originally published in 2 vols. 1794–1795.

Reff, Daniel T. 1991. *Disease, Depopulation and Culture Change in Northwestern New Spain, 1518–1764*. Salt Lake City: University of Utah Press.

Riley, Carroll L. 1971. "Early Spanish-Indian Communication in the Greater Southwest." *New Mexico Historical Review* 46(4): 285–314.

Rodriguez, Sylvia. 1996. *The Matachines Dance: Ritual Symbolism and Interethnic Relations in the Upper Rio Grande Valley*. Albuquerque: University of New Mexico Press.

Roseberry, William. 1994. "Hegemony and the Language of Contention." In *Everyday Forms of State Formation: Revolution and the Negotiation of Rule in Modern Mexico*, edited by Gilbert M. Joseph and Daniel Nugent, 355–66. Durham, NC: Duke University Press.

Rospide, Maria Margarita. 1995. "La Real Cedula del 10 de mayo de 1770 y La Enseñanza del Castellano: Observaciones sobre su aplicacion en el Territoriao Altoperuano." *Memoria del X Congreso del Instituto Internacional de Historia del Derecho Indiano* 1995:1415–48.

Servin, Manuel P. 1978. "The Legal Basis for the Establishment of Spanish Colonial Sovereignty: The Act of Possession." *New Mexico Historical Review* 53(4): 295–303.

Shaul, David L. 2014. *A Prehistory of Western North America: The Impact of Uto-Aztecan*. Albuquerque: University of New Mexico Press.

Spell, Lota M. 1927. "Music Teaching in New Mexico in the Seventeenth Century: The Beginnings of Music Education in the United States." *New Mexico Historical Review* 2(1): 27–37.

Spicer, Edward H. 1962. *Cycles of Conquest: The Impact of Spain, Mexico, and the United States on the Indians of the Southwest, 1533–1960*. Tucson: University of Arizona Press.

Texas Beyond History. 2008. "Indians, Missionaries, Solderies, and Settlers: History of the El Paso Valley." http://www.texasbeyondhistory.net/paso/history.html.

Trujillo, Michael L. 2008. *Aztlán: A Journal of Chicano Studies* 33(2): 91–99. http://www.academia.edu/231413/Onates_Foot_Remembering_and_Dismembering_in_Northern_New_Mexico.

Vélez-Ibáñez, Carlos G. 1996. *Border Visions: The Cultures of Mexican Cultures of the Southwest United States*. Tucson: University of Arizona.

———. n.d. "The Hegemony of Languages and Their Discontents of Southwest North America: From the Spanish Colony to the Present." Tucson: University of Arizona Press, under review.

Weigand, Phil C. 1997. "La turquesa." *Arqueologia Mexicana* 5(27): 26–33.

———. 2008. "Turquoise: Formal Economic Interrelationships Between Mesoamerica and the Southwest United States." In *Archeology Without Borders*, edited by Laura D. Webster and Maxine E. McBrinn, 343–53. Boulder: University of Colorado.

Williams, Raymond. 1977. *Marxism and Literature*. Oxford: Oxford University Press.

Yetman, David. 2010. *The Ópatas: In Search of a Sonoran People*. Southwest Center Series. With an appendix on the languages of the Opatería by David Shaul. Tucson: University of Arizona Press.

7

SPANISH-ENGLISH BILINGUALISM IN UNEVEN AND COMBINED RELATIONS

JOSIAH HEYMAN AND AMADO ALARCÓN

INTRODUCTION

WE EXAMINE FLUENT Spanish-English bilingualism on the U.S.-Mexico border from the perspective of uneven and combined relations, as developed in chapter 2. Such relations connect unequal social, economic, and political positions, both producing differentiation and inequality and requiring social-cultural and linguistic interaction. As François Grosjean (2010, 29) writes, summarizing a long tradition in sociolinguistics, "Bilinguals usually acquire and use their languages for different purposes, in different domains of life, with different people." Our concern is with *combinations* spanning those differences, where the linked differences involve inequalities of economy and social power. For example, poorly paid labor in Mexican export assembly plants (maquiladoras) is recruited and managed in Spanish, but executive, financial, technical, and other corporate operations, including international coordination, is conducted in English (in some cases, in languages such as Japanese, Korean, etc., with English as a lingua franca for North American operations). In-plant office activities vary between Spanish and English. These arrangements are clearly uneven, due to the wage differential between speakers and sites of the two languages, but are combined to obtain profits in the global economy. That combination requires linguistic brokerage (verbal interpretation mainly but sometimes written translation) performed by bilingual people.

Fluent bilinguals often enact such vertical combinations, transmitting power between English-dominant private and public sector institutions and Spanish-dominant or bilingual workers, customers, and targets of control. We will discuss this through studies of U.S.-side bilingual call centers, the health and public safety sectors in the U.S. borderlands, and the Mexican maquiladora sector. We do provide, however, a different analysis for the Mexican side, with Spanish-dominant public and private sector institutions. Language attitudes are consistent with the apartheid-like border inequalities described in chapter 2. English is most valued, and Spanish-English bilingualism[1] has a subordinate value as a tool of access and control. Spanish monolingualism is stigmatized (this differs, of course, for Mexico, where within Spanish prestige and stigma are distributed across class registers). However, these hierarchical attitudes are cross-cut by alternative border values, in which fluent bilingualism and especially code-switching are valued for horizontal relationship building and creativity. In uneven and combined perspective, then, bilingualism constitutes a prism for seeing the borderlands, exposing paradoxical inequalities and equalities.[2]

A distinctive and important feature of our approach is that we take into consideration the full range of language options in the Southwest North American (SWNA) region—Spanish, Spanish-English bilingualism, and English—rather than the narrower phenomenon of code-switching, which has absorbed the most attention in cultural and linguistic border studies. Code-switching is alternating utterances between the two languages. Certainly, we acknowledge the linguistic and cultural-political interest of code-switching, but bilingualism (let alone the totality of border language use) should not be reduced to code-switching. Bilingualism is not only hybridization; it also is used in segmented speech and writing performances, such as interpretation and/or translation between different sources and recipients. Often, though not always, border language options are unequal: English the language of superior economic power[3]; Spanish the language of the control of labor; English or Spanish the language of institutional and governmental sites depending on the nation-state involved, with a secondary language to serve some clients; and bilingualism mediating between these domains (occasionally, shifting into full code-switching between fluent bilingual speakers). Hence, uneven and combined monolingual practices as well as bilingual ones are important to the performance of power, governmentality, and exploitation in the borderlands. Analyzing the full field of coexisting, sometimes bounded, sometimes linked multiple-language speakers, domains, and practices brings consideration of the way language is part of and a clue to unequal social structure in each country and between the two countries; conversely, addressing more narrowly border code-switching foregrounds cultural hybridity that defies the national linguistic and cultural ideologies of Mexico and the United States.

Language is certainly not the whole of culture; it is a relatively autonomous domain. Still, it is an operational way to address key questions that have arisen in the analysis of U.S.-Mexico border society and culture, applicable with modifications to other borders and with implications for general border theory. On the one hand, border cultures have been viewed as creative hybrids of otherwise bounded national cultures (García Canclini 1995; O. Martínez 1994). These hybrids, in turn, have been understood as the cultural ground of solidarity against dominant national, racial, and other hegemonies (Anzaldúa 1987). At the same time, critical social analysis of the U.S.-Mexico border emphasizes the extreme inequalities enacted there (e.g., Heyman 1994). Both views of the border are correct (Heyman 2012) not just because the place is complex and contradictory (though it is) but precisely because uneven and combined relationships produce creative, horizontal hybridization in the interstices of exploitation, domination, and control.

To understand this paradox, we first will look at cases where bilingualism is used in relations of economic and sociopolitical power, including several key sectors in contemporary neoliberalism. We begin with a longer examination of the Mexican-side maquiladoras, which involve linguistic as well as economic brokerage of unequal levels of capital and wages across the border. We then turn to a U.S.-side instance, bilingualism in call centers in the United States, where heritage-based bilingual skills are used by businesses in the service economy without extra cost (we also briefly take note of English-language call centers in Mexico). We then examine the role of bilingual brokerage in health and public safety services on the U.S. side, which are both means of improving service access and yet also Foucauldian forms of biopower and governmentality (this analysis applies less often to the Mexican side, where most service providers and recipients share Spanish but there are a few English-dominant speakers, such as returning migrants). While varied, across most of the cases we take note of the relations of power extending from English-dominant actors, largely accorded economic value and social prestige, toward Spanish-dominant actors, largely placed in exploitative and social devalued roles, and the role of bilingualism in forging and maintaining such unequal connections.

We then discuss a different view of bilingualism: its role in bonding horizontal relationships and the kinds of cultural creativity that emerge in its performance. This material is, admittedly, briefer than our discussion of bilingualism and occupations, in part because in other works the relative emphasis is reversed (G. Martínez 2006). We pay particular attention to "Spanglish," a local meaningful label on the border but not a linguistically precise label, and within that, code-switching. While limited code-switching can occur with dominant skills in one language and limited borrowings from the other, intensive code-switching requires extensive production/reception capabilities in both languages, hence fluent bilingualism. We propose that intensive code-switching performs horizontal solidarity between bilinguals. It thus occurs in a distinctive sociolinguistic domain reproduced and promoted by combined border practices (Hidalgo 2001).

LANGUAGE AND BROKERAGE: ECONOMIC AND POLITICAL

Unsurprisingly, but importantly, U.S. and Anglophone Canadian corporations use bilingual linguistic brokers to coordinate central finance, management, and technology sites with operations management and workers in low-wage production sites in Mexico. These brokers may be Northamericans of non-Mexican origin, U.S. Mexicans, or Mexicans, as long as they can communicate up and down the corporate hierarchy. Such bilingual brokers can occupy posts in plant management, in technical staff, or at the top of the production hierarchy (such as area supervisors). We interviewed bilingual plant managerial staff who confirmed this description of their role. What is at least as telling is a case study of a technical staff member, assigned to Mexico by a U.S. corporation, who effectively could not speak Spanish. While he relied in part on mutual understanding of mathematical and graphic representations in engineering documents, he told us that he definitely required bilingual interpretation assistance to do his job, which included tracking the quality of products and identifying process problems—activities that are essential to utilizing high-quality and -productivity but low-wage Mexican labor.

Another telling example is a Mexican national (recently a legal immigrant in the United States) with very good abilities in English, who managed parts supplies. His job entailed global communication not only between the factory in Mexico and the home office in the United States but also with parts suppliers in the United States, Canada, France, and Taiwan. They coordinated via English as a lingua franca, even when no one involved was a native speaker of English. English as a manufacturing lingua franca is not especially unique to the Mexican border, but it is notable that it was facilitated by an educated, English-speaking Mexican who rose up from the ranks in the Mexican factory system.

Melissa Wright (2006), in turn, provides observations of the social-linguistic ideologies of superiority and domination that mark language in these settings. She observes that in the factories, English was a code for higher value and affiliation with (e.g., career paths into) U.S. corporate management. Spanish was part of a set of signs of lower value and disposability, and a ceiling to career advancement. Her narrative focuses on the distinction between the two unequal symbolic sets. Yet, at the same time, vertical linkage from one set to the other must also have been important, including Spanish-English bilingualism. This is indicated by her case study of a supervisor who used subtle local knowledge of workers' social and geographic backgrounds, encoded in informal Spanish, to maximize productivity on behalf of an oblivious English-speaking corporate management.

Uneven and combined relationships of Spanish and English occur in other workplaces. Our study of call centers (Alarcón and Heyman 2013) in El Paso, on the U.S. side, found that bilingualism helped recruiters identify inexpensive but relatively educated and literate workers for workplaces where such qualities are key. This contrasts with previous eras of relatively silent labor filled by limited-English-proficient workers. Fluent bilinguals are mostly educated in the United States, literate, and good call center workers but come from a disadvantaged social group, U.S. Mexicans (especially second generation), who typically earn slightly less than English-only workers, even with comparable qualifications (Alarcón et al. 2014b). Furthermore, by recruiting such workforces, call centers obtain Spanish-language functionality without any added cost, treating it as a "natural" product of the border environment, a "heritage language" from family and community, not a compensable skill.[4]

Building on this analysis, we note an interesting phenomenon of uneven and combined language in call center capitalism. In the design of operations, Spanish and English can be kept separate. Callers can select one language and be directed to operators exclusively in that language. But, in practice, El Paso call centers deal with complicated bilingual publics who move between Spanish and English. Their initial choices may well indicate only part of the conversation. So, bilingualism is valuable for flexible capitalism. Furthermore, we found that operators and customers often collaborate on using informal (working-class) registers of Spanish or using various dimensions of Spanglish (code-switching, English borrow words, and formations in Spanish). Admittedly, the operators are speakers mainly of northern Mexican Spanish, while the multilingual customers use a variety of national-origin Spanish accents, but we found that more important is how customer-relationship confidence emerges from use of relaxed, informal registers by El Paso bilinguals as opposed to the social distance implied by educated registers. Almost always, the home offices of the corporations were English dominant. At no extra cost, then, bilingual workers supply to English-dominant management: (1) Spanish-language skills as such, (2) Spanish-English flexibility, and (3) positive customer service by means of linguistic cues of solidarity.

There are also English-language call centers in Mexico, on the northern border and the interior, and in Central America and the Caribbean. We did not research them, but clearly they take advantage of lower wages in Mexico. Anecdotally, an important component of staffing is deported Northamericans, whose labor is devalued by deportation from the United States to Mexico. Bilingualism, in summary, plays an important role in characteristic neoliberal economic sectors.

Our qualitative and quantitative research (Alarcón and Heyman 2014; Alarcón et al. 2014a) also examined language in service occupations on the U.S. side of the border, in particular health services and public safety. We found that fluent bilinguals concentrate in intermediate occupations that interact directly with a multilingual public, such as medical office staff and police officers. Management and professions were disproportionately monolingual English speaking, while low-skill service providers (e.g., home health aides) and manual laborers were disproportionately limited English proficient (we controlled for many other factors, such as education, gender, etc.).

This statistical pattern was confirmed ethnographically. For example, in one private doctor's office, the doctor himself was originally Mexican and spoke Spanish as well as English (this office dealt with many occupational injuries and had a substantial limited-English-proficient clientele). But a key technical staff member, a nurse with an advanced university degree, responsible for collecting medical information, writing official medical records, and treating patients, spoke almost no Spanish. Oral interpretation and information gathering from Spanish speakers was performed by a bilingual (first language Spanish, second language English) medical assistant with an associate degree, whose formal responsibilities were medical data entry but whose functional role was more flexible, complex, responsible, and caring. The front office also had a fluent bilingual receptionist (dual first language, somewhat preferentially English speaking). Hence, key mediating roles were bilingual.

In U.S. health services and policing, linguistic brokerage helps construct and reproduce biopolitical power. Obviously, public institutions and business services on the Mexican side differ in being conducted almost entirely in Spanish (with diversity of register, dialect, etc.). Bilingualism is not used for biopolitical power in Mexico as it is used in the United States. But keeping in mind the importance of bilingualism to transnational economic power penetrating Mexico, we can say with confidence that overall, bilingualism is central to uneven and combined power in the border region.

BILINGUALISM: AUTONOMOUS PHENOMENA

While our analysis concentrates on bilingualism in vertical relations of power, this needs to be tempered with attention to the relatively autonomous side of bilingualism. This is not necessarily resistant to power (though sometimes it is) so much as it is slantwise to it, emerging from everyday activities without intentions of either domination or resistance (Campbell and Heyman 2007). Nevertheless, it presents a palpable alternative to the dominant national language ideologies and institutions of the United States and Mexico, which are formal and exclusive English and Spanish, respectively, and to the hierarchical arrangement of English above Spanish in overall regional formations.

The folk terminology, especially on the U.S. side, is "Spanglish." Spanglish is a linguistically imprecise term, but a socially meaningful one. Linguistically, Spanish and

English interact in many ways: borrowed morphemes (words and meaningful word parts, such as *guachate* in Spanish, from the English verb "to watch," reworked as a Spanish command equivalent to "watch out"), calques and other borrowed phrases and morpheme-semantic sets (such as "the job was very ugly," not as a description of appearance but of moral disapprobation, from the semantics of the Spanish *feo*), prosody (borrowed sound patterns, such as Spanish rising inflections at the end of English declarative phrases, giving what sounds in English to be a more musical utterance), and so forth. But the most important component is code-switching, including utterances from one language within speech in the other; at its most intensive, code-switching can involve nearly equal alternation of utterances in the two languages. Only fluent bilinguals can produce sustained code-switching of this kind, and while incompletely bilingual speakers can decode it, that is challenging and imbalanced; a truly effective code-alternating dialogue requires multiple fluent bilinguals. It is thus a core phenomenon in social relationships between bilinguals, though not obligatorily so.

Indeed, Spanglish of all kinds deviates from the two institutionalized formal languages. It thus has a social implication of defying linguistic ideologies of nation-states, even if this is not fully intended in a particular speech situation. For example, trainers and supervisors in U.S. bilingual call centers in some cases instructed workers (often ineffectively) not to use English borrow words and phrasings in Spanish, to preserve a pure code, though others recognized that such performances benefited the business by connecting to clients who also spoke that way. Spanglish in the U.S. borderlands is often associated with sentiments of horizontal solidarity among people of Mexican origin. A medical receptionist (described earlier), when asked, "Who speaks Spanglish?" laughed, paused, and answered, "We do, the children of immigrants." The generational model she described has some truth, though it is overly simple, but the more important point in her statement is the use of the pronoun "we." She identifies herself as part of a group. Notably, in the interview she did not identify with monolingual-English staff but also expressed dislike and resentment of limited-English-proficient clients, even though her dual linguistic skill allowed her to serve them (and indeed, their presence may have been a reason for her employment). And this was hardly the only instance of horizontal identifications among fluent bilinguals revealed in our fieldwork.

An interesting case was provided by a former call center operator. He admitted code-switching, even though he was "not proud of it" because his mother, a certified English-Spanish legal interpreter originally from Mexico, had taught him to keep the languages separate, in her mind an important element of national purity (see Hidalgo, discussed below). Despite this, he ended up code-switching with his siblings and then transferred this speech practice to fellow workers in the call center, where relaxed, joking, casual conversations often were performed in bilingual code-switching. Although the examples used in Limón (1989) are entirely in Spanish, the broader phenomenon of horizontal solidarity in these carnivalesque (anti-formal) speech acts is quite similar.

Those examples of code-switching come from the U.S. side of the border and thus are subject to Pablo Vila's (2003) criticism that the topic of border cultural hybrids is U.S. centered and neglects the Mexican side.[5] Indeed, work on Spanish-English bilingualism on the Mexican side of the border is sparse, although our work has examined bilingual brokerage occurring in the maquiladoras. Jorge Bustamante (1982) found that English-language influences within a comparative set of Mexican border and interior cities ranged from the most frequent (Ciudad Juárez) to the least frequent (Matamoros) in border cities. Using fine-grained ethnography, Rihan Yeh (2016) identifies two routes to English: one through working-class labor migration to and return from the United States and the other through middle- and upper-class education, consumption/visiting, and migration to the United States. Margarita Hidalgo (1984, 1986) finds that learning English in Juárez is partly motivated by the kinds of economic relationships we have identified (maquiladoras and cross-border commerce and tourism), but she also found non-instrumental motivations to develop relations with Northamericans. Hidalgo found that Juarenses expressed disapproving attitudes toward English-Spanish mixes though actual behavior varies; Yeh makes this more complex by finding disapproval of working-class uses of English, while middle- and upper-class versions of such speech forms are seen more approvingly. Possibly, at the top end of the social order, English and "Spanglish" connect to social dominance of people who study English (sometimes in the United States) for its use in Mexico's economic and political relationship to the colossus of the north and thus derive prestige from that vertical relation. Lower on the social ladder, English and "Spanglish" is associated with transnational labor migration and deportation, the stigmatized side of this U.S.-Mexican relationship. Asymmetrical transnational connections, combined with strong class and race inequalities in Mexico itself, shape Mexican-side hybridities and linguistic ideologies.

CONCLUSION

Fluent Spanish-English bilingualism is implicated in both vertical and horizontal relations at the U.S.-Mexico border. Its mediating role is pervasive on the U.S. side, where bilingualism helps to coordinate a socially divided capitalist economy where workers and poor consumers are disproportionately dominant in Spanish while owners and managers are disproportionately dominant in English or bilingual and a socially divided state apparatus where many clients of services and enforcement are disproportionately dominant in Spanish while state decision-makers and institutional codes are disproportionately dominant in English or bilingual. Services to border-crossing visitors (consumers and others) from Mexico whose class backgrounds vary widely, but whose dominant language mostly is Spanish (some are bilingual), reinforce these linguistic patterns. Bilingualism's mediating role in Mexico is limited, because the state apparatus operates in Spanish and domestically oriented enterprises likewise, but the important maquiladora industry, the transnational economic core of the region, does require language brokerage between international English-speaking capital and local production that operates in Spanish. At the same time, creative hybrids of Spanish and English continually emerge in everyday practice in both countries, with locally recognized implications of defiance of linguistic nationalism on each side of the border. That defiance is reinforced by border-crossing processes, such as authorized and unauthorized migration to the United States and return migration to Mexico, both voluntary and forced by deportation.

While language is a distinctive domain, it provides valuable insights into wider questions of social relations and cultural process in the borderlands and generally in complex societies (our perspective is shared by Vélez-Ibáñez in chapter 6). The borderlands are notable for the simultaneity of vertical relations of power and horizontal relations of creativity and interchange. The border culture debate, which has influenced culture theory generally (summarized ably in chapter 4), tends to focus on one or the other side of this dichotomy. The study of bilingualism at the border helps us progress beyond this division. Bilingualism is uneven and combined, coordinating vertical relations of power (both capitalist and biopolitical) but also expressing horizontal bonding and encouraging cultural play that defies nationalist power orders. Approaches that emphasize border hybridities and alternatives to nation-state hegemonies have some hold on the evidence, but they should not be put forward romantically, without also being attentive to vertical relations of power and exploitation that in other ways are crucial to the bilingualism. Spanish-English bilingualism thus has several valences, and only through sensitive social analysis can we understand its role in simultaneous power and autonomy characteristic of borders and complex and unequal linguistic and social-cultural settings generally.

NOTES

1. In El Paso County, Texas, in 2013, the American Community Survey (http://factfinder.census.gov/faces/nav/jsf/pages/index.xhtml, query El Paso County Texas, query Language Spoken at Home, using the 2009–2013 5-Year Estimates) reports that 27.0 percent of the population speak English at home and 73.0 percent speak another language.

Spanish is spoken by 71.0 percent of all persons, composing almost all the home speakers of languages other than English. Of those Spanish-at-home speakers, 57.2 percent speak English "very well" (this is 40.6 percent of the whole population), a conservative estimate of fluent bilinguals that does not include home speakers of English who speak Spanish very well or home speakers of Spanish who speak English "well."

2. The causes of fluent bilingualism are complicated, involving a variety of forms of language acquisition and retention, but the phenomena described in this chapter may help explain the notable persistence of Spanish-English bilingualism in U.S. border communities in the face of generational change and other forces of Spanish language loss (Bills, Hernández-Chávez, and Hudson 1995; Hidalgo 2001). In one of our case studies was a fourth-generation Mexican American construction contractor whose fluency in Spanish, though based on family and neighborhood linguistic socialization, was much reinforced by linguistic brokerage between English-dominant clients and Spanish-dominant workers, which was key to his business.
3. There are some Spanish-dominant large businesses in Mexico, of course.
4. This is the general pattern we found, but there are centers where Spanish-speaking operators earn modestly more than English-only ones; however, bilingual flexibility by non-designated staff is particularly not recognized or compensated.
5. Liliana Lanz Vallejo (2011, 2015) found evidence that Spanish-English code-switching in Tijuana is creative and that English expresses intense feelings among horizontal confidants. However, her material comes from "tweets," which involve informal expression, and from educated youth, which fits Yeh's understanding of the social-status performative role of English use.

REFERENCES

Alarcón, Amado, and Josiah McC. Heyman. 2013. "Bilingual Call Centers at the U.S.-Mexico Border: Location and Linguistic Markers of Exploitability." *Language in Society* 42:1–21.

———. 2014. "From 'Spanish-Only' Cheap Labor to Stratified Bilingualism: Language, Markets and Institutions on the US-Mexico Border." *International Journal of the Sociology of Language* 227:101–17.

Alarcón, Amado, Antonio Di Paolo, Josiah Heyman, and María Cristina Morales. 2014a. "The Occupational Location of Spanish-English Bilinguals in the New Information Economy: The Health and Criminal Justice Sector in the US Borderlands with Mexico." In *The Bilingual Advantage: Language, Literacy, and the Labor Market*, edited by Rebecca M. Callahan and Patricia C. Gándara, 110–37. Clevedon, UK: Multilingual Matters.

———. 2014b. "Returns to Spanish–English Bilingualism in the New Information Economy: The Health and Criminal Justice Sectors in the Texas Border and Dallas-Tarrant Counties."

In *The Bilingual Advantage: Language, Literacy, and the Labor Market*, edited by Rebecca M. Callahan and Patricia C. Gándara, 138–59. Clevedon, UK: Multilingual Matters.

Anzaldúa, Gloria. 1987. *La Frontera/Borderlands = The New Mestiza*. San Francisco: Spinsters/Aunt Lute.

Bills, Garland D., Eduardo Hernández-Chávez, and Alan Hudson. 1995. "The Geography of Language Shift: Distance from the Mexican Border and Spanish Language Claiming in the Southwestern U.S." *International Journal of the Sociology of Language* 114:9–27.

Bustamante, Jorge. 1982. *Uso de idioma español e identidad nacional*. Tijuana, Mexico: Centro de Estudios Fronterizos del Norte de México. https://www.colef.mx/?estudiosdeelcolef=uso-del-idioma-espanol-e-identidad-nacional.

Campbell, Howard, and Josiah McC. Heyman. 2007. "Slantwise: Beyond Domination and Resistance on the Border." *Journal of Contemporary Ethnography* 36:3–30.

García Canclini, Néstor. 1995. *Hybrid Cultures: Strategies for Entering and Leaving Modernity*. Minneapolis: University of Minnesota Press.

Grosjean, François. 2010. *Bilingual: Life and Reality*. Cambridge, MA: Harvard University Press.

Heyman, Josiah McC. 1994. "The Mexico-United States Border in Anthropology: A Critique and Reformulation." *Journal of Political Ecology* 1:43–65. http://www.library.arizona.edu/ej/jpe/volume_1/HEYMAN.PDF.

———. 2012. "Culture Theory and the US–Mexico Border." In *A Companion to Border Studies*, edited by Hastings Donnan and Thomas Wilson, 48–65. Malden, MA: Wiley-Blackwell.

Hidalgo, Margarita. 1984. "Attitudes and Behavior Toward English in Juárez, Mexico." *Anthropological Linguistics* 26:376–92.

———. 1986. "Language Contact, Language Loyalty, and Language Prejudice on the Mexican Border." *Language in Society* 15:193–220.

———. 2001. "Spanish Language Shift Reversal on the US-Mexico Border and the Extended Third Space." *Language and Intercultural Communication* 1:57–75.

Lanz Vallejo, Liliana. 2011. "El cambio de código español-inglés como creatividad lingüística y presentación de la imagen en tweets escritos por tijuanenses." In *Memorias de las 1as. Jornadas de Lenguas en Contacto*, edited by Saúl Santos García and José Luis Quintero Carrillo, 64–73. Tepic, Nayarit: Universidad Autónoma de Nayarit. http://www.cucsh.uan.edu.mx/jornadas/modulos/memoria/lanz_cambio_codigo.pdf.

———. 2015. "'Tijuana Makes Me Happy': El cambio de código español-inglés en la expresión de emociones de tijuanenses." In *Lenguas en Contacto español, inglés y lenguas mexicanas*, edited by Saul Santos García, 61–73. Tepic, Nayarit: Universidad Autónoma de Nayarit.

Limón, José E. 1989. "Carne, Carnales, and the Carnivalesque: Bakhtinian Batos, Disorder, and Narrative Discourses." *American Ethnologist* 16:471–86.

Martínez, Glenn A. 2006. *Mexican Americans and Language: Del dicho al hecho*. Tucson: University of Arizona Press.

Martínez, Oscar J. 1994. *Border People: Life and Society in the U.S.-Mexico Borderlands*. Tucson: University of Arizona Press.

Vila, Pablo. 2003. "Conclusion: The Limits of American Border Theory." In *Ethnography at the Border*, edited by Pablo Vila, 306–41. Minneapolis: University of Minnesota Press.

Wright, Melissa W. 2006. *Disposable Women and Other Myths of Global Capitalism*. New York: Routledge.

Yeh, Rihan. 2016. "Commensuration in a Mexican Border City: Currencies, Consumer Goods, and Languages." *Anthropological Quarterly* 89:63–92.

8

SOUTHWEST NORTH AMERICAN LANGUAGE DYNAMICS AND THE CREATION OF BORDERING

A Commentary

ROBERT R. ÁLVAREZ

IN ADDITION TO language dynamics and the creation of bordering, the chapters in this volume illustrate the broad dynamics and changing social topography of an area that has long been contained in geographic and disciplinary frameworks. Vélez-Ibáñez, Hill, Heyman, and Alarcón help us emerge from the conceptual walls and structure of the template we have defined as the border and the borderlands. Redefining "the Border" has become a trope in and of itself (see Álvarez 2012; Wilson and Donnan 2012; Plascencia, chapter 12); these chapters provide new perspectives that expand yet go beyond the metaphorical. Vélez-Ibáñez's Southwest North American region (SWNA) illustrates recent anthropological trends toward a broader analysis of the historical processes that help define the social-cultural, political-economic dynamics of the region. We draw our understandings of the present and the past not only by the geography of the region but also in relation to the movement of people, commodities/trade, and ideological persuasions. Hill's paleo-linguistic analysis illustrates the importance of finer and more inclusive interdisciplinary engagement in reinterpreting our most fundamental notions of diffusion and contact. She repositions our central assumptions of the Southwest and its people, while challenging the important suppositions we hold of Mesoamerica. For example, in relocating the mythical Chicano Aztlán and placing it squarely in central Mexico, she confronts and challenges our current parameters of the borderlands and Southwest. SWNA comes into focus as a dynamic that we have yet to explore in its entirety. Heyman and Alarcón's focus on Spanish-English bilingual speakers illustrates the complex relational dimensions of social process, power, and brokerage used by people and institutions. They remind us that these processes are not always symmetrical or asymmetrical but also uneven, combined, and conflicting. The irony of the border and its processes is highlighted by such revelation.

The ideological and theoretical premises of the three chapters are drawn from contrastive methodologies and foci. However, language is the central "tool" used to examine essential questions that relate to human process and power that is embedded in the SWNA. These authors identify specific circumstances and the everyday activities of people in the past and present that underlie and define the broader patterns and the texture of life in this region. Vélez-Ibáñez's historical Spanish colonial rendering of hegemonic language patterns is complemented by Hill's deep linguistic genealogy that ties the notion of the SWNA clearly to pre-Hispanic connections far beyond what we have termed the Southwest borderlands and the U.S.-Mexico border. Heyman and Alarcón's focus on bilingual speech-behavior adds a graphic example of the interplay and utilization of language in wages, profits, and the global economy. Their interpretation is as much about finance as it is about language usage. Together these chapters produce new insights and a needed realignment to border studies and in particular to the SWNA.

To this reader, at least four fundamental human processes/concepts stand out as essential: migration, innovation, commodity/trade, and hegemony/agency. These processes not only illustrate the regional dynamic of the SWNA but also lend "community" and network formation and human response and interaction to the broader understanding of human behavior. For example, differential trade and the introduction of the sacred trinity of corn, squash, and beans along with innovations of irrigation and cultivation tell of a dialogic continuum and uneven pattern of human and commodity diffusion.

Migration is among the most primary of human activities, yet we continue to decipher this type of human "mobility" as an aberration of human settlement. Given the present political-economic conditions of the world, im/migration continues to be marked as a current issue reflecting national and international ideological, political-economic, and labor struggles. Viewed in the *long dureé*, migration is fundamental to human existence and to understanding the SWNA. However, we continue to define the region's populations as permanent clusters rather than recognizing the flow not only of goods but also of people who migrate, settle, and resettle, "bumping" and in interrelation with one another. These chapters illustrate the continuous relational quality of the peoples of the region. Rather than viewing the inhabitants of the SWNA as geographic entities, Vélez-Ibáñez, Hill, and Heyman and Alarcón provide a convincing view of these folks as interactive through trade, migration, and language use, in and over time and history.

We might argue that the "dormant" (i.e., strictly geographic) perspective stems from the Spanish hegemony that Vélez-Ibáñez describes. Indeed, when the Spanish arrived, Native settlements were defined as closed geographic entities (also recall the persistence of anthropology's culture areas) as much as they were viewed as contained by language. Viewed in relation to the SWNA, these are but part of the deeper fabric of ongoing mobility and migration directly related to the political ecology of the region. Both the notion of "bumping" and Hill's "leapfrogging" indicate migratory and settlement patterns that were innovative and centered on agency even though framed by natural (climate and overpopulation) and political (force and conquest) events. There is no doubt that hegemony influenced and perhaps "structured" relationships, but the actions and decisions of people themselves also stand out. In addition to stressing the various processes in the SWNA—exchange systems, trade, and redistribution—human settlement itself as an innovation is not often a consideration. And as illustrated by Heyman and Alarcón, even innovation in this schematic can be harmonious, uneven, and conflicting.

Although focusing on language, Hill's analysis is based on a political-ecological model in which Proto-Uto-Aztecan (PUA) cultivators were forced out of central Mexico due to demographic pressures as a result of specific innovations—cultivation and agriculture. Her argument utilizes social, cultural, and biogeographical evidence that "reconstructs" the PUA period. For example, she illustrates how elements of maize vocabulary were present throughout the Proto-Uto-Aztecan SWNA. The reevaluation of the dispersed introduction of maize, squash, and beans forces a chronological revision not only of trade but also of the *process* of settlement itself. Similarly, water management and irrigation not only evolves in the region but also is part of the innovation as people "leapfrogged" from river valley to river valley, bringing cultivation with them. Such leapfrogging also alters our early theoretical notions concerning migration. People did not just trickle north, but strategically aimed for specific ecological niches. This process also informs the larger historical importance of commodity and agricultural dispersal.

Vélez-Ibáñez accurately defines the Spanish *entrada* (entry) and linguistic hegemony as part of colonial historical processes. Whereas Hill's analysis is deeply diachronic, Vélez-Ibáñez's is more syncretic—focusing on "recent" hegemonies and conflict, power, and force. This historical dimension illustrates not only the imposition of language and literacy as a hegemonic force but also the agency and resistance of indigenous peoples. Such resistance, as Vélez-Ibáñez states, is part of the capacity to not only maintain culture and language but also survive the harsh reality imposed by the Spanish.

A central aspect of these chapters is the strategic use of language for both hegemonic and innovative purposes. Heyman and Alarcón discuss bilingualism on the border in specific instances of brokerage and business management and in social bonding among bilingual speakers through code-switching. The complex usages of bilingual expertise in Spanish-English speakers rest, as the authors indicate, not solely in social-cultural performance but also in economic relations related to labor and finance. This analysis illustrates the adaptive quality of bilingualism in both horizontal (social bonding) and vertical power relationships directly related to the hierarchy of labor and the broader relational attitudes embedded in racial ideologies.

These chapters provide important relational and comparative analysis, illustrating continuity, conflict, and complexity in the SWNA. As we continue to engage this region, new visions and understandings continue to develop, as pointed out in the introduction. The broad strokes painted by Vélez-Ibáñez combine with the specific examples of language hegemony and those provided by both Hill, and Heyman and Alarcón. This I believe is the central importance of redefining the region: breaking out of the structure of "border studies" and illuminating the cadences and connections and the contrasts and challenges of time, human life, and ideologies in broad patterns over time.

There is, however, a vestige of and reinforcement of the notion of the "Spanish borderlands." The border and even the SWNA are cast in the Spanish-indigenous and (Mexican) mold of Spanish-indigenous and to a lesser degree Mexican. The Southwest has always been marked as Spanish, Mexican, and indigenous. What escapes the Spanish provincial view is that blacks (and in particular Spanish-speaking blacks) have been a central part of the Southwest. They were present when Hernán Cortés marched against the Aztecs in 1519 (and when Francisco Pizarro attacked the Incas twelve years later) (Wood 2010, 24). In 1598 the first contingent of five hundred colonists to New Mexico included persons of varied racial backgrounds and social ranks. The first Afro-Latino historical personage, immortalized in the memorable *Relación* of Alvaro Núñez Cabeza de Vaca, was the famed Estevanico El Negro, who in 1528 joined Cabeza de Vaca on the trek across the continent and in 1539 was with the Fray Marcos de Niza expedition to New Mexico and the legendary city of Cíbola (Román and Flores 2010, 5). Black soldiers, servants, and sailors were among the first settlers of the Southwest. They included black and mulatto men and women, both enslaved and "free" (Wood 2010, 25). A royal official asserted in 1774 that the Hispano population of northern Mexico were of Negro, Indian, and European ancestry and were so intermixed as to make it difficult for anyone to trace their ancestry (Forbes 2010, 28). The black-mulatto element reinforces the complexity, unevenness, and hegemonic perceptions of the region. But it is an element that has not received due attention.

Although Heyman and Alarcón discuss bilingualism in relation to uneven and relational contexts (discussing both sides of the U.S.-Mexico border), their fine analysis also reinforces the interpretation of a primary division with English-Spanish speakers on the U.S. side and Spanish speakers in Mexico. The questions they raise and identify, such as Mexican Spanish–English bilingualism, are crucial to understanding not only language but also the historical relations of the region. In addition to Mexico, examples from other regions illustrate strong Spanish-Mexican usage far north of the border. A good example is the U.S.-Mexico produce trade among the *fruteros* of the Los Angeles Wholesale Market (LAWM), as well as urban centers such as La 24 in Chicago and downtown Los Angeles. Not only is Spanish dominant but also the use of Spanish becomes a creative mechanism that is related to trade and hierarchy. In the LAWM a specific hierarchy exists among Mexicanos—primary Spanish-language speakers engaged in the produce trade. The trade itself has specialized vocabulary and signifiers that identify types of vendors and their association to the life of the frutero. Similarly, as noted by these authors, English-Spanish has not been the primary language south of the international border (as it is in the United States). Yet, there are distinct examples of strong English usage and bilingualism in Mexican "border" cities. Megalí Muría (2010) discusses the use of English and "Spanglish" in the city of Tijuana, Baja California. This city's distance from the mainland, separation from government, and economic trends until very recently tied its inhabitants to the commerce and daily activities of San Diego in the United States. Indeed, many original Tijuanenses spoke English. This usage was derived from listening to U.S. radio and trips for commerce, shopping, and social connections with kin and friends. Tijuana was oriented toward the United States until the more recent planned reintegration of Tijuana into the Mexican nation after the 1950s.

On my first reading of these chapter titles, I was baffled by what seemed to be differing themes, yet what they illustrate is the actual congruence and interrelations of the region defined here as the SWNA. The subtleties of each chapter produce a picture that spills over the frame we have called the borderlands. The borderlands and the region can no longer be viewed as simple nuances and conflicts of the two nations, or of the historical trends of settlement tied to geography. The SWNA is filled with perplexity, nuances, asymmetry, and human agency. The greatest value of these chapters is that they open new doors and incite new questions.

REFERENCES

Álvarez, Robert R. 2007. *Mangos, Chiles and Truckers: The Business of Transnationalism*. Minneapolis: University of Minnesota Press.

———. 2012. "Reconceptualizing the Space of the Mexico-U.S Borderline." In *A Companion to Border Studies*, edited by Thomas M. Wilson and Hastings Donnan, 538–56. Sussex, UK: Wiley-Blackwell.

Forbes, Jack D. 2010. "Black Pioneers: The Spanish-Speaking Afro-Americans of the Southwest." In *The Afro-Latin@ Reader*, edited by Miriam Jímenez Román and Juan Flores, 27–37. Durham, NC: Duke University Press.

Muría, Megalí. 2010. "Enforcing Borders: Globalization, State Power and the Geography of Cross-Border Consumption in Tijuana, Mexico." PhD dissertation, Department of Communication, University of California, San Diego.

Román, Miriam Jímenez, and Juan Flores, eds. 2010. *The Afro-Latin@ Reader*. Durham, NC: Duke University Press.

Wilson, Thomas M., and Hastings Donnan. 2012. *A Companion to Border Studies*. Sussex, UK: Wiley-Blackwell.

Wood, Peter H. 2010. "The Earliest Africans in North America." In *The Afro-Latin@ Reader*, edited by Miriam Jímenez Román and Juan Flores, 19–26. Durham, NC: Duke University Press.

PART III

PEOPLES, POLITICAL POLICIES, AND THEIR CONTRADICTIONS

9
THE ETHICS OF CULTURE AND TRANSNATIONAL HOUSEHOLD STRUCTURE AND FORMATION REVISITED

ANNA OCHOA O'LEARY

INTRODUCTION

WHILE THEORETICAL FRAMEWORKS afford us a deeper understanding of the geopolitical and economic processes by which regions evolve and nation-states are connected, showing how these translate into opportunities and inequalities "on the ground" is fundamentally an anthropological endeavor. And, while social science research may be imperfect, it is also known for its patient inquiry into patterns of human interaction that deepen our understanding of the sweeping meta-narratives of our times, not the least of which is the asymmetrical integration of what were parts of Mexico into what is now the U.S. Southwest or, as suggested in this volume, is the Southwest North American (SWNA) region and the resulting incorporation of Mexican-origin populations into the U.S. side of the regional social fabric (see chapters 1 and 2).[1] Indeed, the ensuing, dramatic demographic shifts on both sides of the region—primarily due to migration—is a story of emerging inequality, poverty, hunger, and insecurity (Acuña 2007; Zavella 2011). In this chapter, contemporary struggles to overcome these, the actions taken, and justifications articulated continue to trace and put a human face on one of the most remarkable demographic developments of the modern age.[2]

In recent years, immigration has become a highly contentious issue in the United States. An unprecedented number of anti-immigrant measures—numbering in the thousands—have been passed in state legislatures since 2005 (Harnett 2008).

Depending on the state or federal government's interpretation of these laws, immigrants living in the United States may be denied a license, a bank account, and access to social welfare services as if they did not exist or have families to worry about (Wilson 2000). The term "living in the shadows" has popularly been used to refer to the relative invisibility of the estimated 11.1 million undocumented immigrants that these measures are intended to control. Moreover, because they are always at risk of deportation, this presents a paradox because by any other definition their settlement in the United States is real, and permanent. Counter-narratives thus make their permanence visible and shed light on the glaring asymmetries that they contend with on a daily basis (see also chapters 3, 11, 12, and 16). Immigrant stories also reveal meaningful dialogues about values and value systems—systems that articulate and make palpable, among other things, a reliance on households and familiar mores: duty, obligation, and reciprocity, in what might be collectively referred to as an ethical commitment to others. And, as Zavella (2011) has argued, these dialogues take place regardless of whether they are "here" in the United States or "there" in communities of origin, serving to transmit the societal expectations of both. Outside the work of scholars of the Southwest or those engaged in Chicana/o, Latina/o, and ethnic studies, the infusion of this ethos into the United States from outside our nation's borders has remained largely ignored or devalued. However, the extent of its influence on the nation's social tapestry—the nation immigrants increasingly call "home"—cannot be overestimated.

How does this infusion occur? For this chapter, I rely on research conducted from 2006 to 2007 to provide some insight. After a brief description of this study, consisting of interviews with recently repatriated migrant women, I use a selection of narratives to illustrate various patterns of social organization that have given rise to the transnational household structure. Transnationalism refers to the long-term maintenance of cross-border ties between immigrants and their communities of origin that allows for their influences on behavior, practices, and identity to move in both directions (Mouw et al. 2014). Following Mouw and colleagues, I contend that the transborder practices, ideas, and relations that make transnationalism real and visible influence even those who have never migrated (those left behind in the community of origin) and *even if* those who have migrated return home infrequently. This last point becomes particularly salient in discussing the transnational movement of migrants in spite of the increased militarization along the U.S.-Mexico border (chapter 3) intended to dissuade and control the unauthorized crossing of migrants into the United States.

Border enforcement notwithstanding, I argue that patterns of thought and action continue to center around a range of cooperative spheres of activities essential to household form and structure. These include productive, distributive, and reproductive activities (including care of the young, the sick, and the elderly and those activities that transmit values) and coresidence (Netting, Wilk, and Arnould 1984). Migration also imparts important gendered changes with respect to how these activities are carried out and how they are thought about (Hirsch 2002; Cohen, Rodriguez, and Fox 2008). Hirsch (2002) argues that some of the changes in gender roles reflect a greater emphasis on cooperation between men and women (*ayudar* [helping]) that erodes traditional roles for men and women in both sending and settlement communities (see also Wilson 2009). In this chapter, my goal is to use a gendered perspective to further make visible how such changes are manifested through the transnationalization of household forms, within which women play key roles:

- For many migrant women, economic production has become rooted in the United States, but this productive activity continues to be tied—through mores, affect, and function—to the support of households left behind. In other words, while parental or spousal ties may be stretched across borders and across great distances, these ties do not necessarily break.
- Transnational household ties also contract when those left behind (children or spouses) leave their home communities to follow in the footsteps of those who have left for the United States.
- Migrant women, many with U.S.-citizen children, have settled in the United States, although they themselves remain undocumented. The threat of deportation inherently transnationalizes their U.S. households.
- For those settled in the United States, various responsibilities related to household function continue to tie them to their communities of origin.

THE RESEARCH

The narratives and examples used in this chapter come from research[3] conducted at a migrant shelter, Albergue San Juan Bosco, in Nogales, Sonora, Mexico. Nogales, a Mexican border city fifty-five miles south of Tucson, Arizona, lies within a major migration corridor for those in their quest for the opportunities that lie in the United States. Like other migrant shelters along the border, Albergue San Juan Bosco is dedicated to the humanitarian aid of repatriated migrants who have been released from the custody of U.S. authorities and often find themselves alone and vulnerable in a strange city.

Data were gathered using rapid appraisal (RA) techniques (Beebe 2001), which included a semistructured questionnaire for interviewing recently repatriated migrant women. The interviews were conducted in Spanish and, with the interviewees' approval, were tape-recorded. RA techniques also included the use of triangulation to establish validity, which is particularly useful when gathering data from highly mobile and hard-to-reach populations or those engaged in clandestine or extralegal activities where there are incentives to deny them (O'Leary, Valdéz-Gardea, and Sánchez 2013). Triangulation consisted of the comparison and contrasting of information provided by a variety of sources (migrant women, shelter administrators, volunteers, and community leaders) about a range of activities known to impact the migratory experiences. RA also entails a process in which data collection is punctuated by periodic reflection about the data. In this manner a total of 129 repatriated women were interviewed between September 1, 2006, and June 30, 2007. The recorded interviews were transcribed and entered into SIL Fieldworks, a qualitative data analysis software program. Content analysis was performed by searching keywords to identify patterns of thought and action as related by the women interviewed.

One of the objectives of the research was to use the data to theorize cultural transformation subsequent to the migratory experience. A review of the literature indicated that contemporary migration by women may be less motivated by the desire to join husbands than before (Donato 1994; Cerrutti and Massey 2001; Woo Morales 2001). For example, the growing research on domestics, one of the fastest-growing labor sectors and one that undocumented women are most likely to engage in, shows that more Latina women are increasingly migrating as primary wage earners (Wilson 2009). By caring for families in the United States, they often leave their own children behind in the care of others (Hondagneu-Sotelo 1994). In addition, once women begin migrating, they are virtually assured of migrating again, replicating established patterns of circular migration of their male counterparts (Donato 1994).[4] However, my asking women about their migration experience involved more than inquiring about their decisions. It also aimed to understand what their thoughts were during the perilous journey and how those thoughts might have empowered them, strengthened their resolve, or helped them reason and cope with the isolation, fear, and possible death that comes with the migration journey (Marroni and Meneses 2006; O'Leary 2008, 2009a). A section in my field notes devoted to these insights, "Theorizing the Intersection," was used to collect my reflections about these narratives so that I could review them later. For example, my interview with Guadalupe[5] on March 22, 2007, prompted me to write:

> An important dimension of being temporarily suspended in the intersection is poverty, as the present case shows. Another dimension . . . is binationality (for lack of a better term). Take for instance how Guadalupe who, in spite of her U.S. legal residency (and in spite of her twenty years of living and working in the U.S.), has very real connections to Mexico still . . . there is motherhood, family ties, and "things" that need to be taken care of there . . . and the need, desire to belong to both worlds.

Later, an interview with Maria brought out a similar observation, when the topic turned to how she schooled her children about their duties, obligation, and "love" of their culture:

> Upon hearing her children say in English that they hated Mexico, she lectured them on how they can say that if in fact their own mother is Mexican and their father is also Mexican (he lives in Guanajuato). This for now seems to parallel other discussions with other women whose children are U.S. born (or who have children from both nations) about identity and nationhood, leading me to think that the intersection zooms in one's sense of dividedness and resistance to it. The nature of border identity is represented here by the need and desire to belong to both places, and in fact, the ability to do so, thus facilitating the physical and psychological negotiation of the different sides. Thus, although lines and legal definitions attempt to split bodies and individuals from each other, there may be a counter-sensibility that sees the opposites as reconcilable. Maria, in attempting to now belong to Mexico [as the result of her husband's deportation], in spite of her never having lived there, may be incomprehensible for many people.

In this way, the narratives thus helped identify the social and economic contexts that drove women north to cross the U.S.-Mexican border in search of greater opportunities (the mechanics of migration), as well as their thoughts and reasoning. In the sample of 129 women who were interviewed, 125 were women originating from Mexico. Among these 125, there were 73 examples that reflected patterns of thought and deed (shown in table 9.1) that I contend are consistent with how households are theoretically formed and structured, even in the face of the profoundly disruptive and separating process of migration. Each of these patterns will be discussed and illustrated in turn.

TABLE 9.1. Number of Women Reflecting Selected Features of Transnational Households

FEATURE	NUMBER
Economic production, rooted in the United States, is tied to the support of households left behind.	37
Household ties contract when those left behind (children or spouses) leave to join those who now live in the United States.	17
Migrant women, many settled in the United States and with U.S.-citizen children, remain undocumented.	12
For those settled in the United States, various other responsibilities continue to tie them to their communities of origin.	7
Total	73

THE HOUSEHOLD

In the seminal volume by Netting, Wilk, and Arnould (1984), the household is described as the most basic of social units. It operates at the most primordial level of social aggregation larger than the individual. As a strategic social grouping of individuals who may be, but not necessarily are, co-sanguinely related, households are task orientated and the most fundamental of decision-making structures. As such, individual decisions inevitably impact the entire unit. As a well-established sociological unit of analysis, households are theorized as having four continuously operating primary spheres of activity that help delineate the behaviors of its members and give the household its form and structure.[6] These spheres of visible behavior (listed below) allows for the empirical research of actions, values, and symbols that surround this group (Wilk and Netting 1984):

- Production: human activities (remunerated and unremunerated) that increase the value of resources
- Distribution: the movement of material from producers to consumers
- Reproduction: not limited to the sexually pairing of household members, marriage, and the bearing of children but including the socialization and enculturation of younger household members
- Coresidence: evidence of individuals living under one roof or, where this is lacking, the degree of cooperation in production

To this last point, Wilk and Netting (1984, 19) note:

> That a household can operate effectively with some members who are not coresident for extended periods of time is a tribute to the moral imperatives of kinship and reciprocal obligation that flourish in the household context. . . . Those emigrants who send back more money than they expend on themselves at the work place often consider themselves members of the household and expect eventually to return for full-time residence there. . . . households must be examined for the presence of *intermittent coresidents* whose economic contributions adapt local productive and reproductive units to the demands of larger, money-based exchange systems.

In keeping with this theoretical outline of the household, it is necessary to lay claim that a transnationalized form of the household exists due to migration, and in spite of migration. To illustrate, an example of a household where all spheres fundamental to household form and function can be seen operating, but which has not yet become "transnationalized," is illustrated by the following narrative obtained on April 5, 2007:

> Rosalva (18), came from a farming village in Oaxaca, Bajos de Coyula, in the *municipio* of Hautulco. She had finished the *secundaria* and perhaps because of this education had been able to find a job at a pharmacy where she received some more training. She worked for two years at the pharmacy in Oaxaca to help support her family. Her mother worked from the home processing the nopales[7] from her cactus garden and some of the fruit from her trees. She sold her products, for income. Some of the products included *licuado de nopal, nopales a la mexicana*, and *ensalada de fruta*. The mother was also away from the home a lot when she had to go to sell her products. For many years, Rosalva helped her mother take care of the younger siblings. These younger children were now 14, 12, and 7. There were six children in all in their family. Several years ago, Rosalva's father became ill. She did not know what his illness was but only that he had undergone four operations and was unable to work. This is why her mother became essentially the sole support of the household, until Rosalva began working at the pharmacy. However, the pharmacy did not pay well, which is why she saw herself compelled to try something else. Hardship had thus befallen Rosalva's household. To pay for her father's operation they sold some land that had been used for farming, two goats, some of their furniture, and a car. They had been left with only their house. Her older brother had left school to work to help the family. Rosalva thus decided to migrate, despite her mother's opposition.

In its "transnationalized form," Rosalva's household will come to experience the benefits of productive activity ("resource enhancement") that takes place in the United States by way of remittances. In fact, production is enhanced with greater opportunities and higher wages. With the arrival of remittances, household distribution functions (the paying of medical bills and feeding the children) are possible. Rosalva is also fulfilling and transmitting the "moral imperative" of a producer. There is evidence that while women may earn less than men and therefore remit less overall, they are likely to remit more regularly (Cohen, Rodriguez, and Fox 2008). In Oaxacan communities, remittances were shown to go toward the costs of living in the sending household, home construction or renovation, education expenses, and consumer goods (Cohen, Rodriguez, and Fox 2008).

TRANSNATIONAL HOUSEHOLD FORM AND FUNCTION

STRETCHING HOUSEHOLD TIES

At the migrant shelter, it was common to find migrants with family members already working in the United States. Some of those interviewed had in fact been encouraged by these family members to join them in the United States, where they were promised help in finding jobs. If they succeeded in crossing into the United States, the households of these migrants are likely to become transnationalized. A good illustration of this comes from my interview of Paula (18) from San Francisco Tlaloc, Puebla, in April 2006. She was five months pregnant when I met her at the shelter. Her plan was to go to California to join her husband, who had been working there for eight years. With the money her husband had been sending from the United States, they were able to build a house in their hometown, and they planned to return there eventually.

However, the process by which economic production becomes firmly implanted enough to help maintain households in distant places begins with poverty and the "necessary evil" to leave loved ones behind in search of work (Hirsch 2002, 371). For many, this was an emotionally painful experience, such as for Veronica (26) from Guerrero, a soft-spoken woman who was present at the shelter in May 2007. When I first saw her she had a rather large gash on the right side of her forehead. While it is not unusual to see women with many scratches on their faces and arms (the result of plowing through thick brush as they go through the desert, often in the dark, and as they run from agents), this gash was unusually long and deep. There was a small blood clot still caked on the lower end of the gash. She related to me why she had migrated:

> I have three girls. One is 3 years old, and the others are 4 and 5, and my son will be 7 soon . . . my husband earns very little and I sell chickens in the streets. I don't have a home. If I sell a chicken, I have money to buy something to eat. If not, I have to find something to fill the stomachs of my children. We are living in my mother's house and she doesn't want us there. I had to take my daughter out of school because the teacher says I need to get her shoes. Well, I couldn't buy them for her.[8]

With her last utterance, Veronica broke into a tearful sob.

Veronica's situation contrasts with that of Paula's (above) because hers is a household not yet transnationalized with economic production in the United States. Once rooted in the U.S. economy, return migration becomes a driving force, such as in the case of Juana (24), who had come from San Pedro Conchutla, Oaxaca. Of athletic build and engaging personality, Juana considered it her good fortune not to have been robbed by the bandits who routinely prey on migrants and not to have been mistreated by the apprehending U.S. Border Patrol officers. This was her second attempt at crossing, and of the conditions in San Pedro Conchutla, she said there was everything there except prosperity. Economically, there is nothing and not enough for her family. She left her four children with her ex-mother-in-law. The children's father migrated to the United States four years ago but abandoned Juana for another woman. Juana had already worked in the United States. She had merely returned to

Oaxaca because she had become pregnant and wanted to give birth there. After a year, she was ready to return to the United States and to her job in construction putting up sheetrock, an occupation that might be considered by many Oaxacan communities as threatening to the idealized notions of womanhood (Cohen, Rodriguez, and Fox 2008). However, she was well paid in this job, earning between $18 and $20 an hour. When she first started, she earned $10 an hour. But as she improved, she earned more. She was obviously proud of this accomplishment and confident in her abilities. She was jovial and laughed while saying:

> Soy muy vaquetona y en donde sea pues yo no me rajo. Ya ahorita cuando cruce la segunda vez y ya no pude, dije que la tercera vez . . .
>
> [I am very hardy and where ever I may be, well, I don't give up. Like now, having failed to cross on my second attempt I said (to myself), on the third . . .]

Juana, similar to some of the working migrant women in Atlanta, Georgia, interviewed by Hirsch (2002, 365) was a woman who had achieved a measure of autonomy, "*valerse por si misma*" (roughly translated as "having self-worth").

As for many others, Juana's rationale for reaching the United States in spite of the risks is essentially economic in nature: most of the women interviewed at the shelter were migrating because there were few opportunities in their home community to help them support their children (see also Cohen, Rodriguez, and Fox 2008), and their children were suffering as a result. In contrast, the continued economic growth of the United States economy and its demand for labor have attracted migrants, beckoning them to cross the border. In this way, and perhaps with some measure of determination and persistence, economic production becomes embedded in the United States. Above all, these examples illustrate how this process is fundamentally linked to the provisioning of households left behind and show how parental ties may be stretched across borders and across great distances, while not necessarily breaking.

IN THE FOOTSTEPS OF THOSE WHO HAVE GONE BEFORE

There is no reason to believe that those left behind will stay behind indefinitely. In Hirsch's research (2002), migrant women living in Atlanta were daughters and granddaughters who had worked picking cotton in Texas, and in this way, Mexican communities had been integrated into the orbit of the U.S. economy and influenced by its culture. In the research by Cohen and colleagues (2008), 60 percent of the migrant women interviewed who were bound for the United States followed a relative who had already migrated there. Similarly, in the sample of women I interviewed, there was evidence of women migrating north to join their husbands, adult children migrating to join their parents who are living and working in the United States, and to a lesser degree, parents migrating to join their adult children living in the United States.[9] These examples provide further evidence that parental and kinship ties—for however long and however far—are being kept intact.

Keeping households intact can be sustained for years with the help of sheer will and determination. In some cases, years go by before wives and husbands entertain plans to be together. Yadira (23) was mother to a young son, Adrian, age four, who was with her at the shelter. They had come from a small agricultural town in Chiapas. She was migrating to the United States to join her husband who had been away for five years and did not even know his son. Although she could not remember what the name of their destination was, her objective was clear: father and son would be reunited and know each other. The boy had been very brave and remarkably strong in keeping up with his mother in a group of around twenty-four migrants. They had traveled on foot for two days and two nights before they were arrested by enforcement agents.

Children migrating north to be with parents—both unaccompanied and with other adults—is a common pattern in this process of transnationalization (Heidbrink 2014). In 2013, the number of unaccompanied youth from Central American nations surpassed the numbers coming from Mexico (figure 9.1) (U.S. Customs and Border Protection 2015). Up until then, the percentage of Mexican children dominated this pattern (figure 9.2). Among the adult women interviewed for the study, several were bringing adolescents with them to join mothers. For example, Esmeralda (20) from Jalapa, Veracruz, was bringing with her a younger family member, Margarita (16), who was not her child. Also interviewed was Lucila (18), who had plans of reaching Chicago after delivering her young cousin, Alva (9), to her mother. Alva had not seen her mother since she was three years old. Alva's older brother (15) had managed to cross into the United States earlier. In another example, Rosita, interviewed in February 2006, was an eighteen-year-old mother of a seven-month-old infant. She, her husband, and her child were part of a larger group apprehended by the U.S. Border Patrol, which included a cousin, a couple with three children (ages 2, 3, 5), and a childless couple. Rosita was on her way to Oregon where the rest of her family lived. Her parents had left their children in Paracho, Michoacán, ten years ago when they migrated to the United States when Rosita was nine and the oldest of four children. The children were left with Rosita's grandmother and aunts and Rosita helped raise her younger siblings. At that time, the youngest was a little over one year old. Over the years, Rosita's parents had made arrangements with a trusted *coyote* to bring the children to the United States to be with their parents. Rosita was the last of the siblings to make the journey.

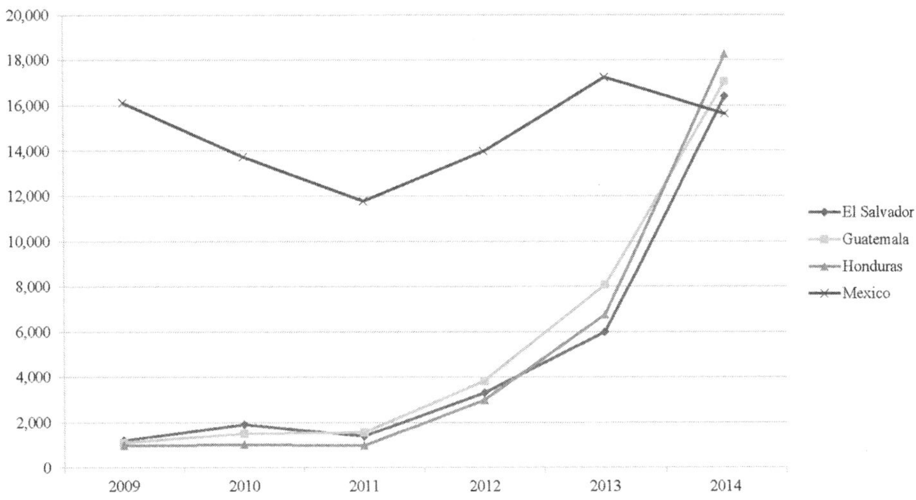

FIGURE 9.1. Unaccompanied children apprehended FY 2009–2014 by country of origin.

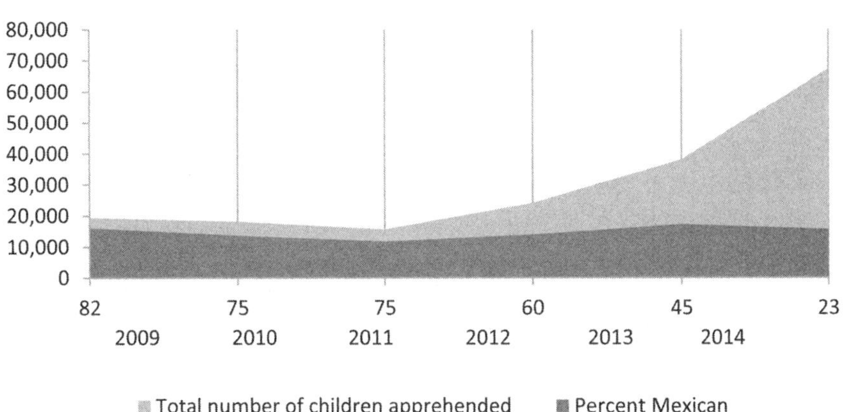

FIGURE 9.2. Unaccompanied Mexican children apprehended as percent of total by fiscal years 2009–2014. Source: U.S. Customs and Border Protection (2015).

Through this course by which households are transnationalized, immigrant stories of family reunification and commitment to each other also articulate culturally meaningful dialogues about values and value systems—systems that articulate and make palpable among other things a reliance on a sense of duty and obligation to care for and protect those made vulnerable by the ravages of poverty (also see chapter 17). This ethical stance is arguably a safeguard against the consequences of losing household members to the trappings of materialism, to new freedoms from the constraints of traditions—the values that undergird a capitalist society premised on individualism and consumerism. These values compete with those that call for sacrifice and familial devotion, and the expectations that ultimately socialize children, who may someday migrate also. About this process, Hackenberg, Murphy, and Selby (1984, 188) have argued:

> The state needs a skilled and disciplined work force to man its industries in the formal economy of modern capitalist firms and enterprises. These needs are met through recruitment of members from households of the poor. . . . The households of the poor which lose their members also lose their battle for economic betterment. . . . Sometimes the household wins, and through the combined efforts of . . . generations of kinfolk or grown children living together and working for the common good they are able to rise from destitution to a tolerable level of poverty and to achieve the beginnings of a decent life for all the members.

What is to prevent those who have migrated from abandoning the common, collective goals that define the household? Cohen and colleagues provides some insight that addresses this question that comes from his research in Oaxacan communities. His research shows that migrants typically follow family or friends to the United States, and these resources help cover the costs of migration once they settle in the United States and translate into material benefits for sending households by way of remittances (Cohen, Rodriguez, and Fox 2008). These innately social networks of support represent the social resources necessary for migration, including the networks needed to facilitate migration (Singer and Massey 1998; Granberry and Marcelli 2007; Wilson 2009). Household members who migrate and invest their time and energy to assure the welfare of their domestic groups are rewarded with additional resources, including the much-needed "trust" and "access" that has the potential to cut across kin and non-kin ties and transcend borders and geographical distances (O'Leary 2012). On the other hand, those who neglect their commitments, and hoard their resources as their economic status rises, limit the strength, prestige, and visibility of their family—both for those who remain at home and for those in settlement communities—risking a withering away of social resources (Cohen 2001).

UNDOCUMENTED, AND (UN)SETTLED IN THE UNITED STATES

The intensification of border enforcement in recent years, and especially since 9/11, has disrupted cyclical migration (Hines 2002), through which kinship ties are renewed and strengthened (Cohen, Rodriguez, and Fox 2008). Migrants who succeed in finding jobs in the United States are thus more inclined to settle into what resembles a permanent residency there, were it not for their undocumented status, which predisposes them to deportation if apprehended by law enforcement agents. The quasi-permanent state of living in the United States has resulted in a growing number of children who are born in the United States and are therefore U.S. citizens. Inherent contradictions thus result from the incorporation of undocumented immigrants into the United States in this way (Ngai 2007). As early as 1988, Chavez drew scholarly attention to this phenomenon by pointing out that undocumented immigrants often form families in the United States, resulting in children who are U.S. citizens within what he referred to as "binational families." Thus, measures directed at controlling undocumented immigrants who are also parents of children living in the United States—measures that may in fact result in their removal from the country—logically impacts all those who are household members regardless of immigration status (Fix and Zimmermann 2001; Romero 2008; O'Leary and Sánchez 2011; Castañeda and Melo 2014) and in particular those who are economically dependent on those parents for support. Contending with the possibility of being forcibly returned to Mexico brings out the transnationalized nature of such households.

In the sample of women interviewed, there were twelve women who had U.S.-born children, but the phenomenon may be more widespread. In research by Slack and colleagues, half of the respondents (deported migrants) reported having left U.S.-citizen children behind in the United States (Slack et al. 2013). Here I briefly summarize the narratives of three women that best illustrate the transnationalization of their households, even after families have settled in the U.S. side of the border. In the first interview, with Lucia, I learned that she had been living in the United States for twenty years, after having entered through the Mexicali area as an undocumented immigrant. She now had two daughters, ages twenty and three. She and her husband had returned lately to Mexico to visit her husband's ailing mother. She was at the shelter alone, wondering where her husband was. She sobbed at the thought that perhaps he was still detained because presently she did not know where he was. He had not shown up at the shelter. She shared with me that she hoped that her older daughter, who is a U.S. citizen, could help her get a permit to reenter the United States. Her own mother, also living in the United States, was taking care of the younger daughter.

I also interviewed Sara, a U.S. citizen who was at the shelter because her husband, an undocumented worker, had been deported. She was visibly upset and hardly interacted with the other women there. She stated that she and her husband lived in New Mexico, where they had three children together. He was arrested crossing the border in the Douglas area after visiting his family in Mexico, and now she had spent all of the money they had to come to Nogales to pick him up. She would be here at the shelter until her husband could cross over again. He had plans to try to cross the border wall as soon as he could from a place there in Nogales. But Sara had suggested to him that they instead all move to Agua Prieta where his family has a house. From there, she could send her children to Douglas (right across the border from Agua Prieta in Arizona) to attend school. She did not want to continue to live in fear that he would risk arrest and face extended jail time.[10]

Finally, I interviewed Maria who was at the shelter not because she had been apprehended but because her husband had been arrested and deported two days ago. After this event, Maria brought her two children with her from Phoenix in the family van. They were at the shelter attempting to resolve their predicament. Maria did not want her husband to attempt to return to the United States without authorization because she was afraid that if arrested, he would be sentenced and imprisoned. The children were not happy about their situation but appeared to be trying to make the best of it. What is interesting about Maria is that her mother is a U.S. citizen and all of her siblings were born in the United States. Maria, for reasons that are unclear, was born in Mexicali. Her mother took her to the United States when Maria was two months old. Therefore, Maria was not U.S. born and she had never lived in Mexico. Just before the interview, Maria had just learned that her husband had found work in Nogales, Sonora. Now Maria was planning on settling here (in Mexico) along with her children so that she can be with her husband and keep her family together.

In these narratives, both separation and reunification can be seen as different sides of the same coin (O'Leary 2009b; also see chapter 2). The rival tensions are reconciled in what may be described as transnational household forms, which are the basis for the cross-border organization of household functions, upon which migrant mobility systems, family ties, and settlement depend.

OTHER RESPONSIBILITIES RELATED TO HOUSEHOLD FUNCTION

In the sample of 125 Mexican migrant women interviewed, there were 7 who had voluntarily left their homes in the United States to return to their home communities. When I interviewed them, they were attempting to return to the United States after a brief stay in their communities of origin. Hirsch (2002) explains that in periods when the U.S. economy was strong, women could quit their jobs in November to return to their home communities to celebrate the Christmas season with family, confident that upon their return, they would easily find another job (Hirsch 2002). Among the women interviewed, there were other, non-celebratory reasons that the women had for returning to Mexico. For example, Elizabeth took her children from their home in Mississippi to flee her alcoholic and abusive husband. She returned home to recuperate her health and reassess her situation. Juana returned to her home community to give birth, and Lucia had gone with her husband to visit her ailing mother-in-law. Minerva had returned after years of living with her family in the United States to finish her education back in her community of origin in Puebla. What is important to note is that very often the different spheres of activities related to a transnationalized household overlap, as the following example illustrates:

> Catalina and Angeles were present at the shelter when I arrived on October 12, 2006. The women had attempted to cross three times. The conversation was quite animated, punctuated with frequent laughter as the women reflected on their experiences and the comedic nature of the Border Patrol agents in hot pursuit of migrants in the desert in the dark. They intended to reach "las Carolinas" where they had friends working in agriculture. They were unclear about whether or not they would attempt to cross again, although Angeles stated that on a previous occasion she had been deported three times before making it through on the fourth attempt. Both had children who had been left in Mexico with grandparents. Angeles had family, including her father, who lived in New York. She had lived in New York and in Los Angeles for several years, having come to the United States at age 14. She had lived there twelve years. During those years she worked as a housekeeper and live-in nanny to children of a Jewish family. Angeles had been living in Mexico now for several years. . . . She has three children. The youngest is a little girl that was born in the United States.

To a lesser degree, my subsample of Mexican migrant women indicated that a few returned periodically to their communities of origin to attend to any one of several life cycle events and rituals (such as funerals) known to fulfill symbolic functions of household organization. This may have been due to the economic downturn of the time, from 2006 to 2007. However, Cohen (2001) has documented the periodic return of Oaxacan migrants, many of whom belong to peasant indigenous communities, averaging two or three trips over their career in fulfillment of obligations related to the ritual life of their communities. Many of the funds needed to support these community rituals come from wages earned by migrants in United States.

CONCLUDING THOUGHTS

In the various ways described in this chapter, transnationalized households defy borders and are maintained across geographies. The different but often-overlapping spheres of household activity help make visible a range of behaviors and values that infuse this domestic group with purpose and tenacity.

These narratives show that women are central to household form and function, so an examination of their roles is an opportunity to identify these activities that may not otherwise be considered essential to integration and nation-building. The idea that women contribute to these macro-level processes, through their roles in household formation and function, is thus key to reconceptualizing schemes of analysis that have made the quotidian invisible. Moreover, conventional approaches to understanding migration often erroneously assume the enforceability of political boundaries and also often assume that processes taking place within national boundaries can be easily separated from those outside (Wimmer and Schiller 2003). That increased border enforcement traps migrants in, making the immigrant household a quasi-permanent feature of U.S. society, is only but one factor in a multifaceted process that starts with poverty. Growing inequality (chapter 10) and weakened confidence that household members will ever be fully absorbed by the existing economic order reinforce important ideological components intrinsic to households, among which are the ethical commitments to keep members close, safe, protected, nurtured, and buoyed with hopes for a better future. Ultimately, basic principles of household organization strengthen the linkages and systems of migrant mobility, and this undermines the state and its authoritative structures (O'Leary 2009b).

Deepening economic instability in Mexico has heightened the importance of migration, and with the increased migration of women, women's roles also become elevated in importance. Hirsh (2003) has argued that for women, migration has been a natural extension of household responsibilities. In acknowledging the importance of their roles, agency is restored to them and they become more than mere reflections of the macro-structural. Instead, they are shown as instrumental in contesting and giving shape to the relations of power and dominion that impinge on their lives. For example, for some immigrant women working as eldercare providers, the workplace provides an important place where humane ideals about the care for kin, assistance, respect for elders, and the presence of others—the "ethics of care"—is played out. This set of culturally and historically circumscribed behaviors offer Mexican immigrant women the opportunity to model behavior and to teach others the "right" way of being human (Ibarra 2003). Just as important in this regard, the roles of migrant women coalesce with the broader trends of working women in general, trends that reflect how women who are also caregivers strategically and simultaneously accommodate economic production activities (Romero 2000). This situates the household—regardless of the borders and distances that stretch its resources and ties—as the site of reorientation: a central node from which the production, maintenance, and diffusion of an ethos emerge and which holds promises for influencing the nation's identity and attitudes, especially with regard to the impoverished, the destitute, the young and vulnerable, the sick and elderly, and the foreigner and newcomer. Despite the drop in the fertility rates among immigrant (primarily Mexican) immigrant mothers in the United States, foreign-born women still represent a significant portion of all mothers giving birth in this country (Livingston 2012). The ethics of their cultural formation—or at least some version of it—thus follow. Together with the declining birthrates of the non-immigrant population in the United States, this demographic shift will provide structural opportunities for immigrant populations and their descendants. In the end, the shift assures that a rethinking about certain societal values around family, household, and belonging will take place and will work to challenge and reconstitute political spheres in years to come.

NOTES

1. For example, well-researched histories such as that by Acuña (2007) document how Mexican workers routinely toiled in the United States for starvation wages, suffering discrimination and humiliation in the process. Resistance to such inequities was kept at bay throughout the U.S. Southwest through violence, policing, unjust laws, residential segregation, and occupational segregation and discriminatory wage systems (the "adobe ceiling") in principal sectors of employment such as mining and agriculture (Acuña 2007, 171).
2. Between 1990 and 2005, the increase in the number of migrants in the North America region grew at an average rate of 3.2 percent per year, faster than in any other region in the world (United Nations 2006). Within this region, the United States was destination to more migrants than any other nation—for an estimated 44.1 million (in 2010)—four times higher than for any other country in the world (Connor and López 2016). Over the past four decades, the single largest group of Latin American immigrants in the United States has been from Mexico, topping out at 40 percent of all immigrants in this country today (Gonzalez-Barrera and López 2013).
3. Funding for this research was provided by a Fulbright Garcia-Robles award, 2006–2007.
4. Donato (1994) points out that recent policy changes intended to curb migration have proven ineffective because they are unable to curb the ties between migrants and their U.S. employers that institutionalize and make self-sustaining the cyclical nature of migration.

5. All names of the women interviewed have been changed to pseudonyms to protect their identities.
6. A fifth, "Transmission," is mentioned and considered less relevant for this paper, and is defined as a node in the household history related to the intergenerational transmission of wealth and property, and patterns of authority that defend and confer inheritance rights to property.
7. Nopales are the pads from the prickly pear cactus. These pads are plucked from the plant, scraped clean of their small splinters, and then diced and sold in bags for cooking. The raw diced nopales can then be cooked in water and mixed with other ingredients (such as chiles or eggs) for a savory dish.
8. Her words are translated from the Spanish.
9. This research did not include interviewing minors under the age of 18. According to U.S. immigration enforcement authorizes, unaccompanied migrant children who are apprehended are to be turned over to consulate authorities for removal to appropriate agencies in Mexico not to nongovernmental shelters such as where the interviews for the research took place.
10. With each successive arrest, immigrants face longer jail time (Alvarado 2004).

REFERENCES

Acuña, Rudolfo F. 2007. *Corridors of Migration: The Odyssey of Mexican Laborers, 1600–1933*. Tucson: University of Arizona Press.

Alvarado, Jeanette E. 2004. "The Federal Consequences of Criminal Convictions: Illegal Reentry After Removal." Unpublished manuscript prepared for the State Bar of Arizona.

Beebe, James. 2001. *Rapid Assessment Process: An Introduction*. Walnut Creek, CA: AltaMira.

Castañeda, Heide, and Milena Andrea Melo. 2014. "Health Care Access for Latino Mixed-Status Families: Barriers, Strategies, and Implications for Reform." *American Behavioral Scientist* 58(14): 1891–1909.

Cerrutti, Marcela, and Douglas S. Massey. 2001. "On the Auspices of Female Migration from Mexico to the United States." *Demography* 38(2): 187–201.

Cohen, Jeffrey H. 2001. "Transnational Migration in Rural Oaxaca, Mexico: Dependency, Development, and the Household." *American Anthropologist* 103(4): 954–67.

Cohen, Jeffrey H., Leila Rodriguez, and Margaret Fox. 2008. "Gender and Migration in the Central Valleys of Oaxaca." *International Migration* 46(1): 79–101.

Connor, Phillip, and Gustavo López. 2016. "5 Facts About the U.S. Rank in Worldwide Migration." http://www.pewresearch.org/fact-tank/2016/05/18/5-facts-about-the-u-s-rank-in-worldwide-migration/.

Donato, Katherine M. 1994. "Current Trends and Patterns of Female Migration: Evidence from Mexico." *International Migration Review* 27(4): 748–72.

Fix, Michael, and Wendy Zimmermann. 2001. "All Under One Roof: Mixed-Status Families in an Era of Reform." *International Migration Review* 35(2): 397–419.

Gonzalez-Barrera, Ana, and Mark Hugo López. 2013. "A Demographic Portrait of Mexican-Origin Hispanics in the United States." Washington, DC: Pew Research Center. http://www.pewhispanic.org/files/2013/05/2013-04_Demographic-Portrait-of-Mexicans-in-the-US.pdf.

Granberry, Phillip J., and Enrico A. Marcelli. 2007. "'In the Hood and On the Job': Social Capital Accumulation Among Legal and Unauthorized Mexican Migrants." *Sociological Perspectives* 50(4): 579–95.

Hackenberg, Robert, Arthur D. Murphy, and Henry A. Selby. 1984. "The Urban Household in Dependent Development." In *Households: Comparative and Historical Studies of the Domestic Group*, edited by Robert McC. Netting, Richard R. Wilk, and Eric J. Arnould, 187–217. Berkeley: University of California Press.

Harnett, Helen M. 2008. "State and Local Anti-Immigrant Initiatives: Can They Withstand Legal Scrutiny?" *Widener Law Journal* 17:365–82.

Heidbrink, Lauren. 2014. *Migrant Youth, Transnational Families, and the State: Care and Contested Interests*. Philadelphia: University of Pennsylvania Press.

Hines, Barbara. 2002. "So Near Yet So Far Away: The Effect of September 11th on Mexican Immigrants in the United States." *Texas Hispanic Journal of Law and Policy* 8 (37): 37–46.

Hirsch, Jennifer S. 2002. "'Que, pues, con el pinche NAFTA?' Gender, Power and Migration Between Western Mexico and Atlanta." *Urban Anthropology and Studies of Cultural Systems and World Economic Development* 31(3/4): 351–89.

Hondagneu-Sotelo, Pierrette. 1994. *Gendered Transitions: Mexican Experiences of Immigration*. Berkeley: University of California Press.

Ibarra, Maria de la Luz. 2003. "The Tender Trap: Mexican Immigrant Women and the Ethics of Elder Care Work." *Aztlán: A Journal of Chicano Studies* 28(2): 87–112.

Livingston, Gretchen, and D'Vera Cohn. 2012. "U.S. Birthrate Falls to a Record Low: Decline Is Greatest Amongst Immigrants." Washington, DC: Pew Research Center. http://www.pewsocialtrends.org/files/2012/11/Birth_Rate_Final.pdf.

Marroni, Maria da Gloria, and Alonso Meneses. 2006. "El fín del sueño americano: Mujeres migrantes muertas en la frontera México-Estados Unidos." *Migraciones Internacionales* 3(3): 5–30.

Mouw, Ted, Sergio Chavez, Heather Edelblute, and Ashton Verdery. 2014. "Binational Social Networks and Assimilation: A Test of the Importance of Transnationalism." *Social Problems* 61(3): 329–59.

Netting, Robert McC., Richard R. Wilk, and Erik J. Arnould. 1984. Introduction to *Households: Comparative and Historical Studies of the Domestic Group*, edited by Robert McC. Netting, Richard R. Wilk, and Eric J. Arnould, xiii–xxxviii. Berkeley: University of California Press.

Ngai, Mae M. 2007. "Birthright Citizenship and the Alien Citizen." *Fordham Law Review* 75:2521–30.

O'Leary, Anna Ochoa. 2008. "Close Encounters of the Deadly Kind: Gender, Migration, and Border (In)Security." *Migration Letters* 15(2): 111–22.

———. 2009a. "In the Footsteps of Spirits: Migrant Women's Testimonios in a Time of Heightened Border Enforcement." In *Violence, Security, and Human Rights at the Border*, edited by Kathleen Staudt, Tony Payan, and Z. Anthony Kruszewski, 91–112. Tucson: University of Arizona Press.

———. 2009b. "*Mujeres en el cruce*: Remapping Border Security Through Migrant Mobility." *Journal of the Southwest* 51(4): 523–42.

———. 2012. "Of Coyotes, Cooperation, and Capital." In *Political Economy, Neoliberalism, and the Prehistoric Economies of Latin America*, edited by Ty Matejowsky and Donald C. Wood, 133–60. Bingley, UK: Emerald Group Publishing Ltd.

O'Leary, Anna Ochoa, and Azucena Sánchez. 2011. "Anti-immigrant Arizona: Ripple Effects and Mixed Immigration Status Households Under 'Policies of Attrition' Considered." *Journal of Borderlands Studies* 26(1): 115–33.

O'Leary, Anna Ochoa, Gloria Ciria Valdéz-Gardea, and Azucena Sánchez. 2013. "Reflections on Methodological Challenges in a Study of Immigrant Women and Reproductive Health in the U.S.-Mexico Border Region." In *Uncharted Terrains: New Directions in Border Research Methodology, Ethics, and Practice*, edited by Anna Ochoa O'Leary, Colin M. Deeds, and Scott Whiteford, 184–205. Tucson: University of Arizona Press.

Romero, Mary. 2000. "Bursting the Foundational Myths of Reproductive Labor Under Capitalism: A Call for Brave New Families or Brave New Villages?" *Journal of Gender, Social Policy and the Law* 8:177–95.

———. 2008. "The Inclusion of Citizenship Status in Intersectionality: What Immigration Raids Tells Us About Mixed-Status Families, the State, and Assimilation." *International Journal of the Family* 34(2): 131–52.

Singer, Audrey, and Douglas S. Massey. 1998. "The Social Process of Undocumented Border Crossing Among Mexican Migrants." *International Migration Review* 32(3): 561–92.

Slack, Jeremy, Daniel E. Martinez, Scott Whiteford, and Emily Pieffer. 2013. "In the Shadow of the Wall: Family Separation, Immigration Enforcement and Security: Preliminary Data from the Migrant Border Crossing Study." Tucson: Center for Latin American Studies, University of Arizona.

United Nations. 2006. *United Nations International Migration Report 2006: A Global Assessment. Part I: International Migration Levels, Trends and Policies.* New York: Population Division, United Nations Department of Economic and Social Affairs.

U.S. Customs and Border Protection. 2015. "Southwest Border Unaccompanied Alien Children Statistics FY2015." https://www.cbp.gov/newsroom/stats/southwest-border-unaccompanied-children/fy-2015.

Wilk, Richard R., and Robert McC. Netting. 1984. "Households: Changing Forms and Functions." In *Households: Comparative and Historical Studies of the Domestic Group*, edited by Robert McC. Netting, Richard R. Wilk, and Eric J. Arnould, 1–28. Berkeley: University of California Press.

Wilson, Tamar, D. 2000. "Anti-immigrant Sentiment and the Problem of Reproduction/Maintenance in Mexican Immigration to the United States." *Critique of Anthropology* 20(2): 191–213.

———. 2009. *Women's Migration Networks in Mexico and Beyond*. Albuquerque: University of New Mexico Press.

Woo Morales, Ofelia, 2001. *Las mujeres también nos vamos al Norte*. Guadalajara, Jalisco, Mexico: Universidad de Guadalajara.

Zavella, Patricia. 2011. *I'm Neither Here Nor There: Mexicans' Quotidian Struggles with Migration and Poverty*. Durham, NC: Duke University Press.

10

NEOLIBERAL POLICIES AND THE RESHAPING OF THE U.S.-MEXICO BORDER

The Case of Arizona

JAMES GREENBERG AND
LUMINIȚA-ANDA MANDACHE

SINCE REAGAN AND THATCHER became advocates of neoliberalism in the 1980s, there has been a rampant increase in the application of its policies. Despite its record of exacerbating inequalities in many countries, conservatives in the United States are championing their application. Neoliberal policies are being tried where Republicans control the state legislature, Arizona being a prime example.

This chapter is divided into three major sections. The first section provides a theoretical frame for understanding North American forms of neoliberalism and how its advocates seek to use numbers and statistics to rationalize and justify these policies. The second section examines Arizona's experiment with neoliberalism, with specific attention to how neoliberal values have shaped state budgets and legislation since 1980. The final section documents the impacts that neoliberal cuts and budget priorities have had on the people of Arizona in education and law enforcement and in increasing racism. Finally, this case study raises questions about neoliberal policies as a form of governance and the inequality these foster in our democracy. In analyzing Arizona's budget and cuts to spending, we argue that following neoliberal practices, Republicans favor numbers that appear to justify "economic growth" but also deploy rhetorics of fear and racism against (illegal) immigrants as justifications for greater investment in security, e.g., policing and prisons. The neoliberal discourse has also been used to justify cuts to social programs and other so-called "nonproductive sectors." As well, neoliberal ideas about privatization stand behind attempts to privatize public lands and appear to motivate cuts in funding to public schools, state universities, and colleges as part of an effort to push their privatization and operations on market principles. In Arizona, they have been also used to advance the privatization of state prisons. In implementing these policies, the champions of neoliberalism ignore other high numbers such as rising tuition costs, or the racial and ethnic disparity in rates of incarceration, or the fact that the United States has more incarcerated people than any other country.

NORTH AMERICAN FORMS OF NEOLIBERALISM

Neoliberalism is a form of market fundamentalism that arose as a right-wing reaction to the ideas of the British economist John Maynard Keynes, which guided President Franklin D. Roosevelt's New Deal. Its roots lie in the work of Friedrich Hayek, an economist at the London School of Economics. In 1944 Hayek wrote *The Road to Serfdom*, a critique of Keynesian economics, which, he argued, smacked of socialism, centrally planned economies, and totalitarianism. In the United States Hayek's ideas inspired a group of economists, historians, and philosophers whose ideas became entrenched in the so-called Chicago School. This movement gained increasing legitimacy when the Noble Prize for Economics was awarded to Hayek in 1974 and to Milton Friedman in 1976. During the 1980s under Reagan in the United States and Thatcher in the United Kingdom, neoliberalism became regent (Greenberg et al. 2012, 34–35). At neoliberalism's core is a faith that competition in a free market is the most efficient way to allocate scarce resources and that government attempts to regulate the free functioning of markets are misguided. Because neoliberals advocate free markets and free trade, in their view government is too large, too far-reaching, and too costly, so taxes are too high. Guided by this credo, neoliberals favor privatization, deregulation of markets, and the elimination of the concepts of "public good" or "community" (Martinez and Garcia 2000). Specifically, they advocate downsizing government by cutting government spending for social programs and welfare services, and privatizing any government services that can be provided by private firms competing in the marketplace (Ross and Gibson 2006).

What is hidden in their high-sounding language about free trade and competition in free markets is that if goods are allocated this way, access to resources quickly becomes simply a matter of the ability to pay. While the neoliberal argument that competition will bring down costs may work in economic models, in actual markets this may or may not be true, because goods may not be competitive or open to all. Because neoliberals expose an extreme form of individualism, they show little concern over issues of equity or with "equal opportunities" (World Bank 2006, xi). Our main critique of neoliberal ideology is its obsession with certain numbers and its narrow understanding of economy as reduced to mathematics. As Sarah Babb (2005) observed in earlier intellectual debates between supporters of modernization and dependency theorists, although the relationship between poor and wealthy nations divided their discussion, both sides advocated for strong government involvement. With the neoliberal turn, both the World Bank's structural adjustment plans and the International Monetary Fund's policies fell in line with the new conventional wisdom that "demanded a dramatic downsizing of many government interventions . . . and suggested that it was only through liberating the market forces that the poor countries could grow and catch up to the developed world" (Babb 2005, 200). Babb adds that while under the older paradigm theorists came from all across the social sciences, the debate over the new model has been held primarily among economists; consequently, it is economists who have done most of the impact studies of these policies.

Often lurking behind neoliberal policies are large-scale transfers of resources into private hands. Commonly, the impacts of such privatizations are devastating for those who had enjoyed their usufruct. David Harvey (2003) has argued that such transfers constitute massive exercises in "accumulation by dispossession" and that neoliberal policies, rather than helping the poor, simply perpetuate and magnify existing power relations and inequalities. Ross and Gibson describe neoliberalism as an ideological monoculture where "a relative handful of private interests are permitted to control as much as possible of social life in order to maximize their personal profit" (2006, 2). They go on to argue that neoliberal policies of free markets pushed by private interests and a complicit state have contributed to increasing inequalities. Weaver et al. (2012) have also documented the profound impacts that neoliberal policies (such as the North American Free Trade Agreement [NAFTA] and the Central American Free Trade Agreement [CAFTA]) have had in Mexico on local economies, revealing how these policies have undermined rural smallholders, causing a mass out-migration both into Mexican cities and to the United States. While the record of neoliberalism is clear and needs no clarification, as political process its practices and experiments deserve close scrutiny: how neoliberalism is politically implemented, we argue, is just as important as its underlying ideas.

The implementation of the neoliberal policies has run parallel to the increase in global inequality. Presently, the top 1 percent of households in United States own 40 percent of nation's wealth. Despite our "strong economy," the number of Americans without health insurance rose from 1 million in 1999 to 44.3 million in 2006 (Ross and Gibson 2006), although under Obama, it has come down to 33 million (Henry J. Kaiser Family Foundation 2015). President Obama in his State of the Union Address in 2014 underlined how a serious economic and social inequality remains:

> Today, after four years of economic growth, corporate profits and stock prices have rarely been higher, and those at the top have never done better. But average wages have barely budged. Inequality has deepened. Upward mobility has stalled. The cold, hard fact is that even in the midst of recovery, too many Americans are working more than ever just to get by—let alone get ahead.

In this regard Arizona presents a particularly interesting and potentially instructive case. Because Republicans have long dominated the state legislature, they have had a free hand to do pioneering experiments in implementing neoliberal ideas. Of the fifty states, Arizona has pioneered deep cuts in education and public services. Unfortunately, the violence along the U.S.-Mexico border has also served a pretext in Arizona for the resurgence of identity politics in which poverty and crime stand as code words for race and class. In this chapter, we will document the increasing privatization of state services (key examples being education and prisons) and look closely at the long-term human and economic costs of these decisions. In doing so, we argue that neoliberal policies legitimized their discourse by making ideologically driven assumptions about reality that both define assumed problems and shape the policies meant to address them. More precisely, we argue that there is a dialectical relationship between their numbers and their construction of reality. Neoliberalism as practiced by Republicans in Arizona uses statistics on immigrants and crime that play upon strong nationalist and anti-immigrant sentiments to justify ever-higher investments in border security and prisons. Neoliberal emphasis on privatization and security, however, necessarily ignores their high costs because they are correlated with cuts from what is defined as the "unproductive sectors" of the state's budget. Arizona's experience in this regard bears a remarkable resemblance to the World Bank and the International Monetary Fund's implementation of structural adjustment policies while ignoring their social costs. Similarly, such loans were used to pressure nations to further privatize state resources even as poverty levels increased, creating in this way the conditions for new loans that were justified by the same discourses of economic growth and poverty alleviation. In a world dominated by the language of econometric models, numbers are the international vocabulary for decision-making; so, we need to look critically at how numbers and statistics are used politically. What needs to be understood is that in decision-making numbers are not simply a reflection of "reality" but are important in defining it and, consequently, in assessing "needs" and proposing "solutions." In this political process, numbers are in a constant and dialectical relationship with what happens on the ground. Hence statistics on poverty, violence, and wealth actually help to mold these phenomena. Therefore, our analysis examines both the understanding of the strategic and selective use of numbers and statistics, as well as how they are used politically to fuel fears and to encourage more spending on security issues. This is especially true in the case of Southwest North America, as theorized in chapter 2.

THE HIGH POLITICS OF (SOME) NUMBERS

Because statistics about Arizona's budgets form the basis of our argument, before we pursue our analysis, a critical understanding of the use of numbers is important. Under economic measurements stand coherent ideologies and axiomatic understandings about the functioning of politics and economy. The measurement of development is the best example in this case: what is measured counts and matters; what is not measured is by default nonexistent. When Arizona governor Doug Ducey took office he announced that his goal would be to "grow the economy" (Office of the Governor Doug Ducey 2015). This statement takes for granted that economy must constantly grow, and so it has a normative charge that rushes policies meant to follow it. If the economy must grow, any stagnation or growth is taken immediately as a sign of crisis that creates panic and the fear that another terrible crisis might follow. Ironically, under the current paradigm, growing the economy has become a goal in itself instead of a means of achieving a more sustainable, resilient, and democratic economy. Although Governor Ducey may declare that "a strong and vibrant economy is essential to an Arizona that will provide opportunity for all" (Office of the Governor Doug Ducey 2015), even a growing economy does not necessarily guarantee a fair distribution of resources. Growing the economy is not correlated with a fair share of this economic gain nor, as research has shown, is economic growth correlated with equality or poverty reduction (World Bank 2006). In focusing on economic growth, other relevant statistics about the population and its "security" are left behind: for example, the fact that among developed nations the United States has the highest number of firearm deaths, that it is the "world's leader in incarceration with 2.2 million people currently in the nation's prisons, a 500 percent increase over the past thirty years" (The Sentencing Project 2016), or the racial and ethnic disparity in incarceration with a black:white ratio of 5.6:1 and a Hispanic:white ratio of 1.8:1 (The Sentencing Project 2016).

Defining goals, measuring, and creating categories and measurements that inform, reform, support, and justify policies remain an ongoing exercise of power. Few social scientists, however, seem to critically consider the "magic" of numbers, and as a result, discussions about development indicators rarely address their limits and incapacities to capture the ground reality and, thus are far from meeting the intentions of institutional decision-making. The statistics used to enumerate people have their own laws, and in a statistical society (Hacking 1990), these laws "carry with them the connotations of normality and deviations from the norm" (Hacking 1999, 5). As Ian Hacking (1975) notes in his study that traces the emergence of probability, the first correlations between numbers and an axiomatic understanding of politics occurred around 1650; thus, the emergence of probability appears to parallel the advent of capitalism and the beginning of the bourgeois individualism. Greenberg and Heyman (2012) have made an analogous observation, noting that as in mathematics, capitalism began to look at the elements of enterprise as discretely calculable, and investments began to be judged in increasingly abstract terms, "not simply as commitments to profit making in particular enterprises but as numerical calculations on rates of return on alternative investments across a wide range of comparisons" (Greenberg and Heyman 2012, 244). The magic trick here is that by attaching numbers to things, disparate and noncomparable things can be categorized and assembled into spreadsheets, accounts rendered, and decisions made. In eighteenth-century Germany, as Scott (1998) argues, the rise of scientific forestry gave the use of numbers increasing legitimacy as a tool of management. Hence, as Scott (1998) argues, to be countable is to be legible. One of the preoccupations of modern states has been how to measure things as numbers become the basis of governance and the means for the exercise of power.

Porter (1995) argues similarly that quantification is an essential tool for measurements and statistics and numbers, even for democratic governments, and constitutes proof of their actions. Annual statistics are published as proof that elected officials are doing their job, reporting to the electorate, and continuing to follow democratic practices. What is not published can only be hidden, and it is usually something that contravenes democratic principles of governance. Porter considers quantification—through numbers, graphs, and formulas—to be a technology and strategy for communication at distance. He argues that quantification in science and politics means that "the rules for collecting and manipulating numbers are widely shared, they can easily be transported across oceans and continents and used to coordinate activities or settle disputes" (Porter 1995, viii). Consequently, "in science, as in political and administrative affairs, objectivity names a set of strategies for dealing with distance and distrust" (Porter 1995, ix). Although Porter does not name the question of power and the practice of its expansion, he holds that "quantification is well suited for communication that goes beyond the boundaries of locality and community" (Porter 1995, ix). Porter's concept of communication, it should be observed, does not encompass the assertive and axiomatic meanings that may be attached to a message. His concept of "communication" is thus politically neutral and seems to be more apt to science than to politics. The reason why numbers seem to fit scientific communications better is that in science there are strict canons for their interpretation. Even in commerce, numbers must add up; there is a bottom line. However, in politics this canon goes out the window; numbers are more open to interpretation and political manipulation. For instance, as Nancy Scheper-Hughes notes, the child mortality rate is an artifact of public records: official censuses, birth certificates, baptismal marriage and divorce records, and death or burial certificates. So whatever these statistics may be, "there are no 'pure,' 'accurate,' or 'objective' sources of information.' Nor are they politically neutral. But, they do reveal a society's system of classification and its basic values including what is considered hardly worth tracking or counting at all" (Scheper-Hughes 1996, 891).

Statistics and numbers "allow the discovery or the creation of entities that support our description of world and the way we act on it" (Desrosieres 1998, 3). Based on evidence in the anthropological literature (for instance, Brian Silverstein's understanding of statistics as "less a technology and more a methodology of governance" [Silverstein 2014, 638]), we argue that numbers have a dialectical relationship with reality. Numbers are drawn from and simultaneously make reality. And, reality is the product and the source of numbers. On the ground reality is made up by and makes numbers. In the budget of the state of Arizona, immigrant numbers, be they legal or not, are used to justify investment in "border security," as "aliens" are perceived literally as a threat. These initiatives, where implemented, reshape realities and become the object of new claims expressed in numbers. Fueled by racism and fear, anti-immigration policies are wrapped in a nationalistic discourse calling for more private investment in security mechanisms. As the Arizona government puts it in its mission statement: "Government's number one responsibility is keeping its citizens and homeland safe. Governor Ducey has made public safety a top priority, with significant new investments in child safety, an enhanced partnership with local and federal law enforcement, and initiatives to combat human trafficking, drug smuggling, and the scourge of drug addiction" (Office of the Governor Doug Ducey 2015). In effect, the Republican discourse, by mobilizing popular fears and prejudices, has pushed policies that simultaneously criminalized undocumented immigrants and has used high numbers to justify investments in private prisons, further reinforcing these fears and prejudices.

Besides turning a blind eye to the role our immigration policy has played in keeping both Mexican migrants vulnerable and their labor cheap, this fixation on Mexican migrant numbers (see chapters 11 and 12) hypocritically ignores the larger international picture in which neoliberal policies instituted in Mexico (with promises by the United States of free trade and development) sharpened inequalities both within Mexico and between Mexico and the United States that induced migrants to come here in the first place. With the downturn in the economy (because of our own neoliberal policies of deregulation), numbers have become the scapegoat used both to increase funding for border security and to justify a wide range of cuts to Arizona's budget, including cuts in education.

NEOLIBERALISM: THE PROCESS IN ARIZONA

Between 1979 and 2013 several sectors of the Arizona State budget have experienced dramatic cuts. Figures 10.1, 10.2, 10.3, 10.4, 10.5, 10.6, 10.7, and 10.8 show both the changes in percentage of budget allocated to sectors and, beneath each graph, the line items for each these sectors.

Given neoliberal antipathy to government regulation and preference for privatization, and environmental priorities by 2013, some of the items have been zeroed out of the state budget: Agricultural Employment Relations Board, Registrar of Contractors, Occupational Safety and Health Review Board, Medical Board of Arizona, the Pharmacy Board, Department of Transportation, Commission on the Environment, Game and Fish Department, Department of Mines and Mineral Resources, Oil and Gas Conservation Commission, Parks Board, and Solar Energy Commission. Given their hard-line, mandatory sentencing, and pro–law enforcement ideologies, some of the following items also have been eliminated: Committee on Appellate Trial Court Appeals, Commission on Judicial Conduct, Grand Jury, Criminal Justice Commission, Drug and Gang Prevention Resource Center, Drug Control District, and Justice Planning Agency. Some of the areas that have had significant cuts include Environmental Quality, Department of Agriculture, Corporation Commission, generally state universities, but also Department of Juvenile Corrections and the Land Department. By contrast, security is one sector that has shown significant growth in the percentage of state dollars allocated to the areas of protection and safety, and this includes both law enforcement and prisons. Because this list is too long to detail the implications of cuts to each of the areas, we shall only focus on education and prisons.

In making these cuts, legislators make use of a couple of common strategies when going after a program or agency they wish, usually for ideological reasons, to eliminate. If the program or agency has some support or if its sudden defunding would be disruptive or create political backlash, they will reduce its funding. Generally this has two effects—it stops further growth and expansion and forces the program to economize. A slow death by a thousand cuts follows, until the program or agency is so weak, small, or dysfunctional that its elimination looks rational. The second strategy is a variation of the first, and it is used to weaken an institution from public funding and so push its increasing privatization—the prime example in Arizona are its state universities and colleges. We also see elements of this same strategy at work in the funding of K–12 public schools. When one looks across this period, another pattern stands out: cuts are more easily justified when the economy is in crisis and more radical measures find increased support. During the credit recession that began in 2007, tax revenues fell and the state legislature continued slashing the K–12 budget, until finally Arizona's

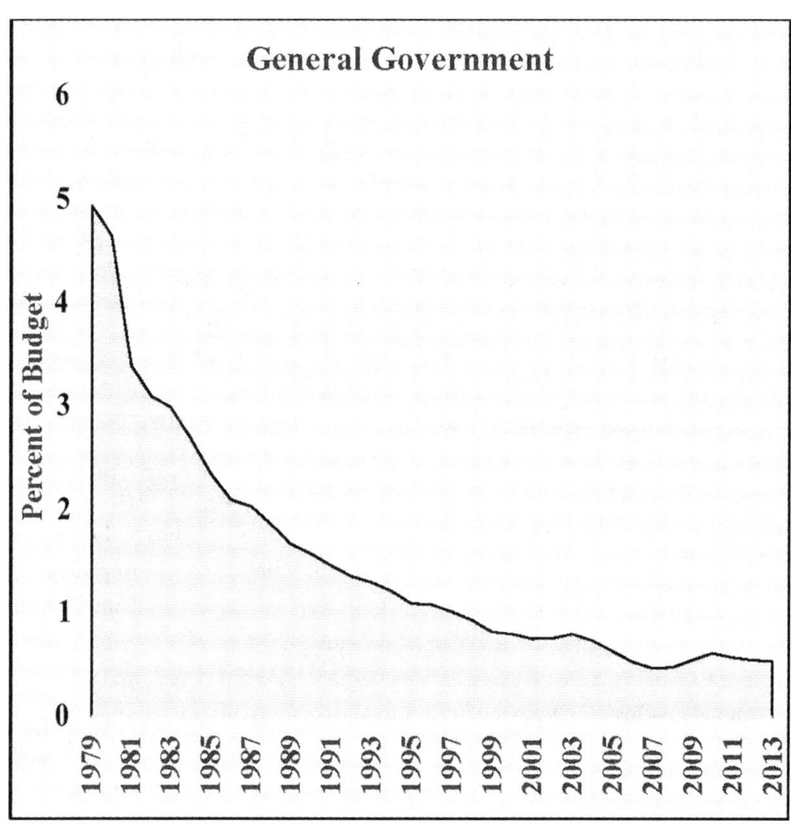

FIGURE 10.1. Percent Arizona state budget spent on general government expenditures, 1979–2013. Underlined items were zeroed out by 2013; italicized items were significantly cut between 2003 and 2013. General government expenditures include Department of Administration, Administrative Hearings Office, Attorney General, Department of Commerce, Commerce Authority, Constitutional Defense Council, County Funding, Courts, Committee on Appellate Trial Court Appeals, Commission of Judicial Conduct, Grand Jury, Governor's Office of Equal Opportunity, State Board of Education, Government Information Technology Agency, *Office of the Governor*, Governor's Office for Excellence in Government, Governor's Office of Management and Budget, Governor's Office of Strategic Planning and Budgeting, Independent Redistricting Commission, Law Enforcement Merit System, Council for State Legislature, Other Joint Committees, Lottery Commission, Military Airport Preservation Commission, Personnel Board, Public Safety Personnel Retirement, Retirement System, *Department of Revenue*, *Secretary of State*, Tax Appeals Board, Office of Tourism, *Treasurer*, Commission on Uniform State Laws. Source: Arizona State Legislature, Joint Legislative Budget Committee (2015).

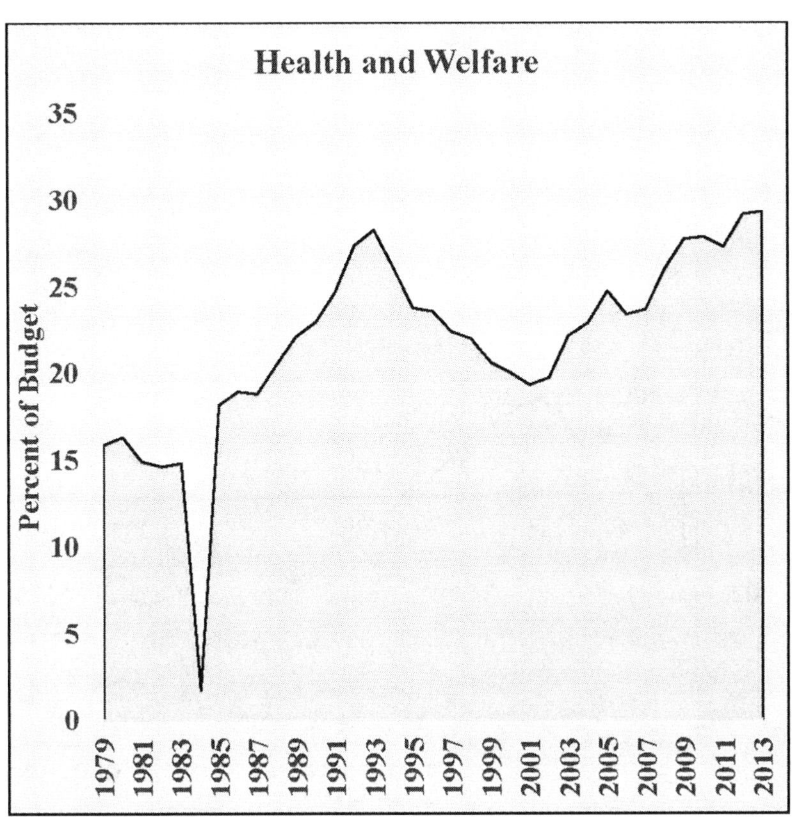

FIGURE 10.2. Percent of Arizona state budget spent on health and welfare, 1979–2013. Underlined items were zeroed out of budget by 2013; italicized items were cut significantly between 2003 and 2013. Health and welfare costs include Arizona Cost Containment System, Biomedical Research Commission, Committee for the Deaf and Hard of Hearing, Department of Economic Security, *Department of Environmental Quality*, Department of Health Services, Commission of Indian Affairs, *Pioneer's Home*, Rangers Pension, Department of Veteran's Services. Source: Arizona State Legislature, Joint Legislative Budget Committee (2015).

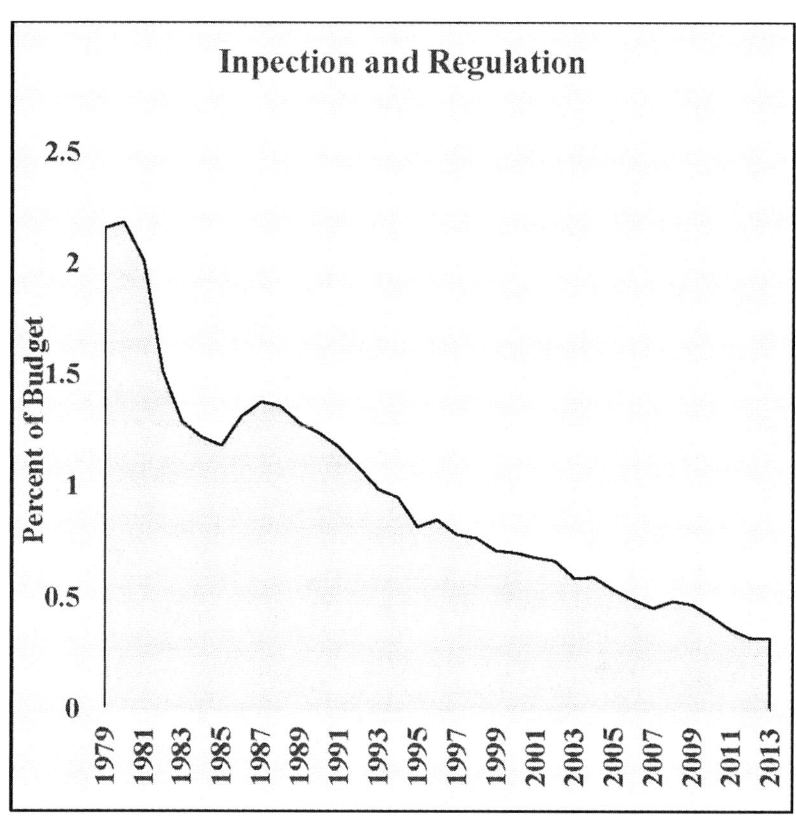

FIGURE 10.3. Percent of Arizona state budget spent on inspection and regulation, 1979–2013. Underlined items were zeroed out by 2013; italicized items cut significantly between 2003 and 2013. Inspection and regulation includes Agricultural Employment Relations Board, *Department of Agriculture*, Agriculture and Horticulture, Boxing Commission, Registrar of Contractors, *Corporations Commission*, Dairy Commissioner, State Department of Financial Institutions, *Department of Fire, Building, and Life Safety*, Department of Gaming, Industrial Commission, Department of Insurance, Department of Liquor License and Control, Department of Livestock Board, Office of Manufactured Housing, Mine Inspector, Occupational Safety and Health Review Board, Department of Racing, Radiation Regulatory Agency, Department of Real Estate, Department of Weights and Measures. Source: Arizona State Legislature, Joint Legislative Budget Committee (2015).

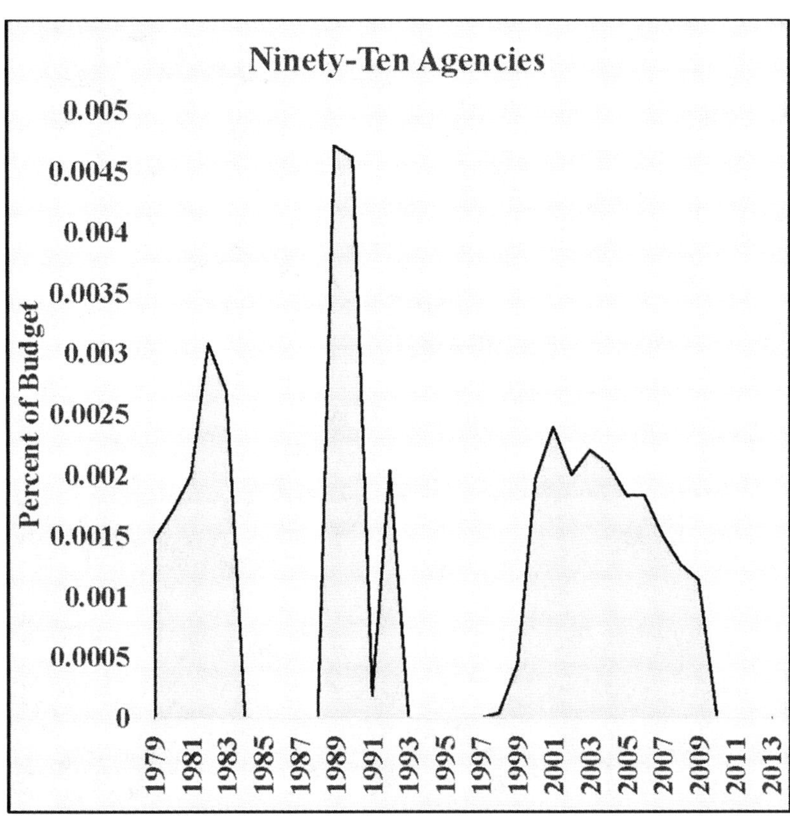

FIGURE 10.4. Percent of Arizona state budget spent on Ninety-Ten Agencies, 1979–2013. Underlined items zeroed out of the state budget by 2013. Percent state expenditures on Ninety-Ten Agencies include Board of Accountancy, Board of Acupuncture Examiners, Board of Appraisers, Board of Barbers, Board of Behavioral Health Examiners, Board of Chiropractic Examiners, Board of Cosmetology, Board of Dental Examiners, Board of Egg Inspection, Board of Funeral Directors and Embalmers, Board of Homeopathic and Integrated Medicine Examiners, Board of Massage Therapy, Arizona Medical Board of Naturopathic Physicians, Board of Nursing Care, Board of Institutional Nursing Care, Board of Administrators, Board of Occupational Therapy Examiners, Board of Opticians, Board of Dispensing, Board of Optometry, Board of Osteopathic Examiners, Office of Pest Management, Pharmacy Board, Physical Therapy Examiners Board, Podiatry Examiners Board, Board for Private Postsecondary Education, Board for Psychological Examiners, Board of Respiratory Care Examiners, Board of State Boards, Office of Technical Registration, Board of Veterinary Medicine Examining Board. Source: Arizona State Legislature, Joint Legislative Budget Committee (2015).

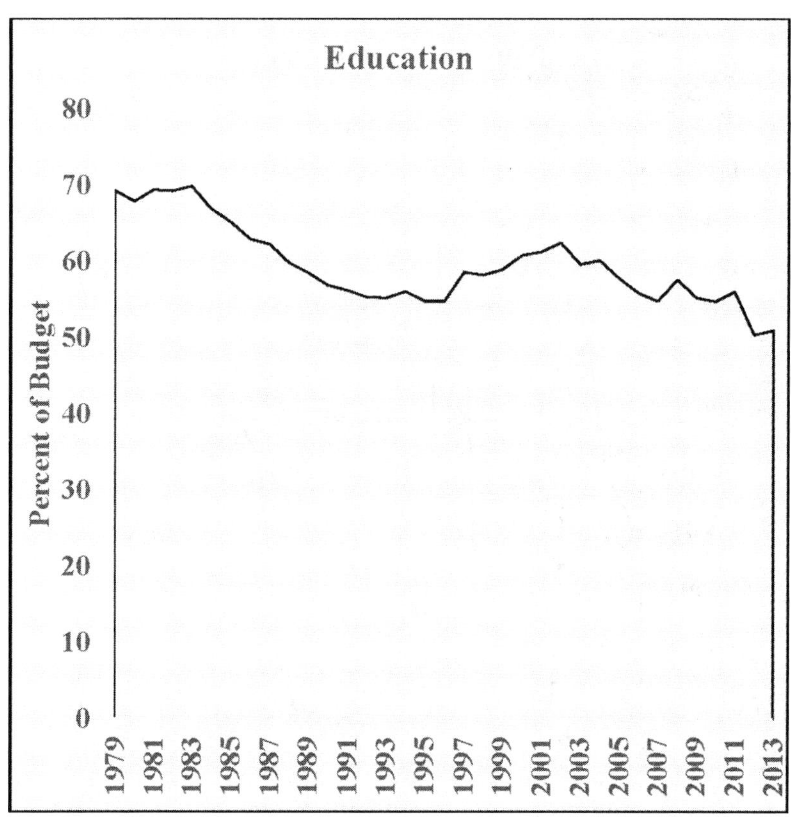

FIGURE 10.5. Percent of Arizona state budget spent on education, 1979–2013. Underlined items zeroed out by 2013; italicized items significant cuts between 2003 and 2013. Education includes Arizona Commission on the Arts, State Board for Charter Schools, *Arizona Community Colleges*, School for the Deaf and Blind, Department of Education, *Arizona Historical Society*, Prescott Historical Society, Board of Medical Student Loans, Committee for Postsecondary Education, State Board for School Capital Facilities, School Facilities Board, Board of University Regents, *Arizona State University, Tempe*, Arizona State University, East Campus, *Arizona State University, West Campus*, Arizona State University, Other, *Northern Arizona University*, *University of Arizona, Main Campus*, *University of Arizona Health Sciences Center*, University of Arizona, Other, University Medical Center, Board of Post Secondary Education. Source: Arizona State Legislature, Joint Legislative Budget Committee (2015).

FIGURE 10.6. Percent Arizona state budget spent on protection and safety, 1979–2013. Underlined zeroed out by 2013; italicized significant cuts between 2003–2013. Protection and safety includes Automobile Theft Authority, Capital Postconviction Public Defenders Office, Department of Corrections, Criminal Intelligence Systems Agency, Criminal Justice Commission, Resource Center for Drug and Gang Prevention, Drug Control District, Department of Emergency and Military Affairs, Board of Executive Clemency, *Justice Planning Agency*, *Department of Juvenile Corrections*, and Department of Public Safety. Source: Arizona State Legislature, Joint Legislative Budget Committee (2015).

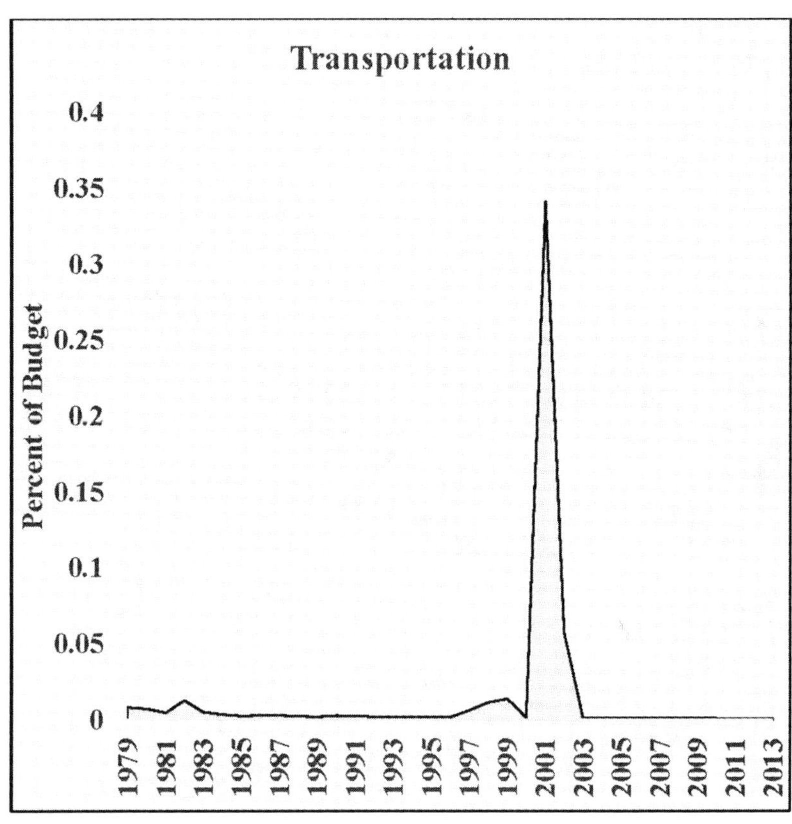

FIGURE 10.7. Percent of Arizona State Budget Spent on Transportation, 1979–2013. Underlined items zeroed out by 2013; italicized items significantly cut between 2003–2013. Transportation includes *Department of Transportation*. Source: Arizona State Legislature, Joint Legislative Budget Committee (2015).

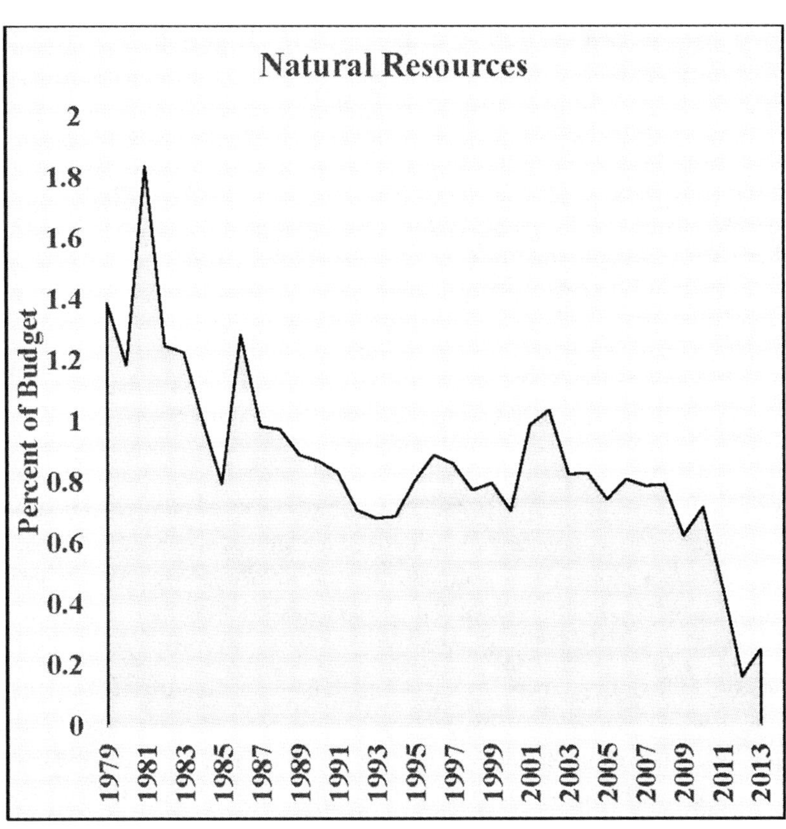

FIGURE 10.8. Percent of Arizona State Budget Spent on Natural Resources, 1979–2013. Underlined items zeroed out of the state budget by 2013; italicized items significantly cut between 2003–2013. Natural resources include Commission on the Environment, State Forester, Department of Game and Fish, Geological Survey, *Land Department*, Department of Mines and Mineral Resources, *Navigable Stream Adjudication Committee*, Oil and Gas Conservation Commission, Parks Board, Solar Energy Commission, Department of Water Resources. Source: Arizona State Legislature, Joint Legislative Budget Committee (2015).

per-student allocation was the lowest in the country. Having engineered a crisis in K–12 education, in 2015 Republican Governor Doug Ducey, taking a page from the neoliberal playbook, proposed increasing funding to public schools without raising taxes by privatizing millions of acres of public land (Arizona State Land Department 2016). Federal lands in the western United States represent a tremendously valuable resource: one that neoliberals have long eyed, private interests—developers, logging, mining, and oil and gas companies—have long coveted, and that conservationists and environmentalists, among others, have sought to protect.

INSTITUTIONALIZED RACISM AND INCREASES IN SECURITY SPENDING

In Arizona race and citizenship, national origin, and other social categories have long histories of intersection and have become ever more nuanced in the twentieth century as segregation became institutionalized in the educational system (Powers 2013). Two laws that exemplify the increasingly racialized politics of fear in Arizona are the anti-immigration law SB 1070 and HB 2281, intended to ban ethnic studies in the K–12 schools. According to Soto and Joseph, "The HB law actually prohibits classes to do the following: promote overthrow of US government; promote resentment towards a class of people; are designed for pupils of a particular ethnic group; advocate ethnic solidarity instead of treatment of pupils as individuals" (Soto and Joseph 2010, 55). As these authors observe: "A degree once a mark of the educated citizen necessary to a democracy, appears to have become the mark of dead citizenship for those participants" (Soto and Joseph 2010, 49).

The larger context for the increasingly overt racism in Arizona lies in the institution of neoliberal policies in Mexico, as previously mentioned. The imposition of neoliberal policies in Mexico during the 1990s wreaked economic havoc and destabilized the Mexican countryside, causing increasing out-migration and fostering the rampant growth of the drug economy (Weaver et al. 2012). In reaction, the U.S. border with Mexico has been increasingly militarized, including the expansion of the size of the Border Patrol, deployment of National Guard troops to the Arizona border in 2010 and 2011, and the spending of billions on fencing and electronic surveillance. Although border enforcement has been effective in slowing unauthorized entries, by making crossing more difficult, it has also pushed migrants' crossings into more remote and more dangerous terrain. Between 1998 and 2012, the Border Patrol found 5,595 bodies (Anderson 2013). On average around 200 migrants lose their lives trying to cross Arizona's deserts each year in Pima County alone! Between 1991 and 2012 the Pima County Office of the Medical Examiner examined remains of 2,238 migrants with the numbers ranging from 8 bodies in 1990 to 225 corpses in 2010. These years coincide with the implementation of NAFTA in 1994 and with increased spending for border security. But, these numbers do not count in the larger realm of decision-making. The numbers that matter are those that can justify the expansionary needs of the market and can lead to "economic growth."

Putting free trade agreements—NAFTA and CAFTA—into place has "created the conditions for US to become a magnet for cheap, exploitable, and 'illegal' migrant labor. State-sponsored violence becomes integral, not incidental, to both dislocation and dispossession of millions of working people and militarization at the US-Mexico border and, beyond that, is a necessary component to disciplining the working class on both sides of the border" (Green 2009, 328). Pushed by a politically inspired right-wing rhetoric that painted immigrants as "illegals," as mules for drug smugglers, and as taking jobs from citizens, the militarization of the border, the credit crises, and the downturn in the economy that began in 2007 created the conditions for virulent racisms and anti-Mexican migrant sentiments to come to the fore.

Led by such sentiments, the Arizona state legislature enacted a series of anti-Mexican migrant measures designed to marginalize this population economically, to create fear, to inhibit their movements, and to encourage their departure. Such measures include laws that make citizenship or legal residency a requirement to obtain a driver's license but also make driving without a license or using fake identification cards in applying for work a criminal act. Such measures both made it increasingly problematic for those without proper identification to find work and increased the "illegality" of populations who tried to do so. One of the laws fueling "prison economics" has been SB 1070, passed into law in 2010. Arizona state senator Russell Pearce, who claimed this law was his idea, in arguing for SB 1070 declared that "enough is enough. . . . People need to focus on the cost of not enforcing our laws and securing our border. It is the Trojan horse destroying our country and a republic cannot survive as a lawless nation" (Sullivan 2012). This law not only requires "aliens" to have documents but also requires state and local officials to enforce federal immigration laws. In effect, SB 1070, which permits local police to demand papers from anyone they have "a reasonable suspicion" of being illegal, has institutionalized racial profiling (Miller 2010).

Even before SB 1070, anti-Mexican migrant rhetoric was already on the rise. In 2005, the Arizona House passed HB 2259, the so-called "Anti-Coyote Law," that made smuggling immigrants a felony (O'Leary 2014, 30). The following year thirty-seven anti-immigration related bills flooded the state legislature (30). This anti-migrant climate led Phoenix sheriff Joe Arpaio to decide to focus on enforcement of immigration laws and to target local migrant populations (Archibald 2005) by encouraging vigilantes, such as the Minutemen, to "defend" our borders.

The Minutemen's case is interesting because it reflects the contradictions and complexities of the neoliberal policies. The Minutemen's first important project took place in 2005, when with the Civil Homeland Defense they conducted a one-month watch near Tombstone, Arizona. Although Minutemen were opposed to many of the effects of neoliberal policies, such as permeable borders and "Big Government," they supported many of its ideological underpinnings, such as ideologies of personal responsibility (Molina 2011, 8). They also combined "anti-immigration ideology with border security tactics in ways that challenge and support state action" (Molina 2011, 13). The action of the Minutemen reveals just how ambiguous the relationship between the state and civil society in a neoliberal context can be. The terrain for this 2010 law was prepared during the 2005 Operation Streamline, which targeted first-time border crossers and charged them with felonies. In 2011, Miller documents that 70 people were convicted and sentenced in Arizona alone. According to his figures 17,850 undocumented people came before a judge each year in Tucson alone, of whom almost 7,000 received prison sentences ranging from thirty days to six months, with those convicted of reentry being given sentences from two to twenty years (Miller 2010, 4). Such enforcement measures have helped to swell Arizona's prisons. So, now Arizona ranks third in the nation and first among U.S. western states in its average annual prison population growth rate between 2000 and 2008 (AFSC 2012, 13). While some other factors might have contributed to this growth, according to Arizona's auditor general, the number of felony adult offenders in Arizona state prisons grew by nearly twelvefold between 1979 and 2009 (AFSC 2012, 13).

Following neoliberal principals, Arizona has experimented with privatizing its prisons. Its experiment with for-profit incarceration began in the early 1990s when the state faced the first of many prison overcrowding crises (AFSC 2012, 10). The State of Arizona currently operates ten prison complexes. "There are five additional state prisons . . . managed by for-profit prison corporations" (AFSC 2012, 11). There are six other private prisons in Arizona (housing inmates from other states), but they do not contract with the State of Arizona. The number of private prisoners held by institutions that have contracts with the Arizona Department of Corrections has grown dramatically between 2001 and 2013 (Arizona Department of Corrections 2015). In 2012, Arizona housed 20.1 percent of its prisoners in private facilities (AFSC 2012, 10). The conditions in these private prisons have not been monitored. In 2011 the American Friends Service Committee (AFSC) filed a suit against Governor Jan Brewer and the Arizona Department of Corrections for failing for more than two decades (since 1981 approximately) to comply with state law that requires the review of private prisons yearly (AFSC 2012, 2). At the state level the increasing expenditures on security measures have been used to justify cuts in other parts of the budget, including education.

CUTS IN EDUCATION

Between 1979 and 2013, State of Arizona expenditures on universities and regents has fallen from almost 20 percent of the state budget to around 8 percent (see figures 10.9 and 10.10). The University of Arizona initially attempted to deal with annual budget cuts through belt-tightening; when no fat remained then attempts at restructuring were made and a pattern of restructuring and cuts ensued. Beginning with President Peter Likens (1997–2006), the administration's strategy to cope with cuts turned on "focused excellence," identifying "the areas in which the UA was best positioned, strategically, to maintain or achieve excellence" (University of Arizona, Executive Office of the President 2016a). When the credit crisis hit in 2007, then-president Robert N. Shelton (2006–2011), again using the rhetoric of "focused excellence," offered a transformational plan that led to a profound restructuring of the university involving merging or elimination of whole colleges, schools, departments, and programs (University of Arizona, Executive Office of the President 2016b). When Ann Weaver Hart (2012–) became president, state contributions to the university budget were minimal, and the university had been, for all intents and purposes, privatized. Under President Hart a new system of budgeting based on Responsibility Centered Management (RCM) was adopted in 2014 (University of Arizona 2016). Developed by private colleges and universities in the 1970s and 1980s, RCM claims to be a transparent, decentralized, approach to budgeting that promotes the values expressed in the university's strategic plan (business model) to reward productivity, effectiveness, and entrepreneurship. Under RCM budgets, following neoliberal principles, central administration allocates revenues to colleges and departments, who become also responsible for expenditures including the costs of office space, phones, etc., on the principle that local units, like local government, can make smarter decisions that can upper administration or distant government. Under RCM, decision-making becomes increasingly driven by quantifiable measures like student-faculty ratios, faculty teaching loads, class size, numbers of degrees granted, and numbers of hours worked per week per teaching assistant, ultimately these measures being central to management.

The problems with RCM are analogous to those faced by scientific forestry. In the eighteenth century, measurements of forest production of board feet ultimately proved to be problematic—because they failed to account for many factors that make forests productive, such as biodiversity, given measurements may not capture what needs to be measured. Just as putting a price on a forest flattens a complex phenomenon, to make it calculable, equating universities to firms presents analogous problems of oversimplification. While accounting and ledger books that divide costs from revenues, logically led to ideas of balancing books, they can also lead to calculations of costs of producing a degree in English as opposed to physics. The problem is that such

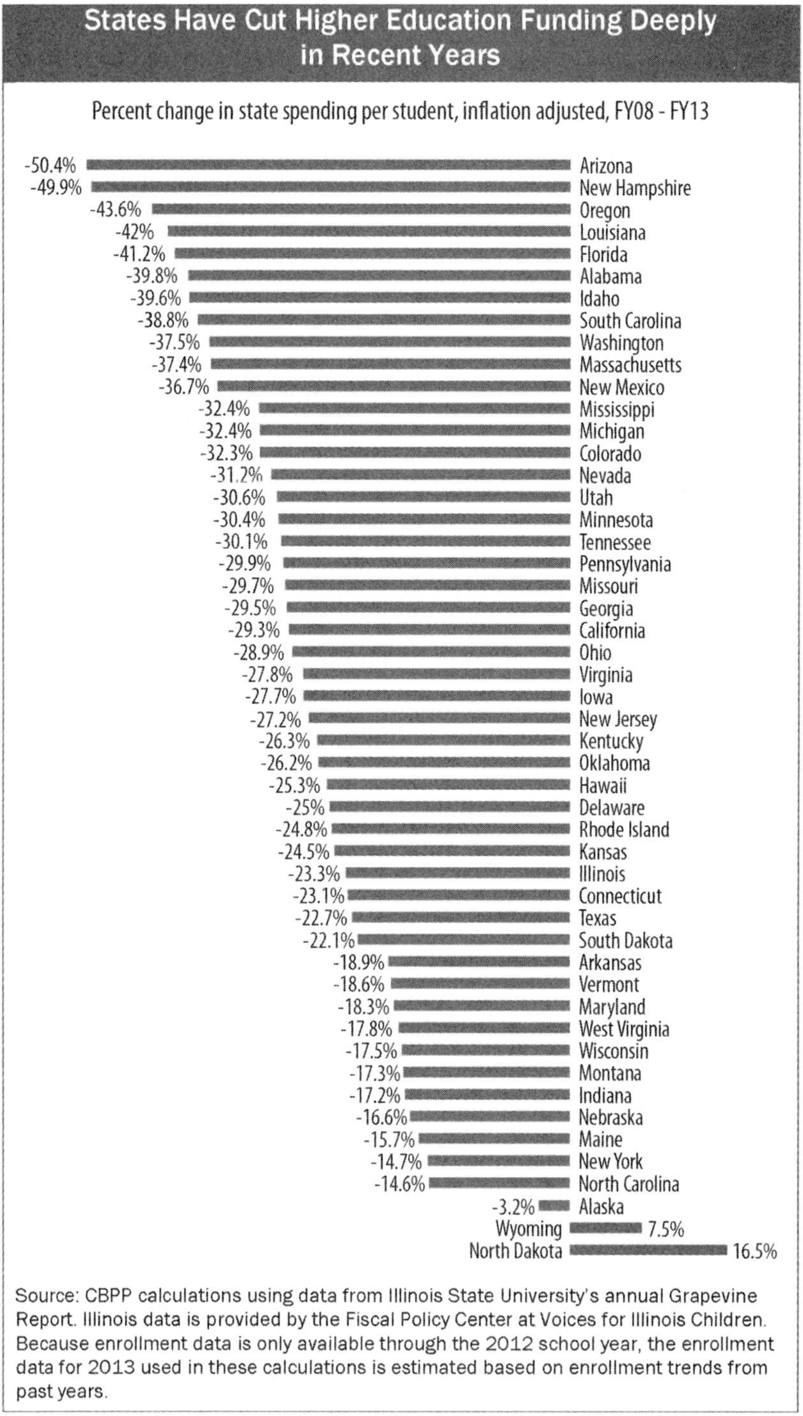

Percent change in state spending per student, inflation adjusted, FY08 - FY13

Arizona	-50.4%
New Hampshire	-49.9%
Oregon	-43.6%
Louisiana	-42%
Florida	-41.2%
Alabama	-39.8%
Idaho	-39.6%
South Carolina	-38.8%
Washington	-37.5%
Massachusetts	-37.4%
New Mexico	-36.7%
Mississippi	-32.4%
Michigan	-32.4%
Colorado	-32.3%
Nevada	-31.2%
Utah	-30.6%
Minnesota	-30.4%
Tennessee	-30.1%
Pennsylvania	-29.9%
Missouri	-29.7%
Georgia	-29.5%
California	-29.3%
Ohio	-28.9%
Virginia	-27.8%
Iowa	-27.7%
New Jersey	-27.2%
Kentucky	-26.3%
Oklahoma	-26.2%
Hawaii	-25.3%
Delaware	-25%
Rhode Island	-24.8%
Kansas	-24.5%
Illinois	-23.3%
Connecticut	-23.1%
Texas	-22.7%
South Dakota	-22.1%
Arkansas	-18.9%
Vermont	-18.6%
Maryland	-18.3%
West Virginia	-17.8%
Wisconsin	-17.5%
Montana	-17.3%
Indiana	-17.2%
Nebraska	-16.6%
Maine	-15.7%
New York	-14.7%
North Carolina	-14.6%
Alaska	-3.2%
Wyoming	7.5%
North Dakota	16.5%

Source: CBPP calculations using data from Illinois State University's annual Grapevine Report. Illinois data is provided by the Fiscal Policy Center at Voices for Illinois Children. Because enrollment data is only available through the 2012 school year, the enrollment data for 2013 used in these calculations is estimated based on enrollment trends from past years.

FIGURE 10.9. Cuts in education nationwide and in Arizona. Source: Oliff (2013).

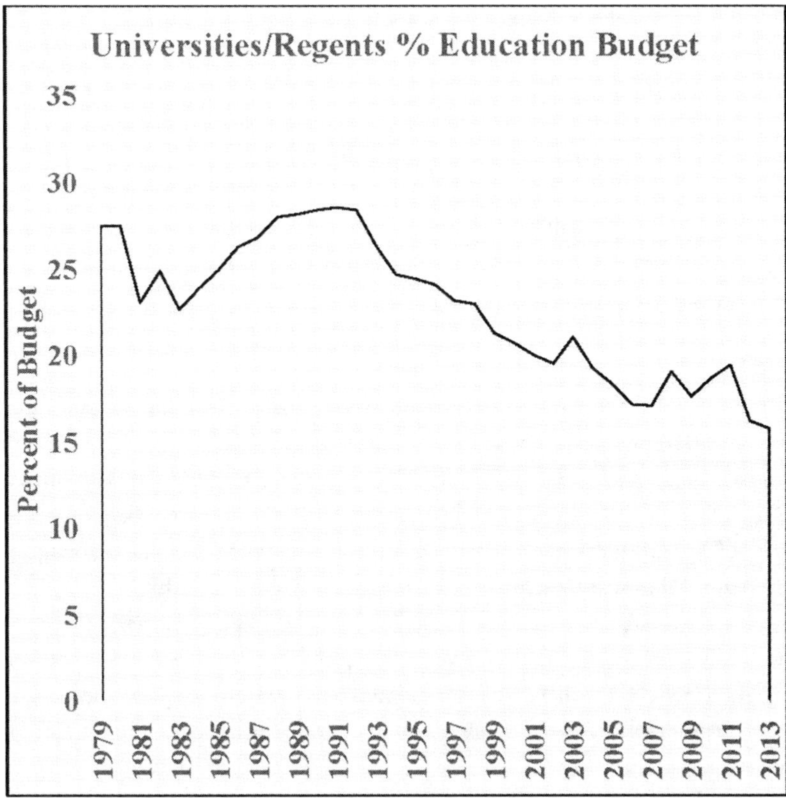

FIGURE 10.10. Regents and universities expenditures as percent of education in the Arizona state budget, 1979–2013. Source: Arizona State Legislature, Joint Legislative Budget Committee (2015).

calculations do not capture a university's value to a state, any more than board feet captures the biodiversity of a forest. How does one quantify the cumulative effect of having a more educated populace on the economy or having the expertise that makes a broad range of investments productive? Ultimately, such metaphors are dangerous in that they lead to misguided attempts to manage universities in the same way that businesses are managed. While such forms of accounting may be rational for a company producing widgets, if the illusions of rationality that accounting provides are allowed to drive the missions of universities, much of what universities offer society may be lost. Maybe the best way to illustrate this problem is to imagine an accounting in which the allocation of credit dollars followed students. Such a system would create a market for student's credit dollars that would put departments and faculty into competition with one another. Followed to its logical conclusions, those departments and faculties that do not attract sufficient numbers of students should be cut. The outcome doubtlessly would lead to elimination of specialized departments and less popular fields and would also seriously undermine academic incentives for cooperation and cross-disciplinary research. Albeit this is not how RCM at the University of Arizona is set up—where allocations are poured into a bigger set of buckets, its colleges; colleges may face the same dilemma—and ultimately, accounting rationalities are likely to drive administrators at all levels to look to and base decisions on "numbers."

COSTS OF PRIVATIZATION TO THE CITIZENS OF ARIZONA

As the University of Arizona has become increasingly privatized, in-state tuition has gone up from $1,828 per year in 1995 to $10,013 per year in 2013; out-of-state tuition has gone from $7,434 to almost $26,231 over the same period. A sharp increase occurred between 2009 and 2011 when tuition increased more than $5,000 (Arizona Board of Regents n.d.). In 2010, for example, 28 percent of the operating budgets of the Arizona University system came from tuition fees; by 2014 this figure had risen to 47 percent (Arizona Board of Regents n.d.). As these figures suggest, tuition costs are rapidly putting an education beyond the reach of many otherwise qualified Arizona residents—particularly for those with modest means, which given the racial and ethnic realities of this state, becomes a great obstacle for these minorities. Not only have state cuts in support for education driven up the costs of education for students and their families but also these cuts affect the quality of education in Arizona. A lily-white, upper-class student body is a disservice both to the people of Arizona and to the students who are denied the benefits of diversity. In Arizona alone these cuts have led to cutting more than 2,100 positions and the merging, consolidation, or elimination of 182 colleges, schools, programs, and departments and the closure of eight extension campuses. Many would blame these cuts on the economic recession that began in 2007; however, while state cuts to university budgets have driven tuition rates up throughout the United States, only seven states have increased tuition for higher education by more than 50 percent, the highest being in Arizona and California, where tuition has increased by almost 70 percent (Oliff et al. 2013). In Arizona, at least, the better explanation is that its conservative legislature has been the bastion of neoliberal ideology and has, through steady cuts to their budgets each year, pushed state universities to become self-sustaining institutions long before the recession. The recession merely provided conservatives the political excuse to move more aggressively toward the virtual privatization of higher education.

Cuts to education in Arizona have not been to higher education alone; public schools also have been a target of such cuts. In 2013, Arizona's average allocation of

$6,949 per K–12 student was the lowest in the United States (National Education Association 2015). This when, as Hoffman and Rex (2009) point out, in Arizona, with its high percentages of minorities and immigrants, and low educational attainments of parents, the investment per pupil needs to be greater than the national average, not less. Why, one might ask, have such cuts been made? While possible answers include the recession and the fact that the political voice of those most affected populations is weak, in Arizona the simpler answer may be that such cuts are consistent with neoliberal ideologies of privatization. To encourage the upper middle class to put their children into public schools, the state legislature has created state tax credits to help students attend private and parochial schools. The political strategy appears to be to make private schools an attractive alternative by underfunding public schools and pushing them into crisis. Unfortunately, such deep cuts in K–12 education, aside from encouraging the exit of the middle class into private schools, leave those who cannot afford private education in poorly funded public schools and so reinforces the state's already nasty identity politics.

As parochial schools have not been eligible for direct public funding, the Arizona legislature in 2011 created a new tax credit program that covers private schools (regardless of faith). Individuals may make state tax–deductible contributions to public schools to cover school-sponsored extracurricular activities that require enrolled students to pay a fee in order to participate or to private schools to be used for scholarships to attend them (State of Arizona State of Arizona Department of Revenue 2016). The Arizona State Senate passed a bill in February 2016 that would provide state vouchers that would allow state tax dollars to be used to attend private and parochial schools—those opposing this bill note that if enacted it would be devastating to the public school system (Fisher 2016).

NUMBERS THAT DON'T MATTER: THE HUMAN COSTS OF NEOLIBERAL POLICIES

Under neoliberal policies, inequality has grown rapidly. Gini coefficients (where 0 equals perfect equality and 1 represents complete inequality) indicate that the United States has moved toward greater inequality, with Gini coefficients rising from 0.44 in 2005 to 0.53 in 2013 (World Bank 2015). Gini figures in Arizona also show sharpening inequality, going from 0.454 in 2006 to 0.468 in 2013 (U.S. Census Bureau 2007, 2013). The relation between privatization of education and inequality is well documented nationally. In his 2014 State of the Union Address, President Obama made numerous references to the increasing problem of access to education, underlining the direct link between increasing inequality, access to education, and getting a job.

Because historically Arizona had very low tuition rates until about 2005, student debt remained fairly low as compared to the rest of the country. Even so, in 2013, 55 percent of Arizona graduates were in debt, and average student debt in Arizona was $22,253 (Institute for College Access & Success 2015). A study conducted in 2013 documenting the impact of the deep cuts to higher education on Arizona's economy notes that "funding cuts have made it harder for public colleges and universities to staff classrooms with full time, tenure-tracked professors, which might threaten student outcomes" so "many schools have turned to part time and non-tenure track faculties as a measure of cost-saving" and "increased classroom size and larger student loads for faculty negatively affect student assessment of class quality" (Oliff et al. 2013, 16). Moreover, increasing student debt is costly for the entire economy: higher levels of debt lower the chances of home ownership. As college costs have risen, it is the most economically vulnerable sector of the population that is affected first. It is not just that access to college education is being priced beyond the reach of many lower- and middle-income families but also that even those who manage to find the money are graduating with increasing levels of debt. This in turn limits how they can spend or invest their capital—for instance to purchase a home—and because they have less money to spend as consumers, the systemic consequences are that business revenues suffer as well. They can afford fewer employees and may have less earnings, all of which may affect tax revenues.

CONCLUSION

In this chapter we aimed at understanding the logic behind Arizona's conservative policies in the past several decades. In doing so, we have focused on Arizona state's budgets between 1979 and 2013 and more precisely on the strategic use of numbers and statistics using an "economic growth" argument to justify investments in "productive sectors" and cuts to less productive sectors, such as education. We have argued that in Arizona the field for this conservative discourse over funding priorities was "prepared" by a longer history of intricate ties between ethnicity and citizenship, motivated by the U.S.-Mexico border. We began this chapter with a discussion on North American forms of neoliberalism, contextualized by the larger global tendency of reducing economics to mathematical formulas and less with the social impacts of the "economic growth" driven policies. The second part of this chapter focuses on the strategic use of numbers and statistics. Here we argue that the Republican discourse, by mobilizing popular fears and prejudices, has pushed policies that simultaneously criminalized undocumented immigrants and has used their high numbers to justify investments in private prisons, further reinforcing these fears and prejudices. In the third part of this chapter we have shown how the neoliberal policies have been put in practice in Arizona. Our analysis focuses on the increased spending on security mechanisms and the racialized rhetoric behind it. Pushing investments in privatized and state-sponsored security mechanisms lead to cuts in the state budget from the less "productive" sectors such as education. Discussion about cuts in education inevitably call for an understanding of the social costs associated with these policies. The last part of the chapter explores the long-term costs of the neoliberal policies on the economy, such as increased inequality and a problematic economic growth (processes illustrated in chapters 15, 16, and 17).

In our attempt to place this material within a larger framework, we have argued that neoliberalism is an attempt to use market principles to allocate resources and can be seen as a logical progression of a capitalist logic of discretization that seeks to rationalize its investments. Discretization (a term used in mathematics) refers to reducing geometries to discrete numbers to render them more calculable. As capitalism has followed an analogous path toward abstraction, enterprises are seen as being composed of increasingly abstract sets of elements that are discretely calculable and substitutable. Where once enterprises were constituted by men and women doing concrete things in particular places, discretization has transformed these into increasingly abstract categories.[1] Under this logic men and women cease to be treated as individuals and become a category of labor in a spreadsheet, calculable across industries, sectors, and nations. In such spreadsheets definitions mask differences: professors of chemistry and anthropology may be lumped together as faculty. Citizens in state budgets are likewise abstracted into categories and subject to numerical discipline.

The underlying problem with this approach, and arguably the principal problem with neoliberalism, is that what counts and what doesn't are equally artifacts of ideologically loaded cultural categories and metaphors. For example, Republicans' rhetoric against state debt and in favor of a balanced budget often uses the metaphor of a checkbook to argue that expenses should balance revenues, but what counts on the plus and minus sides of their ledger isn't as straight forward as it might sound. To illustrate this point, when you buy a house, the outlay is certainly an expenditure—and for most of us creates a debt that we must pay off. What is not captured in this example is the house is also an asset that goes forward in time, just as debts do, and debts must be considered against assets.

At a deeper level, Republican definitions of economic benefits and costs are products themselves of conservative ideologies, ones particularly colored by business analogies. Unless government expenditures are self-liquidating[2] and pay for themselves, they are classified as unproductive consumption. Republican ideology certainly places government spending on social welfare on the expense side of the ledger. Despite some recognition that an educated population is an asset to the state, and that investments in human capital creates wealth over the long term, in the battle for state tax dollars short-term gains seems to trump long-term returns. The underlying problem is that education competes for tax dollars with the business community, so they feel educational expenditures are too high and come at their expense. Neoliberal ideology offers Republicans a way out of this dilemma, holding that anything that government does can and should be privatized, and privatization is preferable to using tax dollars.

Because state budgets are quintessentially the product of political processes, what is funded or not is not simply a matter of neoliberal or conservative ideologies but of the tactics politicians and political parties use to get elected and curry favor with voters. Unfortunately, as we document in this chapter, Arizona politics has been infused by fear and racism. Appeals to fear and racism fuel popular support for Republican anti-immigrations measures, as well as for increased government spending for security—police and prisons—and as these become priorities, they are used to justify state budget cuts in other areas such as education, or social programs.

NOTES

1. A similar argument has been advanced by Franco Moretti and Dominique Pestre (2015).
2. The criterion of being self-liquidating is used by banks to distinguish between productive commercial loans and unproductive consumer loans.

REFERENCES

AFSC (American Friends Service Committee), Arizona Program. 2012. "Private Prisons: The Public's Problem. A Quality Assessment of Arizona's Private Prisons." https://afsc.org/sites/afsc.civicactions.net/files/documents/AFSC_Arizona_Prison_Report.pdf.

Anderson, Stuart. 2013. "How Many More Deaths? The Moral Case for a Temporary Worker Program." National Foundation for American Policy. http://www.nfap.com/pdf/NFAP%20Policy%20Brief%20Moral%20Case%20For%20a%20Temporary%20Worker%20Program%20March%202013.pdf.

Archibald, Randal. 2005. "Arizona County Uses New Law to Look for Illegal Immigrants." *New York Times*, May 10.

Arizona Board of Regents. n.d. "Arizona's Public Universities." *Reports-ABOR Annual Reports 2010–2014*. http://www.azregents.edu/reports/default.aspx.

Arizona Department of Corrections. 2015. "FY 2010 Operating Per Capital Cost Report: Cost Identification and Comparison of State and Private Contract Beds. Bureau of Planning, Budget and Research." http://archive.azcentral.com/ic/pdf/0904prison.pdf.

Arizona State Land Department. 2016. https://land.az.gov.

Arizona State Legislature, Joint Legislative Budget Committee. 2015. "Fiscal History." http://www.azleg.gov/jlbc/fiscal.htm.

Babb, Sarah. 2005. "The Social Consequences of Structural Adjustment: Recent Evidence and Current Debates." *Annual Review of Sociology* 31:199–222.

Desrosieres, Alain. 1998. *The Politics of Large Numbers: A History of Statistical Reasoning.* Cambridge, MA: Harvard University Press.

Fisher, Howard. 2016. "Senate Approves Voucher Plan Decried as 'the End of Public Education in Arizona.'" *Arizona Capitol Times*, February 22. http://azcapitoltimes.com/news/2016/02/22/arizona-senate-votes-for-vouchers-for-all-school-students/.

Green, Linda. 2009. "The Fear of No Future: Guatemalan Migrants, Dispossession and Dislocation." *Anthropologica* 51:327–41.

Greenberg, James B., and Josiah McC. Heyman. 2012. "Neoliberal Capital and the Mobility Approach in Anthropology." In *Neoliberalism and the Commodity Production in Mexico*, edited by Anne Browning-Aiken, James B. Greenberg, Thomas Weaver and William L. Alexander, 241-68. Boulder: University Press of Colorado.

Greenberg, James B., Thomas Weaver, Anne Browning-Aiken, and William L. Alexander. 2012. "The Neoliberal Transformation of Mexico." In *Neoliberalism and the Commodity Production in Mexico*, edited by Anne Browning-Aiken, James B. Greenberg, Thomas Weaver, and William L. Alexander, 1–31. Boulder: University of Colorado Press.

Hacking, Ian. 1975. *The Emergence of Probability: A Philosophical Study of Early Ideas About Probability, Induction and Statistical Inference.* London: Cambridge University Press.

———. 1990. *The Taming of Chance.* Cambridge: Cambridge University Press.

———. 1999. *The Social Construction of What?* Cambridge, MA: Harvard University Press.

Harvey, David. 2003. "Accumulation by Dispossession." In *The New Imperialism*, edited by David Harvey, 137–82. Oxford: Oxford University Press.

Henry J. Kaiser Family Foundation. 2016. "Key Facts About the Uninsured Population." http://kff.org/uninsured/fact-sheet/key-facts-about-the-uninsured-population/.

Hoffman, Dennis, and Tom Rex. 2009. *Education Funding in Arizona: Constitutional Requirement and the Empirical Record. A Report from the Office of the University Economist.* Tempe: Arizona State University.

Institute for College Access & Success. 2015. "Project on College Debt." http://ticas.org/posd/home.

Martinez, Elizabeth, and Arnoldo Garcia. 2000. "What Is 'Neo-Liberalism'?" *Global Exchange.* February 26. http://www.globalexchange.org/resources/econ101/neoliberalismdefined.

Miller, Todd. 2010. "Arizona, the Anti-Immigrant Laboratory." *NACLA Report on the America*, July/August, 3–4.

Molina, Devin T. 2011. "A Comment on the Minutemen Militia of the U.S. and Neoliberal State Activity." *New Proposals: Journal of Marxism and Interdisciplinary Inquiry* 4(2): 7–14.

Moretti, Franco, and Dominique Pestre. 2015. "Bankspeak: The Language of World Bank Reports." *New Left Review*, March, 75–99.

National Education Association. 2015. "Rankings of the States 2013 and Estimates of School Statistics 2014." http://www.nea.org/home/rankings-and-estimates-2013–2014.html.

Office of the Governor Doug Ducey. 2015. http://azgovernor.gov/governor/priorities.

O'Leary, Anna Ochoa, ed. 2014. *Undocumented Immigrants in the United States: An Encyclopedia of Their Experience*. Santa Barbara: ABC-CLIO-LLC.

Oliff, Phil, Vincent Palacios, Ingrid Johnson, and Michael Leachman. 2013. "Recent Deep State Higher Education Cuts May Harm Students and the Economy for Years to Come." Washington, DC: Center on Budget and Policy Priorities. http://www.cbpp.org/research/recent-deep-state-higher-education-cuts-may-harm-students-and-the-economy-for-years-to-come.

Porter, Theodore M. 1995. *Trust in Numbers: The Pursuit of Objectivity in Science and Public Life*. Princeton, NJ: Princeton University Press.

Powers, Jeanne M. 2013. "From Extralegal Segregation to Anti-immigrant Policy: Reflections on the Long History of Racial Discrimination and Colorblindness in Arizona." *Aztlán: A Journal of Chicano Studies* 38(2): 191–205.

Obama, Barack. 2014. "State of the Union Address." http://www.whitehouse.gov/the-press-office/2014/01/28/president-barack-obamas-state-union-address.

Ross, Wayne, and Rich Gibson. 2006. "Introduction." In *Neoliberalism and Education Reform*, edited by Wayne Ross and Rich Gibson, 1–14. Creskill, NJ: Hampton Press.

Scheper-Hughes, Nancy. 1996. "Small Wars and Invisible Genocides." *Social Sciences Medicine* 45(5): 889–900.

Scott, James C. 1998. *Seeing Like a State: How Certain Schemes to Improve the Human Condition Have Failed*. New Haven: Yale University Press.

The Sentencing Project. 2016. http://www.sentencingproject.org.

Silverstein, Brian. 2014. "Statistics, Reform, and Regimes of Expertise in Turkey." *Turkish Studies* 15(4): 638–54.

Soto, Sandra K., and Miranda Joseph. 2010. "Neoliberalism and the Battle over Ethnic Studies in Arizona." *Thought and Action*, Fall, 45–56.

State of Arizona, Department of Revenue. 2016. https://www.azdor.gov/taxcredits/schooltaxcreditsforindividuals.aspx.

Sullivan, Laura. 2012. "Prison Economics Help Drive Ariz. Immigration Law." National Public Radio, April 4. http://www.npr.org/2010/10/28/130833741/prison-economics-help-drive-ariz-immigration-law.

The Sentencing Project. 2016. http://www.sentencingproject.org.

University of Arizona. 2016. "Responsibility Centered Management. Frequently Asked Questions." http://rcm.arizona.edu/faq-page.

University of Arizona, Executive Office of the President. 2016a. "Peter Likens." http://president.arizona.edu/president/peter-likins.

———. 2016b. "Robert Neal Shelton." http://president.arizona.edu/president/robert-neal-shelton.

U.S. Census Bureau. 2007. *Income, Earnings, and Poverty Data from the 2006 American Community Survey*. https://www.census.gov/prod/2007pubs/acs-08.pdf.

———. 2014. *Household Income: 2013*. American Community Survey Briefs. https://www.census.gov/content/dam/Census/library/publications/2014/acs/acsbr13-02.pdf.

Weaver, Thomas, James B. Greenberg, William L. Alexander, and Anne Browning Aiken. 2012. *Neoliberalism in Mexico: A Commodity Approach*. Boulder: University of Colorado Press.

World Bank. 2006. *World Development Report: Equity and Development*. New York: The World Bank and Oxford University Press.

11

BEYOND IL/LEGALITY

Persistent Inequality and Racialized Borders of U.S. Citizenship

RUTH GOMBERG-MUÑOZ

INTRODUCTION

THE POLITICAL BORDERS that bracket nation-states not only map territorial boundaries but also constitute an element of governance in the national body. They also bifurcate regional ecologies of what may be regarded as the Southwest North American (SWNA) region as characterized by Vélez-Ibáñez in this volume (chapter 1). Borders and immigration policies determine who can legally enter and remain in a national territory, while citizenship policies confer certain rights on some of those people and not on others. That is, not everyone who is physically present in a nation-state is eligible for legal residence or citizenship there. This mismatch gives rise to a social hierarchy in which law is used to deny certain people rights and resources, leaving them politically disempowered and especially vulnerable to insecurity, exploitation, and deportation (also see chapters 3, 9, 12, and 16, and the broader framework in chapter 2).

Insofar as immigration and citizenship policies regulate who is welcome in a nation-state and who is not, they reflect dominant ideas about what the nation is and what it ought to be. As these ideas shift, so too do policies, including and excluding different groups over time. In the United States, immigration and citizenship policies have historically been tied to concerns about the racial, class, and gendered composition of the nation-state—the "borders" of U.S. citizenship have always been more easily penetrable by some than by others.

This chapter traces legacies of conquest and colonization of the U.S. Southwest border region with a consideration of the role of immigration and citizenship policies in differentiating Mexican and Mexican American communities. I show how racialized ideas about Mexican workers drove mid-twentieth-century U.S. immigration programs that promoted mass migration of Mexican farmers to agricultural fields and construction sites in the U.S. Southwest. By the latter decades of the twentieth century, Mexico-U.S. migration patterns provided vital outlets for farmers and workers whose livelihoods in Mexico were undermined by globalization, while U.S. immigration policies turned increasingly restrictive. This history provides the foundation for a consideration of immigration enforcement policies and practices at the turn of the twenty-first century. I explore how accelerated enforcement measures have increasingly characterized Mexico-U.S. migration as "illegal" and "criminal," and I discuss recent immigration reform programs that grant temporary reprieve from deportation for select immigrants. Taken together, these sections historicize and complicate contemporary discussions about migration in the United States, challenging the notion that immigration policies and statuses are divorced from wider racial, gendered, and class-based ideologies.

FROM BRACEROS TO "ILLEGALS": U.S. IMMIGRATION POLICY OF THE TWENTIETH CENTURY

Contemporary nation-state borders largely arose from colonial configurations, themselves the result of campaigns of conquest. The United States, for example, rapidly transformed from a colony of Great Britain to an empire of its own with westward campaigns of colonization driven by an ideology of "manifest destiny" in the decades following the American Revolution. The current border between the United States and Mexico was not established until 1854, as a result of the U.S. invasion and conquest of Mexico's northern territory. As a result of that war, Mexico ceded its entire northern province to the United States, along with the 75,000 to 100,000 Mexican citizens who resided there (Gutierrez 1995, 13; De Genova and Ramos-Zayas 2003).

Treaty stipulations guaranteed that Mexicans living in the conquered territory would have access to U.S. citizenship, but U.S. citizenship was limited to "free white persons" at that time. Rather than expand citizenship to include non-whites, Mexicans in the United States became legally classified as "white" (Gutierrez 1995). In spite of their legal whiteness, Mexicans were widely derided and relegated to an inferior "caste-like" status in the developing social structure of the U.S. Southwest (Gutierrez 1995; Pedraza and Rumbaut 1996; De Genova and Ramos-Zayas 2003). The influx of gold prospectors in California in the early 1850s forced many Mexican *californios* from the goldfields, and Mexican Americans throughout the Southwest were steadily displaced from their lands, subject to massive civil rights violations, and forced into low-wage, low-status work in agriculture, mining, and construction (Gutierrez 1995; De Genova and Ramos-Zayas 2003). In a system sometimes called "Juan Crow" segregation, Mexicans were racially segregated from whites in housing, schooling, and public facilities throughout the Southwest (Menchaca and Valencia 1990; Gutierrez 1995). This segregation was justified by a doctrine of white racial supremacy that cast Mexicans as inferior racial "hybrids" (Menchaca and Valencia 1990; Pedraza and Rumbaut 1996). And while the legal "whitening" of Mexicans exempted them from the wholesale denial of citizenship rights that applied to non-whites at the time, their designation as U.S. citizens would be both legally contested and politically undermined for much of the next century and a half.

By the late 1800s, U.S. businesses began recruiting Mexican migrant labor in earnest in response to labor shortages brought about by restrictions on Chinese immigration (Massey 2009). To tap this labor reserve, recruiters traveled deep into the heart of Mexico's populated north-central valleys, where they enlisted Mexicans to work in agriculture, construction, and industry across the U.S. Southwest and in cities such as Chicago, Cleveland, and Pittsburgh (De Genova and Ramos-Zayas 2003). By the 1920s, Mexican workers (both migrants and Mexican Americans) comprised as much as 75 percent of the agricultural workforce in California and the unskilled construction labor force in Texas (Gutierrez 1995). By the turn of the twentieth century, occupational discrimination had become institutionalized into a dual-wage system, in which Mexican workers were consistently paid less than their white counterparts (Hondagneu-Sotelo 1994; Gutierrez 1995). With this growing reliance on low-paid Mexican workers, Mexicans in the United States became widely associated with undesirable manual labor. Stereotypes of Mexicans as "dirty" and unambitious, but usually industrious, workers became popular (Glenn 2002). Mexicans were also considered especially desirable as workers because of their propensity to return to Mexico, and the proximity of Mexico to the United States made it relatively easy to deport Mexican workers when demand for their labor eased.

Prior to this period, ethnic Mexicans on both sides of the border favored regional and class-based identities over a Mexico-oriented one (Gutierrez 1995). In response to discrimination and displacement after the Mexican-American War, Mexican Americans began to shift from local allegiances to a more general ethnonational solidarity (Gutierrez 1995). As with earlier groups of immigrants, Mexican immigrants from disparate backgrounds learned to think of themselves as Mexicans by being treated as such in the United States (Gutierrez 1995; Portes and Rumbaut 1996, 104). Within the Mexican barrios that sprang up throughout the Southwest, ethnic Mexicans insulated themselves from the affront of discrimination and harassment, continued to speak Spanish, and observed Roman Catholicism and Mexican cultural practices (Gutierrez 1995; Portes and Rumbaut 1996, 104). Excluded from U.S. institutions and relegated to the bottom of the labor market, many Mexican communities established *mutualistas*, mutual-aid organizations that pooled resources to fund events and provide social insurance for households facing hardship (Gutierrez 1995; Portes and Rumbaut 1996, 104). A Mexican ethnic identity was also fostered by attempts of the Mexican government to reach out politically to México de Afuera (Mexico of the Outside) and was promoted in popular Spanish-language newspapers in the Southwest (Garcia 1985; Pedraza and Rumbaut 1996). By the turn of the twentieth century, a sense of identity had emerged that bound Mexicans on both sides of the border as members of La Raza, a people with ties rooted in ethnic Mexican-ness (Gutierrez 1995).

The conception of Mexicans as a laboring class of the United States had become politically established by the 1920s. During congressional hearings leading up to the first general immigration bill in 1924, Mexicans were identified as a labor force whose racial characteristics made them especially suited for arduous and low-paying agricultural work (Gutierrez 1995; Pedraza and Rumbaut 1996). And when the Immigration Act of 1924 restricted immigration from southern and eastern Europe, Asia, and Africa, it exempted nations of the Western Hemisphere from immigration quotas, allowing an unlimited number of visas to be granted to Mexican nationals. The 1924 act also established the U.S. Border Patrol, whose function was not to restrict migration over the U.S.-Mexico border so much as regulate it according to seasonal labor needs. In fact, the Border Patrol was initially a unit of the Bureau of Immigration, itself part of the U.S. Department of Labor (Ngai 2004). The 1924 act did require Mexicans to pay a head tax and avoid being deemed "likely to become a public charge," but in all, restrictions on European and Asian immigration would augment U.S. reliance on Mexican labor throughout the mid-twentieth century (Daniels et al. 2001).

By 1930, the U.S. Census Bureau officially established "Mexican" as a distinct racial category (De Genova 2005), and throughout the 1930s, criminalization and deportation of Mexicans was explicitly based on their "race" and not citizenship (De Genova and Ramos-Zayas 2003). Of the 500,000 "Mexicans" deported during the Great Depression, for example, as many as half were U.S.-born U.S. citizens (Daniels and Graham 2001).

Following the Great Depression, the onset of World War II accelerated demand for migrant labor, as women and southern African Americans were recruited to work in industry throughout the north. Mexican workers were imported to agricultural fields of the U.S. Southwest, where they harvested the food that would sustain industrial workers and the families of soldiers abroad. To ensure an unhindered labor supply, the United States and Mexico signed a binational treaty in 1942 that came to be known as the Bracero Program. The Bracero Program was a contract-worker program that brought an estimated five million workers from Mexico to labor in the agricultural fields, construction sites, and factories across the southwestern United

States and in cities such as Chicago (De Genova and Ramos-Zayas 2003). The program was initially conceived as an emergency wartime measure, but it proved to be so important that Congress extended it several times before it was finally terminated in 1964—after a period of twenty-two years.

"POST-RACIAL" U.S. IMMIGRATION POLICY

Just one year after the Bracero Program ended, the immigration system was reformed to address racial biases in the national origins quota system. The Immigration and Nationality Act of 1965 (Hart-Celler Act) equalized the quota system such that each country would receive the same number of visas, and it subjected nationals of Mexico and other Latin American countries to numerical restriction for the first time ever. Over the next fifteen years, the number of visas available to Latin American workers was reduced from an unlimited number to just 20,000 per country per year (Nakano Glenn 2002). These restrictions on legal immigration, in conjunction with the interrelationships established during the Bracero Program and instability fomented by globalization in Mexico, rapidly pushed the prevalence of unauthorized immigration from Mexico to the United States skyward.

By the 1980s, fears of an "alien invasion" were inflamed by media outlets and politicians seeking to bolster support for their political campaigns (Massey et al. 2002; Chavez 2008). In 1986, Congress passed the very first bill that targeted unauthorized migration: the Immigration Reform and Control Act, or IRCA. This made the employment of undocumented workers illegal for the first time, though provisions in the law largely protected employers from prosecution (Calavita 1994; Massey et al. 2002). IRCA also doubled funding for the Border Patrol, but it included an amnesty provision through which some 2.7 million undocumented people were able to legalize their status (Calavita 1994; Meyes 2005). A decade later, Congress passed the Illegal Immigration Reform and Immigrant Responsibility Act (IIRAIRA) of 1996, which is widely considered to be the most punitive and draconian U.S. immigration bill to date. The IIRAIRA put measures in place that blocked many undocumented people from ever changing their immigration status, and it facilitated the deportation of lawful permanent residents. Since IIRAIRA's passage, the rate of deportation of noncitizens has increased nearly eightfold, from 50,924 in 1995 to 419,384 in 2012 (U.S. Department of Homeland Security 2013).

The 1990s also marked a major shift toward militarization of the U.S.-Mexico border region. Throughout the 1990s, the U.S. Border Patrol built miles of steel fencing, new roads, and lighting along the southern border that was guarded with hundreds of new agents and high-tech detection systems (Meyers 2005). The Border Patrol also launched a series of highly publicized "operations" on the U.S.-Mexico border, which made unauthorized border crossings more dangerous (Massey et al. 2002). Like caps on visas, border militarization did not stop migration, but it has rerouted migrant trails from more populated areas into vast stretches of desert, dramatically increasing the cost and risk of unauthorized border crossings (Jimenez 2009).

The timing of IIRAIRA and U.S. border militarization is significant, because the 1990s also ushered in a proliferation of free trade agreements between the United States and Mexico. These agreements, such as the General Agreement on Tariffs and Trade (GATT; entered into by Mexico in 1986) and North American Free Trade Agreement (NAFTA; entered into in 1994), lifted restrictions on the movement of capital, goods, money, and businesses at the same time that IIRAIRA and border "operations" restricted the movement of Mexican labor (Massey et al. 2002). These free trade agreements devastated the working and living conditions of many Mexicans, as cheap, mass-produced U.S. grains and goods flooded Mexican markets, pushing farmers off their land and undermining the ability of Mexican craftspeople to sell their wares. The Mexican economy contracted in the 1980s and again, following NAFTA's passage, in the 1990s; the Mexican peso fell to a fraction of its pre-1970 value, while unemployment, debt, and crime all rose steeply (Greider 1997). After decades of migration, Mexican workers faced historic restrictions on their movement at the same time that free trade agreements undermined their ability to stay home and make a living as workers, farmers, and small business owners. Not surprisingly, Mexican migration to the United States continued in the decades to come, but it became ever more characterized as illegal (De Genova 2005).

CRIMINALIZATION AND DETENTION: U.S. IMMIGRATION POLICY OF THE TWENTY-FIRST CENTURY

Currently, some 11.2 million people live in the United States without authorization, more than 50 percent of whom are of Mexican origin (Passel and Cohn 2014). While U.S. immigration politics of the twentieth century can be largely characterized by policies that created, then targeted, undocumented immigrants, the early decades of the twenty-first century suggest a shift in strategy that involves ratcheting up the terror in immigrant communities via record-breaking deportations, coupled with a push to regularize the undocumented without removing their risk of deportation.

Following the attacks on the World Trade Center and Pentagon on September 11, 2001, immigration enforcement came under the auspices of the Department of Homeland Security (DHS) and its Immigration and Customs Enforcement agency

(ICE), signaling a broader shift toward the association of undocumented migration with terrorism and the criminalization of undocumented immigrants. Since 2001, immigration enforcement measures have expanded both within the U.S.-Mexico border region and throughout the U.S. interior, driving record-breaking deportation rates. For most of the twentieth century, deportation rates fluctuated between 10,000 and 20,000 thousand per year, reaching highs of 30,000 to 36,000 during the sweeps of the Great Depression (1924) and Operation Wetback (1954) (U.S. Department of Homeland Security 2013). In 1997, one year after IIRAIRA's passage, deportation rates reached more than 100,000 for the first time, and they have gone up fairly steadily ever since. Between 1997 and 2012 alone, more than 4.2 million people were deported from the United States—more than double the total number of all prior deportations in the history of the United States (Golash-Boza and Hondagneu-Sotelo 2013).

It is not just the magnitude of U.S. immigration enforcement that has increased but its gravity as well. In particular, there has been a rhetorical and political coupling of immigration violations, historically categorized under civil law, with criminal offenses (Inda and Dowling 2013). Currently, unlawful *presence* in the United States is not a crime but a civil violation, and expulsion is not considered a punishment but an administrative solution. Yet, since 2005, the U.S. Border Patrol has been aggressively prosecuting unauthorized *entry* as a federal crime: a misdemeanor for the first attempt and a felony charge for any additional attempts. Between 1992 and 2012, the number of federal convictions for unlawful reentry into the United States increased twenty-eight-fold, from 690 cases in 1992 to 19,462 in 2012 (Light et al. 2014). By 2012, criminal prosecutions for immigration violations made up more than half of all federal charges brought by the U.S. government, and three-quarters of all criminal prosecutions for unlawful entry and reentry occurred in just five southern states (Linker 2013; Light et al. 2014). Because these prosecutions are concentrated on the U.S.-Mexico border, they disproportionately ensnare Latin American entrants, and the share of Latinos among federally sentenced offenders rose from 23 percent in 1992 to 48 percent in 2012 (Light et al. 2014). On average, these migrants spend twenty-four months in jail prior to deportation (Light et al. 2014). Criminal prosecution for unlawful entry is but the latest iteration of the long-standing concentration of immigration enforcement measures on the U.S.-Mexico border, a practice that continues to reinforce the association of Mexican immigrants with "illegality" in the United States (De Genova 2005; Massey 2009; Heyman 2013).

As enforcement on the U.S.-Mexico border region has expanded, so too has immigrant policing within the U.S. interior. The most pervasive interior policing program is known as Secure Communities (U.S. Department of State 2015). This program links the databases of local police agencies with the DHS and FBI. When a person is arrested and fingerprinted, their fingerprints are run through the DHS database, and if there is a "hit" (often the result of being caught at the border), ICE can deport them whether or not they are ever charged or convicted of a crime. In fact, even though ICE states that it targets "dangerous criminals," many deportations from the U.S. interior result from simple traffic stops (Guelespe 2015). As a result of Secure Communities, any contact with police anywhere in the United States can, and increasingly does, result in an undocumented immigrant's deportation. In 2014, Obama announced that DHS would end Secure Communities in favor of a more "targeted" interior enforcement program.

In addition to federal programs such as Secure Communities, states and municipalities have increasingly pursued their own immigration-related agendas. Nearly 1,600 pieces of immigration legislation were introduced at state capitols in the first eight months of 2011 alone—an all-time record (National Conference of State Legislatures 2011). Punitive immigration policies have been enacted in Arizona, Georgia, Alabama, and South Carolina, while more "immigrant-friendly" bills granting in-state college tuition or driver licenses to undocumented immigrants have been implemented in California, Connecticut, Illinois, and Colorado. Immigration policymaking has also proliferated at the local level. Between 2006 and March 2011, ordinances targeting undocumented immigrants had been passed and/or considered in over 130 U.S. cities (Varsanyi 2011). Many of these policies seek to regulate and persecute everyday behaviors associated with undocumented immigrants, and they range from English-only laws to limits on the number of adults who can reside in a household to bans on sitting in public spaces (Quesada et al. 2014).

A final component of the immigration enforcement apparatus is the growing immigrant detention system. More than 30,000 immigrants, including children, are currently held in detention on any given day, an increase of 84 percent over 2005 (Selway and Newkirk 2013). This number is driven by a congressional directive, known as the "bed mandate," that requires ICE to keep an average of 34,000 immigrants in detention per day. About two-thirds of all immigrant detainees are held in privately owned facilities, at an average cost to taxpayers of $120 per day (Selway and Newkirk 2013). Two of the five private corporations that hold immigration contracts spent more than $15 million on political lobbying between 2005 and 2013, and these corporations have been major campaign contributors to the legislators behind enforcement-oriented immigration bills (Selway and Newkirk 2013).

While ICE has taken an official stance condemning racial profiling (U.S. Immigration and Customs Enforcement 2015), emerging evidence indicates that U.S. immigration enforcement measures especially target Latin Americans. For example, while deportations have increased for all national-origin groups since the 1990s, the rise has been especially sharp for Mexicans and Central Americans (Golash-Boza and Hondagneu-Sotelo 2013). Nationwide, immigrants from Latin America make up about 75 percent of the total undocumented immigrant population, but they have accounted for over 90 percent of deportees since 2000 (Fussell 2011). Mexicans make up 59 percent of the undocumented population but have constituted between 65 and 80 percent of deportees each year between 2000 and 2009 (Passel and Cohn 2009; Fussell 2011). Tanya Golash-Boza (2012, 89) found that Central American immigrants are many times more likely to be deported than Asians, who make up just under a quarter of the undocumented population. She reports that undocumented Hondurans have a 10 percent chance of being deported and undocumented Guatemalans have a 5 percent chance; in contrast, undocumented Vietnamese, Koreans, Filipinos, Indians, and Chinese all have less than a 1 percent chance of deportation (Golash-Boza 2012). And while deportation patterns reveal ethnoracial bias, their gender bias is especially pronounced: even though roughly half of all undocumented people are women, upward of 90 percent of deportees are men (Golash-Boza and Hondagneu-Sotelo 2013).

Disproportionate arrests on the U.S.-Mexico border do not account for this disparity alone; in fact, 93 percent of those arrested through Secure Communities in 2011 were Latino (Kohli et al. 2011). This suggests that racial disparities in deportation rates are at least partially driven by local policing practices. One study conducted in Irving, Texas, by the Chief Justice Earl Warren Institute on Law and Social Policy found that, following the 2006 establishment of a partnership between local law enforcement and ICE, arrests of Latinos for minor offenses, particularly traffic violations, increased markedly. The study also found that local police arrested Latinos for misdemeanor offenses in significantly higher numbers than they arrested whites and African Americans. The authors conclude that there is "strong evidence" to support the charge that local law enforcement officials used racial profiling of Latinos to screen them for immigration violations (Gardner and Kohli 2009).

Much as twentieth-century immigration policies created, then illegalized, mass Mexico-U.S. migration, so too have early twenty-first-century policies criminalized it. This criminalization is not evenly distributed, especially targeting Latin Americans.

PERMANENTLY DEPORTABLE

While the overwhelming majority of U.S. immigration resources, funds, and personnel are dedicated to enforcement measures, roughly 1 million people are processed in the United States as new lawful immigrants every year (Nwosu et al. 2016); in fact, the United States admits more legal immigrants annually than any other country in the world. The 1965 Hart-Celler Act prioritized family reunification as a basis for lawful immigration, and two-thirds of immigrant visas are allotted to family members of U.S. citizens and lawful residents, while employment and humanitarian visas make up most of the rest. The family preference system involves a complex hierarchy of family relationships and citizenship statuses that, while privileging heterosexual nuclear families, appears largely consistent with "post-racial" U.S. values.

Even so, the quota system's caps on visas mean that relatives of U.S. citizens who are eligible for a visa can wait many years for one to become available. All countries get the same number of visas for non-immediate relatives, and wait times for these visas range from a few months to more than two decades, depending on which "line" a person is in and how many of their co-countrymen are in that line already. Paradoxically, the stronger the family ties between any particular country and the United States, the more demand there is for these visas, and the longer people in those places will have to wait to be reunited with their U.S. family members. People from Mexico, India, China, and the Philippines encounter especially long wait times (U.S. Department of State 2013). For example, in July 2014, the U.S. Department of State (DOS) was processing applications for adult unmarried children of U.S. citizens that had been filed in April 2007—an average worldwide wait time of seven years. But for adult unmarried Filipino children of U.S. citizens, the DOS was processing applications that had been filed in January 2003—an eleven-year wait. Visa applications for adult unmarried Mexican children of U.S. citizens were being processed from February 1994—a whopping twenty-year wait time for them. It should not be surprising that many people from these nations have forfeited the wait and attempted reunification with their U.S. family without the benefit of a visa.

Furthermore, current immigrant policies prevent most undocumented people who are already in the United States from ever changing their status—even when they have U.S.-citizen relatives. Under current law, only undocumented people with U.S.-citizen or lawfully resident spouses or parents are eligible to change their status, and for those select few, the path to lawful status diverges according to their mode of entry. Undocumented people who entered the United States lawfully with a temporary visa or through the U.S. Visa Waiver Program can typically adjust their status from within the United States if they have qualifying immediate relatives (U.S. Department of Homeland Security 2014). Undocumented people who entered the United States unlawfully by crossing a border without permission must leave the United States and apply to be admitted; when they do, all but a few are barred from returning for a period of ten years. In some cases, a U.S.-citizen spouse or parent can petition to have the bar waived if they can prove that a ten-year separation would cause them "extreme hardship," but the process is expensive and onerous, and it incurs the risk of prolonged family separation (Gomberg-Muñoz 2016).

Disproportionately punitive treatment of unauthorized border crossers is tied to broader ethnoracial and class inequalities. Citizens of many of the world's wealthiest nations—including most European countries, such as England, France, Germany, Sweden, Austria, the Netherlands, Finland, Greece, and Spain, as well as Australia and New Zealand and select Asian nations, including Japan, Taiwan, and South Korea—are part of the U.S. Visa Waiver Program. People from these countries do not need a visa to come to the United States; they can enter lawfully and stay up to ninety days without a visa (U.S. Department of State 2013), and this makes them very unlikely to ever enter the United States unlawfully. For the rest of the world, whether a person can procure a temporary visa to visit the United States is often based on their "assets" in the home country. Ample assets are considered evidence that visitors will return home promptly after a visit, making middle-class and wealthy people more likely to be granted visas to visit the United States than poor and working-class people (Gerken 2013). In all, the history of migration between Latin America and the United States, coupled with the likelihood that prospective Latin American immigrants will be working poor, makes undocumented Latin Americans more likely to be unlawful border crossers than undocumented people from elsewhere in the world (Coutin 2000; Pew Hispanic Center 2006; Heyman 2013). Thus, onerous legalization criteria for unauthorized border crossers disproportionately burden undocumented Latin Americans.

Between border policies that hem them in and immigration policies that keep them "illegal," there are more undocumented people settled in the United States than ever before. More than two-thirds of the U.S. undocumented population has lived in the United States for ten years or more, and the majority live in households with immediate family members (Taylor et al. 2001). Calls to reform the immigration system and grant a pathway to lawful status for some of these people have come from both the political right and left, but comprehensive immigration legislation has repeatedly stalled in Congress. In fact, no comprehensive bill has been passed since 1986's IRCA, and the undocumented population of the United States has been building steadily ever since. In this legislative void, administrative actions on immigration have offered temporary protection against deportation to select undocumented people. While administrative actions on immigration have a long history in U.S. politics, the scale of such action grew dramatically with the implementation of two programs: DACA in 2012 and DAPA in 2014.

The administration of President Barack Obama launched DACA, or Deferred Action for Childhood Arrivals, in 2012. DACA allows unauthorized youth who arrived in the United States when they were sixteen years old or younger, and who have graduated from or are enrolled in high school, to apply for a three-year deferral of deportation and a work permit. While DACA has provided significant relief for hundreds of thousands of undocumented youth, it does not provide a pathway to lawful permanent residency or U.S. citizenship, and it maintains ineligibility for federal financial aid, health care coverage under the Affordable Care Act, and most other public services. Because DACA is an executive action, the executive branch can cancel it at any time without approval from Congress, and in 2016, President-Elect Donald Trump vowed to end the DACA program on his first day in office.

In 2014, following the failure of a comprehensive immigration reform bill in the U.S. House of Representatives, the Obama administration once again sought to take executive action on immigration. The new program, called Deferred Action for Parental Accountability, or DAPA, would expand the key provisions of DACA to include select parents of U.S. citizens and lawful permanent residents. To qualify for DAPA, applicants must have qualifying children and be able to prove continuous residence since January 1, 2010. Like DACA, DAPA eligibility is predicated upon a largely "clean" criminal record and, thus, may leave out people with prior deportations, as well as return migrants with immigration-related criminal records. And because program participants must reapply every three years, they would be monitored closely for behaviors that could make them ineligible. Following Obama's announcement of the DAPA program, twenty-six states sued to stop DAPA, and implementation of the program has since been held up in the Fifth Circuit Court of Appeals. With an incoming Trump presidency, the program is unlikely to go forward in the foreseeable future.

Together, DACA and DAPA would bring millions of undocumented people "out of the shadows" and under the purview of the state, where they would be fingerprinted, registered, and either detained and deported or surveilled and regulated for a prolonged and indefinite period. Programs such as these shift the risks of deportation from random and unpredictable encounters with immigration enforcement to a pervasive and routine surveillance by agents of the state, expanding the population of U.S. immigrants who are able to work legally but remain permanently blocked from accessing lawful permanent residency and U.S. citizenship. Much as the diffusion of immigration enforcement throughout the U.S. interior has "thickened" U.S. borderlands (Rosas 2006), blocked access to lawful permanent residency "thickens" the boundaries of U.S. citizenship, pushing it ever further out of reach for most undocumented people. Furthermore, because they are the result of executive action and not legislation, these programs can be ended at any time and thus confer some legal legitimacy without any long-term security, rendering program participants both eligible to work legally and permanently deportable.

CONCLUSION

Together, this review of the U.S. immigration system shows how immigration policies are neither rigid nor static but rather built on the shifting sands of prevailing social values. As these values change over time, so too do the policies that are shaped by them. With the perspective of history, biases in law become apparent and overt discriminatory policies are no longer considered socially acceptable. Today, U.S.

immigration policies sanction and enforce discrimination against undocumented people, a practice widely considered to be race neutral. Yet, the likelihood that a person will become and remain undocumented is tightly linked to U.S. economic and foreign policy strategies that affect some people more than others. Moreover, emerging evidence suggests that immigration status and race are not easily unlinked: racial stereotypes continue to influence immigration in ideology and in practice and especially so in the SWNA region, whose populations are the focus of much of the racialized discourse of those policies.

Finally, in spite of meaningful shifts in U.S. immigration policy over time, this history also reveals some remarkable consistencies. Throughout U.S. history, welcome immigrants are imagined to more fully embody "American" values and traditions, while unwelcome immigrants are considered both inassimilable and criminal—invaders who constitute a threat to both public safety and national identity. Legislatively, undesirable characteristics are glossed as a lack of "morality," attributing exclusion to personal characteristics of immigrants rather than to prevailing social values of the U.S. elite.

REFERENCES

Calavita, Kitty. 1994. "U.S. Immigration and Policy Responses: The Limits of Legislation." In *Controlling Immigration*, edited by Wayne Cornelius, Philip Martin, and James Hollifield, 55–82. Stanford, CA: Stanford University Press.

Chavez, Leo. 2008. *The Latino Threat: Constructing Immigrants, Citizens, and the Nation*. Stanford, CA: Stanford University Press.

Coutin, Susan Bibler. 2000. *Legalizing Moves: Salvadoran Immigrants' Struggle for U.S. Residency*. Ann Arbor: University of Michigan Press.

Daniels, Rogers, and Otis L. Graham. 2001. *Debating American Immigration, 1882–Present*. New York: Rowman and Littlefield.

De Genova, Nicholas. 2005. *Working the Boundaries: Race, Space, and "Illegality" in Mexican Chicago*. Durham, NC: Duke University Press.

De Genova, Nicholas, and Ana Y. Ramos-Zayas. 2003. *Latino Crossings: Mexicans, Puerto Ricans, and the Politics of Race and Citizenship*. New York: Routledge.

Fussell, Elizabeth. 2011. "The Deportation Threat Dynamic and Victimization of Latino Migrants: Wage Theft and Robbery." *The Sociological Quarterly* 52(4): 593–615.

Garcia, Mario T. 1985. "*La Frontera*: The Border as Symbol and Reality in Mexican-American Thought." *Mexican Studies/Estudios Mexicanos* 1(2): 195–225.

Gardner, Trevor, II and Aarti Kohli. 2009. "The C.A.P. Effect: Racial Profiling in the ICE Criminal Alien Program." Policy brief. The Chief Justice Earl Warren Institute on Race,

Ethnicity and Diversity, Berkeley Law School, University of California. https://www.law.berkeley.edu/files/policybrief_irving_0909_v9.pdf.

Gerken, Christina. 2013. *Model Immigrants and Undesirable Aliens: The Cost of Immigration Reform in the 1990s*. Minneapolis: University of Minnesota Press.

Golash-Boza, Tanya. 2012. *Immigration Nation: Raids, Detentions, and Deportations in Post-9/11 America*. New York: Paradigm Publishers.

Golash-Boza, Tanya, and Pierrette Hondagneu-Sotelo. 2013. "Latino Immigrant Men and the Deportation Crisis: A Gendered Racial Removal Program." *Latino Studies* 11:271–92.

Gomberg-Muñoz, Ruth. 2016. *Becoming Legal: Immigration Law and Mixed Status Families*. New York: Oxford University Press.

Greider, William. 1997. *One World, Ready or Not: The Manic Logic of Global Capitalism*. New York: Simon and Schuster.

Guelespe, Diana M. 2015. "From Driving to Deportation: Experiences of Mixed-Status Immigrant Families Under Secure Communities." In *Living Together, Living Apart: Mixed-Status Families and US Immigration Policy*, edited by April M. Schueths and Jodie Lawston, 198–213. Seattle: University of Washington Press.

Gutierrez, David G. 1995. *Walls and Mirrors: Mexican Americans, Mexican Immigrants, and the Politics of Ethnicity*. Berkeley: University of California Press.

Heyman, Josiah. 2001. "Class and Classification at the U.S.-Mexico Border." *Human Organization* 60(2): 128–40.

———. 2013. "Constructing a Virtual Wall: Race and Citizenship in U.S.-Mexico Border Policing." In *Governing Immigration Through Crime: A Reader*, edited by Julie Dowling and Jonathan Xavier Inda, 99–114. Stanford, CA: Stanford University Press.

Hondagneu-Sotelo, Pierrette. 1994. *Gendered Transitions: Mexican Experiences of Immigration*. Berkeley: University of California Press.

Inda, Jonathan Xavier, and Julie A. Dowling. 2013. "Introduction: Governing Migrant Illegality." In *Governing Immigration Through Crime: A Reader*, edited by Julie Dowling and Jonathan Xavier Inda, 1–36. Stanford, CA: Stanford University Press.

Jimenez, Maria. 2009. "Humanitarian Crisis: Migrant Deaths at the U.S.-Mexico Border." Report of the ACLU of San Diego and Imperial Counties and Mexico's National Commission of Human Rights. https://www.aclu.org/files/pdfs/immigrants/humanitariancrisisreport.pdf.

Kohli, Aarti, Peter L. Markowitz, and Lisa Chavez. 2011. "Secure Communities by the Numbers: An Analysis of Demographics and Due Process." Research report. The Chief Justice Earl Warren Institute on Law and Social Policy, Berkeley Law School, University of California. https://www.law.berkeley.edu/files/Secure_Communities_by_the_Numbers.pdf.

Light, Michael T., Mark Hugo Lopez, and Ana Gonzalez-Barrera. 2014. "The Rise of Federal Immigration Crimes." Washington, DC: Pew Research Center's Hispanic Trends Project.

Linker, Jodi. 2013. "A 'S.A.F.E.' Approach to Defending Illegal Reentry Cases." Winning Strategies Seminar, Orlando, FL, Jan. 17–19. https://www.fd.org/docs/select-topics/common-offenses/immigration/safe_approach_illegal_reentry.pdf.

Massey, Douglas. 2009. "Racial Formation in Theory and Practice: The Case of Mexicans in the United States." *Race and Social Problems* 1:12–26.

Massey, Douglas, Jorge Durand, and Nolan J. Malone. 2002. *Beyond Smoke and Mirrors: Mexican Immigration in an Era of Economic Integration*. New York: Russell Sage Foundation.

Menchaca, Martha, and Richard Valencia. 1990. "Anglo-Saxon Ideologies in the 1920s–1930s: Their Impact on the Segregation of Mexican Students in California." *Anthropology & Education Quarterly* 21:222–49.

Meyers, Deborah W. 2005. "U.S. Border Enforcement: From Horseback to High Tech." *Migration Policy Institute Insight* 7.

Nakano Glenn, Evelyn. 2002. *Unequal Freedom: How Race and Gender Shaped American Citizenship and Labor*. Cambridge, MA: Harvard University Press.

National Conference of State Legislatures. 2011. "Immigration-Related Laws and Resolutions in the States (January–June)." *Immigration Policy Report*, September 19. http://www.ncsl.org/issues-research/immig/state-immigration-laws-january-to-june-2011.aspx.

Ngai, Mae. 2004. *Impossible Subjects: Illegal Aliens and the Making of Modern America*. Princeton, NJ: Princeton University Press.

Nwosu, Chiamaka, Gregory Auclair, and Jeanne Batalova. 2016. "Frequently Requested Statistics on Immigrants and Immigration in the United States." *Migration Policy Institute*, April 14. http://www.migrationpolicy.org/article/frequently-requested-statistics-immigrants-and-immigration-united-states.

Passel, Jeffrey, and D'Vera Cohn. 2009. "A Portrait of Unauthorized Immigration in the United States." Washington, DC: Pew Hispanic Center. http://pewhispanic.org/files/reports/107.pdf.

———. 2014. "Unauthorized Immigrant Totals Rise in 7 States, Fall in 14." Washington, DC: Pew Research Center.

Pedraza, Silvia, and Ruben G. Rumbaut. 1996. *Origins and Destinies: Immigration, Race, and Ethnicity in America*. New York: Wadsworth.

Pew Hispanic Center. 2006. "Fact Sheet: Modes of Entry for the Unauthorized Migrant Population." http://www.pewhispanic.org/2006/05/22/modes-of-entry-for-the-unauthorized-migrant-population/.

Portes, Alejandro, and Ruben Rumbaut. 1996. *Immigrant America: A Portrait*. Berkeley: University of California Press.

Quesada, James, Sonya Arreola, Alex Kral, Sahar Khoury, Kurt C. Organista, and Paula Worby. 2014. "'As Good as It Gets': Undocumented Latino Day Laborers Negotiating Discrimination in San Francisco and Berkeley, California, USA." *City & Society* 26(1): 29–50.

Rosas, Gilberto. 2006. "The Thickening Borderlands: Diffused Exceptionality and 'Immigrant' Social Struggles During the 'War on Terror.'" *Cultural Dynamics* 18:335–49.

Selway, William, and Margaret Newkirk. 2014. "Congress Mandates Jail Beds for 34,000 Immigrants as Private Prisons Profit." *Bloomberg*, September 24. http://www.bloomberg.com/news/2013-09-24/congress-fuels-private-jails-detaining-34-000-immigrants.html.

Taylor, Paul, Mark Hugo Lopez, Jeffrey S. Passel, and Seth Motel. 2011. "Unauthorized Immigrants: Length of Residency, Patterns of Parenthood." Pew Research Center, *Hispanic Trends*, December 1. http://www.pewhispanic.org/2011/12/01/unauthorized-immigrants-length-of-residency-patterns-of-parenthood/.

U.S. Department of Homeland Security, Security Office of Immigration Statistics. 2013. "Yearbook of Immigration Statistics: 2012." Washington, DC: U.S. Department of Homeland Security, Security Office of Immigration Statistics.

———. 2014. "Visa Waiver Program." http://travel.state.gov/content/visas/english/visit/visa-waiver-program.html.

U.S. Department of State, Bureau of Consular Affairs. 2014. "Visa Bulletin for October 2014." http://travel.state.gov/content/visas/english/law-and-policy/bulletin/2015/visa-bulletin-for-october-2014.html. Washington, DC: Bureau of Consular Affairs, U.S. Department of State.

U.S. Department of State, Immigration and Customs Enforcement. 2015. "Secure Communities: Get the Facts." https://www.ice.gov/secure-communities/get-the-facts.

Varsanyi, Monica. 2011. "Neoliberalism and Nativism: Local Anti-immigrant Policy Activism and an Emerging Politics of Scale." *International Journal of Urban and Regional Research* 35(2): 295–311.

12

WHERE IS "THE BORDER"?

The Fourth Amendment, Boundary Enforcement, and the Making of an Inherently Suspect Class

LUIS F. B. PLASCENCIA

INTRODUCTION

U.S. ATTORNEY GENERAL Eric H. Holder Jr. released the U.S. Department of Justice's long-awaited policy document on "racial profiling" on December 8, 2014, the *Guidance for Federal Law Enforcement Agencies Regarding the Use of Race, Ethnicity, Gender, National Origin, Religion, Sexual Orientation, or Gender Identity* (2014).[1] There is a general consensus that the 2014 guidance is an improvement over the 2003 *Guidance Regarding the Use of Race by Federal Law Enforcement Agencies* (U.S. Department of Justice 2003). The 2014 *Guidance* expands the protected classes to include gender, gender identity, national origin, religion, ethnicity, and sexual orientation. Under the 2014 *Guidance*, federal law enforcement agents are prohibited from *solely* using *one* of the listed categories to initiate a police action upon a civilian. State and local police are not covered by the *Guidance* unless they are participating in a federal law enforcement task force.[2]

What is most relevant for the discussion here is footnote 2 on page two of the 2014 *Guidance*. Footnote 2 indicates, "This Guidance does not apply to interdiction activities in the *vicinity of the border*, or to protective, inspection, or screening activities" (*Guidance* 2014, 2; my italics).[3] In other words, the *Guidance* exempts the "vicinity of the border," marine ports, permanent checkpoints, and airports (i.e., places where protective, inspection, and screening actions also take place) from restrictions against "racial profiling" by federal law enforcement officers. Stated more directly, the U.S. Department of Justice authorizes "racial profiling" in the "vicinity of the border" and at a significant number of other sites where inspection and screening take place.[4]

The 2014 *Guidance* and the stated exception serve to index key issues addressed in this chapter: (1) the long-standing presumed meaning of "the border," even if undefined. A historical process that has come to associate "the border" with only one of hundreds of possible borders: the Mexico-United States boundary area or, as termed in this volume, the Southwest North American (SWNA) region (chapter 1); (2) the development of a long-established "border exception" wherein the protections afforded in the "interior" of the United States by the Fourth Amendment to the Constitution are eroded in the vicinity of the boundary area; (3) the juridical construction of "border functional equivalents," that is, airports and permanent checkpoints, that are elements in constituting "the border" and are national in scope.

The aim of this chapter is to present a genealogy of how juridical actions, and noncitizen and citizen legal challenges to the actions of Border Patrol officials, specifically those drawing on the Fourth Amendment, have been central in shaping the police powers of the Border Patrol, and the definition of what constitutes the spatial composition of "the border" (relatedly, see chapter 3). In this chapter I present four arguments: (1) since the early 1920s, the policy assumptions and police practices regarding border enforcement have been narrowly constructed to mean the apprehension and deportation/removal[5] of persons with "Mexican appearance/descent"; (2) boundary law enforcement has a parallel formation that aims to "secure the border" and this has come to mean securing only one boundary; (3) the enforcement apparatus, border exceptions, and similar political decisions have been salient in the making of a inherently suspect class (i.e., individuals classified as possessing a "Mexican appearance/descent"; also see chapter 11); and (4) Latinos, particularly Mexican-origin persons, have used federal courts as the primary sites of contestation of State police powers regarding racialized policing.

The chapter is divided into five parts. The first part summarizes the formation of the intrinsic association between the concept of "the border" and the Mexico-U.S. boundary area. The second part outlines the development of the salient juridical notion of "border exception," also referred to as "border search exception." Included in the section is a discussion of how the vicinity of the border came to be arbitrarily defined as the area within one hundred air miles from an external boundary—a classification not created by the U.S. Congress. The third part outlines the importance of understanding the creation of the "land border patrol," its origins, and how the law enforcement focus and practices implemented since 1925 established the foundation of present practices. In the fourth part, the discussion turns to legal challenges to Border Patrol actions by U.S. citizens and noncitizens. Part five brings together the material presented to suggest how Border Patrol practices and ongoing legal challenges to their discretionary power have sought to disrupt the political imaginary that created and sustains the view of persons with a "Mexican appearance/descent" as an inherently suspect class. In other words, the Border Patrol, though not necessarily a product of a strategic, calculated state policy, represents the "fruit of a poisonous tree" from which it traces its origins and which produced a federal law enforcement agency that is a de facto Mexican Border Patrol or, parallel to the older "Chinese Inspectors," an agency of Mexican Inspectors.[6] Irrespective of the label selected, there is no doubt that the agency's focus is on stopping, questioning, and investigating persons deemed to possess a "Mexican appearance/descent" or "Hispanic appearance" because of an a priori assumption that they are neither U.S. citizens nor do they belong in the United States. This is a de facto form of racial profiling, even though the Ninth Circuit Court of Appeals ruled in *United States v. Montero Camargo* (2000) that due to the demographic composition in the Southwest, Border Patrol officials "*may not* . . . consider . . . [Hispanic appearance as] a relevant factor where particularized or individualized suspicion is required" in carrying out boundary enforcement along the Mexico-U.S. region (2000, 6; my italics). With reference to persons with Mexican/Latino appearance residing or traveling in the northern segment of the SWNA region as well as beyond the region, the footnote number two exception in the 2014 Department of Justice *Guidance* conflicts with the dictum in *Montero Camargo* in the geographic jurisdiction of the Ninth Circuit Court of Appeals.[7]

LOCATING "THE BORDER"

Academic, media, government, and popular discourse in the United States on the Mexico-U.S. "border" bear the weight of a hegemonic trope. It is a trope that, to paraphrase Pierre Bourdieu, "goes without saying because it comes without saying" (1977, 167). Its taken-for-granted nature is anchored deeply in the imagination of users, and thus it is evoked without much reflection. Multiple academic books and journal articles, conferences, print and television media, and migrant civil rights activists, as well as the White House, Congress, and other federal agencies, regularly evoke the notion of "the border" as an unambiguous term. It is a label that has been naturalized as indexing an unspecified space near the Mexico-U.S. boundary.

On more than one occasion in my borderlands course and at an international Mexico-U.S. border conference in Arizona, I asked the rhetorical question if any in the audience had visited or been to the border. Not surprisingly a number of hands were quickly raised. No one asked me to clarify which "border" I was referring to in my question. My ambiguous question was interpreted as a specific, factual question related to the Mexico-U.S. boundary area, although I had not specified this. It could be argued that in the SWNA region the response was a logical one; however, if we factor in that residents and businesses in Detroit, Michigan, a city that is across from Windsor, Canada, do not define themselves as "border" residents or Detroit as a "border/*frontière*" city suggests that it is not simply location, but rather has more to do with a different historical and political imaginary. The fact that Detroit residents live across from Canada does not automatically make them borderlanders/*frontalier*.

The commonly invoked concept of "the border" in the United States has no intrinsic or singular referent—it is a historically contingent floating signifier.[8] The current United States of America has hundreds of borders. Its land border with Canada, approximately five thousand miles, dwarfs the southern land border. It also possesses Hawai'i, American Samoa, Guam, Northern Mariana Islands, Puerto Rico, and the U.S. Virgin Islands, as well as the thousand-mile-long Aleutian archipelago. In addition, it has a 1,500-mile Alaska-Canada boundary (approximately three-fourths the length of the Mexico–United States boundary), and it has three lengthy coastal borders on the continental states. Moreover, juridically created borders are not generally included in discussions of "border" issues, yet within migration and boundary enforcement apparatuses, they are important and have real material consequences for individuals and the degree of constitutional rights afforded to nationals and non-nationals.

Despite the complex reality of the political territory of the United States and its multiple borders, the Mexico-U.S. boundary has been arbitrarily coded as "the border." While some may argue that the label "the border" is simply a shorthand form for the "Mexico-U.S. border," and thus there is no reason to make our communication more complex than it needs to be, this overlooks the political implications of the label. The hegemonic position of the label, I argue, has to be factored into our analysis of political discussions at the federal, state, and local level regarding issues such as the regulation of migration and migrants, the degree of boundary enforcement needed, detention, and removal. In a discussion of "border security," for example, advocates for a more militarized boundary zone as well as migrant advocates opposed to that militarization may present opposing views, but both rely on the same underlying premise. Both sides strongly dispute the needed level of military and law enforcement but do not question the spatial reference of the debate. Within the contemporary debate regarding "comprehensive immigration reform," the "secure the border first" position makes clear that before any amnesty or path to citizenship can proceed, only one of the hundreds of U.S. borders needs to be secured. Oddly enough, nothing is said about the rationale or logic for why the "security" of all the other borders is irrelevant to national homeland security.

The aforementioned reality should lead us to raise questions such as the following. Why is the Mexico-U.S. border the only border that needs to be secured? Why is it that the label "border security" is only applied to the southern land border? Should walls be built along all our coastal areas and islands, and at the edge of territorial waters, to ensure greater homeland security? Why is the idea of a "border wall," such as that proposed by Republican presidential candidate Donald J. Trump, only applicable to the Mexico-U.S. border? Is it that our Canadian neighbors would be insulted if we build a border wall along our entire five-thousand-mile northern land and water border? Do U.S. officials and public hold different perceptions and evaluations of our two neighbors? Why do academics and non-academics deploy an unstated preference for the label the "U.S.-Mexico border"—a label that gives sequential preference to the U.S.—rather than the Mexico-U.S. border (a label that gives preference to the alphabetical order of names)? These and similar questions are issues that require attention and reflection, rather than deployed uncritically as a priori assumptions or unmarked, self-indexing categories.

The heightened attention on the southern land boundary is also important in shaping our understanding of the "undocumented" migrant population (what I refer to as the "informally authorized" migrant population; Plascencia 2009[9]) and U.S. visions on how to "solve" the "problem." What I am referring to is the common view that the estimated eleven to twelve million "undocumented" migrants are persons subject to removal because they entered the United States without formal authorization—based on the assumed premise that they entered through the southern land boundary. The corresponding solution is of course to "secure the border" (i.e., the Mexico-U.S. boundary area) through higher expenditures for Border Patrol agents, drones, and other high-tech instruments of surveillance and mobility control. Yet, Government Accountability Office (GAO) reports, and Department of Homeland Security (DHS) officials testifying before Congress, have over many years noted that they estimate that the total "undocumented" migrant population is made up of two groups: those who entered U.S. territory without formal authorization and those who entered the U.S. with a nonimmigrant visa (e.g., student, tourist, entertainer, business visitor, temporary contract agricultural worker) or with a border-crossing permit but who may have either violated the conditions or time limits of the respective visa.[10] The violation of visa conditions converts the person to one subject to removal—i.e., in common discourse, the person becomes an "undocumented" migrant subject to removal. What is not commonly noted is that the estimated proportion of the two groups is approximately 50:50 (Pew Hispanic Center 2006).[11] This means that whatever level of U.S. dollars, personnel, and drones allocated to "secure" the southern boundary, or height of the "border wall," they only address half of the expressed policy concern. A fully militarized southern boundary will have little impact on about half of the population subject to removal.

I would argue that the above issue regarding the 50:50 split in the "undocumented" migrant population in the United States has become almost invisible in policy debates because of the overriding centrality of the southern boundary and because of the pattern since the early 1970s that forged the association in the political imaginary in the United States among the Mexico-U.S. border, Mexican "silent invasion/invasion," and "illegal aliens." The over four-decade-long conflation of these issues has been key in shaping how scholars, government officials, media, and the public imagine the issue of Mexican migration to the United States.[12] Thus, it is not surprising that one impact of the fusion of the issues has fostered the notion of the Mexico-U.S. boundary as "the border" and the view that the solution to the "undocumented" migrant problem is "border security" along the southern boundary. The conflation has also contributed to producing the racialized notion that the labels "illegal alien" or "undocumented immigrant" are synonymous with Mexican migrants—persons perceived as "Mexicans" have become an inherently suspect racialized class. Informally authorized migrants from Ireland and Poland, for example, are not an enforcement priory for Immigration and Custom Enforcement (ICE) or the Border Patrol; they remain largely outside the enforcement gaze.

Having foregrounded some of the central limitations in the contemporary discourse regarding "the border," I turn to examining the determination of what constitutes "the border," the development of the "border exception," and the juridical construction of "functional border equivalents."

WHERE IS THE UNITED STATES, WHAT ARE ITS BORDERS, AND WHAT IS THE BORDER EXCEPTION?

As suggested above, it is not easy to provide a concise answer to the question, "Where is the border?" U.S. nationals, even if U.S. born and educated, tend to believe that they know what constitutes the territory of the United States of America, and presumably its borders.[13] Internal and external territorial issues further complicate the actual question of what constitutes the territory of the United States. Federally recognized Native American/Indian reservation land belongs to the respective indigenous community; thus it is land that does not belong to the United States, though U.S. federal agents have jurisdiction within those national sovereign territories. Moreover, the land occupied by the United Nations and foreign embassies in Washington, DC, are formally not under the jurisdiction of the United States; simultaneously, land occupied by U.S. embassies in other countries is considered U.S. sovereign territory. This also applies to the over one thousand U.S. military installations throughout the globe. Entering such sovereign spaces means that a non-U.S. national who enters a military base has crossed "the border" and entered U.S. sovereign territory.

A distinctive marker of a boundary on land is a customs/port-of-entry structure, and on coastal areas there are ports. The United States operates 483 land ports of entry and 149 international marine ports on the continental states. Each of these nodes represents a point where a non-U.S. national can be inspected before being allowed to enter the territory.[14] In addition, U.S. law classifies airports designated as "international" airports as "functional border equivalents," and thus they are a formal category of "border."[15] The United States has a total of 154 international airports located from coast to coast, including facilities in non-continental territories. Taken together, "the border" ultimately represents a combination of land and water boundaries, as well as a multiplicity of points in and outside the continental United States that demarcate a political and legal space of exception, particularly in the full application of the Fourth Amendment.

Although the reader might expect that the important concept of "functional equivalent" of the border was congressionally legislated, this is not the case; it was the creation of the U.S. Supreme Court. In the *Almeida-Sánchez v. United States*, 413 U.S. 266 (1973) case, the U.S. Supreme Court considered a Border Patrol agent's warrantless search of an automobile driven by a Mexican national with a valid work permit approximately twenty-five miles north of the Mexico-U.S. boundary and traveling on a west–east axis. The court reversed the conviction imposed by the Ninth Circuit Court of Appeals and noted:

> Whatever the permissible scope of intrusiveness of a *routine* border search might be, searches of this kind may in certain circumstances take place not only at the border itself, but at its *functional equivalents* as well. For example, searches at an *established station [i.e., permanent checkpoint]* near the border, at a point marking the *confluence of two or more roads* that extend from *the border [north–south axis]*, might be functional equivalents of border searches. For another example, a search of *passengers* and cargo of an airplane arriving at a St. Louis *airport* after a nonstop flight from Mexico City would clearly be the functional equivalent of a border search. (1973, 3; my italics)

The *Almeida-Sánchez* opinion reinforced the long-standing practice of treating an actual port of entry as falling under the "border exception" or "border search exception"—that is, giving power to migration officials to conduct a "routine" search at a port of entry involving the person and her luggage and vehicle—but in effect extended the notion of border to a permanent road checkpoint, the confluence of two roads extending from a national boundary, and international airports. The classification of a "routine" search also produced the category of "non-routine" search; while the former largely depends on the agent's discretion, the latter requires an officer to articulate a rational indicator of "probable cause" or "reasonable suspicion."[16]

What is notable in the discussion in the case and in the above quote is that Justice Potter Stewart in writing the majority opinion of the court concentrated his discussion of "the border" as signifying the Mexico-U.S. boundary as the primary reference. Additionally, it is worth observing that the approximate 154 international airports were thought of as functional border equivalents not because they might receive nonstop flights from Canada, England, France, or Israel but because they may receive nonstop flights from Mexico. The Lambert–St. Louis International Airport receives flights from many international points of origin, not only from Mexico.

Based on an important comment in Justice Byron White's dissent in *Almeida-Sánchez* (joined by Chief Justice Burger and Associate Justices Blackmun and Rehnquist), I suggest that the justices misunderstood a central concept in the case. According to Justice White:

> This has also been the considered judgment of three Courts of Appeal whose daily concern is the enforcement of the immigration laws along the Mexican-American border, and who, although as sensitive to constitutional commands as we are, perhaps have a better vantage point than we here on the *Potomac* to judge the practices of *border-area* law enforcement and the reasonableness of official searches of vehicles to enforce immigration statutes. (*Almeida-Sánchez*, 11; my italics)

The reference to the Potomac River as somehow not in the "border area" overlooks the fact that under the one-hundred-air-mile rule from an external boundary demarcation (established in 1954), which is referenced in the introduction to the opinion itself, the Potomac River, the White House, the Capitol, and the Supreme Court building are located in a border area. They are at some distance from the Mexico-U.S. boundary but are completely and without question within the zone classified as "the border." The dissenting justices misrecognized that they lived and worked in a border area and, thus, like all other residents within border areas, such as the "Mexican-American border," were subject to official searches of vehicles and persons in the enforcement of migration and migrant control.

ONE HUNDRED AIR MILES FROM AN EXTERNAL BOUNDARY

The determination of the boundary zone as the area encompassed within one hundred air miles from an external boundary is also not a product of congressional action and has an ambiguous creation.[17] In the same year that General Joseph Swing (commissioner of the Immigration and Naturalization Service [INS]) implemented the short-lived "Operation Wetback" (principally June and July 1954),[18] Commissioner Swing and/or U.S. Attorney General Herbert Brownell Jr. adopted the one-hundred-air-mile rule; however, they failed to post it or provide for public comment, as required by law, in the *Federal Register* in 1954. Three years later, two months after

Brownell's departure, under Attorney General William P. Rogers, the INS filed the requisite posting of the rule on December 6, 1957. *Federal Register* Section 287.1 states:

> (a) . . . The phrase "within a reasonable distance from an external boundary of the United States," as used in section 287 of the [1952] Immigration and Nationality Act, means within a distance of not exceeding 100 air miles from any external boundary . . . (*Federal Register* 1957, 9808)[19]

The significance of the "reasonable distance" definition is that it created a zone wherein we can safely speculate most residents do not perceive that they are borderlanders/ *fronterizos/frontalier* or that their Fourth Amendment protections are diluted if confronted by a Border Patrol or Immigration and Customs Enforcement (ICE) officer who may suspect them of being unauthorized "aliens." As graphically presented in figure 12.1, residents in Baltimore, Washington, DC, Chicago, Eugene, Houston, Augusta, and many other cities and towns across the continental United States live within a "border" area, even though that fact is not part of their conscious everyday lives. Moreover, the entire state of Hawai'i and island colonies such as Puerto Rico are border territories; there is in effect no "interior" area within these.

The map in figure 12.1 provides a visual representation of the border zone and the fact that close to two-thirds of the United States population lives in "the border." To gain a more comprehensive optic of the spatial dimension, however, one must overlay a map of international airports in the "interior" (the area not encompassed by the boundary zone) such as those in Chicago, Denver, Salt Lake City, Dallas–Fort Worth, etc., and location of all permanent checkpoints to grasp the significance of the combined border area and functional border equivalents. Citizens and noncitizens traveling through a border zone or functional equivalents can be stopped, questioned, and inspected by a Border Patrol/ICE agent as part of "routine" and "non-routine" searches and seizures.

THE BORDER EXCEPTION

The importance of knowing the juridical boundaries of the border zone is not simply to gauge the physical location but also its linkage to the border exception/border search exception. On July 31, 1789, the First Congress enacted an important provision that remains in effect to the present. Section 23 specifies "that it shall be lawful for the collector, or other officer of the customs, after entry made of any goods, wares or merchandise, on suspicion of fraud, to open and examine" the belongings of persons seeking to enter the United States (1 Stat. 29, 43). This provision is codified as 8 U.S.C. §1357 (a)(3):

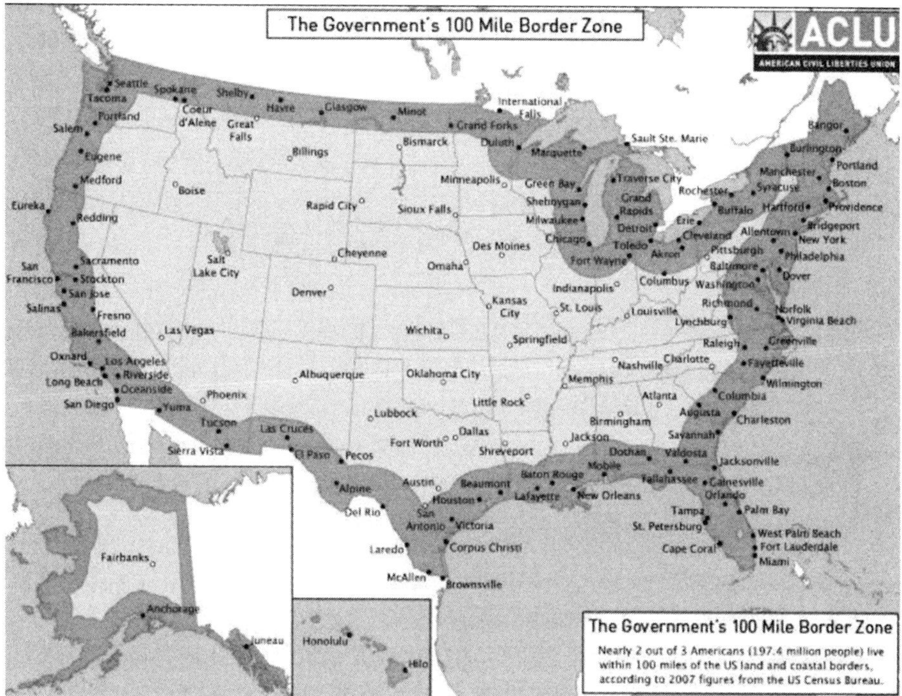

FIGURE 12.1. ACLU, one-hundred-mile border zone. Source: American Civil Liberties Union (2016). Copyright (c) 2016 American Civil Liberties Union.

> [W]ithin a reasonable distance from any external boundary of the United States, [a migration officer shall have the power] to board and search for aliens any vessel within the territorial waters of the United States and any railway car, aircraft, conveyance, or vehicle, and within a distance of twenty-five miles for any such external boundary to have access to private lands, but not dwellings, for the purpose of patrolling the border to prevent the illegal entry of aliens into the United States.

The First Congress granted federal officers the power to search and seize persons, goods, and beasts entering the territory without the standards of *reasonable suspicion* or *probable cause* that is said to apply to areas in the interior (1 Stat. 29, 43). The fact of location is central in determining the full or limited application of the Fourth Amendment; border searches are deemed to be inherently "reasonable" and, if classified as "routine," do not require probable cause or reasonable suspicion. Contemporary migration and boundary enforcement are grounded on the principle that U.S. citizens and noncitizens do not enjoy full Fourth Amendment protection in the space defined as "the border"; thus, Customs, migration, and Coast Guard officials possess greater discretion than other federal agents within the border zone. Stated differently, about two-thirds of the U.S. population, both nationals and non-nationals, reside in a juridical zone that diminishes Fourth Amendment protections.[20]

BORDER ZONE AND FUNCTIONAL EQUIVALENT ENFORCEMENT

The aim of this section is not to present a full historical account of the Border Patrol; to do so is beyond the scope of this chapter and would entail repeating the excellent foundation laid by Andreas (2009), Hernández (2002, 2006, 2010), Heyman (2001, 2002), Maril (2004), and Nevins (2010). Instead, it aims to draw attention to the links between its origins and contemporary operations. Although it is commonly noted that the Border Patrol was created in 1924, what is often overlooked are its statutory creation and law enforcement roots.[21] The May 28, 1924, Labor Appropriations Act included a provision related to the Department of Labor that specified "that at least $1,000,000 of this amount shall be expended for additional land border patrol of which $100,000 shall be immediately available" (43 Stat. 205, 240).[22] What is notable in the provision is that it did not specify its enforcement focus, mission, enforcement and territorial jurisdiction, arrest powers, cross-deputation, etc. The initial 450 land border patrol agents hired in 1925, as noted by Hernández (2010), were simply given a gun and a holster and told to go out and do their job.[23] Congress provided the initial charge for the land border patrol nine months later:

> That hereafter any employee of the Bureau of Immigration authorized so to do under regulations prescribed by the Commissioner General of Immigration with the approval of the Secretary of Labor, shall have power without warrant (1) to arrest any alien who in his presence or view is entering or attempting to enter the United States in violation of any law or regulation made in pursuance of law regulating the admission of aliens . . . (2) to board and search for aliens any vessel within the territorial waters of the United States, railway car, conveyance, or vehicle, in which he believes aliens are being brought in to the United States. (43 Stat. 1014, 1049–50)

The 1925 directive and subsequent amendments refined the border search powers of the Border Patrol and thus formulated law enforcement practices to implement the broad guidelines enunciated in 1789. These directives formalized what is now considered "routine" searches at "the border" and functional equivalents: the power of federal agents to stop and seize persons and goods at "the border" without need of a warrant, probable cause, or reasonable suspicion.

According to the historian Kelly Lytle Hernández (2010), many within the initial cohort of 450 agents hired in 1925 had been Texas Rangers prior to becoming land border patrol agents. The primary policing practices of the Texas Rangers in the 1840s and 1850s was on "ridding the Texas territory of thousands of Mexicans and for terrorizing into submission those who survived" (Samora, Bernal, and Peña 1979, 2).[24] Ernesto Galarza characterized the work of the Texas Rangers as one of "gunpowder justice" or what is popularly known as "shoot first, ask questions later."[25] Thus, for Hernández, aims and practices in the Texas Rangers were informally transplanted to the new land border patrol. The multiplicity of recent high-profile local police killings of African American and Latino males in cities across the United States and Border Patrol killings of Mexican migrants on both the northern and southern section of the SWNA region are contemporary examples of the long-standing continuity of gunpowder justice.

Human and civil rights abuses of persons of Mexican descent along the southern boundary have been well documented.[26] Since the early 1970s, local and national organizations documented and published a variety of reports noting multiple forms of violence carried out by Border Patrol agents: from stops with a lengthy detention, verbal abuses, assault, battery, sexual assault (including rape), negligence in providing medical care, and use of excessive force to the use of deadly force. It is reported that between 2004 and 2014, Border Patrol agents killed forty-six individuals. More recently, the American Civil Liberties Union (ACLU) published its *Record of Abuse: Lawlessness and Impunity in Border Patrol's Interior Enforcement Operations* (2015) report based on information obtained through a Freedom of Information Act (FOIA) regarding complaints in the Tucson and Yuma sectors filed between 2011 and 2014 with the U.S. Customs and Border Protection (CBP) and the DHS. The authors conclude from the approximately six thousand pages provided by the DHS that there were egregious violations of human rights against residents in the border area, that these complaints are more numerous than officially reported, that there is a general absence of accountability, and that basic data collection processes that would allow the detection and correction of problem practices are largely absent. Data provided to ACLU indicate at least eighty-one Fourth Amendment complaints. Although not highlighted in the report due to the redacting of the name of the complainants, the actual racio-ethnic and sex/gender of the complainants is unknown, but given the location of the two sectors, it is safe to assume that most are Latinas/os.

One indicator of the clear emphasis within the Border Patrol and ICE on identifying persons of "Mexican appearance/descent" is the data on apprehensions, deportations/removals, the proportion of apprehensions in the Mexico-U.S. "border region," and those deported/removed to Mexico.[27] Tables 12.1, 12.2, and 12.3 summarize the continued focus on the stopping, questioning, and apprehending persons of Mexican descent.

Over the twenty-eight-year period from 1927 to 1954, from close to three-fourths (71 percent) to 99 percent of all apprehensions took place in the Mexico-U.S. boundary area. As insightfully noted by Hernández (2010), the early years of the Border Patrol produced a "net of surveillance" throughout the Mexico-U.S. boundary area. The surveillance apparatus encompassed a political imaginary that constituted persons of Mexican descent as the subjects of surveillance and detection—a parallel to the post-1875 period that made persons of "Chinese appearance" the targets of surveillance—as well as placing the majority of Border Patrol agents after 1943 along the Mexico-U.S. border. What is often overlooked in the debate regarding "border security" and the citation of the substantial number of Mexican migrants apprehended or removed is that the number is a product of state political arbitrary decisions regarding the location of enforcement personnel.[28]

Apprehensions are one indicator of the actions and impact of Border Patrol activities. What is not addressed is the high volume in the number of residents and travelers in the Mexico-U.S. boundary area who are ensnared in the surveillance net. Hernández (2010) presents a series of tables (1, 2, 4, 5, and 6) that summarize the low proportion of actual apprehensions for violations of migration laws, from all persons questioned in the same area. Between 1926 and 1944, a total of 22.4 million individuals were "questioned," and of these 1.1 percent were apprehended for potential violations of migration laws. In the period covering 1945 and 1954, the number increased to 7.2 percent, and of the 147.3 million questioned between 1955 and 1974, 2.01 percent were apprehended. This suggests that the surveillance apparatus is not simply about capturing those who violated a migration law, but more importantly, its aim is in monitoring and controlling the larger population (principally those of Mexican origin) who live or travel in the Mexico-U.S. boundary area. Citizens, permanent residents, asylees, refugees, nonimmigrants with valid visas, and other formally authorized migrants have to pay the social costs of living or traveling in the "vicinity of the border." They are part of the inherently suspect class.

While table 12.1 underscores the spatial dimension of boundary enforcement, table 12.2 foregrounds the fact that persons of Mexican descent are the clear targets of apprehensions over the fifty-nine years between 1955 and 2013 (the most recent year for which data are available). It is noteworthy that in fifty-three of the fifty-nine years, Mexican-origin persons made up more than half of all apprehensions. The most recent year for which Mexicans were less than half of the total apprehended was 2011

TABLE 12.1. Total Apprehension and Proportion at Border Region, 1925–1954

YEAR	TOTAL APPREHENDED	APPREHENDED, MEXICAN BORDER REGION	PERCENT AT MEXICAN BORDER REGION
1925	22,199	N/A	N/A
1926	12,735	N/A	N/A
1927	16,393	13,759	84%
1928	23,566	19,850	84%
1929	32,711	28,805	88%
1930	20,880	17,027	82%
1931	22,276	18,072	81%
1932	22,735	17,648	82%
1933	20,949	16,950	81%
1934	10,319	7,637	74%
1935	11,016	8,430	77%
1936	11,728	9,010	77%
1937	13,054	9,544	73%
1938	12,851	9,263	72%
1939	12,037	8.879	74%
1940	10,492	7,438	71%
1941	11,294	N/A	N/A
1942	11,784	8,708	74%
1943	11,175	11,775	105%
1944	31,174	28,173	90%
1945	69,164	64,368	93%
1946	99,591	92,107	92%
1947	193,657	183,832	95%
1948	192,779	180,774	94%
1949	288,253	279,379	97%
1950	468,339	459,289	98%
1951	509,040	501,713	99%
1952	543,535	517,805	95%
1953	885,587	827,440	93%
1954	1,089,583	1,022,374	94%

Sources: U.S. Department of Homeland Security, Office of Immigration Statistics 2014, table 33 (1925–2013); Hernández 2010 for data on Mexican border region

TABLE 12.2. Total Apprehended and Mexican Nationals Apprehended, 1955–2013

YEAR	TOTAL APPREHENDED	MEXICAN NATIONALS APPREHENDED	MEXICAN NATIONALS, PERCENT
1955	254,096	221,674	87%
1956	87,696	62,625	71%
1957	59,918	38,822	65%
1958	53,474	32,556	61%
1959	45,336	25,270	56%
1960	70,684	22,687	32%
1961	88,823	23,109	26%
1962	92,758	23,358	25%
1963	88,712	31,910	36%
1964	86,597	35,146	41%
1965	110,371	44,161	40%
1966	138,520	71,233	51%
1967	161,608	86,845	54%
1968	212,057	113,304	53%
1969	283,557	159,376	56%
1970	345,353	219,254	63%
1971	420,126	290,152	69%
1972	505,949	355,099	70%
1973	655,968	480,588	73%
1974	788,145	616,630	78%
1975	766,600	579,448	76%
1976	1,097,739	678,356	62%
1977	1,042,215	792,613	76%
1978	1,057,977	841,525	80%
1979	1,076,418	866,761	81%
1980	910,361	734,219	81%

TABLE 12.2. *(continued)*

YEAR	TOTAL APPREHENDED	MEXICAN NATIONALS APPREHENDED	MEXICAN NATIONALS, PERCENT
1981	975,780	797,923	82%
1982	970,246	795,382	82%
1983	1,251,357	1,076,345	86%
1984	1,246,981	1,104,429	89%
1985	1,348,749	1,218,695	90%
1986	1,767,400	1,635,702	93%
1987	1,190,488	1,123,725	94%
1988	1,008,145	928,278	92%
1989	954,243	891,147	93%
1990	1,169,939	1,103,353	94%
...	...	...	...
2004	1,264,232	1,142,807	90%
2005	1,291,065	1,093,340	85%
2006	1,206,412	1,057,222	88%
2007	960,772	854,275	89%
2008	1,043,799	884,043	85%
2009	889,203	731,218	82%
2010	796,587	632,034	79%
2011	678,606	517,472	76%
2012	671,327	468,766	70%
2013	662,483	424,978	64%

Source: U.S. Department of Homeland Security, Office of Immigration Statistics 2014, table 33 (1925–2013) and 1991–1997 "all aliens located" by country of origin

TABLE 12.3. Expulsions and Proportion for Mexico, 1993–2013

YEAR	TOTAL DEPORTATIONS/ REMOVALS	TOTAL DEPORTATIONS/ REMOVALS TO MEXICO	MEXICO, PERCENT
1993	42,542	27,094	64%
1994	45,674	30,062	66%
1995	50,924	34,586	68%
1996	69,680	50,813	73%
1997	114,432	86,208	75%
1998	174,813	139,392	80%
1999	183,114	149,775	82%
2000	188,467	150,644	80%
2001	189,026	141,565	75%
2002	165,168	109,648	66%
2003	211,098	139,597	66%
2004	240,665	175,865	73%
2005	246,431	169,031	69%
2006	280,974	186,726	66%
2007	319,382	208,996	65%
2008	359,795	247,263	69%
2009	391,597	276,850	71%
2010	382,265	273,150	71%
2011	387,134	288,078	74%
2012	418,397	303,745	73%
2013	438,421	314,904	72%

Source: U.S. Department of Homeland Security, Office of Immigration Statistics 2014

(46 percent). This was the product of the Great Recession and the important shift in Mexican migration to the United States, including formally authorized migration. In 2013, migrants from China and India overtook Mexicans for those who have resided for one year or less.

Table 12.3 highlights a parallel pattern regarding actual expulsions (deportations/removals). From 1993 to 2013, U.S. migration officials have expelled a substantial number of persons to Mexico. Of the 4.9 million expelled from 1993 to 2013, 72 percent of these were removed to Mexico.

LOCAL CHALLENGES TO UNREASONABLE SEARCH AND SEIZURES

According to the Fourth Amendment, "The right of *the people* to be secure in their persons, houses, papers, and effects, against *unreasonable* searches and seizures, shall not be violated, and *no Warrants shall issue, but upon probable cause*, supported by Oath or affirmation, and particularly describing the place to be searched, and the persons or things to be seized."[29] It is important to note that the Fourth Amendment does not protect persons from searches and seizures, it only protects against "unreasonable" ones. Much of Fourth Amendment case law and debate regarding migrants and "the border" has centered on three issues: (1) the question of whether "undocumented" migrants or Mexican nationals not residing in the United States are protected by the Fourth Amendment (i.e., whether "undocumented" migrants fall under "the persons" construction in the Constitution, particularly the Fourteenth Amendment)[30]; (2) the distinction between reasonable and unreasonable searches and seizures; and (3) the link between reasonable/unreasonable searches and seizures and the requirement that all warrants of search, seizure, and arrest must be based on probable cause.

The substantial literature on Fourth Amendment cases, and on cases related to border searches and border functional equivalents, makes it difficult to succinctly summarize all cases in the space provided here; consequently, I focus on presenting a small set of cases covering the period from 1927 to 2013. The cases were selected from the cases reviewed (see the list of cases at the end of the references section). Each of the cases was selected to foreground a different though related issue.

MARIANO MARTÍNEZ AND JESÚS JASO (1927)

According to Hernández, on March 23, 1927, Border Patrol agents Pete A. Torres and George W. Parker "were driving slowly up the El Paso–Las Cruces Highway when this Ford Car and the two Mexicans in question passed us going north." Torres communicated to Parker, "I believe the two in the case are Mexicans; let us go and see if they are wet aliens." The officers stopped the car and discovered the two individuals were transporting liquor and proceeded to arrest both individuals for violating federal liquor laws. The attorney for the defendants argued that the evidence should be excluded because the stop was an illegal arrest and seizure. The commissioner of immigration hearing the case upheld the actions of the agents (Hernández 2010, 47–48). In doing so the commissioner upheld the authority of agents to stop cars based on the "Mexican appearance" of the driver and/or passengers. In this case the sole criterion of "Mexican appearance" constituted sufficient grounds to investigate the driver and passengers of a vehicle in the vicinity of "the border" and to search the car and seize property found in the car.

ALMEIDA-SÁNCHEZ V. UNITED STATES (1973)

Mr. Almeida-Sánchez, a Mexican citizen who held a valid U.S. work permit, was stopped by the Border Patrol twenty-five air miles north of the Mexican border in the Imperial Valley. Mr. Almeida-Sánchez's car was stopped and searched, and in the trunk, the officer found a bundle of marijuana; however, Mr. Ameida-Sánchez did not consent to the search. The Supreme Court reversed Mr. Almeida-Sánchez's drug conviction based on the facts that the road where the stop was made was not a north–south road linked to Mexico and that although the stop took place within "reasonable distance" from the boundary, defined as one hundred air miles (*Federal Register* 1957), the officer did not have *probable cause* to search the vehicle. In addition, the court formulated the concept of "functional equivalent" of the border. This meant that Border Patrol has the authority to carry out searches and seizures in places beyond the immediate area of the boundary, such as a road intersection away from the boundary but that extends from the boundary, permanent checkpoints, and airports. However, they could not simply carry out roving patrols to indiscriminately stop and search cars without probable cause. The discussion of the justices makes clear that the danger of the southern boundary, and functional equivalents of "the border," is the link to the perceived threat posed by "Mexicans."

UNITED STATES V. BRIGNONI-PONCE (1975)

Mr. Brignoni-Ponce was stopped by Border Patrol agents on Interstate Highway 5, south of San Clemente, California. The checkpoint was closed at the time because of weather conditions. Border Patrol officers spotted the car driven by Mr. Brignoni-Ponce, who appeared to be "Mexican"—his actual birth was Puerto Rico. Two additional passengers also appeared to be of "Mexican" descent. The Border Patrol agents indicated that they stopped the car because of the appearance of the driver. The Supreme Court concluded in 1975 that "Mexican" appearance alone could not justify a stop, but since Mexico is a source of persons who enter without formal authorization, the Border Patrol could use Mexican appearance *as one factor* in making the decision to stop a vehicle within "reasonable distance" from the border or in border "functional equivalents."[31] The decision formalized a practice of racialized-class profiling, as long as Border Patrol agents do not make the mistake of indicating on paper or other discoverable form that they stopped an individual *solely* because the person appeared to be "Mexican." Consequently, as long as they could identify an actual or nonexistent violation, they could initiate the stop and carry out a "reasonable" search and seizure. At the *Ortega Melendrez v. Joseph M. Arpaio* bench trial in 2013, deputies for the Maricopa County Sheriff's Office repeated on more than one occasion that if they follow a car for fifteen or so minutes, they can identify a reason for stopping the car. The attorneys for Sheriff Arpaio articulated a class-based reason for stopping a car, though they did not label it as such. They noted that since Hispanic/Mexican migrants tend to own older cars, in a short period of time they could identify a mechanical or "safety" reason for stopping a particular vehicle driven by someone with a "Mexican appearance" (e.g., malfunctioning license plate light, cracked windshield, non-functioning brake or turning signal light bulb, etc.), and so the latter would be the justification for the stop. Such a stop, according to the defense attorneys, cannot be interpreted as a form of "racial profiling."[32] Maricopa County sheriffs did not stop suspected "aliens" solely because of Mexican appearance, as argued by Sheriff Arpaio's attorneys; they stopped drivers who were driving cars with a mechanical or safety problem. The documentation showing that most of those stopped under the "crime suppression sweeps" were Mexicans was argued to be of secondary importance.

UNITED STATES V. MAGAÑA (1986)

Mr. Magaña was stopped immediately north of Eugene, Oregon—about 1,500 miles from the Mexico-U.S. boundary. He is a permanent resident, but four passengers in his truck were "undocumented" Mexican migrants. INS officers suspected Mr. Magaña and the four passengers were of Mexican descent and that the "occupants were illegal aliens" based on their visual inspection while Magaña's vehicle was traveling at seventy miles per hour on Interstate Highway 5. Mr. Magaña's attorney sought to defend him on Fourth Amendment grounds. A federal district judge ruled against Mr. Magaña, and the Ninth Circuit Court of Appeals upheld the conviction. What is striking about the case was that the judges framed the case as being about a suspect stopped 1,500 miles from the Mexico-U.S. boundary. The Ninth Circuit Court of Appeals panel acknowledged the point argued by Magaña's attorney that the stop was made 1,500 miles from Mexico but cited that under Brignoni-Ponce an officer may stop a car beyond the border if she/he is "aware of specific articulable facts" and is supported by "the totality of the circumstances." In this case, it was Mr. Magaña's and the passengers' "Mexican" appearance that indexed the stop as a reasonable form of enforcement beyond the one-hundred-mile distance from the southern boundary. However, it is particularly noteworthy that the appellate judges did not note that the stop actually took place in the "vicinity of the border": the entire Eugene area falls within one hundred miles from the coastal border and thus there was no need to rely on Brignoni-Ponce to justify the stop. They also did not comment on the fact that the stop took place 361 miles from the Canadian boundary; instead, their attention was on the question of distance from the Mexico-U.S. boundary area. Magaña's and his passengers' "Mexican appearance" made them suspects of being "illegal aliens" who did not belong in the United States. He was marked as a member of an inherently suspect class and thus was stopped accordingly. This case also suggests that in the case of Mexicans, "the border" is embodied in their persons: it is not simply a geographic marker. In other words, "the border" is a portable sociopolitical attribute that is perceived as residing within the bodies of Mexicans.

MURILLO ET AL. V. MUSEGADES ET AL. (1992)

In light of sociologist Timothy J. Dunn's full thirty-page discussion of the *Murillo et al. v. Musegades et al.* case (2009, 20–50), here I want to highlight a central part of the complaint against the El Paso Border Patrol. The question of widespread abuse of the Fourth Amendment rights of "Hispanic" staff and students at Bowie High School was a key concern of the citizens and permanent residents in the class of plaintiffs who filed suit against the Border Patrol. Plaintiffs in the suit produced a long list of abuses such as Border Patrol agents stopping vehicles with their guns drawn, conducting vehicle searches without consent, stopping the same individual several times, physical and verbal abuse by Border Patrol agents, knocking down and kicking a female student, and others. The federal district judge ruled in favor of the plaintiffs and issued an injunction against the Border Patrol for its persistent and abusive practices toward persons of "Hispanic" appearance. Dunn makes a convincing case that the success in the case was directly linked to modifications in Border Patrol practices in the El Paso sector, specifically the development of the 1993 Operation Blockade (later renamed Operation Hold the Line). Operation Blockade became the model for later operations such as the 1994 Operation Gatekeeper, authorized by President Clinton, in the Tijuana–San Ysidro sector and later repeated in Arizona and Texas. The *Murillo* case indexed the long-standing practice of El Paso Border Patrol agents focusing on stopping and questioning persons of Mexican descent. Border Patrol agents, according to the complaint, carried out searches and seizures without much concern regarding Fourth Amendment protections. The inactions by Border Patrol sector chiefs, regional INS directors, and administrators in Washington, DC, ultimately sanctioned the racial profiling and abuses of Fourth Amendment protections of citizens and noncitizens in the El Paso area. The federal court is the space utilized by the Mexican-descent persons to challenge Border Patrol's racial profiling and long-standing discriminatory practices in violation of Fourth and Fourteenth Amendments protections.

UNITED STATES V. MONTERO CAMARGO (2000)

Mr. Montero Camargo and a second car driving in tandem were observed making U-turns immediately after a sign indicating that the checkpoint was open in the El Centro, California, area. Border Patrol agents stopped them and arrested both parties. One party had a bundle of marijuana and the second was in possession of ammunition. The Federal District court found them guilty of criminal activity. The Ninth Circuit Court of Appeals supported the conclusion of the lower court but found that it erred in allowing "Hispanic appearance" to be included among the grounds supporting the reasonable suspicion that led to the arrest. The appellate court reasoned that the Border Patrol could not use "Hispanic appearance" as the sole factor in a community where over 70 percent of the population was "Hispanic." In short, the court revised the Brignoni-Ponce standard. Theoretically, since the year 2000 the Border Patrol must not use Mexican/Hispanic appearance as a factor in justifying a vehicle stop (at least within the area covered by the Ninth. However, as late as 2009, the ICE training manual being used to train Maricopa County officers under the Immigration and Nationality Act 287(g) provision still used the 1975 Brignoni-Ponce standard, rather than the 2000 Ninth Circuit Court of Appeals ruling in *Montero Camargo*. The issue of improper ICE training was one line of defense by defendants in the *Ortega Melendres v. Arpaio* case.

IN RE ENRIQUE SOTO-GARCÍA (2013)

Mr. Soto-García was stopped at the Arizona-California highway checkpoint. He was a passenger in a truck driven by a friend. A Border Patrol officer had waved the car through the checkpoint, but shortly thereafter they were pursued and stopped by the Border Patrol. Three of the individuals provided proof of their authorized presence and were allowed to continue on their way; Mr. Soto-García was detained. One of the Border Patrol officers told the occupants of the truck that he "could smell undocumented aliens"—this is what they were trained to be able to do. The federal immigration judge upheld the stop as not being a violation of the Fourth Amendment and ignored the multiple errors in the identification of the vehicle and the names of the passengers. The case was appealed to the Executive Office for Immigration Review, and the judge hearing the appeal remanded the case back to the immigration judge for review. However, it was not for the olfactory reasonable suspicion but because of the other errors in the names of the defendants and year and brand of vehicle involved. Although not explicitly addressed in the case, and given the location of the stop and the Mexican descent of the individuals stopped, the olfactory training noted by the Border Patrol officer presumably refers to the smell of a Mexican undocumented migrant not to the presumed smell of Canadian or other undocumented migrants. The Soto-García case suggests that racial profiling is not limited to visual recognition of "Mexican appearance/descent."

JANE DOE V. THE EL PASO COUNTY HOSPITAL ET AL. (2013)

The case of Ms. Jane Doe represents an example of a particularly abusive case on the part of Border Patrol agents; however, its extremeness underscores the extent of state authority in implementing a series of dehumanizing, demeaning, and highly invasive acts on a U.S. citizen returning to the United States at a port of entry. It also underscores the real consequences of the implementation of the "border exception" and what a non-routine inspection can entail. Although the ancestry or descent of Ms. Jane Doe is not noted, the context of the case suggests that she is likely of Mexican descent.

Ms. Doe is a fifty-four-year-old U.S. citizen who was returning from a brief visit to a friend in Ciudad Juárez. She regularly visited her friend in Ciudad Juárez, and so this was not the first time she had made the brief trip. Over the course of six hours of detainment, Ms. Doe, based on a false alert on the part of a drug-sniffing dog (false alerts are not uncommon),[33] was strip-searched, then underwent a manual and flashlight inspection of her vagina and anus by a Border Patrol officer. Since no drugs were found, Ms. Doe was then ordered to undergo an observed bowel movement. This also did not produce any drugs. Ms. Doe was then taken in handcuffs to a local hospital in El Paso where she was X-rayed, then vaginally examined with a speculum, and had a second rectal exam. Again no drugs were identified. Finally, after a CT scan revealed that she was not carrying any drugs within her body, she was released. All of the exams at the Border Patrol station and the hospital were done without her consent. Prior to being released, Ms. Doe was asked to sign a consent form, which she refused to sign. The El Paso Medical Center then billed Ms. Doe for $5,000 for the "services" they performed. In July 2014, the Medical Center reached a settlement for $1.1 million with Ms. Doe. The case against the Border Patrol is still pending. The Ms. Jane Doe case reveals the extent of non-routine inspections that can take place in the one-hundred-air-mile border zone or at an international airport, a permanent checkpoint, a port of entry, or a port. A citizen or noncitizen can undergo a highly invasive and demeaning inspection if a Border Patrol agent alleges reasonable suspicion or probable cause to carry out the non-routine inspection. As long as there is an assertion of a documentable reasonable suspicion or probable cause, the non-routine inspection is allowed under the border exception guideline. Inspections such as that undergone by Ms. Jane Doe are juridically interpreted as "reasonable" under the Fourth Amendment because of Section 23 in the 1789 Act and subsequent case law related to the border exception.

DISCUSSION

The eight cases presented represent a small sample of cases filed by citizens and noncitizens in federal courts, including the Supreme Court, to challenge Border Patrol actions that they felt violated their constitutional rights, particularly the protection against "unreasonable search and seizure." While some outcomes were favorable to plaintiffs, most were not. This is not surprising. Similar to state cases regarding abuse of police powers by individual police officers, even cases involving the killing of civilians, judges and juries are generally reluctant to convict police officers. Federal judges also tend to support "law and order" discourses and thus tend to side with Border Patrol officers who are portrayed as honest, professional law enforcement officers who are simply carrying out their federal mandate, and presumably possess no biases regarding persons with a "Mexican appearance."

Although there is evidence of a significant volume of illegal actions by Border Patrol and other federal law enforcement officers—encompassing human smuggling, drug smuggling, accepting bribes, selling of classified law enforcement information, and multiple other criminal acts (Plascencia 2010)—local, regional, and federal supervisors commonly deploy the "tiny handful" or "few bad apples" explanation to characterize the problem. Based on FOIA court data collected by the Transactional Records Access Clearinghouse (TRAC) at Syracuse University, however, a better metaphor would be "tip of the iceberg." Between 1986 and 2009, an annual average of 322 federal officers were convicted for violating federal law (Plascencia 2010). Consequently, federal courts appear to disavow potential officer-based problems and thus adhere to an idealized characterization of officers in adjudicating Fourth Amendment and other challenges to Border Patrol actions.

The cases presented, and cases listed in the references, highlight a second important point. Federal courts represent the space of contestation for citizens and noncitizens seeking to secure constitutional protections. Citizens and noncitizens deployed a "war of position" struggle to assert their individual liberties and presumed protections afforded by the Constitution.[34] While the strategy has not been successful in all cases, the challenges have resulted in curbing some Border Patrol practices. The Fourth and Fourteenth Amendments have been central to the contestation.

This chapter has also foregrounded the importance of Fourth Amendment case law as an avenue for examining the construction of key concepts such as "the border" and "border enforcement" and how persons perceived as "Mexican" have become the sine qua non of the national boundary enforcement apparatus and made a large portion of the nation the site for surveillance of a racialized class: persons with "Mexican appearance/descent" (also see chapter 11).

The eight cases summarized and related cases underscore the centrality of "Mexican" appearance/descent in organizing the practices of the Border Patrol. It is a central factor dating back to the creation of the land border patrol. Border Patrol work is one whose primary orientation is to search for individuals suspected of violating entry restrictions—specifically, persons perceived as "Mexicans." The link between the practices of the Texas Rangers and the initial cohort of land border patrol agents, as discussed above, provides evidence for understanding the present work and orientation of the Border Patrol. It is a process wherein persons defined as "Mexican" came to be imagined as the inherently suspect class and whose pursuit has produced an unprecedented enforcement apparatus. And as shown in the three tables, the dominant orientation of the agency is to question persons evidencing "Mexican" appearance and initiating the removal of those deemed not to be lawfully present. Historically, removal here refers to both the offering of "voluntary departure" as well as formal deportation/removal.

Footnote 2 in the 2014 Department of Justice *Guidance* regarding racial profiling by federal law enforcement officers ultimately sanctions the continuation of racial profiling of persons of "Mexican appearance/descent" not only in the vicinity of the Mexico-U.S. boundary but also through the entire "vicinity of the border" area identified in figure 12.1, as well as the multiplicity of spaces designated as border equivalents. Despite the general sensitivity of President Obama and Attorney General Loretta Lynch toward reducing racial profiling across the nation, particularly in reference to the police killings of African Americans/blacks, the promulgation of footnote 2 in the 2014 Department of Justice *Guidance* marks an unfortunate sanctioning of racial profiling where two-thirds of the U.S. population reside, but particularly more so in the SWNA region. Persons of Mexican origin living in or traveling through the southern boundary area will remain an inherently suspect class that is targeted for stopping, questioning, and lengthy vehicle detention because of the long-standing aim of boundary enforcement organized to apprehend and question persons perceived as possessing a "Mexican appearance/descent."

Lastly, the discussion presented here regarding "the border" as a juridical, social, and political construct that has changed since the early days of the nation is also important in the conceptualization of the SWNA region as initially proposed in chapter 1. While it is true that a significant portion of the Latino/Mexican population resides within the SWNA region, the federal construction of the "vicinity of the border" produces a significantly larger "border" area. It is an area that encompasses about two-thirds of the total U.S. population, including persons of Mexican descent who reside outside the SWNA region. Moreover, because of the de facto law enforcement practice that characterizes persons with "Mexican appearance" as embodying "the border" irrespective of where they reside, this suggests the need to examine the articulation between the embodied border, the larger national "border" area, and the SWNA region. The challenge is how to better integrate a geographically delimited area and spatial mobility of individuals within and outside the SWNA region.

NOTES

1. The 2003 *Guidance* had been "under review" since 2009, but the police killing of Michael Brown in Ferguson, Missouri, Eric Gardner in Staten Island, New York, and other racialized individuals appear to have prompted the Obama administration's release of the 2014 *Guidance*.
2. The result of this is that local police and sheriff units possess a de facto discretion to implement police practices based on racial profiling, until local residents legally challenge such practices or the Department of Justice steps in to challenge the practices on constitutional grounds. It is important to note that a key term in the *Guidance* is "solely." This translates to a warning for agents to be wise and use more than one factor, such as claiming that an individual was acting suspicious.
3. The 2003 *Guidance* contained essentially the same qualification, though it was stated in broader and longer terms: "II. *National Security and Border Integrity*. The above standards do not affect current Federal policy with respect to law enforcement activities and other efforts to defend and safeguard against threats to national security or integrity of the Nations' borders, to which the following applies: In investigating . . . (including the performance of duties related to air transportation security) or in enforcing laws protecting the integrity of the Nation's borders, Federal law enforcement officers may not consider race or ethnicity except to the extent permitted by the Constitution and laws of the United States" (2003, 2).
4. Although there is no precise definition in law, "racial profiling" is the label that emerged in the 1990s to index the near-exclusive selection of subjects racialized as "minorities" (principally African Americans and Latinos) to deploy police discretion to stop a vehicle driven by such a subject or to "stop-and-frisk" individuals standing in a public space. Law scholar and criminologist David Harris suggests that "racial Profiling is a crime-fighting strategy—a government policy that treats African Americans, Latinos, and members of other minority groups as criminal suspects on the assumption that doing so will increase the odds of catching criminals" (Harris 2002, 11).
5. It should be noted that in 1996 Congress altered the linguistic reference from "deportation" to "removal."
6. The concept of "fruit of the poisonous tree" refers to the juridical principle that evidence obtained through unlawful means does not shed its taint, even if it produces evidence relevant to a prosecution. In other words, a poisonous tree will produce poisonous

fruit. The principle was first stated in general terms in *Silverthorne v. United States*, 251 U.S. 385 (1920) and then explicitly named by Justice Frankfurter in *Nardone v. United States*, 308 U.S. 338 (1939). I also should note that the Border Patrol can be thought of a largely Mexican Patrol in an ironic sense: although its primary focus is the detection and apprehension of persons of "Mexican appearance" who may be subject to removal, about 52 percent of the total of close to twenty-two thousand Border Patrol agents are classified as Latinos and the majority of these are of Mexican descent. For a unique discussion of the latter issue and how Immigration and Naturalization Service (INS) officers of Mexican descent distance themselves from the migrants they are seeking to control, see Heyman 2002.

7. The Ninth Circuit Court of Appeals encompasses Alaska, Arizona, California, Hawai'i, Idaho, Montana, Oregon, and Nevada, as well as Guam and Northern Mariana Islands.
8. The current and past territory of the U.S. Empire is vastly different from the area encompassed by the thirteen British colonies that became the United States of America.
9. Plascencia (2009) examines the development of the two problematic terms of "illegal" and "undocumented" migrant, and offers the alternative of "formally authorized" and "informally authorized" migrant. The latter term recognizes the role of the state in the formation of political statuses.
10. Under *border-crossing permit*, I am including the short-term permits authorizing travel within twenty-five miles of the boundary and commuters who reside in Mexico and travel to work in the United States.
11. The 50:50 proportion is an estimate because neither the previous Immigration and Naturalization Service (INS) nor the current DHS or the State Department have procedures or methods to accurately identify the violation of visa conditions or departures. As reported by Dion Nissenbaum (*Mercury News*), during Arnold Schwarzenegger's campaign for the California governorship, Schwarzenegger appears to have violated both his B-1 visa as an entertainer and his H-1B visa as a temporary contract worker. He later was granted permanent residency status, and then U.S. citizenship (Nissenbaum 2003a, 2003b). If INS officials had investigated the visa violations, Schwarzenegger would have been subject to deportation after the violations. Moreover, if Schwarzenegger had truthfully divulged his earlier visa violations, his permanent residency and naturalization would have been denied.
12. Three classic discussions of these processes are found in Andreas 2009, Chávez 2001, and Nevins 2010.
13. The chapter uses the terms "citizen" and "national" as synonyms. All U.S. citizens are formally considered nationals of the United States, though some nationals, such as those born in American Samoa, are considered nationals but not citizens.
14. It is a common misconception that U.S. authority ends at the edge of U.S. territory. There are several instances where U.S. officials operate outside U.S. territory and implement

U.S. laws. The U.S. Department of Agriculture, for example, has fruit inspectors located in production areas and carry out U.S. laws regarding what fruit can be shipped to the United States. At Canadian international airports, U.S. Customs officials carry out inspection of individuals intending to travel to the United States and clear their entry into U.S. territory from their posts in Canada.

15. The U.S. classification of airports involves several codes related to "enplanement" (volume of traffic); thus, some airports may receive international commercial flights but not international passengers, and not all international airports may include the label "international" in its name. Because of this, the actual count of "international" airports may range from 107 to 154.
16. While the label "non-routine" search and seizure may sound like a minor inconvenience to a citizen or noncitizen entering the United States or crossing a "border," it can include demands such as a complete strip search and inspection of body cavities by Border Patrol officials.
17. Federal rules define an "external boundary" as "the land boundaries and the territorial sea of the United States extending twelve nautical miles from the baseline of the United States" (8 C.F.R. 287.1(a)(1)).
18. In light of the common misconception in the media and popular sources and among some scholars that the 1954 "Operation Wetback" apprehended and removed a million Mexican migrants, it is important to note that ultimately the actual operation deported a small fraction of migrants. Its media campaign about its success was, however, quite a success. After the two-month campaign, in January 1955, Commissioner Swing announced, "The day of the wetback is over." The best discussion of actual apprehensions under the operation, in contrast to the alleged one million, can be found in Hernández 2002, 2006, and 2010. For the classic discussion of the Operation see García 1980.
19. Although the core rule is relatively precise, the rule also allows border enforcement agents to exceed the one hundred air miles "because of unusual circumstances" (*Federal Register* 1957, 9808).
20. The core issue of how the Supreme Court has allowed Congress to diminish one of the rights in the Bill of Rights in the Constitution without a serious challenge remains an important one but one that is beyond the scope of this chapter. Theoretically Congress should not determine what part of the Constitution applies to one geographic space and not in another—particularly because of the magnitude of its coverage (i.e., two-thirds of the population).
21. In addition, it should be noted that scholars and others at times confuse the 1924 Labor Appropriations Act and the 1924 Immigration Act (45 Stat. 153) and erroneously attribute the creation of the land border patrol to the latter.
22. The $1,000,000 appropriation is without doubt a substantial amount in current dollars; however, when compared to the 1925 appropriation for the Narcotics Division within

the Prohibition Unit of $11,341,779 or the Coast Guard ($12,000,000), the land border patrol was relatively small (Hernández 2010, 33).

23. According to the Border Patrol, as of September 20, 2014, the total Border Patrol force consisted of 20,863 agents, and 18,127 were assigned to the Southwest Border Sector (U.S. Border Patrol 2014).
24. The account of the violence carried out by Texas Rangers and local law enforcement on Mexican-origin communities has been addressed in multiple books and articles; thus, it is not repeated here. For a sample of such discussions, see Acuña 1972; Hall and Coerver 1988; McWilliams 1968; Paredes 1958; Rosales 1999.
25. Dr. Galarza's phrase was the source for the title of the book by Samora, Bernal, and Peña (1979, acknowledgments).
26. A sample of the many reports and academic discussions of Border Patrol abuses can be found in Samora, Bernal, and Peña (1979); U.S. Commission on Civil Rights (1980); Comisión Nacional de Derechos Humanos (1991); Human Rights Watch/Americas (1992); Americas Watch (1993); Hing (1995); Rosales (1999); Luibheid (2002, particularly chapter five); Vargas (2002); No More Deaths (2014); American Civil Liberties Union (2015).
27. It should be noted that almost all of those expelled to Mexico are Mexican citizens, but an unknown number are Latin Americans that were able to convince U.S. migration officials that they were "Mexicans" and thus should be returned to nearby Mexico.
28. If federal policy was enacted to place the majority of Border Patrol agents on the Canada-U.S. boundary area, the data on apprehensions and removal would without doubt change. And if the apprehension priority was placed on locating and removing Irish and Polish migrants subject to removal, or another OTM (in INS parlance, "other than Mexican") group, then apprehension and removal statistics would be significantly different.
29. https://www.law.cornell.edu/constitution/fourth_amendment
30. For useful discussion of issue of "the people" and whether "undocumented" migrants fall under the protections of the Fourth Amendment, see *Harvard Law Review* 2013; Medina 2008a, 2008b; Richezza 1991; and Romero 1992. The Supreme Court has judged that the search of a home outside the United States by U.S federal officials without a warrant is not a violation of the Fourth Amendment (see *United States v. Verdugo Urquídez*, 494 U.S. 259, 1990). And in the case related to the torture and murder of Drug Enforcement Agency (DEA) agent Enrique Camarena Salazar in 1985, the U.S. federal courts did not question the illegal kidnapping (i.e., seizure) of Humberto Álvarez Machain (a physician), and Javier Vásquez Velasco by bounty hunters who brought the two men to the United States.
31. The other eight factors include a) characteristics of the area; b) proximity to the border; c) usual patterns of traffic; d) information about recent unauthorized border entry; e) driver's behavior; f) aspects of the vehicle; g) persons trying to hide; and h) characteristics of appearance (e.g., "Mexican").

32. Material from the trial is based on notes taken during the two-week trial.
33. The ACLU report (2015) notes that there are recurrent false alerts by canines and that the DHS refused to release information related to canine training and certification, as well as what procedures are in place regarding dogs with a record of repeated false alerts. The DHS also refused to release the names of service canines, thus making it impossible to ascertain the pattern of false alerts (11).
34. The "war of position" concept is taken from Gramsci's *Selections from the Prison Notebooks* (1971).

REFERENCES

Acuña, Rodolfo. 1972. *Occupied America: The Chicano's Struggle Toward Liberation*. San Francisco: Canfield Press/Harper & Row.

Adams, Jon. 2004. "Applying More Restrictive Search and Seizure Requirements Under State Constitutional Law in Federal Courts Using *Michigan v. Long* and *Erie v. Tompkins*." *Temple Political and Civil Rights Law Review* 14:201–23.

———. 2005. "Rights at United States Borders." *BYU Journal of Public Law* 19:353–71.

American Civil Liberties Union (ACLU). 2015. *Record of Abuse: Lawlessness and Impunity in Border Patrol's Interior Enforcement Operations*. Phoenix: ACLU of Arizona.

———. 2016. "Know Your Rights: The Government's 100-Mile 'Border' Zone–Map." https://www.aclu.org/know-your-rights-governments-100-mile-border-zone-map?redirect=national-security-technology-and-liberty/are-you-living-governments-border-zone.

Americas Watch. 1993. *United States Frontier Justice: Human Rights Abuses Along the U.S. Border with Mexico Persist amid Climate of Impunity*. https://www.hrw.org/sites/default/files/reports/US935.PDF.

Andreas, Peter. 2009. *Border Games: Policing the U.S.-Mexico Divide*. 2nd ed. Cornell Studies in Political Economy. Ithaca, NY: Cornell University Press.

Bernsen, Sam. 1975–76. "Search and Seizure on the Highway for Immigration Violations: A Survey of Law." *San Diego Law Review* 13:69–81.

Bourdieu, Pierre. 1977. *Outline of a Theory of Practice*. Cambridge: Cambridge University Press.

Brown, Penny J. 1982. "Immigration Roving Border Patrols: The Less Than Probable Cause Standard for a Stop." *American Journal of Criminal Law* 10:245–64.

Chávez, Leo R. 2001. *Covering Immigration: Popular Images and the Politics of the Nation*. Berkeley: University of California Press.

Clark, James P. 1977. "*United States v. Martínez-Fuerte*: The Fourth Amendment—Close to the Edge?" *California Western Law Review* 13:333–57.

Comisión Nacional de Derechos Humanos. 1991. *Report on Human Rights Violations of Mexican Migratory Workers on Route to the Northern Border, Crossing the Border and Upon*

Entering the Southern United States Border Strip. Mexico City: Comisión Nacional de Derechos Humanos.

Compton, Nina H., and Garrett T. Newland. 1992. "The Functional Border Equivalent." *Journal of Borderlands Studies* 7(2): 73–92.

Connell, James G., and René L. Valladares. 1997. "Search and Seizure Protections for Undocumented Aliens: The Territoriality and Voluntary Presence Principles in Fourth Amendment Law." *American Criminal Law Review* 34:1293–1352.

Dacey, Jennifer J. 1997. "U.S. Citizens' Fourth Amendment Rights: Do They Extend Only to the Waters' Edge? *United States v. Barona*." *George Mason Law Review* 5(4): 761–97.

Dorsey, Margaret E., and Miguel Díaz-Barriga. 2015. "The Constitution Free Zone in the United States: Law and Life in a State of Carcelment." *PoLAR: Journal of the Association for Political and Legal Anthropology* 38(2): 204–25.

Dunn, Timothy J. 2001. "Waging War on Immigrants at the U.S.-Mexico Border: Human Rights Implications." In *Militarizing the American Criminal Justice System: The Changing Roles of the Armed Forces and the Police*, edited by Peter B. Kraska, 65–81. Boston: Northeastern University Press.

———. 2009. *Blockading the Border and Human Rights: The El Paso Operation That Remade Immigration Enforcement*. Austin: University of Texas Press.

Escobar, Edward J. 1999. *Race, Police, and the Making of a Political Identity: Mexican Americans and the Los Angeles Police Department, 1900–1945*. Berkeley: University of California Press.

Ettinger, Patrick. 2006. "'We Sometimes Wonder What They Will Spring on Us Next': Immigrants and Border Enforcement in the American West." *Western Historical Quarterly* 37(2): 159–81.

Federal Register. 1957. Title 8—Aliens and Nationality 22(236): 9808.

Fragomen, Austin T., Jr. 1975. "Searching for Illegal Aliens: The Immigration Service Encounters the Fourth Amendment." *San Diego Law Review* 13:82–124.

———. 1976. "Procedural Aspects of Illegal Search and Seizure in Deportation Cases." *San Diego Law Review* 14:151–92.

———. 1978. "The 'Uncivil' Nature of Deportation: Fourth and Fifth Amendment Rights and the Exclusionary Rule." *Brooklyn Law Review* 45:29–52.

García, Juan Ramón. 1980. *Operation Wetback: The Mass Deportation of Mexican Undocumented Workers in 1954*. Westport, CT: Greenwood Press.

Getrich, Christina M. 2013. "'Too Bad I'm Not an Obvious Citizen': The Effects of Racialized US Immigration Enforcement Practices on Second-Generation Mexican Youth." *Latino Studies* 11(4): 462–82.

Gowie, Renata Ann. 2001. "Driving While Mexican: Why the Supreme Court Must Reexamine *United States v. Brignoni-Ponce*, 422 U.S. 873 (1975)." *Houston Journal of International Law* 23(2): 233–54.

Gramsci, Antonio. 1971. *Selections from the Prison Notebooks*. Edited and translated by Quintin Hoare and Geoffrey Nowell Smith. New York: International Publishers.

Graybill, Andrew. 2004. "Texas Rangers, Canadian Mounties, and the Policing of the Transnational Industrial Frontier, 1885–1910." *Western Historical Quarterly* 35(2): 167–91.

Hall, Linda B., and Don M. Coerver. 1988. *Revolution on the Border: The United States and Mexico 1910–1920*. Albuquerque: University of New Mexico Press.

Harris, David. 2002. *Profiles in Injustice: Why Racial Profiling Cannot Work*. New York: New Press.

Harvard Law Review. 2013. "Note: The Meaning of 'the People' in the Constitution." *Harvard Law Review* 126:1078–99.

Hernández, Kelly Lytle. 2002. "Entangling Bodies and Borders: Racial Profiling and the U.S. Border Patrol, 1924–1955." PhD dissertation, Department of History, University of California, Los Angeles.

———. 2006. "The Crimes of Illegal Immigration: A Cross-Border Examination of Operation Wetback, 1943 to 1954." *The Western Historical Quarterly* 37(4): 421–44.

———. 2010. *Migra! A History of the U.S. Border Patrol*. Berkeley: University of California Press.

Heyman, Josiah McC. 2001. "Class and Classification at the U.S.-Mexico Border." *Human Organization* 60(2): 128–40.

———. 2002. "U.S. Immigration Officers of Mexican Ancestry as Mexican Americans, Citizens, and Immigration Police." *Current Anthropology* 43(3): 403–507.

Hing, Bill Ong. 1995. "Border Patrol Abuse: Evaluating Complaint Procedures Available to Victims." *Georgetown Immigration Law Journal* 9:757–99.

Human Rights Watch. 1995. *Crossing the Line: Human Rights Abuses Along the U.S. Border with Mexico Persist Amid Climate of Impunity*. New York: Human Rights Watch. http//www.refworld.org/docid/45d2f3672.html.

Human Rights Watch/Americas. 1992. *Brutality Unchecked: Human Rights Abuses Along the U.S. Border with Mexico*. New York: Human Rights Watch. https://www.hrw.org/sites/default/files/reports/US925.PDF.

Johnson, Kevin R. 2010. "How Racial Profiling in America Became the Law of the Land: *United States v. Brignoni Ponce* and *Whren v. United States* and the Need for Truly Rebellious Lawyering." *Georgetown Law Journal* 98:1005–77.

Keller, Ken. 1975. "Border Searches Revisited: The Constitutional Propriety of Fixed and Temporary Checkpoint Searches." *Hasting Constitutional Law Quarterly* 2(Winter): 251–75.

Kikawa, Gail T. 1991. "Casenote: *Verdugo-Urquídez*: How the Majority Stumbled." *Houston Journal of International Law* 13:369–88.

Lalmalani, Spana G. 2005. "Extraordinary Rendition Meets the U.S. Citizen: United States' Responsibility Under the Fourth Amendment." *Connecticut Public Interest Law Journal* 5(1): 1–29.

Leahy, James E. 1974. "Border Patrol Checkpoint Operation Under Warrants of Inspection: The Wake of *Almeida-Sánchez v. United States.*" *California Western International Law Journal* 5:62–71.

Lippman, Matthew. 1989. "The Decline of Fourth Amendment Jurisprudence." *Criminal Justice Journal* 11:293–356.

———. 1992. "The Drug War and the Vanishing Fourth Amendment." *Criminal Justice Journal* 14:229–308.

Luibheid, Eithne, 2002. *Entry Denied: Controlling Sexuality at the Border*. Minneapolis: University of Minnesota Press.

Maril, Robert Lee, 2004. *Patrolling Chaos: The U.S. Border Patrol in Deep South Texas*. Lubbock: Texas Tech University Press.

McWilliams, Carey, 1968. *North from Mexico: The Spanish-Speaking People of the United States*. New York: Greenwood Press.

Medina, M. Isabel 2008a. "Exploring the Use of the Word 'Citizen' in Writings on the Fourth Amendment." *Indiana Law Journal* 83:1557–88.

———. 2008b. "Ruminations on the Fourth Amendment: Case Law, Commentary, and the Word 'Citizen.'" *Harvard Latino Law Review* 11:189–203.

Mirandé, Alfredo, 2002. "Is There a 'Mexican Exception' to the Fourth Amendment?" *Florida Law Review* 55:365– 89.

Nevins, Joseph, 2010. *Operation Gatekeeper and Beyond: The War on "Illegals" and the Remaking of the U.S.-Mexico Boundary*. New York: Routledge.

Nissenbaum, Dion, 2003a. "Abuse of Actor's 1960s Visa Suggested: Schwarzenegger Aides Defend Record." *Mercury News*, September 13.

———. 2003b. "New Schwarzenegger Visa Issue: '71 Construction Work Appears to Be Violation." *Mercury News*, September 21.

No More Deaths. 2014. "Shakedown: How Deportation Robs Immigrants of Their Money and Belongings." http://nomoredeaths.org/wp-content/uploads/2014/12/Shakedown-with cover.pdf.

Paredes, Américo. 1958. *"With His Pistol in His Hand": A Border Ballad and Its Hero*. Austin: University of Texas Press.

Pérez, Javier. 2011. "Note: Reasonably Suspicious of Being *Mojado*: The Legal Derogation of Latinos in Immigration Enforcement." *Texas Hispanic Journal of Law and Policy* 17(1): 99–108.

Pew Research Center. 2006. *Modes of Entry for the Unauthorized Migrant Population. Fact Sheet*. Washington, DC: Pew Hispanic Center.

———. 2015. "What We Know About Illegal Immigration from Mexico." http://www.pewresearch.org/fact-tank/2015/11/20/what-we-know-about-illegal-immigration-from-mexico/.

Plascencia, Luis F. B. 2009. "The 'Undocumented' Mexican Migrant Question: Re-examining the Framing of Law and Illegalization in the United States." *Urban Anthropology* 38(2–4): 375–434.

———. 2010. "Corruption at the Gates: Challenges in Researching Misconduct Among U.S. Government Officials on the Mexico-United States Borderlands." Paper presented at the Between the Lines: Border Research Ethics and Methodologies Conference, University of Arizona, Tucson, April 22–23.

———. 2012. *Disenchanting Citizenship: Mexican Migrants and the Boundaries of Belonging.* New Brunswick, NJ: Rutgers University Press.

———. 2013. "Attrition Through Enforcement and the Elimination of a 'Dangerous Class.'" In *Latino Politics and International Relations: The Case of Arizona's Immigration Law SB1070*, edited by Lisa Magaña and Eric Lee, 93–127. New York: Springer.

———. 2015. "Racialized Policing, Violence and Latinas/os." *Anthropology News* (26 January). http://www.anthropology-news.org/index.php/2015/01/26/racialized-policing-violence-and-latinasos/.

Ricchezza, Joseph. 1991. "Are Undocumented Aliens 'People' Persons Within the Context of the Fourth Amendment?" *Georgetown Immigration Law Journal* 5:475–504.

Romero, Victor C. 1992. "Whatever Happened to the Fourth Amendment? Undocumented Immigrants' Rights After *INS v. López-Mendoza* and *United States v. Verdugo-Urquídez.*" *Southern California Law Review* 65:999–1034.

———. 2000a. "The Domestic Fourth Amendment Rights of Undocumented Immigrants: On *Gutiérrez* and the Tort Law/Immigration Law Parallel." *Harvard Civil Rights-Civil Liberties Law Review* 35:57–101.

———. 2000b. "Racial Profiling: 'Driving While Mexican' and Affirmative Action." *Michigan Journal of Race and Law* 6:195–207.

———. 2010–11. "Decriminalizing Border Crossings." *Fordham Urban Law Journal* 38: 273–302.

Rosales, F. Arturo. 1999. *¡Pobre Raza! Violence, Justice, and Mobilization Among México Lindo Immigrants, 1900–1920.* Austin: University of Texas Press.

Rosenzweig, Paul. 1985. "Functional Equivalents of the Border, Sovereignty, and the Fourth Amendment." *University of Chicago Law Review* 52:1119–45.

Samora, Julian, Joe Bernal, and Albert Peña. 1979. *Gunpowder Justice: A Reassessment of the Texas Rangers.* Notre Dame, IN: University of Notre Dame Press.

Sosa, Steve. 1990. "An Introduction to Search and Seizure Under the Immigration Reform and Control Act of 1986." *Chicano Law Review* 10:33–46.

Susman, Barbara A. 1987. "The Immigration Reform and Control Act of 1986 ('IRCA'): Impact Upon Employer/Employee Fourth Amendment Protections Against Search and Seizure." *Hofstra Labor Law Journal* 5(1): 1–44.

Sutis, Robert W. 1974. "The Extent of the Border." *Hastings Constitutional Law Quarterly* 1:235–50.

U.S. Border Patrol. 2014. "Border Patrol Agent Staffing by Fiscal Year [1992–2014]." http://www.cbp.gov/sites/default/files/documents/BP%20Staffing%20FY1992-FY2014_0.pdf.

U.S. Commission on Civil Rights. 1980. *The Tarnished Golden Door: Civil Rights Issues in Immigration*. Washington, DC: Government Printing Office.

U.S. Department of Homeland Security, Office of Immigration Statistics. 2014. *2013 Yearbook of Immigration Statistics*. https://www.dhs.gov/sites/default/files/publications/ois_yb_2013_0.pdf.

U.S. Department of Justice. 2003. *Guidance Regarding the Use of Race by Federal Law Enforcement Agencies*. https://www.justice.gov/sites/default/files/crt/legacy/2010/12/15/guidance_on_race.pdf.

———. 2014. *Guidance for Federal Law Enforcement Agencies Regarding the Use of Race, Ethnicity, Gender, National Origin, Religion, Sexual Orientation, or Gender Identity*. https://www.justice.gov/sites/default/files/ag/pages/attachments/2014/12/08/use-of-race-policy.pdf.

U.S. Department of Justice, Immigration and Naturalization Service. 1991–1997 and 2004. *Statistical Yearbook of the Immigration and Naturalization Service*. Washington, DC: Government Printing Office.

Vargas, Jorge A. 2002. "U.S. Border Patrol Abuses, Undocumented Mexican Workers, and International Human Rights." *Immigration and Nationality Law Review* 23:1–92.

Viña, Stephen. 2002. "Virtual Strip Searches at Airports: Are Border Searches Seeing Through the Fourth Amendment?" *Texas Wesleyan Law Review* 8:417–39.

Yale Law Journal. 1968. "Border Searches and the Fourth Amendment." 77:1007–18.

Young, Stewart M. 2003. "Comment: *Verdugo* in Cyberspace: Boundaries of Fourth Amendment Rights for Foreign Nationals in Cybercrime." *Michigan Telecommunications & Technology Law Review* 10:139–74.

Zagaris, Bruce, and David R. Stepp 1992. "Criminal and Quasi-criminal Customs Enforcement Among the U.S., Canada, and Mexico." *Indiana International Comparative Law Review* 2:337–83.

CASES (CHRONOLOGICAL ORDER)

Boyd v. United States, 116 U.S. 616 (1886).

Weeks v. United States, 232 U.S. 383 (1914).

Silverthorne Lumber Co., Inc. v. United States, 251 U.S. 385 (1920).

Carroll v. United States, 267 U.S. 132 (1925).

Mariano Martínez and Jesús Jaso (1927).

Landau v. United States Attorney for Southern District of New York, 82 F.2d 285 (1936).

Nardone v. United States, 308 U.S. 338 (1939).

Brinegar v. United States, 338 U.S. 160 (1949).

Rochin v. California, 342 U.S. 165 (1952).

Cervantes v. United States, 263 F.2d 800 (1959).

Ruvalcaba Ramírez v. United States, 263 F.2d 385 (1959).

Fuentes v. United States, 283 F.2d 537 (1960).
Murgia et al. v. United States, 285 F.2d 14 (1960).
Barrera v. United States, 276 F.2d 654 (1960).
Mansfield v. United States, 308 F.2d 221 (1962).
Fernández v. United States, 321 F.2d 283 (1963).
Alexander v. United States, 362 F.2d 379 (1966).
Terry v. Ohio, 329 U.S. 1 (1968).
Bloomer v. United States, 409 F.2d 869 (1969).
Roa-Rodríguez v. United States, 410 F.2d 1206 (1969).
Valenzuela-García v. United States, 425 F.2d 1170 (1970).
The People v. González Herrera, 12 Cal. App. 3d 629 (1970).
United States v. Sepeda Salinas, 439 F.2d 376 (1971).
United States v. Pequeño De León, 462 F. 170 (1972).
Almeida-Sánchez v. United States, 413 U.S. 266 (1973).
United States v. Quiroz-Rivera, 500 F.2d 1223 (9th Cir. 1974).
United States v. Ortiz, 422 U.S. 891 (1975).
United States v. Brignoni-Ponce, 422 U.S. 873 (1975).
United States v. Barbera, 514 F.2d 294 (1975).
United States v. Martínez-Fuerte, 428 U.S. 543 (1976).
State of Arizona v. Castro, 27 Ariz. App. 323 P.2d 919 (1976).
United States v. Medina, 543 F.2d 553 (5th Cir. 1976).
United States v. Ramsey et al., 431 U.S. 606 (1977).
United States v. Maxwell, 565 F.2d 596 (9th Cir. 1977).
State of Arizona v. Guerrero, 119 Ariz. 273 P2d 734 (Ct. App. 1978).
United States v. Rivera, 595 F.2d 1095 (5th Cir. 1979).
Torres v. Puerto Rico, 442 U.S. 465 (1979).
United States v. Cortez, 449 U.S. 411 (1981).
United States v. Hernández, 739 F.2d 484 (9th Cir. 1984).
Immigration and Naturalization Service (INS) v. Delgado, 466 U.S. 210 (1984).
Immigration and Naturalization Service (INS) v. López-Mendoza, 468 U.S. 1032 (1984).
United States v. Montoya de Hernández, 473 U.S. 531 (1985).
United States v. Magaña, 797 F.2d 777 (9th Cir. 1986).
United States v. Verdugo-Urquídez, 494 U.S. 259 (1990).
Murillo et al. v. Musegades et al., 809 F. Supp. 487 (1992).
United States v. Padilla et al., 508 U.S. 77 (1993).
United States v. Rodríguez-Sánchez, 23 F.3d 1488 (1994).
González-Rivera v. Immigration and Naturalization Service, 22 F.3d 1441 (1994).
United States v. López, 514 U.S. 549 (1995).
United States v. Soto-Camacho, 58 F.3rd 408 (9th Cir. 1995).

United States v. Bojórquez-Gastelum, 94 F.3d 656 (1996).
United States v. Alarcón-González, 73 F.3d 289 (1996).
United States v. Morales, 191 F.3d 578 (5th Cir. 1999).
United States v. Montero Camargo, Nos. 97–50643, 97–50645 (9th Cir. 2000).
United States v. Chávez-Chávez, 205 F3d 145, No. 99–40072 (5th Cir. 2000).
Gutíerrez v. Texas, 22 S.W.3d 75 (2000).
United States v. Zapata-Ibarra, No. 99–50156 (5th Cir. 2000).
United States v. Machuca-Barera, 261 F.3rd 425 (5th Cir. 2001).
United States v. Arvizu, 534 U.S. 266 (2002).
United States v. Moreno-Vargas, 315 F.3rd 489 (5th Cir. 2002).
United States v. Chacón, 330 F.3rd 323 (5th Cir. 2003).
United States v. Angulo, 328 F.3rd 449 (8th Cir. 2003).
United States v. Flores-Montaño, 541 U.S. 549 (2004).
United States v. Manzo-Jurado, 457 F.3rd 928 (9th Cir. 2006).
Ortega Melendres v. Arpaio (2007).
In re Enrique Soto-García, Executive Office for Immigration Review (2013).
Jane Doe v. The El Paso County Hospital et al. (2013).

STATUTES AND CONSTITUTIONAL AMENDMENTS

1789 *An Act to Regulate the Collection of Duties . . .*, 1 Stat. 29 (1789).
Fourth Amendment, http://constitution.findlaw.com/amendment4/amendment.html.
8 U.S.C §1357(a)(3).
1924 *Appropriations Act*, 43 Stat. 205 (1924).
1925 *Appropriations Act*, 43 Stat. 1014 (1925).

13

PEOPLES, POLITICAL POLICIES, AND THEIR CONTRADICTIONS

A Commentary

ROBERT R. ÁLVAREZ

THESE CHAPTERS REVIEW recent policy and law that have had a strong effect on people and social process in the Southwest North American (SWNA) region. Significantly, each author relates specific laws that are aimed at controlling immigrants and the international demarcation of the U.S.-Mexico border. Social scientists, and anthropologists in particular, continue to identify the local-regional interactions and responses of immigrants, settlers, and citizens, yet it is not often that we recognize the greater "reach" or, utilizing O'Leary's term, "stretch" of the connections. In addition to outlining changes in immigration law, state policy, and governance, these chapters also illuminate strategic processes employed by individuals and immigrant communities in surviving catastrophic hurdles and life crisis. The conflict and crisis are contained within the broader social reality of the region. The context of SWNA provides a substantive framework in understanding these contradictions and connections and adds depth to the concept of "the borderlands" or the U.S.-Mexico border region. SWNA has deep historical as well as extensive connections that are interrelational, often conflicting and influencing social and institutional behavior in myriad ways (see my commentary for part 2 of this volume).

The work of O'Leary, Greenberg and Mandache, Gomberg-Muñoz, and Plascencia illustrates the many strands of the legal/political process as well as both a cross-cutting social process and a substantive control. The cross-cutting is the dialectical and contradictory effects of law and policy on the region's people. But the control or, better put, "organized control" is a condition that we have yet to identify as universal and systemic. All the folks—immigrants, citizens, families, individuals, communities, and the populations of the entire region—are affected by the rules and regulations discussed by these authors. The process of litigation, creation of the law, and policy appear on the one hand as separate from one another and specific, but there is also a systemic quality to the creation, nature, and practice of laws and policy described by the authors in part 3 of this book.

The regulation and control of immigrants, citizenship, deportees, and the incarcerated, as well as of commodities, business, and trade, might best be viewed in terms of the systemic process that is embedded in the transnational/transborder architecture of this region. Identifying the deep connections and cadences of Vélez-Ibáñez's SWNA helps us see the interconnectivity of law and policy not in just the local or on "the border" but as part of the transnational/transborder social topography and architecture of the region. The obvious results of Arizona's neoliberal policy described by Greenberg and Mandache, Gomberg-Muñoz's explanatory treatise of recent immigration laws, and the implications of Plascencia's identification of "the Border" illustrate the controlling aspects of these laws and policy aimed specifically at the southern border (U.S.-Mexico) and specific groups of immigrants (those connected with the southern border). O'Leary induces thinking about the "ethos" not only of immigrant households but also of a broader ethos that infiltrates law and policy. Identifying the region as a transnational/transborder social system underlines the effects of law and policy not solely on U.S. soil but also throughout the region and beyond. These authors illustrate the actual effects of these laws and policy on the populations through increased deportations, the multiplying incarceration of immigrant Latinos, increased surveillance and fluidity of law enforcement aimed at the undocumented, heightened neoliberal trade, heightened drug traffic, and other social-political ramifications. However there is also a not so subtle range of control that is part and parcel of the transnational topography that marks the region.

Focusing on the local and the ethnographic, anthropologists have illustrated how people react to, manipulate, adapt, and create processes in various social-cultural scenarios. Looking from the ground up, we see how people live and create adaptive social processes. We continue to speak of the transnational as a varied process evident in numerous social forms such as "the household" and the family and in trade and commerce. At the same time, we agree that transnational process affects everyone and the entire region. O'Leary's women's narratives, for example, illustrate the various patterns of social organization that have given rise to transnational household structure. The transnational nature of the region may seem obvious, but we have yet to acknowledge the web of connection and influence of transnationalism. I would argue that the region is clearly connected systemically. These papers clearly illustrate the connections and effects of policy and law in SWNA. For example, Gomberg-Muñoz in her fine outline and fleshing out of immigration law illustrates how seemingly separate policy has affected the region. This includes the Illegal Immigration Reform and Immigrant

Responsibility Act of 1996 (IIRAIRA), the shift toward militarization of the U.S.-Mexico border, the beginning of trade agreements (General Agreement on Tariffs and Trade [GATT] and the North American Free Trade Agreement [NAFTA]), and the rapid increase of deportation. These processes and the current diffusion of immigration enforcement throughout the U.S. interior have, she states, "thickened" the U.S. borderlands. When we connect the pieces—these various social and juridical forms of the household, trade, law, and policy—it should come as no surprise that this is not an ad hoc assemblage. All of this is tied to the ethos of control. This is a broader systemic that overlaps the everyday, the local, and the regional. People function in this transnational universe utilizing the social-cultural assets they carry with them. The enactment of social networks, "moral" households, and identity are all strategic processes that people (and institutions) utilize in dealing with the complexity and challenges of the transnational system. It is time we recognize this systemic because it is not haphazard but rather organized through the laws and policies at local, regional, and international levels.

Some time ago I argued that the U.S.-Mexico border is a social system characterized by organized flows of personnel (Álvarez 1984). At the time, this referred to network formation, immigration, and the back-and-forth flow of people and goods across the U.S.-Mexico border. In our current world these processes are exacerbated and increasingly controlled as transnationalism with its categorical processes engages not only "nations" but also people and things, overlaying the border, the region, and human process.

Laws and policy on both sides of the "border" channel and organize flows of people, trade, and values. There are indeed conflicting parts and processes, but the encompassing architecture and social topography is the transnational. The foci of singular processes such as the "transnational" in households, or "transnational" trade, sustain the barriers we ourselves challenge about nations, the state, and the border. The constrictions on the border, immigration law, and neoliberal policy work to maintain and create specific flows of people, commodities, and ideologies. The strategies people employ—networks, households, values—are strategic mechanisms based on "social-cultural" foundations of various ethnic groups. In this scenario the border itself becomes a metaphor of control. Border "security" is more than "shutting down the border" or securing the national boundary; it is as much about controlling commodities, flows of people and labor, influence, and as Plascencia illustrates so profoundly, citizenship and human rights. The laws and policy described by these authors result in deportations and the incarceration of specific groups. Importantly, the time period covered by these chapters illustrates the exacerbation of laws of control and policy that not only affect local, regional, and international levels but also channel and control the flow of labor, people, and commodities.

The SWNA is unique in the types of control and contradictions created here because of specific historical patterns and conflict. Other "borderland" regions of the world are infused with contradiction and conflict, as is SWNA, yet differ due to the historical particularities and relationships.

Greenberg and Mandache raise crucial questions not only about the State of Arizona's neoliberalism and its effects on the border but also about the power and reach of the state. They allude to the "implicit state" and focus on the increasing inequalities illustrating how "the numbers"—statistics—not only reflect "reality" but also help shape it. This shaping is also reflected in the discussions of O'Leary, Gomberg-Muñoz, and Plascencia (e.g., quotas, deportations, the U.S. Immigration and Customs Enforcement [ICE] bed mandate, incarcerations, etc.).

The evoking of Scott's *Seeing Like a State* enhances the recognition of the "transnational state" (Álvarez 2006). Much of the literature on globalization and neoliberalism has focused on the inequities and economic dimensions of free trade, especially NAFTA, while ignoring the offshore capacity of the nation-state as participant and organizer of regional-, national-, and local-level adaptations in a variety of sociopolitical processes (in this case across the border in Mexico). The actions, for example, of the U.S. Department of Agriculture and the Food and Drug Administration as well as other U.S. involvement in Mexico and the southern hemisphere illustrate such reach and penetration (Álvarez 2005).

The questions raised by Luis Plascencia in "Where Is 'the Border'?" are crucial in understanding the extensive reach of border law and its effects on citizens, noncitizens, and immigrants. The juridical formation of the actual border encompassing the entire United States and the identification of the "border zone" (one hundred air miles from an external boundary) and "border functional equivalents" reveal the state's massive containment and control. Plascencia illustrates how this has narrowed the individual rights of citizens and noncitizens under the Fourth Amendment. The various identifications and judicial process of "the border" have expanded the police powers of the Department of Homeland Security and expose the wide net of control in law and policy.

These chapters are also instructive in that they forge new areas of research and perspectives that illustrate how bounded our own disciplinary queries have been. Rather than maintain our focus on social-cultural behavior, the limits of the "border," the metaphorical extent of the boundary, and the overworked image of the militarization, violence, and trade, the focus on law and policy, and its effects over time and in the present, are exacting. Such critical analysis is crucially important in understanding the transnational topography and the role of the state and its growing power and control.

REFERENCES

Álvarez, Robert R. 1984. "The Border as Social System: The California Case." *New Scholar* 9:119–35.

———. 2006. "The Transnational State and Empire: U.S. Certification in the Mexican Mango and Persian Lime Industries." *Human Organization* March 65(1): 35–45.

Scott, James C. 1998. *Seeing Like a State: How Certain Schemes to Improve the Human Condition Have Failed.* New Haven: Yale University Press.

PART IV

TRANSBORDER ECONOMIC, ECOLOGICAL, AND HEALTH PROCESSES

14

CO-PRODUCING WATERSCAPES

Urban Growth and Indigenous Water Rights in the Sonoran Desert

LUCERO RADONIC AND THOMAS E. SHERIDAN

INTRODUCTION

RIGHTS ARE PROCESSES, unfolding stories that speak of power relations and changing legal and physical landscapes as people contest access to and control over resources. In the Sonoran Desert, where urbanization is intimately tied to struggles over the control of water resources, indigenous water rights serve as a powerful lens to explore transborder dynamics. The Sonoran Desert stretches over 120,000 square miles across the states of Arizona, Sonora, California, and Baja California. It is in fact one of the major subecologies of the larger regional ecology of what Vélez-Ibáñez has featured in the concept of the Southwest North America (SWNA) region in this volume (chapter 1). On both sides of the international border between Mexico and the United States of America (USA), which was finalized in 1854 when the U.S. Congress approved the Gadsden Purchase, this region is homeland to at least seventeen indigenous groups. For at least 12,000 years, indigenous peoples have lived on and transformed these lands and its resources. For that reason, the term "transborder" welcomes reflections on the relationships between indigenous and non-indigenous cultures and governance structures, and their implications for the production of space in this rapidly urbanizing semi-arid environment. In this chapter we consider how contemporary water rights are reconfiguring power dynamics in Sonora, Mexico, and Arizona, USA, and possibly setting a precedent for a new sociopolitical landscape where tribal governments may become powerful stakeholders in urban development.

The challenge in semi-arid regions has always been how to manage water's spatio-temporal variability. The Sonoran Desert is one of the wettest deserts of North

America, but still its annual precipitation is as low as three inches per year in some locations.[1] In precolonial times, Native American societies developed sophisticated agricultural systems based on irrigation or floodplain-inundation. For example, the Hohokam archaeological culture, which flourished in Arizona between AD 200 and 1450, created the largest irrigation canal system in all of Native North America, including Mesoamerica (Fish and Fish 2008). Until the late nineteenth century, people largely relied upon surface flow, adapting to rivers rather than making the rivers adapt to them (Sheridan 1995). In the twentieth century, however, the waterscape was radically transformed through the construction of dams on all major rivers and later the extraction and overdraft of groundwater resources. On both sides of the U.S.-Mexico border, growth was promoted by a speculative mentality and the conviction that water shortages could be engineered on the supply side. The regulation of the rivers' natural flow regimes, after all, allowed for the control of water availability across large distances and over time.

Both portions of the Sonoran Desert region have followed similar economic, demographic, and political trajectories as capitalist agricultural waterscapes submerged Native ones, only to be submerged by sprawling cityscapes. The term *waterscape* as used here refers to a socio-natural assemblage where social power is embedded in and shaped by material water flows and their representations (see Swyngedouw 1999; Loftus 2007; Budds and Hinojosa 2012). In other words, a waterscape speaks to the enrollment of water under particular ideological and institutional projects that contribute to the reproduction of specific social and ecological relations. From this perspective, water embodies and reproduces forms of power and thus access to water and allocation of water rights are expressions of uneven power relations (Perreault, Wraight, and Perreault 2012). In the twentieth century the Salt River valley in central Arizona and the Yaqui River valley in southern Sonora developed into major zones of irrigated agricultural business, largely with water wrested away from Native farmers. Over the second half of the century, the population across the Sonoran Desert more than tripled, surpassing eight million people by the turn of the century. By the early twenty-first century, explosive urban growth dominates the desert landscape, with the Phoenix Metropolitan Area in Arizona and Hermosillo in Sonora as the foremost examples on each side of the border. The progressive replacement of the agricultural waterscape in favor of modern cities is made possible through the relocation of capital investment from rural to urban areas and its accompanying pull of water toward residential, commercial, and industrial centers. Rapidly growing cities now depend on the import of water resources from across the desert region. Hermosillo and Phoenix, as many other urban areas in the semi-arid Southwest, are outgrowing their place-based water endowments and beginning an at-times creative and at-times violent expansion of their hydraulic reach.

It has been extensively reported that in the SWNA region water flows uphill toward money (Worster 1985; Brown and Ingram 1987; Hundley 1988; Sheridan 1995; Wilder and Whiteford 2006; Sheridan 2012). However, the flow of water, the contours of the landscape, and the location of these "uphill" places vary through time according to changes in capital circulation and institutional arrangements for the allocation and management of water resources. As cities today seek to diversify their water portfolios by expanding their hydraulic reach, they are producing a political ecology configuration that articulates indigenous tribes' historical resource rights with urban real estate development. Indigenous peoples are emerging as important agents in the political ecology of water in the arid Sonoran Desert. But there is one major difference in the emerging political ecology of water in this transborder region. Native tribes in Arizona, including the Akimel O'odham and the Pee Posh, have reestablished rights to some of the waters they lost, making them major players in the Arizona water market. In contrast, in Sonora the Yaqui tribe (the Yoemem) still struggle to secure waters they were allocated in the 1930s. Our two case studies, then, shed stark light on the contrasts between indigenous sovereignty and access to water resources across the urbanizing Sonoran Desert.

In what follows we divide the transformations of the Sonoran Desert waterscape into two periods. The first period corresponds to the non-Native colonization of the Salt River valley in central Arizona and the Yaqui River valley in southern Sonora and the subsequent construction of large-scale hydraulic infrastructure that led to agro-industrial development. In this section we show that reclamation in the United States and modernization in Mexico were parallel representational spaces that played important roles in sociopolitical practices and the modification of water flows and rhythms in the Sonoran Desert. The second period corresponds to the accelerated growth of urban areas, specifically the Phoenix Metropolitan Area and Hermosillo, and their ever-expanding hydraulic frontier. During this period we observe the development of infrastructure and institutional structures to facilitate rural-to-urban water transfers. We introduce the Central Arizona Project (CAP) and Sonora Sistema Integral (SI) as the latest incarnations of a long series of infrastructural strategies to make the desert flourish. Together these centralized infrastructure projects offer an analytical gateway to comparatively study contemporary indigenous water rights in this transborder region.

LARGE-SCALE HYDRAULIC INFRASTRUCTURE FOR AGRO-INDUSTRIAL LANDSCAPES

Beginning in the 1500s, Spanish, Mexican, and, later, Anglo-American settlers began pushing Native peoples out of their riparian oases or diverting their water upstream.

That trend accelerated in the late nineteenth and twentieth centuries, when Native armed resistance largely came to an end and railroad construction linked the Arizona-Sonora borderlands to transnational and global markets. As both newcomers and capital flowed into the region, major zones of commercial irrigated agriculture developed, especially in the Salt River valley of central Arizona and the Yaqui River valley of southern Sonora.

North of the international border, the Desert Land Act was passed in 1877 to encourage settlers to develop arid and semi-arid public lands. The act allowed homesteaders to lay claim to up to 640 acres of public land at twenty-five cents per acre provided that they reclaimed, irrigated, and cultivated the land within three years. Rooted in the prior appropriation doctrine, the Desert Land Act required settlers to acquire and put to beneficial use legal rights to water. Homesteaders were to settle the arid and semi-arid western frontier through irrigation; however, controlling the direction and abundance of surface waters was neither technologically easy nor inexpensive. In the 1890s farmers created joint-stock irrigation and canal companies to build small dams and deviation canals, but by the turn of the century, erratic river flows had shown these structures were inadequate for large-scale agricultural development and the ever-expanding settler population (Sheridan 1995).

With the goal to "Annex Arid America!" —as the motto of the National Irrigation Association proclaimed—in sight, the Reclamation Act was passed in 1902, allocating federal funds to construct and maintain irrigation works for the storage, diversion, and development of western waters. In other words, the hydraulic era of large-scale water infrastructure had begun, with the federal government officially taking the lead in the construction of large dams, reservoirs, and canals. As an institution, reclamation materialized the idea that irrigation works would grant productivity to otherwise useless arid lands, making them available for human use and capital expansion. Reclamation institutionalized what William Cronon (1991) referred to as the "myth of wilderness" through a rhetoric that produced desert lands as areas largely untouched and uninhabited prior to Anglo settlement.

The Roosevelt Dam, inaugurated in 1911, was one of the first projects of the newly formed U.S. Reclamation Service, later the U.S. Bureau of Reclamation. Constructed along the Salt River, the main tributary of the Gila River, the dam was built to control flooding, generate hydroelectric power, and provide irrigation water for the Salt River Project. In the ensuing decades other dams were constructed along the Salt as well as the Verde and Gila Rivers. This created a reliable supply of surface water and allowed agriculture, mining, industry, and population to rapidly expand in the Salt River valley, which later come to be known as the Phoenix Metropolitan Area. In the process, Akimel O'odham and Pee Posh farmers downstream saw their floodplains dry up and their agricultural economy wither. In the mid-1800s, O'odham and Pee Posh had become Arizona's first agricultural entrepreneurs, expanding their production to sell produce to forty-niners, the U.S. military, and the Butterfield Overland Stage. However, by the early twentieth century, they could no longer feed themselves and came to depend on commodity foods provided by federal and state administrations to combat starvation (Rea 1997). The radical change in diet and stress brought about by the loss of surface water contributed to a diabetes epidemic among the Akimel O'odham and Pee Posh (Schulz et al. 2006; Smith-Morris 2006).

South of the border, land colonization and hydraulic development were central to the economic modernization policies of the turn of the century. In Sonora, like in Arizona, state policies encouraged non-Native settlers to carve a new agrarian civilization out of the rich but seemingly idle indigenous territory (Tenorio-Trillo 1996). To allow for the modernization of the nation, indigenous bodies and lands were to be stripped of their indigeneity by turning them into laborious units of work under a capitalist agricultural system; the construction of canals and dams was conceived as the central technology for this transformation. As Banister (2010) explains for the neighboring indigenous Mayo Valley, in the Yaqui Valley the implementation of a grid-based system of irrigated fields via the diversion of water was seen as a necessary battle in Mexico's struggle against the barbarism of the Native people and the semi-arid territory. To this end, the 1883 Mexican Executive Decree on Colonization and Survey Companies set out to establish the boundaries and measure, divide, and appraise vacant and national lands to be put up for sale. The law transferred the responsibility over these tasks to land survey companies who, in exchange for preparing the land for the establishment of settlers, were granted up to one-third of the lands they surveyed. Once measured, divided, and appraised, the lands were sold to foreign and Mexican settlers. While the original law restricted land purchase to 6,177 acres, the 1894 Law for the Occupation and Alienation of Vacant Lands removed the size limit. Together these laws resulted in extensive disenfranchisement of numerous indigenous communities, who were stripped of their territories when their lands were identified as vacant and eligible for colonization (see McGuire 1986; Gómez Estrada 2000; Mora Donatto 2000).

In southern Sonora, in 1890 the federal government granted a Mexican entrepreneur the right to develop the Yaqui River valley and to construct diversion dams and irrigation canals (Aguilar Camín 1977; Evans 1998). Communally held Yaqui lands that were previously cultivated through floodwater irrigation and rights equivalent to one-third of the river's flow were granted as concessions to a U.S.-based company. The legality of these federal concessions was much debated at the time given that the property of water was a matter in dispute until a 1910 law stipulated federal property over water resources (Aboites Aguilar, Birrichaga Gardida, and Trejo 2010). Foreign and Mexican farmers settled along the southern bank of the Yaqui River, and the diversion canals built for irrigation decreased water availability on the north bank, impacting indigenous Yaqui subsistence farming (Dabdoub 1980; Spicer 1980; Evans 1998).

After decades of resource expropriation, indigenous armed resistance, and forced displacement, in 1937 a presidential decree granted the Yaqui tribe exclusive property rights over one-third of their ancestral territory and access to sufficient water for all its population (Spicer 1980). A second presidential decree, ratified in 1940, expanded on the water issue, stipulating the Yaqui tribe could have at its disposal up to half of the volume stored at the Angostura Dam—under construction at the time—and all stream flow not controlled by the dam. In the following two decades, two other dams were constructed downstream from La Angostura, and stream flow was redirected toward Mexican agro-industrial fields. The construction of reservoirs on the Yaqui River system brought nearly 250,000 hectares under cultivation in the Yaqui Valley. Most of that land was farmed by non-Yaquis, who became major wheat producers after Norman Borlaug established one of his Green Revolution wheat-breeding experimental stations in the valley. While highly capitalized Mexican agro-industry boomed on the southern margin of the Yaqui River, indigenous smallholders on the northern margin suffered from the combined effect of capital shortage and water monopolies (Evans 1998; Scott and Banister 2008). Even though the Yaqui tribe is the only Native group in Mexico who has anything resembling a reservation, they have not received the water they were granted by presidential decree in 1937. Nowadays, in a good year, they receive 250 million cubic meters of water, which allows them to have around 25,000 hectares under irrigation.

SHIFTING PARADIGMS: INDIGENOUS WATER RIGHTS IN AN URBANIZING WATERSCAPE

At the dawn of a new century, this semi-arid region has one of the highest economic development and urban population growth rates in Mexico and the United States. As a result, the region has undergone an overwhelming transformation from a rural waterscape dominated by extractive industries and agriculture to an urban waterscape characterized by explosive urban, suburban, and industrial growth (Gober 2006; Hirt, Gustafson, and Larson 2008; Sheridan 2012). In 2015 the Sonoran Desert is home to over eight million people and their associated factories, farms, and suburban tracts; two-million-dollar houses and trailer parks; and shopping malls and ritual grounds, all in need of water.

PHOENIX AND THE GILA RIVER INDIAN COMMUNITY

The Phoenix Metropolitan Area is the largest city in the Sonoran Desert and among the largest metropolitan areas in the United States. This megalopolis is located downstream from the jointure of the Salt and Verde Rivers, which are tributaries of the Gila River. The expansion of the Phoenix Metropolitan Area is closely bound to the Salt River Project (SRP). For the first half of the twentieth century, the SRP was primarily a provider of water for irrigation to rural parts of the Salt River valley. Phoenix and other small towns located within the boundaries of the project's service area supplied their own drinking water with wells. But with the advent of World War II, the agricultural waterscape that dominated the area was radically transformed as military installations and defense industries were established in the area, bringing about an unprecedented urbanization process. Manufacturing businesses and new housing subdivisions soon followed suit, becoming customers of the SRP, who began providing water to budding urban, commercial, and industrial sectors (Salt River Project 2015). From 1950 to 2010, the population in what is today the Phoenix Metropolitan Area increased eight times: from 500,000 to over 4.1 million people.

The Phoenix Metropolitan Area has a relatively diverse water portfolio. Water-supply sources include groundwater, surface water from the Salt and Verde Rivers via the SRP and from the Colorado River via the Central Arizona Project (CAP), and reclaimed water for non-potable uses. In operation since 1986, CAP is a system of aqueducts, tunnels, pumping stations, and pipelines that annually carries 1.5 million acre-feet of Colorado River water to the Phoenix Metropolitan Area, from where it continues to its final destination in southern Arizona. Originally planned to support agriculture, CAP became primarily a municipal and industrial water supplier as urban centers expanded and agriculture declined (Jacobs and Holway 2004; Larson et al. 2005). CAP water provides a viable supplement during normal conditions, but if the federal government estimates there are insufficient supplies to meet the combined allocations of the lower Colorado River and makes an official declaration of shortage, then CAP allocations would be cut. This is because CAP holds junior priority-right status on the Colorado River relative to other right-holders such as the state of California and some indigenous tribes (Pitzer, Eden, and Gelt 2007). The Phoenix Metropolitan Area is constantly searching for alternative water sources to diversify its water portfolio and ensure supply during dry years. Indian water is gaining importance as a water source. Reserved Indian water rights are more secure in times of shortage because they have priority-right status; priority dates are based on the date of the enactment of the treaty, act of Congress, or executive order that established the reservation (Arizona Senate Bill 2007). In this institutional panorama, some cities and towns within the Phoenix Metropolitan Area have already established long-term leases with tribes for water supply. As Colby and Jacobs (2007) explain, an important feature of these leases is that the water retains its Native American priority date even when leased, so non-Indian users have a reliable supply source in times of shortage.

On the southern boundary of the Phoenix Metropolitan Area, the Gila River Indian Community (GRIC) is home to fourteen thousand Akimel O'odham and Pee Posh people. Over the last one hundred years, numerous dams and diversions constructed upstream along the Salt and Verde Rivers—tributaries of the Gila River—reduced segments of the Gila River to a dry riverbed. After eighty years of litigation to regain part of the water they lost to reclamation projects, the Arizona Water Settlements Act was passed in 2004, which included the Gila River Indian Community Water Rights Settlement Act (see Lewis and Hestand 2006). The settlement granted the GRIC an annual allocation of 653,500 acre-feet of water from diverse sources, including CAP, the Gila River, the Salt River, effluent, and groundwater. Although the settlement is for only a fraction of the amount originally claimed by the Community, the Arizona Water Settlements Act is by far the largest Indian water settlement in the history of the United States. Following its enactment, 47 percent of the CAP supply is designated for Indian water rights settlements. The GRIC holds rights to over 311,800 acre-feet from the state's yearly allocation of 2.8 million acre-feet of Colorado River water. In addition, the settlement is conducive to the conversion of paper water into wet water by setting apart funds to refurbish and expand the water distribution network and cover its operation and maintenance costs.

The GRIC's stated long-term goal is to develop a distribution system, agricultural lands, and riparian habitat areas for the beneficial use of water resources (Pima-Maricopa Irrigation Project 2005). Through the development of irrigation infrastructure, the objective is twofold: to restore the agrarian heritage of the Akimel O'odham and Pee Posh and to stimulate a self-sufficient agricultural economy in tribal lands through a combination of heritage crops and cash crops. The plan is to establish an irrigation system composed of over 2,400 miles of canals and pipelines to deliver water to 146,300 acres across the reservation (Pima-Maricopa Irrigation Project 2005). To diversify its economic base and facilitate accomplishing its goals, the GRIC is working with the SRP to store a portion of its CAP water allotment underground to create long-term storage credits, 30,000 acre-feet of which will be made available in the form of one-hundred-year leases to municipal water providers. One-hundred-year lease agreements have already been signed with the cities of Phoenix, Scottsdale, Goodyear, and Peoria in the Phoenix Metropolitan Area. In the short term, the GRIC has agreed to make available up to 100,000 acre-feet of CAP water for purchase by the SRP in years when the utility company is facing cutbacks in its water allocation due to prolonged drought (Salt River Project 2013).

HERMOSILLO AND THE YAQUI NATION

The city of Hermosillo is the largest Mexican city in the Sonoran Desert. Early colonial documents describe the area as an oasis amid arid lands, the last segment where water from the Sonora River flowed on the surface before seeping into the alluvial sands. Over the last three centuries, the structure and function of human settlement in the area underwent numerous permutations, from a small indigenous rancheria in precolonial times to a provincial Mexican capital in the late 1800s. Each reincarnation brought about construction of hydraulic infrastructure to maintain local livelihoods and attract new enterprises to ensure capital expansion. In 1940s the Abelardo L. Rodriguez Dam was built along the Sonora River to prevent flooding and supply water to new agricultural irrigation districts downstream from Hermosillo, where surface water would otherwise not reach. As agro-industrial activity expanded in this part of the desert, Hermosillo's population more than doubled from 1950 to 1960. In the ensuing decades, as the industrial and manufacturing sectors also expanded, population growth continued at an accelerated rate. In six decades the population grew by a multiple of eighteen: from 43,516 in 1950 to 792,000 in 2010. Rapid population growth and high industrial activity translated into higher water demands in an already overtaxed hydrological system (Pineda Pablos 2006; Salazar Adams and Pineda Pablos 2010).

Today, the once-desert oasis is a heat island where asphalt covers the ground and water is brought from deep inside the earth and from a river basin far away. Although located outside the ancestral Yaqui homeland, Hermosillo is tied into Yaqui struggles over self-determination, as water from the Yaqui River is transferred to the city irrespective of unmet Yaqui water rights over the river. In the late 1990s Hermosillo began observing the signs of urban water shortage when the Abelardo L. Rodriguez Reservoir rarely filled over 2 percent of its total capacity and the wells that had come to supply groundwater to the urban population started to dry up. Forced to diversify its water portfolio, Hermosillo expanded its hydraulic reach by buying water rights to groundwater from small-scale agricultural producers upstream in the Sonora River basin, as to not affect the water supply of downstream agro-industry (Scott and Pineda Pablos 2011). In 2012, the state governor announced the construction of the Acueducto Independencia (Independence Aqueduct), presenting it as the long-term solution to the capital's water scarcity problem. The aqueduct would allow for inter-basin water transfers from the Plutarco Elias Calles (or El Novillo) Reservoir along the Yaqui River to the Abelardo L. Rodriguez Reservoir along the Sonora River in Hermosillo. A total of seventy-five million cubic meters would be transferred annually to maintain urban development. The initial plans for this large-scale hydraulic project, however, did not take into account the Yaqui tribe, which has collective water rights over the Yaqui River. The tribe's undelivered water allotment was not accounted for in the hydrometric calculation for the Yaqui River, and tribal members were not meaningfully consulted as part of the environmental impact assessment. This is a continuation of a resource-governance framework that has historically disregarded indigenous sovereignty and disenfranchises indigenous communities (Radonic 2015).

By the time the Acueducto Independencia was announced, Yaqui water rights had gone unmet for over seven decades. Faced by the dismissal of their indigenous rights, the tribe initiated a series of civil lawsuits, inter-ethnic forums on indigenous issues, and mobilizations—most salient of which was the nine-month-long blockade of the international highway connecting Mexico City to Nogales, Arizona. In 2010 and 2011, traditional Yaqui authorities filed two civil lawsuits against the president, the state governor, and the directors of the national and state water commissions on grounds of unconstitutionality for neglecting their right to prior consultation and dismissing their historical water rights. In both instances tribal grievances were based on the state's failure to consult with indigenous peoples according to its obligations under Mexico's General Law of Ecological Balance and Environmental Protection and the International Labor Organization (ILO) Convention 169 (Radonic 2015).

District courts ruled in favor of the tribe, granting them injunctions on the grounds of unconstitutionality that required the state government to halt construction until the Supreme Court of Justice of the Nation heard the case. State authorities, however, disregarded the court's orders continuing construction. In 2013, the aqueduct came into operation, allowing for water to flow from the Yaqui River to Hermosillo. Two years later, in 2015, the Supreme Court sanctioned the aqueduct's operation and the water rights to the Yaqui River allocated by federal and state authorities to the state water commission for inter-basin transfers. Even then, the court declared the environmental impact statement issued for the Acueducto Independencia to be invalid and ordered federal authorities to present another environmental impact statement where the plaintiffs could exercise their right to free and informed, and no longer prior, participation[2] (see Pineda Pablos 2015; Radonic 2015).

INDIGENOUS WATER RIGHTS IN MEXICO AND THE UNITED STATES

The contrasts between these two case studies begin with the creation of what euphemistically is called the reservation "system" in the United States. As non-Native settlers pushed westward, the U.S. government "reserved," i.e., removed, sections of the federal public domain for the exclusive use of Native peoples. That system—an ad hoc assemblage of treaties and military conquests—survived numerous attempts to dismantle it, including the Dawes Act of 1887, which carved many reservations into individual allotments, and termination in the 1950s, which sought to abolish reservations once and for all. Meanwhile, an obscure U.S. Supreme Court decision in 1908 established the Winters Doctrine, which holds that Indian reservations are entitled to enough water flowing through or below them to fulfill the original purposes of their reservation. Federally reserved water rights set out in the Winters Doctrine, as Lewis and Hestand (2006) explain, have become a critical instrument in Indian water rights litigation.

American tribes began recovering their water rights with the Supreme Court decision in *Arizona v. California* (1963), which reasserted the Winters Doctrine while reaffirming Arizona's allotment of the lower Colorado River water under the Colorado River Compact. *Arizona v. California* declared that the statute and executive orders that had created the Indian reservations implicitly reserved water rights for the people, and thus it demanded the quantification of those rights. The result was a formula based on the amount of water necessary for all "practicably irrigable acres" of reservation land. Because of the decision, five tribes along the lower Colorado were granted nearly 1 million acre-feet of the lower basin's allotment of 7.5 million acre-feet. In 2001, the Arizona Supreme Court rejected the practicably irrigable acreage standard as the means for quantification of water reserved for federal lands as limiting and inflexible. Referring back to the Winters Doctrine, in *Gila V* the Supreme Court of Arizona determined that when reservations were created the government impliedly reserved water to meet their purpose as a permanent homeland. Thus, to achieve self-determination and economic self-sufficiency, indigenous tribes and communities should be free to develop their waters for multiple and new purposes, including agriculture; commercial development; and industrial, residential, and recreational uses, as well as cultural purposes, natural resource development, and environmental preservation. In subsequent years Congress passed a series of laws allocating both CAP and groundwater to the Ak-Chin Indian Community, the Salt River Pima–Maricopa Indian Community, the Tohono O'odham Nation, and the Fort McDowell Yavapai Nation in central and southern Arizona. Following these decisions, the tribes quickly diversified their water portfolios. All reserved some of the water for tribal farms; agriculture was part of their cultural heritage even if most tribal members had not farmed for generations. But the tribes also leased portions of their allocations to non-Indian water users within state boundaries, particularly the cities of the Phoenix Metropolitan Area.

While in the United States the initial legal understanding of indigenous water rights as limited to agricultural production was broadened by court decisions that gave room to indigenous self-determination and economic self-sufficiency, south of the border the situation is quite different. Indigenous peoples in Mexico continue to be locked into the perception that they are part of the agrarian legal structure without any collective rights over water outside this framework. In 1992 a constitutional amendment moved to recognize the multicultural composition of the Mexican nation, but it was no more than a declaratory statement of cultural diversity that did not include clear stipulations for the recognition and enforcement of specific indigenous rights. It was only in 2001 that indigenous rights were back on the legislative agenda due to the pressure exerted by the Zapatista Army of National Liberation (Ejército Zapatista de Liberación Nacional; EZLN). Crafted in dialogue with indigenous organizations, the legislative proposal recognized indigenous peoples as new subjects of the law with specific rights.[3] The constitutional amendment passed by the Congress of the Union, however, undermined the intent of the proposal by circumventing indigenous self-determination in matters of territory (Espinoza Sauceda et al. 2001; López Bárcenas 2001a). The amendment to Article 2 recognizes that indigenous people have preferential use and enjoyment of natural resources in spaces they inhabit and occupy, but their right to access, use, and govern these resources remains circumscribed through the forms of property set out in Article 27 of the constitution. Thus, ejidos and agrarian communities remain the only modality of property and legally recognized form of collective organization available to indigenous peoples to claim collective access to land and govern their resources, including water. The status of agrarian community grants indigenous groups legal personality, yet this is not a modality exclusive for indigenous communities. In this regard, as López Bárcenas (2001b) explains, the amendment did not recognize indigenous peoples as new subjects of the law nor did it grant them any specific rights that they did not already possess.

In Mexico, water is the property of the nation, and the federal government working through the National Water Commission has the power to grant private water rights to individuals or collective entities through concessions (Aboites Aguilar 1998; Aboites Aguilar, Birrichaga Gardida, and Trejo 2010). Water concessions, which have a fifty-year limit and are renewable, are in practice equivalent to private property rights (Roemer 1997). Since indigenous groups have no legal standing, their only avenue to obtain water rights is by soliciting a federal concession as ejidos or agrarian communities. Amid neoliberal reforms aimed at reducing the role of government and liberalizing the economy—specifically the land and water markets—Mexico issued the National Water Law in 1992. Neither this new water legislation nor the constitutional amendments that preceded it make any reference to indigenous self-determination and their collective property rights over water. The explicit objective of the new regulatory framework was to strengthen water use right concessions and transfer the administration, distribution, and conservation of water to the private sector and social sector—ejidos and agrarian communities. As part of this process to decentralize decision-making, the law introduced public participation as an important component of water management. This presented a legal pathway for the transformation of the relationship between the state, its citizens, and water (Torregrosa, Saavedra, and Kloster 2005). Despite these legal reforms aimed at reducing the role of the federal government and increasing public participation, the process remains incomplete, with little room for participation by indigenous peoples and other politically underrepresented groups (see Castro, Kloster, and Torregrosa 2004; Wilder 2005; Barreda 2006; Dávila Poblete 2006; Wilder and Romero Lankao 2006; Mussetta 2009).

In contrast to the United States, where water allocations have largely been determined by court decisions, the Mexican federal government actively manages national waters and the courts play a very small role. In this context, the Mexican Supreme Court's resolution in favor of the Yaqui tribe is framed under a broad category of universal rights as listed under the constitution, without directly acknowledging the central role of indigenous sovereignty and water property rights as part of the legal dispute. The 1992 National Water Law promoted decentralization and institutionalized local participation through the establishment of river basin councils, but it excluded collective regulation and management of water resources in indigenous territories. Thus, indigenous communities are accepted as stakeholders in water resource governance only via the river basin councils. These are basin-specific administrative spaces that allow for the participation of water users under an integrated water management framework. In each council, voting seats are granted to representatives from every water sector—i.e., agriculture, industry, public urban, etc.—and to nongovernmental organizations (Diario Oficial de la Federación 1994, 1997). Under this institutional structure, indigenous communities are considered water users analogous to agricultural producers, which largely restricts their water claims to irrigation and dismisses the groups' comprehensive relationship to the Yaqui River water, thus failing to recognize its role as the historical backbone of their traditional Eight Pueblos, a source of life, and the means for self-sufficiency.

CONCLUDING REMARKS

The Sonoran Desert stretches across the states of Arizona, Sonora, California, and Baja California in the United States and Mexico. On both sides of the 1854 international border, the Sonoran Desert is homeland to at least seventeen indigenous groups. In this chapter we have argued that the Sonoran Desert is a transborder socio-ecological assemblage that is produced through cross-cultural power relations embodied in myriad material and textual forms, including water infrastructure and water rights shaped in interactions among Native, Spanish, Mexican, and Anglo-American peoples. In highlighting the power relations that are reflected in and reproduced by the circulation of water, a waterscape perspective fosters a vision of transborder dynamics in the SWNA that transcends the analytical centrality of the geopolitical border between the United States and Mexico in favor of recognizing the cultural diversity within and across the nation-state.

Beginning in the 1500s, Spanish, Mexican, and, later, Anglo-American settlers began pushing indigenous peoples out of their riparian oases or diverting their water upstream. Land colonization policies in hand with centralized water development brought about the consolidation of major nuclei of commercial irrigated agriculture, especially in the Salt and Yaqui River valleys, which had a long history of indigenous O'odham and Yoeme agricultural activity. The expansion of the manufacturing sector after World War II initiated the transformation of the Sonoran Desert from a rural waterscape dominated by extractive industries and agriculture to an urban waterscape characterized by explosive urban, suburban, and industrial growth. In the wake of the twenty-first century, rapidly growing urban communities from Hermosillo to Phoenix depend on the import of water resources from outside areas. As cities seek to diversify their water portfolio by expanding their hydraulic reach and indigenous groups mobilize to ensure their historical water rights are transformed from paper water to wet water, they are co-producing a political ecology that articulates indigenous tribes' historical resource claims with the production of urban centers.

This new waterscape is already evident in the United States where tribes such as the Gila River Indian Community are leasing portions of their water allocations to non-Indian water users, particularly cities along the Sun Corridor that extends from Phoenix south to Tucson. This new trend in water politics is the result of indigenous mobilization and a series of laws passed by Congress in the last decade allocating both CAP water and groundwater to Native communities. These water settlements are reconfiguring the power dynamics in the arid Southwest, setting a precedent for a new sociopolitical landscape where tribal governments are becoming powerful stakeholders in water politics. Historically, the political ecology of water in Sonora has been not that different from Arizona; however, precarious legal infrastructure for indigenous sovereignty in contemporary Mexico tends to overshadow the vital connections between indigenous water rights and urbanization. The fact that the Sonoran Desert region has a shared Spanish colonial legacy, a common ecology, and common environmental challenges but falls under the jurisdiction of two different national governments provides an ideal setting for transborder studies on urbanization and indigenous sovereignty.

NOTES

1. In this paper we follow Forrest Shreve's definition of the Sonoran Desert, which recognizes seven subdivisions within this region, based on the diverse and distinctive vegetation.
2. In 2013 the court had already instructed the Secretariat of Environment and Natural Resources (Secretaría de Medio Ambiente y Recursos Naturales; SEMARNAT) to

consult with the tribe following the international standards for prior and informed consent with indigenous people. As of April 2015, the process had not moved forward.

3. On January 1, 1994, the EZLN staged a rebellion in the state of Chiapas to protest changes to land reform legislation. The Commission of Harmony and Pacification (Comisión de Concordia y Pacificación; COCOPA) was a mediating body created to facilitate dialogue between the EZLN and the federal government and constituted by congressional representatives from Mexico's four main political parties. The COCOPA was responsible for registering the stipulations of the San Andrés Accords—the peace agreement signed between the federal government and the EZLN in 1996—and turning them into the legislative proposal containing the constitutional reforms regarding indigenous rights and culture.

REFERENCES

Aboites Aguilar, Luis. 1998. *El agua de la nación. Historia política de México 1888–1946*. Mexico City: CIESAS.

Aboites Aguilar, Luis, Diana Birrichaga Gardida, and Jorge Alfredo Garay Trejo. 2010. "El manejo de las aguas mexicanas en el siglo XX." In *El agua en Mexico: Cauces y encauces*, edited by Blanca Jiménez Cisneros, María Luisa Torregrosa y Armentia, and Luis Aboites Aguilar, 21–50. Cuernavaca, Mexico: Academia Mexicana de Ciencias.

Aguilar Camín, Héctor. 1977. *La frontera nómada: Sonora y la Revolución Mexicana*. Mexico City: Siglo XXI Editores.

Arizona Senate Bill. 2007. "House Changes to S.B. 1570 House of Representatives." Phoenix.

Banister, Jeffrey M. 2010. "Rio Revuelto: Irrigation and the Politics of Chaos in Sonora's Mayo Valley." PhD dissertation, University of Arizona.

Barreda, Andrés, ed. 2006. *Voces del agua: Privatización o gestión colectiva: Respuestas a la crisis capitalista del agua: Testimonios, experiencias y reflexiones*. Mexico City: Editorial Ítaca & Casifop.

Brown, F. Lee, and Helen Ingram. 1987. *Water and Poverty in the Southwest*. Tucson: University of Arizona Press.

Budds, Jessica, and Leonith Hinojosa. 2012. "Restructuring and Rescaling Water Governance in Mining Contexts: The Co-production of Waterscapes in Peru." *Water Alternatives* 5(1): 119–137.

Castro, Jose Esteban, Karina Kloster, and María Luisa Torregrosa. 2004. "Ciudadania y gobernabilidad en México: El caso de la conflictividad y la participación en torno a la gestión de agua." In *El agua en México vista desde la academia*, edited by Blanca Jiménez and Luis Marín, 199–231. Mexico City: Academia Mexicana de Ciencias.

Colby, Bonnie G., and Katharine L. Jacobs. 2007. *Arizona Water Policy: Management Innovations in an Urbanizing, Arid Region*. Washington, DC: Resources for the Future Press.

Cronon, William. 1991. *Nature's Metropolis: Chicago and the Great West*. New York: W. W. Norton.

Dabdoub, Claudio. 1980. *Breve historia del Valle del Yaqui*. Mexico City: Editores Asociados Mexicanos.

Dávila Poblete, Sonia. 2006. *El poder del agua: ¿Participación social o empresarial?* México: La experiencia piloto del neoliberalismo para América Latina. Mexico City: ITACA.

Diario Oficial de la Federación. 1994. *Reglamento de la Ley de Aguas Nacionales*. Mexico City: Diario Oficial de la Federación. January 12.

———. 1997. *Decreto que reforma el reglamento de la Ley de Aguas Nacionales*. Mexico City: Diario Oficial de la Federación, December 10.

Espinoza Sauceda, Guadalupe, Francisco López Bárcenas, Yuri Escalante Betancourt, Ximena Gallegos Toussaint, and Abigail Zúñiga Balderas. 2001. *Los derechos indígenas y la reforma constitucional en México: Derecho indigena*. Mexico City: Centro de Orientación y Asesoría a Pueblos Indígenas A.C.

Evans, Sterling. 1998. "Yaquis vs. Yanquis: An Environmental and Historical Comparison of Coping with Aridity in Southern Sonora." *Journal of the Southwest* 40(3):363–96.

Fish, Suzanne K., and Paul R. Fish, ed. 2008. *The Hohokam Millennium*. Santa Fe, NM: School for Advanced Research.

Gober, Patricia. 2006. *Metropolitan Phoenix: Place Making and Community Building in the Desert*. Philadelphia: University of Pennsylvania Press.

Gómez Estrada, José Alfredo. 2000. *La gente del delta del Río Colorado, indígenas, colonizadores y ejidatarios*. La Paz: Universidad Autónoma de Baja California.

Hirt, Paul, Annie Gustafson, and Kelli L. Larson. 2008. "The Mirage in the Valley of the Sun." *Environmental History Review* 13(3): 482–514.

Hundley, Norris. 1988. "The Great American Desert Transformed: Aridity, Exploitation and Imperialism in the Making of the Modern American West." In *Water and the Arid Lands of the United States*, edited by Mohamed T. El Ashry and Diana C. Gibbons, 21–84. London: Cambridge University Press.

Jacobs, Katharine L., and James M. Holway. 2004. "Managing for Sustainability in an Arid Climate: Lessons Learned from 20 Years of Groundwater Management in Arizona, USA." *Hydrogeology Journal* 12(1):52–65.

Larson, Elisabeth K., Nancy B. Grimm, Patricia Gober, and Charles L. Redman. 2005. "The Paradoxical Ecology and Management of Water in the Phoenix, USA Metropolitan Area." *Ecohydrology & Hydrobiology* 5(4):287–96.

Lewis, Robert B., and John T. Hestand. 2006. "Federal Reserved Water Rights: Gila River Indian Community Settlement." *Journal of Contemporary Water Research & Education* 133:34–42.

Loftus, Alex. 2007. "Working the Socio-Natural Relations of the Urban Waterscape in South Africa." *International Journal of Urban and Regional Research* 31(1):41–59.

López Bárcenas, Francisco. 2001a. "La diversidad negada: Los derechos indígenas en la propuesta gubernamental de reforma constitucional." In *Globalización, identidad y democracia: México y América Latina*, edited by Julio Labastida, Martín del Campo, and Antonio Camou, 449–63. Mexico City: Siglo Ventiuno Editores.

———. 2001b. *Legislación y derechos indígenas en México*. Mexico City: Centro de Orientación y Asesoría a Pueblos Indígenas AC.

McGuire, Thomas R. 1986. *Politics and Identity in the Río Yaqui: Potam Revisited*. Tucson: University of Arizona Press.

Mora Donatto, Cecilia. 2000. "Aspectos históricos jurídicos del problema agrario en México." *Revista de la Facultad de Derecho de México* 235:161–92.

Mussetta, Paula. 2009. "Participación y gobernanza. El modelo de gobierno del agua en México." *Espacios Públicos* 12(25): 66–84.

Perreault, Thomas, Sarah Wraight, and Meredith Perreault. 2012. "Environmental Injustice in the Onondaga Lake Waterscape, New York State, USA." *Water Alternatives* 5(2): 485–506.

Pima-Maricopa Irrigation Project. 2005. "History of the Gila River Water Settlement Act of 2004." http://www.gilariver.com/settlement.htm.

Pineda Pablos, Nicolás. 2006. "Las tarifas y la autosuficiencia financier, la equidad y la conservación del agua: Un studio comparative de las tarifas urbanas de agua potable en Sonora." In *La busqueda de la tarifa justa*, edited by Nicolás Pineda Pablos, 115–28. Hermosillo: El Colegio de Sonora.

———. 2015. "El acueducto "chueco" del gobierno de la alternancia." In *Sonora 2015: Balance y perspectivas de la alternancia*, edited by Álvaro Bracamonte Sierra, Gloria Ciria Valdéz Gardea, and Alex Covarrubias Valdenebro, 213–42. Hermosillo: El Colegio de Sonora.

Pitzer, Gary, Susanna Eden, and Joe Gelt. 2007. *Layperson's Guide to Arizona Water*. Edited by Sue McClurg. Tucson: University of Arizona Water Resources Research Center.

Radonic, Lucero. 2015. "Environmental Violence, Water Rights and (Un) Due Process in Northwestern Mexico." *Latin American Perspectives* 42(5): 27–47.

Rea, Amadeo M. 1997. *At the Desert's Green Edge: An Ethnobotany of the Gila River Pima*. Tucson: University of Arizona Press.

Roemer, Andrés. 1997. "Derecho y economía: Políticas públicas del agua." Mexico City: Editoria Porrúa.

Salazar Adams, Alejandro, and Nicolás Pineda Pablos. 2010. "Escenarios de demanda y políticas para la administración del agua potable en México: el caso de Hermosillo, Sonora." *Región y Sociedad* 22(47): 105–22.

Salt River Project. 2013. "Gila River Water Storage, LLC." Brown bag presentation, University of Arizona Water Resources Research Center, Tucson, November 7.

———. 2015. "A History of the Salt River Project." http://www.srpnet.com/about/history/default.aspx.

Schulz, Leslie O., Peter H. Bennett, Eric Ravussin, Judith R. Kidd, Kenneth K. Kidd, Julian Esparza, and Mauro E. Valencia. 2006. "Effects of Traditional and Western Environments on Prevalence of Type 2 Diabetes in Pima Indians in Mexico and the U.S." *Diabetes Care* 29(8): 1866–71.

Scott, Christopher A., and Jeffrey M. Banister. 2008. "The Dilemma of Water Management 'Regionalization' in Mexico under Centralized Resource Allocation." *International Journal of Water Resources Development* 24(1): 61–74.

Scott, Christopher A., and Nicolás Pineda Pablos. 1995. "Arizona: The Political Ecology of a Desert State." *Journal of Political Ecology* 2: 41–57..

———. 2011. "Innovating Resource Regimes: Water, Wastewater, and the Institutional Dynamics of Urban Hydraulic Reach in Northwest Mexico." *Geoforum* 42(4): 439–50.

Sheridan, Thomas E. 2012. *Arizona: A History, Revised Edition.* Tucson: University of Arizona Press.

Smith-Morris, Carolyn. 2006. *Diabetes Among the Pima: Stories of Survival.* Tucson: University of Arizona Press.

Spicer, Edward. 1980. *The Yaquis: A Cultural History*. Tucson: University of Arizona Press.

Swyngedouw, Erik. 1999. "Modernity and Hybridity: Nature, Regeneracionismo, and the Production of the Spanish Waterscape, 1890–1930." *Annals of the Association of American Geographers* 89(3): 443–65.

Tenorio-Trillo, Mauricio. 1996. *Mexico at the World's Fairs: Crafting a Modern Nation*. Berkeley: University of California Press.

Torregrosa, María Luisa, Fernando Saavedra, and Karina Kloster. 2005. "Posibilidades y limitaciones de la participación privada en la prestación de servicios de agua y saneamiento: El caso de Aguascalientes, México." *Cuadernos del Cendes* 22(59): 89–109.

Wilder, Margaret. 2005. "Water, Power, and Social Transformation: Neoliberal Reforms in Mexico." *Hors série—VertigO* 1:1–5.

Wilder, Margaret, and Patricia Romero Lankao. 2006. "Paradoxes of Decentralization: Water Reform and Social Implications in Mexico." *World Development* 34(11): 1977–95.

Wilder, Margaret, and Scott Whiteford. 2006. "Flowing Uphill Toward Money: Groundwater Management and Ejidal Producers in Mexico's Free Trade Environment." In *Changing Structure of Mexico: Political, Social and Economic Prospects*, edited by Laura Randall, 341–58. New York: M.E. Sharpe.

Worster, Donald. 1985. *Rivers of Empire: Water, Aridity, and the Growth of the American West.* New York: Pantheon.

15

NEOLIBERAL REGIMES, RESEARCH METHODS, LOCAL ACTIVISM

Border Steel, Environmental Injustice, and Health in a Texas-Mexico Border Colonia

KATHLEEN STAUDT

I BEGIN WITH a thickly described story about health among Mexican Americans in an unplanned settlement (known as a colonia, a settlement type also discussed in chapters 1 and 17) in the Paso del Norte tristate borderlands of 2.5 million people located within ten miles of Mexico, New Mexico, and Texas. In the "Southwest North American region," as Carlos Vélez-Ibáñez analyzes in chapter 1, perhaps 1 million people live in approximately 1,800 colonias. My story starts in 2005 when the grassroots Border Interfaith community organization, affiliated with the Texas Industrial Areas Foundation (IAF), and one of its member faith-based institutions, Inmaculado Corazón de María, took on an issue of grave concern to residents, long burdened by the half-century-old Border Steel plant waste recycling plant and its pollution, noise, and soot that settled in people's homes. I use the word "grave" pointedly, for many colonia residents concluded that people died in "cancer clusters," and Father Pablo publicly stated that he had "never buried so many people" in the time he served there as parish priest. My story ends with analyses of a complex scientific research project that provided weak yet statistically significant causal connections between cancer health outcomes and the length of time people resided in this location (for details, see Staudt, Dane'el, and Márquez-Velarde 2016).

Despite a powerful community organization partnered in this complex community-based research, in the neoliberal regime under which people live in these borderlands, policy neglect will likely occur, whatever the deleterious health outcomes, in this and other colonias and the urban regions surrounding them. The bulk of the analysis offers reasons for probable policy neglect with a focus on four factors: (1) research methods that may give industrial polluters a pass, (2) crowded but narrow academic publication burial grounds in which few activists or policymakers tread (a reason for which I use alternative-to-the-usual academic formatting in this chapter), (3) community organizations whose leaders and major players move onto other issues, and (4) a neoliberal regime that prizes economic growth whatever the externalities (such as deleterious health) residents might bear. My approach involves anticipating the path forward using well-developed grounds, not just diagnosing the past—perhaps an unconventional move, but one that goes beyond the typical academic pattern of waiting long after an issue is locked in place to analyze it.

By neoliberal, I mean the principles and practices of limited government and the reliance on the market and its priorities to drive the economy and social order. In some ways, the neoliberal regime bears similarity to the nineteenth-century mercantilist regime analyzed in chapter 1, with asymmetrical power relations between Mexico and the United States. The state of Texas fits clearly in the neoliberal regime category, with its ideological and partisan commitment to limited government, as evidenced by its low ranking compared to the other forty-nine states on numeric indicators of education, health, income, and well-being (Jillson 2012; Texas House of Representatives 2013). Understanding public policy futures in the border region of Texas requires recognizing the neoliberal context wherein people matter little compared to unfettered foreign investment.

THE RESIDENTS' STORY

Westway colonia with its approximately four thousand residents, 97 percent of them census-identified Hispanic people and located in northwestern El Paso County, sits on one side of Interstate 10 (I-10). On the other side sits the recycling plant, Border Steel, which imports waste from the large industrialized city of Ciudad Juárez in Mexico. The old plant and its operating equipment have been producing since the early 1960s, under different owners from different locales: first the United States, next Mexico, and since 2007, India, by the world's largest steel corporation, ArcelorMittal. The plant operates a round-the-clock operation, day and night, producing noise, soot, and smoke that residents hear, touch on their cars and in their homes, and even videotape during the night. While no one wants job loss in this job-hungry area, residents organized their time and talents into regulatory efforts to reduce pollution and thus improve the environment.

Leaders in the IAF organization, with a dozen member institutions, such as the church in Westway and other faith-based institutions, resolved to address residents' concerns. One leader, a retired environmental engineer in the city of El Paso, identified leverage that could be used to push the plant, political representatives, and/or regulatory agencies to reduce pollution. In reading the fine print of an El Paso newspaper, he saw the public notice that Border Steel was up for license renewal from the Texas Commission on Environmental Quality (TCEQ), a pro-business agency headed by gubernatorial appointees.

For several years, in the typical IAF style of developing relationships with public officials who can be held accountable, leaders held public meetings, gained press coverage, and met with many decision-makers to gain concrete commitments to achieve their goals: county commissioners, the U.S. congressman, the Environmental Protection Agency regional director, and TCEQ officials. Without going into detail already covered (see Staudt, Márquez-Velarde, and Dane'el 2013 and its literature review on community organizing), IAF achieved a victory of sorts. TCEQ required ArcelorMittal to hire and pay an independent firm to generate baseline data on the exact amounts of polluting emissions per year, and then TCEQ would set a standard of, community leaders hoped, reduction from that baseline. Instead, however, TCEQ allowed a 400 percent increase in emissions from that baseline (from 347 tons of carbon monoxide to 1,489 tons annually) (Crowder cited in Staudt, Márquez-Velarde, and Dane'el 2013). ArcelorMittal also committed to investing several million dollars to modernize some equipment.

In the meantime, colonia residents shared their own stories in many meetings and public events about what they perceived to be many deaths from cancer. While stories make deep impressions on others, including politicians, they can easily be discounted by regulatory officials as "mere anecdotes." Thus, Westway and IAF leaders developed an interest in a "scientific" study that, it was thought, would generate irrefutable evidence of environmentally driven harm done in the Westway colonia with credible analysis. With a foot in each of both worlds—a leader in the IAF organization, with deep knowledge of all these events from having participated in and observed them, and an academic analyst, trained in and practitioner of multiple "mixed" methods of research in the borderlands—I applied for funding to hire graduate students to become part of a research team. Ultimately, we engaged in the time-consuming processes of writing the proposal, gaining approval, implementing the complex research design, and analyzing and publishing the results.

RESIDENTS' STORIES AND EXISTING STUDIES IN THE REGION

An avid reader and consumer of interdisciplinary research, I was aware of many indicators and studies that pointed to the border region generally and Westway colonia specifically being "at risk" for health problems such as cancer. Such studies would be important for the "review of the literature" in any grant proposal and any peer-reviewed articles that would emanate from research efforts. Below I summarize studies warning about such risks, perhaps leading some readers to conclude that further research might not be necessary. Yet while much research and publication exist in a crowded field of academic journals, little of it is communicated to decision-makers with the political will, drive, and resources to do something about health warnings.

INDUSTRIALIZATION AND POPULATION IN THE GEOGRAPHIC REGION

People in the Paso del Norte metropolitan region live in what has become a heavily populated river valley region between two mountain ranges. The largest populated area consists of Ciudad Juárez, once Mexico's fifth-largest city and home to at least 1.5 million people, many of whom migrated from north-central Mexico. Next in size is the city and county of El Paso, with approximately 800,000 residents. Going northward from El Paso County, one counts approximately 100,000 in the Las Cruces population. Many smaller towns, villages, and colonias are scattered in between these urban regions.

Ciudad Juárez has been called "the maquila capital of the Americas" (Staudt, Fuentes, and Monárrez Fragoso 2010). Since Mexico's Border Industrialization Program, which began in the 1960s, around three hundred export-processing factories operate there employing between 200,000 and 250,000 workers. While Mexico has fine environmental regulations in its laws, the implementation of those laws is weak, and Grineski and Juárez-Carrillo refer to the "transfer of environmental risk" from the United States to countries to its south (2012). Moreover, industrial waste from U.S. firms in Mexico is imported into the United States not only for disposal but also for commercial purposes, such as in the Border Steel plant that is analyzed in this chapter.

While no inventory of pollution emissions has been published in the binational region, researchers and activists have focused on several firms for the dangers of potential and environmental mishaps. In one example, the Belgian-owned Solvey Chemical Plant, which produces hydrofluoric acid and is located near residential areas of Ciudad Juárez, has, according to Morales, Grineski, and Collins, "the potential to create a Bhopal-type disaster" (2012, 5). Besides earning very low wages (1–2x legal minimum wages, or approximately US$40–50 weekly), workers and neighbors are exposed to "paltry safety precautions," gas releases, and "waste mountains" in a municipality with inadequate equipment and funding to respond to emergencies (Morales et al. 2012, 8, 10, 14). In another example, the copper-smelting plant ASARCO in El Paso had polluted the region for over a century, including an area known as Smeltertown, which housed resident-workers. Despite extensive studies (with mixed results) and activism, what finally appeared to seal the coffin of closure was the fall in world copper prices and the various costs associated with the cleanup. The smokestack, a symbol of El Paso's environmental history, was demolished in 2013. Yet on the other side of El Paso, also embedded in a residential neighborhood near the border, sits Western Refinery. The plant emits pollution and odors, and the nearby elementary school is classified in the top 1 percent most dangerous for air and soil quality of more than 126,000 U.S. public schools in the smokestack study (*USA TODAY* 2007), discussed below.

ENVIRONMENTAL RACISM, ENVIRONMENTAL JUSTICE, AND IMPOVERISHMENT

For several decades, scholars have argued that dirty, polluting industries are often located in regions with impoverished people who are politically marginalized. Such communities may lack the political power to challenge polluting industries. Moreover, in such communities, policymakers might make racist assumptions and/or hold individuals with limited incomes or no insurance responsible for health problems. This literature initially focused on oil refineries built near African American communities but has expanded to include other groups that have experienced long-standing discrimination, such as Mexican Americans. The concept of environmental racism, along with its counterpart, points to a policy rationale, environmental justice, that would reduce excessive pollution, equitably distribute the placement of dirty industries, or set standards to incentivize cleaner industries (see Bullard 1999; Grineski and Juárez-Carrillo 2012).

Many studies in southwestern colonias have pointed to their economic and political marginality (see various chapters in Donelson and Esparza 2010). Moreover, colonias are often populated with a relatively high percentage of undocumented people and/or "mixed households" of citizen children and noncitizen adults (Staudt 1998, chapter 5), who avoid calling political attention to their neighborhoods. Westway is certainly economically marginalized, with a per capita income of $7,781, compared to El Paso's per capita income of $18,100, according to U.S. Census data (Márquez-Velarde 2013, 25). In the entire region, insurance coverage is low, partly due to Texas leadership and its refusal to expand Medicaid after the Affordable Care Act (ACA) of 2010 (unlike New Mexico and Arizona, also with Republican governors). According to estimates from the Austin think tank the Center for Public Policy Priorities (CPPP), if Medicaid had been allowed to expand, one hundred thousand more El Paso County citizen residents would be covered, with $222 million of health business annually (Dunkelberg 2012). However, after 2005, when the Immaculate Heart of Mary church joined the IAF organization Border Interfaith, political marginalization has not been what it once was.

PREDICTED CUMULATIVE CANCER RISK

Official counts of cancer cases are typically reported out in pan-ethnic categories per large units of population on national or state bases. By pan-ethnic, I mean the official U.S. parlance of "Hispanic," a category that includes people of various location heritages to include Puerto Rico, the Dominican Republic, Spain, Mexico, and Cuba (plus other countries in the Americas). Such a category does not do analytic justice to people of Mexican heritage living in the U.S. Southwest and/or borderlands.

Focusing on the El Paso region, Timothy Collins and his co-authors examined conditions that lead to high cancer susceptibility. In 44 census block groups, among the 140 block groups in El Paso County (31 percent of the tracts), they found rates "falling at or above the 90th percentile in cumulative cancer risk" (2011, 338). These data show risk, not the actual existence of cancer. With all the attention to data in the United States, we should, but do not, have disaggregated spatial data on cancer incidence, reoccurrence, treatment, and mortality.

SCHOOLCHILDREN AT RISK

In one of the most compellingly frightening scenarios for the future, the smokestack study (*USA TODAY* 2007) categorized 126,709 U.S. public schools, and two El Paso County elementary schools are located in the top 1 and 2 percentiles for unsafe air and soil. The smokestack study drew from Environmental Protection Agency (EPA) databases posted on right-to-know networks. One school, in the top 1 percent, sits next to Western Refinery in the City of El Paso (mentioned earlier) while the other, in the top 2 percent, is in the research site of Westway colonia. While information sufficiency exists from right-to-know networks and other studies, once again, the political will to act seems nonexistent. Indeed, the regional public was hardly roused, for such information did not make its way into the local media.

Despite rather convincing perspectives and evidence, muddling details and counter-evidence raise questions and lead to uncertainties about actual risk. Such perspectives also open ambiguous doors for future research.

BUT WHAT ABOUT THE "HISPANIC HEALTH PARADOX" AND "IMMIGRANT ADVANTAGE"?

Various health researchers have coined conceptual terms to help explain better-than-expected health outcomes among Hispanics compared to African Americans and whites when controlled for other factors. This has been called the "Hispanic Health Paradox" (Franzini, Ribble, and Keddie 2001; Markides and Eschbach 2005). Also, researchers have noted how immigrants' food preferences and physical activities provide advantages compared with native-born populations, who consume more junk food and lead more sedentary lives, calling this the "Immigrant Advantage" (Zsembik and Fennell 2005). Perhaps cancer incidence would be tempered by such factors or special resilience distributed differently in the population.

However, the "pan-ethnic" Hispanic category and multinational immigrant category may also muddle findings for Mexican Americans located in the Southwest borderlands. Staudt, Dane'el, and Márquez-Velarde develop the term "Border Paradox" (2016) in discussing the advantages of some border people, given the proximity of Mexico and their ability (with appropriate documents and time) to cross the border for health care, lower-cost pharmaceuticals and physicians, and for some, access to Mexico's public (albeit under-resourced) health care program known as Seguro Popular (see details on the program in Homedes 2012). Moreover, bilingual or Spanish-speaking health practitioners are more readily available in Mexico than in the mainstream United States. However, countering this advantage, Zsembik and Fennell note that U.S. mortality data for Hispanics may be underestimated if or when people of Mexican heritage decide to cross the border to their home country when near death (2005).

BUT WHAT ABOUT TRAFFIC ON THE NEARBY INTERSTATE HIGHWAY SYSTEM?

Heavily trafficked highways near communities can confound efforts to establish causation between environmental pollution from vehicles and from dirty industries. Collins and his co-authors estimate that pollution from the I-10 highway that runs through El Paso may account for 60 percent of health outcomes. Westway sits across the I-10 from the Border Steel plant. Furthermore, at fuel stations near the highway in Westway, large trucks park and idle their vehicles, disseminating minute polluting particulates in the air. Also, several dirty industries operate nearby in the area of Vinton, an incorporated village that permits their establishment, perhaps partly for the property tax obtained.

The studies and data reported in this section leave the analytic impression that many in the Paso del Norte region—El Pasoans, Juarenses, and Westway residents—could be at risk for deleterious health outcomes. Yet in health research, it is difficult to attribute causality to environmental factors given the existence of multiple factors that operate and/or mediate a person's exposure to health problems, particularly those health problems such as cancer that generally have a long gestation period. We now turn to the lengthy, multiyear process of conducting laborious field research. Rather than treat risk synergies across interactive multiple variables, researchers often isolate a single causal variable, giving polluters—always anxious about lawsuits—a pass for accountability or responsibility.

FUNDING FOR SCIENTIFIC RESEARCH

With approximately one thousand homes in Westway to canvass and a full-time job, I needed assistance from both the community organization and research assistants for this field research project. Besides, as a teacher, I knew that these MA students, soon to join PhD programs, must augment their CVs with peer-reviewed publications during graduate school if they are to be competitive in academic employment. Also, I had a personal interest in the curious ways officials and researchers gather, count, and report cancer data by region, having recently recovered from harsh treatment in 2011 through 2012. For twenty years, I lived within two miles of Westway in an unincorporated area; I was aware of the dirty industries and several dangerous industrial fires, one that required my family and me to evacuate. The lack of regulation in the state and county governments of Texas brought home the potentially deleterious consequences for residents.

The gestation period for new academic research requires some time. While I participated in Border Interfaith from its inception in the late 1990s and Westway's entry in 2005, where I heard from meetings and actions about residents' concerns, I was finishing a book and two edited volumes on the region about different topics. Thus, movement in a new research direction was a daunting challenge, requiring a great deal of background reading and interaction with a new set of colleagues in the health field.

I knew, however, that existing paradigms in epidemiology favored individualist rather than structural factors in assessing public health outcomes (Brown 2007). In my communication with TCEQ about their studies on the region, they provided reports that focused on smoking or other individual choices rather than pollution and industry regulations. Without nearby air monitors, I was unable to capture data on pollution emissions in different parts of this 1,054-square-mile county divided by a mountain range.

My next steps involved extensive writing to obtain funding and approvals to begin the research. Fortunately, my university had a funded Hispanic Health Disparities Research Center, including funding for environmental health, thus fostering openness to structural factors potentially connected to health outcomes. I applied for pilot funding according to the strict terms in the request for proposals and submitted the many forms common for any funding with agencies affiliated with the National Institutes of Health (NIH). One form asked explicitly about the number of African Americans expected in the sample, and given demographic information from the census, none was expected, thus later raising questions and delays from the federal agency's Washington, DC, office.

NIH funding typically operates under the canons of positivist empirical research, requiring strict attention to sampling, statistical techniques, and causal methods. Had I proposed ethnographic research, it would have decreased the chance that the proposal would have been funded. Based on comments received, the three peer reviewers appeared to be positivist, quantitative researchers (also see Brown 2012). I proposed to generate a random sample of every ninth household to test hypotheses (including one related to voting, civic and organizational behavior, and efficacy) on factors connected to health outcomes and to analyze findings with both descriptive and multivariate statistics. When the Washington, DC–based program officer reviewed the proposal, reviewer comments, and proposed survey instrument, he raised questions about my inclusion of standard indicators of civic participation (voting, contacting officials, organizational affiliations), showing me that the agencies and their peer reviewers rarely operate with paradigms wherein political marginality or power mediate health outcomes. In fact, I have concluded that attention to political activism is rare in scientific health research.

With the proposed community-based research (CBR), far more collaborative interaction was necessary than a mere support letter (see Minkler and Wallerstein 2008). Border Interfaith leaders reviewed the draft survey instrument, both English- and Spanish-language versions, and made several valuable suggestions. Like many colonia residents, Westway had been "burned" before, by researchers from New York State who captured data and left, and no one had ever heard from them again. I met with the new elderly priest, who had just returned from forty years in Latin America, to gain his support and willingness to allow our research team to introduce ourselves and announce the project at church services. Border Interfaith leaders passed the word to neighbors that students would be going door-to-door on the weekends. All this accounted for an extraordinarily high response rate of 82 percent. In the budget, I built in a small stipend for the organization for its time and labor, but the forms necessary to free the money from the university bureaucracy were complex and required tax numbers, generating some anxiety and delay.

The Institutional Review Board (IRB) template for human subjects approval was itself a complicated one, twelve single-spaced pages, copies of the survey instruments in both languages, and the four-page consent letters in Spanish and English. After submission to the IRB, one of the graduate students asked to add a series of questions to tap mental health data, an under-researched topic in colonias, for her thesis. Her good idea meant we had to submit an appended IRB. While the addition of these questions to the survey instrument produced more delays in IRB approval, in hindsight our research team valued these additions for the intriguing findings that were generated about high rates of diagnosed depression and anxiety and their statistically significant connections to worries about the Border Steel plant (Staudt, Dane'el, and Márquez-Velarde 2016).

The data collection process was laborious and time-consuming. I went to the county Road & Bridge Department to get maps of households in order for us to count every ninth household. Because they were full-time students who also had part-time jobs, the research assistants could only interview on weekends. By the end of summer, almost a year after submitting the successful pilot funding proposal, we began entering data for analysis.

The research generated interesting findings from its mixed methods: the contextual analysis, descriptive statistics, multivariate analysis, and occasional stories interviewees told students that added rich detail to their experiences. One example of a story involved a man who was having a heart attack, was dismissed by a U.S.-based health provider, continued having symptoms, and was treated by a medical doctor based in a pharmacy in Ciudad Juárez who saved his life (for approximately US$20). In descriptive statistics we found eleven cases of people with cancer, most of whom lived in quadrants I and II (closer to the Border Steel plant than equidistant quadrants III and IV) and lacked insurance. However, the total number was not large enough to produce statistical significance for the spatial or insurance variable. The only hypothesis support in multivariate stepwise regression analysis at statistically significant levels involved "years living in Westway" (Staudt, Dane'el, and Márquez-Velarde 2016). In the research proposal, I promised to publish two peer-reviewed articles. One of our team's two publications focused on the complexity of CBR in changing political contexts, published in early 2014 (with a 2013 publication date; Staudt, Márquez-Velarde, and Dane'el), while the other required two revisions and explicit formatting like that for positivist research paradigms imposed upon the 2016 article (with a 2015 electronic publication date; Staudt, Dane'el, and Márquez-Velarde). Had no variables confirmed statistical significance, perhaps positivist reviewers would have discounted the overall findings in this mixed-methods approach. In my perusal of health journals, I concluded that most privilege quantitative research.

WHY PROBABLE POLICY NEGLECT?

In this chapter, I have outlined a research story and, behind it, the previous studies and research methods that ultimately led to a community presentation in February 2013, a decision by Border Interfaith to focus on statewide health policy reform, and two peer-reviewed journal publications. With that behind us, still I have predicted probable neglect in policy change in my argument for this article. Why? Below I consider four explanations, beginning with the research methods themselves, followed by academic publication outlets, then the declining interest by the community organization, and finally, the overall neoliberal regime. I then put forward a prognosis for the future.

RESEARCH METHODS

Findings from this research project generated relatively meager conclusions in terms of statistical significance. Part of this can be attributed to the size of the sample. Nevertheless, the variable "years living in Westway" was a causal factor in explaining people's cancer, as noted above. Furthermore, extremely high incidences of diagnosed depression and anxiety became a striking finding, as did the statistically significant connection with a list of respondents' major concerns about Westway, related to the pollution and noise from the Border Steel plant.

Health researchers typically use hypothesis-testing models in deductive, positivist research designs. That our work produced only some support was in some ways disappointing, but in most ways it was a relief when we reported findings in a community setting at the school. We found no "cancer clusters." (In my heart, I wondered if we would have found clusters had we done a sample of *all* households or if community members would have done the research themselves, without regard for funding agencies or peer-reviewed publication opportunities.)

An excellent book by Sylvia Tesh, *Uncertain Hazards*, helped me to understand that this is common in environmental research (2000). She problematizes the particular ways that science as a social construct has led to weak statistical findings amid communities in which grassroots leaders are convinced, through community experiences, of risk. As she relates:

> The populations exposed are usually too small, information about exposure levels is usually too weak, the latency period before cancer shows up is usually too long, and the possible confounding factors are usually too many. (2000, 5)

Tesh critiques EPA paradigms that adopt narrow risk assessment (RA) research and high-validity standards at .05 or .01 levels—sacrosanct levels in which many researchers are trained in most disciplines. Such levels are certainly not adhered to for other risks, such as bomb threats and possible epidemics (2000, 78). Currently, the burden of risk falls on the public to demonstrate proof in high standards, not on industry. Tesh says that much research is conducted as "science for its own sake" (2000, 77), but

> if your aim is to protect public health and a high standard of mathematical certainty both robs you of a scientific rationale for doing so and justifies those who would expose the public to potential harmful substances, the study is unethical. (2000, 77–78)

The U.S. approach appears to privilege business over people's health consequences. Edwards (2008) analyzes European standards, more sensitive to health risks for people than for business costs. Business is at the heart of priorities in a neoliberal regime.

As noted earlier, epidemiological paradigms focus on the individual more than public or structural perspectives (Brown 2007). Even the United States-Mexico Border Health Commission, in its *Healthy Border 2010* goal-oriented report (2010), calls for no measurement, oversight, or reduction of industrial pollution in this industrial manufacturing region, particularly in Ciudad Juárez. Few researchers look at links between economic and political powerlessness and access to health or health outcomes. If researchers are to support their work with funding, to what agencies can they go, with what proposed methods? As noted earlier, causal models using multivariate analyses have value in contemporary, dominant research paradigms, validating findings with .05–.01 statistical significance levels. Context or descriptive statistics are hardly relevant. Yet public health and safety are at potential risk.

CROWDED, NARROW ACADEMIC PUBLICATION OUTLETS

Once researchers analyze data, they typically publish findings in one among many highly specialized peer-reviewed academic journals that delay the disseminations of findings, albeit with the intention of improving the integrity and quality of articles. Accepted articles then enter a queue of articles that await publication. In our experience with this research project, it took almost as many years to organize around pollution (2005–10) as it took to design a research project and get results published. As analyzed above, those who submit articles to many health journals must successfully navigate the quantitative expectations and paradigms of reviewers using positivist research paradigms.

The proliferation of academic journals reflects a market niche into which commercial publishers have moved. Disciplinary associations also offer journals to their members who pay dues. University libraries subscribe to journals in hard-copy or electronic formats. For those readers not affiliated with universities, access to journals is challenging, if not impossible, unless the journal offers open access. Open access typically comes with steep fees with respected journals—the kinds of fees researchers with external funding are able to invest in dissemination. But ultimately, questions remain about readers, connections to political advocacy, and policymakers. Alas, academic journals may be little more than burial grounds for academic visibility and assessment. Graduate students may be steered away from publications in edited book volumes, lacking "impact factor" numeric indicators.

CHANGING COMMUNITY ORGANIZATIONAL AGENDAS

Border Interfaith, like IAF generally and other community organizing models, views "research" as related to the achievement of goals and associated strategies. IAF goals emerge from what it calls "house meetings" that people prioritize in group meetings. After having invested approximately five years in achieving a negotiated goal between TCEQ and the Border Steel plant, however questionable such a victory, the organization moved on to other issues that emerged from house meetings. Yet my communication with the Commission for Environmental Cooperation (a NAFTA side-agreement institution based in Montreal) unearthed data that show continued ArcelorMittal violations of emission standards (see Staudt, Márquez-Velarde, and Dane'el 2013, 198, and other details about the changing context). IAF groups typically work simultaneously on multiple goals, relating to the expansion of Medicaid coverage in the state, the reduction of punitive standardized tests in schools, wage theft, and water or sewer services in colonias, among others. In recent years, Westway leaders have made the construction of a second road into its neighborhood their top priority.

At the community meeting when our research team reported findings in both Spanish and English—with about fifty people in attendance, including some Border Interfaith leaders—some doubted the findings about cancer, but the rates of diagnosed depression and anxiety (double the rates in the county and other colonias) elicited reactions that suggested such findings might have been expected, given the worries and anxieties about the steel plant. Although I never heard Border Interfaith leaders state explicitly that it would be difficult to organize and mobilize efforts around place-based mental illness rates, as a leader myself, I understand the marginalization of mental health issues in U.S. society. Border Interfaith continues, along with the entire statewide IAF network, to push for the expansion of Medicaid coverage (and its associated coverage of mental health). However, those efforts remain an uphill battle in a Republican-controlled state. Despite Medicaid expansion in nearby states with Republican governors, Arizona and New Mexico, the dominant Texas political regime is adamant that health care is mostly an individual responsibility and that more public spending would hurt business.

OVERARCHING NEOLIBERAL REGIMES: ENVIRONMENTAL RACISM AND INJUSTICE

We may be losing the battle for a cleaner environment in African American, "pan-Hispanic," and pan-ethnic communities generally. The ideologues that support limited government, market-generated change, and individual responsibility have triumphed, at least in the state of Texas. Advocates and activists hoped that the well-organized business community would join a coalition chorus of support for Medicaid expansion, given the huge market niche in health care business and jobs (recall the CPPP study cited earlier estimating $222 million annually for El Paso County alone with ACA Medicaid expansion). However, such influential voices have not joined such a chorus, perhaps illustrating the depths of the neoliberal ideology of limited government even at the expense of the likely profitable market niche. Businesses resist government regulations, including those relating to the environment and health. Racism, prejudice, and nativism also affect the ideology and irrationalism of supposed self-interested behavior on the part of businesses. Many of the Texans who would benefit from Medicaid expansion are "persons of color," including Mexican Americans and African Americans. An ideology of individual responsibility prevails in the United States, and especially in Texas, relegating responsibility for health problems to individual behavior, not to public policy or business causes, thus burdening the impoverished. While the Affordable Care Act of 2010 prohibits access to subsidized health care for undocumented people, all too many mainstream white Texans fear what some call an "invasion" of immigrants. Yet within the next two decades, state demographers estimate that white people will be in the minority (as white public school children became in 2013). The prosperity and well-being of the entire state depend on healthy residents, whatever their ethnicity and race.

FROM DIAGNOSIS TO PROGNOSIS: SHORT- AND LONG-TERM FUTURES

Policy neglect will, I predict, aggravate health problems in the Paso del Norte region generally and Westway specifically. Residents who can afford to move elsewhere will do so, while those with scarce resources will be stuck. Many people in the whole region are unaware of industrial pollution and potential environmental health problems; it is hardly a public issue in the media and policy (even to the United States-Mexico Border Health Commission).

It seems that many residents become accustomed to normalized environmental hazards. The same may be true for Westway residents who, understandably, are intent upon improving their community with additional roads and better public services. However, residents may suffer in silence with continuing cancer and mental health problems, attributing them to the national "epidemic" in cancer and supposed individual failures to adjust mentally to the structural violence in their lives. In the border region as a whole, many view the obscene border inequalities in wages and employment safety as key to "global competitiveness," built on the backs of working people in Ciudad Juárez. Environmental health problems will continue and probably grow without systemic attention to the dirty industries and pollution emissions.

Despite the common interests that exist among people on both sides of the U.S.-Mexico border—and indeed the entire North American region—government policies will likely try to contain their population's privileges or burdens in national enclaves. Binational approaches exist for some health issues, such as tuberculosis and HIV/AIDS, but more comprehensive approaches may be decades, even generations away. A European model of open borders and priority to health over business concerns seems far in the distant future.

Influential advocates such as Angela Blackwell and others at Policy Link call for more linkage between grassroots activism and policy change at not only state but also national levels (2012). Yet with a polarized Congress and the two-year cycle of electoral campaigns that resort to lowest-common-denominator negative rhetoric about people and policy, it is difficult to remain hopeful. Those of us who reside and work at borders look to binational or North American solutions, yet these too seem limited given that the political classes in both Mexico and the United States remain tolerant of the ongoing, obscene inequalities of the early twenty-first-century neoliberal era. One certainty from this analysis is that academic researchers can and should do more to communicate their findings to action and policy change with organized constituencies. We are producing much quantitative data, predicting (albeit weakly, using given research standards) deleterious health outcomes, but limited government and hostility to the "R" word, regulation, continues. It is high time that we move toward safety standards in those public policies that allow pollution to hurt people at the border, in colonias, and in the larger region.

REFERENCES

Blackwell, Angela Glover, Mildred Thompson, Nicholas Fruedenberg, Jeanne Ayers, Doran Schrantz, and Meredith Minkler. 2012. "Using Community Organizing and Community Building to Influence Public Policy." In *Community Organizing and Community Building for Health and Welfare*, edited by Meredith Minkler, 371–85. New Brunswick, NJ: Rutgers University Press.

Brown, Phil. 2007. *Toxic Exposures: Contested Illnesses and the Environmental Health Movement*. New York: Columbia University Press.

———. 2012. "Qualitative Approaches in Environmental Health Research." In *Contested Illnesses: Citizens, Science, and Health Social Movements*, edited by Phil Brown, Rachel Morello-Frosch, Stephen Zavestoski, and the Contested Illness Research Group, 33–45. Berkeley: University of California Press.

Bullard, Robert. 1999. "Dismantling Environmental Racism in the USA." *Local Environment* 4(1): 5–19.

Collins, Timothy, Sara E. Grineski, Jayajit Chakraborty, and Yolanda J. McDonald. 2011. "Understanding Environmental Health Inequalities Through Comparative Intracategorical Analysis: Racial/Ethnic Disparities in Cancer Risks from Air Toxics in El Paso County, Texas." *Health & Place* 17:335–44.

Donelson, Angela J., and Adrian X. Esparza, eds. 2010. *The Colonias Reader: Economy, Housing, and Public Health in the U.S. Mexico Border Colonias*. Tucson: University of Arizona Press.

Dunkelberg, Anne. 2012. *Your County and the ACA*. http://library.cppp.org/files/3/HC_2012_11_MedicaidCounty Data.pdf.

Edwards, Nelta. 2008. "An Ounce of Precaution." *Contexts* 7(2): 26–30.

Franzini, L, J. C. Ribble, and A. M. Keddie. 2001. "Understanding the Hispanic Paradox." *Ethnicity & Disease* 11(3): 496–581.

Grineski, Sara, and Patricia Juárez-Carrillo. 2012. "Environmental Injustice in the U.S.-Mexico Border Region." In *Social Justice in the U.S.-Mexico Border Region*, edited by Mark Lusk, Kathleen Staudt, and Eva Moya, 179–98. Dordrecht: Springer.

Homedes, Nuria. 2012. "Achieving Health Equity and Social Justice in the US-Mexico Border Region." In *Social Justice in the US-Mexico Border Region*, edited by Mark Lusk, Kathleen Staudt, and Eva Moya, 109–27. Dordrecht: Springer.

Jillson, Cal. 2012. *Lone Star Tarnished*. New York: Routledge.

Markides, Kyriakos S., and Karl Eschbach. 2005. "Aging, Migration, and Mortality: Current Status of Research on the Hispanic Paradox." *Journals of Gerontology* Series B 60B (special issue II): 68–75.

Márquez-Velarde, Guadalupe. 2013. "Mental Health in the *Colonias*." MA thesis, Department of Sociology and Anthropology, University of Texas at El Paso.

Minkler, Meredith, and Nina Wallerstein, eds. 2008. *Community-Based Participatory Research for Health: From Process to Outcomes*. New York: John Wiley.

Morales, Oscar, Sara E. Grineski, and Timothy Collins. 2012. "Structural Violence and Environmental Injustice: The Case of a US-Mexico Border Chemical Plant." *Local Environment* 17(1): 1–21.

Staudt, Kathleen. 1998. *Free Trade? Informal Economies at the U.S.-Mexico Border*. Philadelphia: Temple University Press.

Staudt, Kathleen, Mosi Dane'el, and Guadalupe Márquez-Velarde. 2016. "In the Shadow of a Steel Recycling Plant in These Neoliberal Times: The Political Economy of Health Disparities Among Hispanics in a Border Colonia." *Local Environment* 21(5): 636–52.

Staudt, Kathleen, César Fuentes, and Julia Monárrez Fragoso. 2010. *Cities and Citizenship at the U.S.-Mexico Border*. New York: Palgrave USA.

Staudt, Kathleen, Guadalupe Márquez-Velarde, and Mosi Dane'el. 2013. "Stories, Science, and Power in Policy Change: Environmental Health, Community-Based Research, and Community Organizing in a US-Mexico Border *Colonia.*" *Environmental Justice* 6(6): 191–99.

Tesh, Sylvia Noble. 2000. *Uncertain Hazards: Environmental Activists and Scientific Truth.* Ithaca, NY: Cornell University Press.

Texas House of Representatives. Legislative Study Group. 2013. *Texas on the Brink.* http://texaslsg.org/texasonthebrink.

United States-Mexico Border Health Commission. 2010. *Healthy Border 2010: An Agenda for Improving Health in the United States-Mexico Border.* http://www.borderhealth.org/files/res_63.pdf.

USA TODAY. "The Smokestack Effect: Toxic Air and America's Schools." 2007. http://content.usatoday.com/news/nation/environment/smokestack/search/TX/~/el+paso+.

Zsembik, Barbara A., and Dana Fennell. 2005. "Ethnic Variation in Health and the Determinants of Health Among Latinos." *Social Science & Medicine* 61:53–63.

16

DIVERTED RETIREMENT

The Pension Crisis Among Elderly Migrant Farmworkers

SARAH HORTON

DON PABLO IS a fairly typical retired farmworker. A seventy-six-year-old who first came to the United States as a bracero at the age of eighteen, he is now an elderly bachelor.[1] He rents a one-room shack on the main drag of Mendota, a small farmworking community in California's Central Valley, for $150 a month. Both don Pablo and his house are relics from the bracero era; just as don Pablo himself has spent the last five decades tending fields throughout the Southwest, many of the low-ceilinged and tumbledown shacks that line the town's main drag—Seventh Avenue—had former lives sheltering the town's braceros.

Beto, the owner of the corner store that serves as a hub for the community of single male sojourners, has directed me to don Pablo because of his age and experience. When I arrive at his house, I find that don Pablo's front door directly abuts the sidewalk. When don Pablo opens the door, I draw in my breath as I enter. Don Pablo has made a bachelor pad of his shack; within the space of a large closet, he has managed to squeeze his bed, a chair for guests, a dresser, a desk with microwave, and a large refrigerator. There is no kitchen sink or stove, and only a foot of floor remains bare. Accessories for grooming and a few belongings are stacked on the dresser at the end of the bed. Meanwhile, tacked up on the inside of his front door, presenting a jarring contrast, is a magazine cut-out of a spacious colonial estate with columns.

Don Pablo remains resolutely proud of his history of work. Before he settled in Mendota, don Pablo had worked as a bracero in Sacramento, California, in Yuma, Arizona, and in California's Imperial Valley. He had worked for the same Filipino contractor for ten years, and the man had praised him for never skipping out on his contract. He had worked weeding tomatoes and picking stone fruit—a job all the more challenging because agriculture was not yet mechanized. "Back then, there were no machines. I had to do pure hard work" (Me tocó puro trabajo duro), he remembers. Elderly migrant men express great pride in their work histories; their loyalty and consistency as workers is central to their identities as men (see Walter, Bourgois, and Loinaz 2004). Even now that he is retired, don Pablo's consistency and his hardiness as a worker remain integral to his masculine identity and key to his conception of his self-worth.

However, retirement unsettled don Pablo's belief in the value of his hard work. When don Pablo went to Fresno to apply for his Social Security pension at the age of sixty-two, he was startled to hear that his forty-four years of farm work had afforded him a pension of only $400 a month. He inquired why his pension was so small, and the eligibility worker replied that it was "simply the misfortune of those who had done fieldwork." "Well, you didn't work in construction, or in restaurants, or driving a truck," she explained. "You only worked in the field. And they pay people in the field very little." "Ehh, well, I suppose that's right," don Pablo responded. So don Pablo returned to the fields for three more years, supplementing his monthly pension with the occasional work he found on crews.

"Retirement"—as understood by the majority of the U.S. populace as the permanent cessation of work—ill-describes the realities that elderly farmworkers face. Only farmworkers with legal status are eligible for a federal pension, and they must be at least sixty-two years old to receive it. Yet even migrant farmworkers with legal status receive pensions that they believe ill-reflect their efforts. This chapter uses retirement dilemmas of elderly unauthorized farmworkers as a means of exploring the long-term consequences of migrants' "legal nonexistence" (see Coutin 2000, and chapters 2, 9, 11, and 12). It explores how migrants' legal absence facilitates what I call "strategies of erasure," as well as the strategies that migrants use to supplement retirements that have been diverted into the pockets of their employers or the coffers of the state and federal governments. In doing so, this chapter contributes to our understanding of the legal and political processes that maintain an artificial divide between spaces of production and social reproduction within this transborder region, in turn cheating migrant farmworkers of a retirement.

STRATEGIES OF ERASURE

As don Pablo's case shows, farmworkers' monthly Social Security payments rarely sustain them in their old age. Because farm work is the second-lowest-paid occupation in the United States (NCFH 2012)—and retirement payments are based on wage deductions—many farmworkers continue to work for as long as they are able to supplement their meager federal assistance. Yet even as farmworkers' low annual incomes condemn them to an insufficient safety net, a period of prior legal nonexistence often erodes the pensions available to them. Unauthorized or temporary workers may eventually adjust their legal status and subsequently retire, only to find that their pensions have been pillaged through what I call *strategies of erasure*—that is, tactics by which individuals, employers, and the state have profited by making workers appear to "disappear" from the employment record.

We have seen that don Pablo's Social Security worker attributed his paltry pension to the everyday "misfortune" of receiving a retirement based on a lifetime of below-poverty-level wages. Yet at the same time, don Pablo's retirement is low in part because his fourteen years as a temporary contract worker did not count toward his retirement; don Pablo was ineligible for Social Security while a bracero. Although braceros were not subject to Social Security or income taxes, the federal government garnished their income by 10 percent to be held in trust by the Mexican government as an incentive for the braceros to return to Mexico after the program was over. Like many other braceros, don Pablo never saw this income (Meissner 2004).

Elderly migrant farmworkers with legal status often find their federal retirement payments low because a variety of agents have profited from their "legal absence" (Coutin 2000). Although in don Pablo's case the Mexican state failed to acknowledge the wage deductions it received for migrant workers, U.S. agents more frequently obscure migrants' labor history. Most frequently, migrants find themselves ineligible for Social Security because their labor supervisors—whether mayordomos (foremen) or contractors—had made them invisible to the state when they were unauthorized.

In California, labor supervisors are often migrants and former field hands. The passage of the Immigration Reform and Control Act (IRCA) of 1986 facilitated former field hands' ascent through the farm labor hierarchy in two different ways. IRCA's Special Agricultural Worker Program (SAW) provided legal status to 1.1 million farmworkers who could provide proof of having performed at least ninety days of farm work between 1985 and 1986 (Massey, Durand, and Malone 2002, 91). In allowing some migrants to adjust their legal status, IRCA also provided them an unprecedented opportunity to apply for federal contracting licenses. In addition, IRCA imposed fines on employers who "knowingly" and "intentionally" hired unauthorized workers (Massey, Durand, and Malone 2002, 119). Thus IRCA encouraged many growers to delegate to contractors the risks of hiring a predominantly unauthorized labor force, creating the subcontracting boom in contemporary agriculture (Martin 1994). Meanwhile, subcontracting itself provides labor supervisors with an incentive to exploit their knowledge of the legal vulnerability of their workforce to make a profit, as growers allot contractors a fixed sum of money to cover their overhead expenses, workers' wages, and their own salaries (see Horton 2016).

Migrants' invisibility is often a cloak for their employers' crime—that is, contractors and mayordomos hide workers' employment to conceal violations of immigration or labor laws from the authorities. Mayordomos giving underage workers loaned work authorization documents to obscure their violation of child labor laws is a prominent example of this (see Horton 2016). Another such example is when labor supervisors require that farmworkers work "under the same ticket" when they are being paid piece rate. Federal law requires that employers pay workers at least the minimum wage when they are working piece rate. Yet because two employees working "under the same ticket"—that is, working under the same name—leads to the appearance of inflated pay, it allows employers to hide their violation of labor laws. As an organizer for California Rural Legal Assistance, Inc., puts it: "When that check comes along, it shows that that person was earning minimum wage even though there were [actually] two working that ticket."

Yet the most common ploy employers use to render workers invisible is when they pay unauthorized workers "off the books"—that is, they hide their employment of unauthorized workers from the state and federal governments to profit from their legal invisibility. One worker in the Mendota branch of a local social service agency says that many elderly migrant farmworkers find themselves without pensions due to such ruses. As she puts it: "Most farmworkers either can't draw [Social Security] because they've worked off the books or the bosses have collected [e.g., withheld payroll deductions] but not paid in. In other words, they've been ripped off."

Ofelia, for example, is a seventy-three-year-old who migrated to the United States from Morelia, Mexico, in 1976. For twelve years, she and her husband had worked for Manuel González, a contractor who had taken advantage of their unauthorized status to pay them entirely in cash (*en efectivo*). "He liked us because we were hard workers; he used to call us and let us know when there was work at different ranches," she remembers. Every two weeks, Mr. González would give Ofelia and her husband an envelope with their wages as well as an approximation of a "check stub": that is, a typed receipt listing the mandatory payroll deductions he had made. Ofelia and her husband found this arrangement mutually agreeable at the time. Because they lacked the official identification required to open up a bank account, they would have had to pay extra to cash their paychecks. "And to think we were so happy because it was in cash," she says now, smiling sadly at her naiveté.

Ofelia worked in the United States for seventeen years. She picked chile; weeded melon, tomatoes, and cotton; and packed pomegranate. She now suffers from arthritis, high blood pressure, diabetes, and cataracts. After years of working "illegally," Ofelia was able to adjust her legal status in 1986 through IRCA's special legalization program for farmworkers. Yet when Ofelia applied for her Social Security pension at the age of sixty-two, the eligibility worker told her that the office had scarcely any record of Ofelia having worked. It was only then that Ofelia realized the cost of her arrangement with Mr. González; he had never in fact paid the federal and state governments the deductions he had listed on her balance sheet. Mr. González had taken advantage of Ofelia's legal absence to conceal her from the government; in so doing, he had cheated her of a retirement.

Ofelia's case shows that migrants' legal ineligibility for employment provides employers with a handy excuse for erasing them from the official record. Employers often justify their erasure of migrants by explaining to them that they wish to "hide" their illegal hire so as to avoid fines and a federal audit. Yet paying workers "off the books" serves a dual purpose, as employers simultaneously leave no trace of the migrant's employment. Having erased unauthorized workers from federal and state records, employers then take advantage of workers' invisibility by appropriating their wage deductions.

Cash payments are not the only vehicle for strategies of erasure; employers have even devised means of making workers invisible to the government when paying them by check. Sulema had experienced this. Sulema told me that one local contractor paid all its employees with checks but routinely neglected to provide to only its unauthorized employees the check stubs listing the mandatory federal and state withholdings from their wages. "They give the check stubs to those with papers. But they erase all those without papers," Sulema says. After puzzling over this fact with several of her colleagues, Sulema decided to ask her supervisor why she had not received her check stubs. "Because your papers are no good," he had replied. Like Mr. González, then, Suelma's employer took advantage of his workers' legal absence to obscure their presence from the government; in so doing, he had made their work and wage histories disappear.

By keeping its employees invisible to the authorities, employers defraud the state and federal governments of taxes. They appropriate for themselves the state and federal withholdings taken directly from workers' wages: income taxes, FICA taxes (which help fund Social Security, Medicare, and federal disability payments), and SDI (State Disability Insurance).[2] They also avoid paying a series of employer taxes on such "invisible" workers: unemployment taxes on their wages, as well as Social Security and Medicare taxes to match employees' deductions. Unauthorized migrants' legal exclusion from the very programs funded by their wage deductions enables such tactics. Because unauthorized migrants are ineligible for Social Security, unemployment, and Medicare, employers often conceive of their wage deductions as money for the taking—as deductions without a rightful recipient.[3]

The erasure of their work histories creates an immediate problem for low-income populations such as farmworkers. Workers must be visible to the state to receive the scant state and federal assistance available to them. Sulema, for example, needed her check stubs as proof of income to receive food stamps and Medicaid for her citizen children; she also needed her W-2 so that she could file her income taxes with her Individual Taxpayer Identification Number (ITIN). Sulema visited the company's office several times to request her missing check stubs—to no avail. It was only when her social worker took the trouble of calling the company himself—in an attempt to get Sulema's family the food stamps they needed—that Sulema's employer eventually faxed over the missing evidence. Yet while the erasure of their work histories presents obstacles to unauthorized migrants' receipt of social assistance, it also robs them of a future. It deprives them of the disability and retirement funds to which they would be entitled should they eventually be able to adjust their legal status.[4]

Ofelia, for example, is recently widowed. Despite her seventeen years of farm work and her legalization under IRCA, she receives only $200 in Social Security assistance a month. Mr. González's pocketing of her wage deductions left Ofelia with a minimal retirement. Ofelia is entirely dependent upon the $600 in monthly Social Security disability payments that her son, *un sordomudo* (deaf-mute), receives. "He gives me half his check to pay the rent and electricity, and that's how we survive," she says. When I ask her whether she still has the receipts Mr. González gave her some thirty years ago as potential evidence in a lawsuit, Ofelia smiles wanly. "Sometimes, when you move apartments so often, all those old papers bother you and you just throw them away," she says.

Thus migrants' shifting legal status over their lifetimes facilitates the obliteration of their work histories. As Susan Coutin has pointed out, "prohibited work that is unreported, unregistered, and untaxed cannot always be proven to have occurred" (2000, 32). Employers' strategies of erasure propel migrants into a space of nonexistence—a space in which their social and physical presence grates against their legal absence. When employers make their migrant employees invisible to the government, they cheat them of a retirement.

THE PROFIT RESERVE

Employers' strategies of erasure highlight the peculiar form of value created by unauthorized migrants' exclusion from state and federal assistance (see also Horton 2015). Migrants' ineligibility for state and federal benefits makes their unclaimed wage deductions and unused employer taxes what I call a "profit reserve"—a source of profit formally accessible only to the government. By rendering workers invisible, employers vie to tap into this "profit reserve" and siphon off such surplus value.

Theorists of "global apartheid" have recently argued that unauthorized migrants' legal and political exclusion from industrialized countries has benefited both states and employers by rendering migrants an "efficient, flexible, and globally competitive workforce" (Sharma 2007, 80; see also Booker and Minter 2001; Sharma 2006; Spener 2009). They draw upon the arguments of sociologist Michael Burawoy (1976), who first compared the position of temporary Mexican laborers in the United States as a cost-effective "labor reserve" to that of African laborers under apartheid who migrated from their *bantustans* (separate reserves) to work in the gold mines of South Africa. In both cases, Burawoy argued, migrants' political and legal exclusion from receiving states serves to displace the costs of labor force renewal—such as paying for workers' health care, unemployment, and retirement—to sending states.

Yet such strategies of erasure suggest that not only do receiving states economize on the reproduction of labor by importing migrants—that is, by externalizing the costs of labor force renewal to sending states—but also each unauthorized worker represents a source of direct surplus value for the receiving state. In short, the legal exclusion of unauthorized migrants from both state and employer benefits appropriates a portion of the value of unauthorized migrants' labor for the state. Migrants' ineligibility for retirement and unemployment benefits does not merely save the state money; rather, it actively transfers value from migrants to the state in the form of wage deductions and employer taxes (see Heyman 1998, 2001).

The chief actuary of the Social Security Administration (SSA) estimates that unauthorized migrants paid a net contribution of $12 billion in 2007 in the form of Social Security wage deductions that are attached to a Social Security number (SSN) that cannot be matched to a verifiable legal name. By 2007, he reports, the Social Security trust fund had received a net benefit of between $120 and $240 billion from unauthorized immigrants (Schumacher-Matos 2010).[5] The state of California also receives unemployment insurance taxes on the wages of each employee, which are deposited in a general fund for unemployment insurance. Thus the ineligibility of unauthorized workers to collect unemployment insurance similarly generates a surplus in the state fund. Adapting Burawoy's concept of the "labor reserve," I suggest that unauthorized migrants' exclusion from state and employer benefits has rendered their unclaimed deductions and unused employer taxes a "profit reserve"—a source of revenue formally accessible only to the state.[6]

Like the concept "labor reserve," the term "profit reserve" implies that unauthorized migrants serve as a source of surplus value that is generally hidden from public consciousness and view. It refers to the fact that unauthorized migrants serve as containers of value that remain inaccessible to them due to their very legal absence (see Horton 2015). Strategies of erasure illustrate employers' awareness of the value associated with unauthorized labor and their attempts to strategically unlock it for their own benefit. Employers disrupt the value transfer created by citizenship laws, deliberately diverting income that would normally enter state and federal coffers into their own pockets.

DIVERTED RETIREMENT

Even as migrant farmworkers with legal status find that their pensions have often been depleted by strategies of erasure, elderly unauthorized migrants are excluded from the Social Security safety net entirely. Thus unauthorized migrants experience what I call "diverted retirements." The phenomenon of "diverted retirement" is one facet of a broader "international transfer of caretaking" that scholars have identified in the global South as its residents' care resources are diverted from their own kin—usually their children—to attend to the needs of elders and children in the global North (see Parreñas 2006). As women from Mexico, Central America, and the Philippines migrate to the global North to serve as domestic workers, nannies, and nurses—filling positions typically vacated by white women—care is systematically transferred from their children who remain in their homelands. Rhacel Parreñas calls this phenomenon "diverted mothering." As Parreñas puts it, the imperatives of the global economy dictate that mothers expend their mothering resources on the children of others. In "diverted mothering," she writes, the emotional resources of mothering are redirected away from those who, "by kinship or communal ties, are their more rightful recipients" (2006, 54).

We have seen that unauthorized migrants' contributions to the SSA have played a key role in postponing the federal government's projected pension shortfall. The Social Security deductions from unauthorized migrants' wages offset the retirement deficit policymakers have long anticipated due to the aging of the U.S. population. Thus elderly unauthorized migrants in the global North experience a crisis of care parallel to that of families in the global South. Unauthorized migrants find their own wage deductions redirected to fund the retirements of legal permanent residents and citizens.

WAITING FOR "ANOTHER AMNESTY"

Elderly unauthorized migrants are only eligible to collect the Social Security taxes deducted from their paychecks should they eventually be eligible to adjust their legal status. The last major legalization program occurred in 1986, when IRCA established the SAW program, which required that applicants demonstrate proof of having performed at least ninety days of farm work between 1985 and 1986. Yet by predicating legal status on proof of work—like most legalization programs—IRCA created obstacles for manual laborers. Some had worked under the table and lacked the required documentation; others had inopportunely sustained injuries that sidelined them from their jobs during the legalization window. Thus some single sojourning men worked in the Central Valley for decades and yet were ineligible for SAW. Many such career migrants decided to wait out their old age in the Central Valley in the hopes that Congress would pass "another amnesty"—as they put it—so that they could eventually access their accumulated pensions.[7]

Don Luis, for example, is an unauthorized sixty-seven-year-old who has been migrating from Las Ánimas, Zacatecas, since 1962. He missed IRCA's legalization program because he threw his back out while picking melon and temporarily returned to Mexico to recuperate. His employer sent him a letter in 1985 to inform him that he could in fact adjust his legal status if he returned that year, but don Luis was unable to walk. He views his employer's letter as proof of his work history, and he has kept it ever since. Don Luis has continued to work in the Central Valley as an unauthorized laborer for another twenty-five years, hoping for a second chance.

When I visit don Luis in the bachelor apartment he shares with his roommate, he walks me through the dim kitchen—with its low, sloping ceiling and the linoleum curling up from the floor in waves—to the bedroom. A naked lightbulb on the ceiling lights the room, and two cots lie opposite one another. Don Luis lifts up the bedcover of one and bends down to fetch one of several plastic shopping bags carefully stored underneath. Don Luis cannot read, but he knows each stack of papers by their size, shape, and distinctive markings. He unfurls one set of papers—curled from age—to reveal every single record from the medical appointments he has had since he first visited the doctor eight years ago: appointment reminders and slips handwritten by clerks to record payment. In the adjacent bag lie his taxes, which he has taken care to pay each year since he returned to the United States after his accident. A third bag holds receipts from his rent and utilities payments. Don Luis has stashed such records under his bed because they are as important as his savings. Should there indeed be "another amnesty," as he puts it, such paperwork will serve as proof of his duration of residence.

Similarly, don Santiago is a sixty-three-year-old migrant from the same region as don Luis who also missed the "amnesty"—in his case, because he had returned to Zacatecas in 1984 to take care of his dying parents. Many of his coworkers and family members in the United States had obtained their "green cards" under IRCA, and they urged him to pay a contractor to falsify documentation stating that he had worked that year so that he too could qualify. Don Santiago refused to engage in such *tranzas* (scams). Yet he often thinks wistfully of the tens of thousands of dollars he has invested in Social Security since 1970—money that he has forfeited simply by having been temporarily absent during the legalization program. "I must have at least $70,000 in there," he tells me. When he was finally able to return to the United States after his parents' death in 1986, he came with the express goal of working until another legalization program might permit him to access the funds the SSA held in his name.

Both don Luis and don Santiago are legal anomalies. Although unauthorized, they had applied for and received valid Social Security cards from the SSA in the early 1970s, before the agency stopped issuing such cards to unauthorized migrants. Although their names and SSNs are officially registered with the federal government, neither man is eligible for the same benefits of citizenship because their unauthorized status makes them ineligible for valid forms of identity documentation, such as green cards or passports. Thus don Santiago and don Luis occupy a form of "liminal legality" (Menjívar 2006).

Aware of the importance of building a wage history attached to a single identifier, both don Santiago and don Luis have assiduously avoided working on other people's papers. Don Santiago takes great pride in the fact that he has worked "only one SSN" ever since he first arrived in the Central Valley. "I never worked another *seguro* [Social Security card] since I have my valid card," he boasts. Similarly, don Luis makes sure to steadfastly work only one of two numbers—the *derecho* (legal one), the number on the card he was initially assigned by the SSA, or the *chueco* (fake one), the one he purchased after immigration officials confiscated the derecho when he was deported in 1973. As an indication of the legitimacy he feels the card grants him, don Luis prefers to work the number of his *seguro derecho* even after the card itself was confiscated; he only works the *seguro chueco* when labor supervisors demand that he present them with physical proof of documentation.

Hoping to one day be able to access the phantom retirement accounts to which they are assiduously contributing, men like don Santiago and don Luis view their valid cards as prized possessions. They assiduously eschew "identity loan" (see Horton 2015, 2016) and accumulate documentation to build a legible record of their presence. Don Luis and don Santiago know that attaining legal status is dependent upon their ability to avoid the space of nonexistence. Although unauthorized workers' legal absence often obscures their wage histories and duration of presence, don Santiago and don Luis know that visibility to the state is a precondition for their legalization.

SUPPLEMENTING DIVERTED RETIREMENTS

Men like don Santiago and don Luis are the human faces of the "profit reserve"—personally responsible for the Social Security surplus due to their lack of legal personhood. Even as their wage deductions pad the balance sheets of the SSA, they must rely on other sources of income to compensate for their lack of federal support. Yet elderly unauthorized men find little gainful employment in the fields because their bodies are *agotados* (used up). Unauthorized senior citizens like don Luis and don Santiago resort to other strategies to survive as they await a hoped-for legalization program: recycling, receiving assistance from family, and—for those who have given up—repatriation.

FAMILY ASSISTANCE

Because of their pension shortfalls, family assistance is crucial for all farmworkers, regardless of legal status. In the absence of sufficient state and federal support, kin often step in to provide food, income, and shelter for aging farmworkers. Many migrant men who had spent a lifetime migrating to the Central Valley indeed did move in with their offspring, sharing beds with grandchildren and dividing grocery expenses.

Don Luis, for example, has had a hard time finding work over the past three years as he waits for "an amnesty." He suffers from severe headaches, high cholesterol, and a persistent, nagging cough; he also suffered strokes in 2005 and 2006. (He describes these strokes—which temporarily paralyzed one side of his body—as "burst nerves," yet his hospital paperwork reveals them as strokes.) He worked until December last year when a job picking almonds—which requires shaking the branches of almond trees with a cane—caused the back of his head to swell. That was six months ago, and he has not found work since. Don Luis tells me that he used to send his wife in Zacatecas $200 a month, but now—as he puts it—he is "drowning in debt" (Me estoy endrogando con el dinero).

Don Luis has four children who live in San Jose, California; they visit him several times a month. This last Sunday, they gave him $500 toward his rent and food. "They know I'm not working because I'm badly off," he says. Beto, who keeps track of the comings and goings of single sojourning men from the window of his store, told me later that don Luis's children took him to buy *carnitas* at the local grocery store, La Fiesta, and returned him to his apartment with several bags of food. "They must have spent $100!" he exclaims.

Don Luis and I sit on the stoop in front of Beto's store as don Luis describes his dilemma. He says that his children often plead with him to leave Mendota and live with them, but the thought of depending on his kids rankles him. He tells me he thinks he still has a few years left of fieldwork in his body—that is, if his health will only bear up. "We'll see if I can hold out," he says.

Don Luis complains that his sons do landscaping in San Jose's suburbs—mowing lawns and trimming trees—rather than the "real work" of farm work. "I'm not used to yard work," he says. "All you do is cut the grass, trim the little flowers [*las florecitas*]. Work in the fields is harder, plus they pay you better because you work more hours." "Landscaping is easier work," sniffs don Luis's friend, who joins him on the stoop. Don Luis nods. "Plus I like the open spaces [Y me gusta andar al aire libre]," he adds. Thus elderly men like don Luis perceive accepting less strenuous jobs in yard work as a blow to their identities as hard, vigorous workers. They perceive working in confined spaces as a surrender of their masculinity (see Horton 2016) and an acknowledgment of their bodies' lack of utility. Likewise, becoming dependent upon the assistance of their family wounds their self-esteem as providers.

Don Santiago has also had difficulty finding work as he waits. After having decided to semi-retire in Mexico in 2003, a son's death in the United States prompted don Santiago to return five years later with a temporary visa. That is how don Santiago unexpectedly found himself newly on the job market at the age of sixty-three, suffering the indignity of competing with "youths" and "boys fresh from Mexico," complaining of high blood pressure and throbbing varicose veins. Don Santiago's daughter, Blanca, fed and housed him as he searched for work, giving him the relative privilege of sleeping on the couch in her living room while his wife shared a bed with Blanca's two daughters.

Blanca was delighted when her husband was able to obtain a job for don Santiago on the small ranch where he worked. "My husband simply explained that his father-in-law was living here and couldn't find work. His boss is very Catholic, and he did it as a favor," Blanca explains. Because there is less strict supervision on ranches and greater autonomy than on labor crews hired by contractors, jobs on small ranches are particularly coveted by elderly farmworkers.

As don Santiago puts it: "Ranchers tell you, 'We don't want anyone racing up and down the field [*carreras*] here. We only want a job well done.'" "It's a calmer job," Blanca had agreed. "My dad just can't spend his day running back and forth in the fields anymore. He's too old to be working on a crew." Yet to both Blanca's and don Santiago's dismay, the ranch owner had "retired" Santiago after only two weeks. He simply needed fewer men to plant pistachios, he had explained.

When I enter Blanca's apartment and find don Santiago on the couch, he dismisses the experience with a wave of his hand. He is quick to distinguish between being temporarily "laid off" (*descansar*) and actually being "fired" (*correr*). "They only let me rest [nada más me descansaron]," he asserts. Thus don Santiago refuses to accept that he may be chronically unemployed and entirely dependent upon Blanca's generosity.

As don Luis's and don Santiago's cases show, there are few job opportunities open to elderly workers, and to unauthorized workers in particular. While particularly fortunate workers with papers may find less harried work in packing sheds and processing plants—work that additionally often carries health benefits and higher pay—elderly unauthorized workers are often consigned to scavenging for work in the fields. Yet elderly workers are employees of last resort. When mayordomos do hire them, they often do so as an act of "charity."

RECYCLING

Each day, hundreds of freight trucks thunder down the highways that comprise the main arteries of Mendota, carrying produce and farm machinery to the Central

Valley's ranches and farms. Alongside them, darting in between pickup trucks and out of the way of the freight trucks with their cargo, ride the city's class of recyclers—elderly men and women precariously perched on used bicycles purchased in yard sales. Some strap garbage bags full of their wares to the metal frame of the bike behind them. Others manage to grip tattered umbrellas to protect themselves from the sun even as they pedal. These senior citizens are *juntando botes* (recycling)—they are gathering aluminum cans, glass bottles, and plastic containers for sale. They forage for wares in the street's gutters and dart into alleys to rifle through dumpsters.

For elderly men like don Luis and don Santiago, informal recycling is one of the few income-generating opportunities they can find. Due to demand, there are three recycling stations in this town of eleven thousand. As one city politician once put it, Mendota—one of the poorest cities in the state—may also ironically be one of California's "cleanest and greenest." The Gutierrez Recycling Center alone ships out two full trucks of recyclables—each carrying two to three thousand pounds—to buyers each week. Strategically positioned around the city's downtown—home to the shacks that house the city's single sojourner men—each station has a regular clientele. All day long, elderly and unemployed men and women ride up to these stations on their bikes, hauling garbage bags full of cans and bottles to be sorted.

Don Luis had even designed a special tool to snag the aluminum cans deposited in the dumpster outside his yard. I discovered this when, to his dismay, I carelessly tossed a can into the dumpster by his house right in front of him. "Wait!" he had protested in vain. Although the can had disappeared into the cavernous space, don Luis was not to be deterred. He darted into his house to retrieve his special implement—a dowel with a nail attached to one end—and succeeded in spearing the can with it.

Recycling fills in the gaps left by the unpredictability of seasonal employment. It provides a source of informal work to both elderly farmworkers and to those who find themselves temporarily unemployed. As they struggle to continue to find work, don Luis and don Santiago find in recycling a reliable, though meager, source of income. Yet in doing so, migrant men trade farm work for a precarious existence scavenging refuse. Because recycling signifies one's lack of capacity to work in the fields, it is a stigmatized livelihood, posing a blow to men's identities as capable workers.

Don Luis, for example, still seeks out farm work. To disguise his age, he diligently dyes his moustache black. The discrepancy only becomes apparent when he doffs his baseball hat to inadvertently reveal gray tufts of hair. He seeks work with mayordomos at the pool hall, waiting for phone calls that frequently never come. He faithfully stands outside the gas station on the highway out of Mendota each morning at 5 a.m., hoping to be invited to join crews on their way to work. Don Luis often works for a few days in different jobs before being laid off; the mayordomos hire him because they know him and they understand his need.

One evening at the pool hall, don Luis happily tells me that he had just returned from a job clearing pomegranates. He had worked for two days, walking up and down the field, using a hoe to clear leaves from the young bushes. Yet, a week later, I find don Luis in the Laundromat on Seventh Avenue at noon on a Friday, despondent. He says that that morning he arose at 4 a.m. as usual to go to work; he went outside to wait on Seventh Avenue for his *raitero*, "ride," but the man never came. "Well, maybe they'll take me on Saturday," he says, ever the optimist. The mayordomo never called, so he doesn't know if they cut him from the crew or if the job itself had ended.

Two weeks later, when I see don Luis at the pool hall, he tells me he spent four days weeding pistachios to fill in for a sick crew member. Yet that job soon ended as well. He says he has talked to three mayordomos he knows about three other jobs—two picking apricots and one weeding cherries. "We'll see who calls me first," he says. In short, don Luis refuses to accept his unofficial retirement. In-between the unpredictable stints of work he finds, recycling provides him with additional income.

Don Santiago also turned to recycling out of necessity. Two weeks after he lost his job at the ranch, he learned from a friend about a mayordomo who needed workers to fill his crew weeding sugar beets. But, don Santiago tells me, the crew consisted of "all young'uns" (*pura gente nueva*)—"kids of twenty and people fresh across the border." It was a May day of ninety degrees and the mayordomo drove them hard, leading them up and down the fields pulling weeds. The mayordomo left the water at only one end of the field, a half mile long, and it took an hour to work his way over to reach it. By the second day, don Santiago began to feel sick. "My stomach started to turn; I think maybe I was getting heat stroke," he says. Dehydration struck him midfield, and by the time he had weeded his way to the edge of the field with the water, he was dizzy and his mouth was parched from thirst. So don Santiago quit. "No, no, I don't want any more of that mayordomo who rushes people [*que da carillas a la gente*]," he tells me.

Unable to find a job befitting his age, don Santiago decided to recycle. He borrows his granddaughter's banana seat bicycle and fishes recyclables out of the city's alleyways and gutters. Blanca, don Santiago's daughter, tells me that her father has found himself in a difficult position; he is unfit for work on *cuadrillas* (labor crews) and yet dreads becoming a "burden" (*una carga*) on his family. Yet the only income-generating activity available—scavenging the refuse left by others—makes him feel ashamed. Blanca had attempted to salve his wounded masculinity and restore his sense of dignity. "He's not hurting anybody!" she exclaims. "I tell him that his job is just as worthy [*digno*] as any other."

Raúl, a middle-aged Salvadoran migrant, also fears that recycling may be in his near future. He recently paid a visit to the Social Security offices in Fresno to find out whether he could begin collecting retirement and discovered that he must wait three more years. Aluminum, he tells me, pays good money right now. But recycling rarely yields more than $20 a day, and carries the stigma of being "all washed up" (*acabado*).

Raúl recounts a story of walking down Seventh Avenue at 3 a.m. one morning as he returned home from the bar. He heard a scuffling on the other side of the street and saw a woman, her face covered by a bandana, gathering bottles and tins in the dead of night. She was dimly lit by the street lamps, and he recognized her as a coworker from the fields. "Carmen!" he had called out, and—though he says she perhaps had later regretted it—she had turned around. Raúl laughs as he tells me now how Carmen had deftly attempted to deflect attention from her obvious need. "Oh, I was just out getting some exercise," she had told him.

Recycling fills in the gaps of scant social assistance and seasonal employment, providing meager sustenance to the families of farmworkers whose bodies are "spent." By engaging in recycling, elderly men like don Luis and don Santiago lessen the stigma of being a perceived "burden" on their families. Yet as they ride children's bikes and scavenge for refuse, former breadwinners grieve the impending reversal of their family role. They face the humiliation of entering the ranks of the "lumpen proletariat" (Bourgois & Schonberg 2009, 17)—that is, of outcasts from productive labor—as they trade one source of shame for another.

REPATRIATION

As we have seen, the sociologist Michael Burawoy (1976) argues that the system of migrant labor in the United States "externalizes" the costs of labor force renewal to Mexico. Comparing Mexico to the African bantustans that subsidized the cost of labor in South Africa under apartheid, he suggests that Mexico has historically served as both "nursery" and "nursing home" for Mexican migrants (see Rouse 1992, 28). Burawoy examined a "system of migrant labor" in which seasonal farmworkers returned to Mexico each winter to rest and recharge. Many elderly and ill unauthorized migrants do indeed return to Mexico. Yet once migrants have left the United States, stepped-up border enforcement makes unauthorized returns cost prohibitive. Due to the tightening of the border, repatriated migrants' returns are often permanent.

For elderly unauthorized migrants, returning to Mexico means not only "hanging up one's gloves" but also forfeiting all hopes of accessing their retirement savings, which the SSA holds in trust. Only those few elderly unauthorized migrants who are fortunate enough to access their pensions by having adjusted their legal status typically remain in the United States. Don Santiago was lucky; his daughter's becoming a naturalized citizen allowed him to become a legal permanent resident and finally access his long-anticipated retirement. Don Luis, on the other hand, was less fortunate.

By his early sixties, don Luis had developed debilitating headaches; he described them as "*tronazos*" or "thunderings" in his head. The thunderings began just after he had suffered his last stroke. When he arose a few days later, it felt like two bones in his head were grating against each other. He demonstrates, moving his fists against one another like tectonic plates. When his head throbs, don Luis tries to right it himself by settling it with his hands. "I settle it myself," he says. Don Luis took a month off work to recover so that he would not have to return to Mexico for good. He sought work shaking almond trees one day in January. When his head swelled up after just one day of work, he decided to seek medical attention.

In January of 2008, I drive don Luis to a MediCal eligibility site in Mendota and a senior citizen resource center in Fresno. It turns out that although many states and counties have restricted health care services for the unauthorized, Fresno County does have a program for the uninsured for which the unauthorized qualify. Yet as we soon found, this program only covers the able-bodied uninsured between the ages of twenty-one and sixty-five; don Luis's age disqualified him from receiving any government help. Excluded from both social assistance and health care, don Luis ultimately eventually decided to return to Mexico.

I was not in Mendota to bid don Luis farewell when he left. Don Santiago was the first to inform me of don Luis's departure and the circumstances that led up to it. Although don Luis had still hoped to bide his time until an amnesty, he could no longer find work—not even during the summer harvest, when there are usually plentiful positions on the mayordomos' crews. "He lagged behind when we were picking melon. Everyone saw it. And people told the mayordomo, 'don Luisito, he's all washed up,'" don Santiago says. The mayordomo fired him and would not take him back.

Beto, who says he had known don Luis as a customer in his store "since [he] was a kid," elaborated on the chain of events precipitating his return. Beto said that sometime in 2009, don Luis's sons came down from San Jose. They told Beto that they were driving don Luis back to San Jose and then flying him back to Zacatecas to be with his wife. Don Luis had been a fixture around Seventh Avenue for four decades, and he had resisted leaving the world he had known. He knew his departure would be permanent. As he had told me in 2008, his body would not tolerate another unauthorized border crossing through the desert. For don Luis, then, leaving meant giving up the hope of his retirement. "He didn't want to go," Beto says. "But his sons said his wife was lonely. And they were tired of supporting him when he couldn't find work."

Don Luis's story illustrates the fate of elderly unauthorized migrants who can find no gainful economic activity as they wait. In the absence of an "amnesty," only those fortunate elderly workers with children who have legal status in the United States find themselves eligible to adjust their own. Yet most single sojourning men—like don Luis—lack children with legal status and therefore find themselves ineligible for legalization.

As Burawoy described, Latin American sending countries do serve as "nursing homes" for their expatriate workers. Their exclusion from social assistance and health care programs, along with the tightening of the U.S.-Mexico border, indeed encourage many elderly unauthorized migrants to return to their homelands. As their legal ineligibility for social assistance repatriates elderly and infirm migrant farmworkers, the United States diverts the cost of their care in their old age to their families abroad and to their sending states. Thus the transborder neoliberal economy without transborder policies for the aged transborder worker is not required to provide the type of social scaffolding necessary for their support. It relies instead on the subsidies provided by local familial networks.

CONCLUSION

Migrant farmworkers' depleted pensions illustrate the perils of remaining invisible to the state. Unauthorized migrants' status as prohibited workers provides employers with an excuse to mask their very existence, in turn erasing their work and benefit histories from the official record. Meanwhile, their exclusion from state and federal benefits serves as the justification for employers' theft, allowing employers to pillage the retirement and disability benefits migrants will need to support them in their old age. Through the lens of the retirement dilemmas of elderly farmworkers, this chapter illuminates the way the legal and political exclusion of migrants from the United States allows for the externalization of the costs of their social reproduction to their homelands (also see chapter 9). Legal nonexistence facilitates the political economic processes that lead to diverted retirements. As well, it provides the basis for the continued subsidy of the state itself by not including transborder aged workers into retirement.

To compensate for scant social assistance, many migrant farmworkers attempt to continue to work past retirement age. Yet elderly workers comprise the last battalion in the reserve army of labor that supervisors call upon to cushion agribusiness's labor demands. As employees of last resort, migrant farmworkers must turn to informal subsistence strategies. Some—like don Santiago—rely upon recycling and family assistance. Others, like don Luis, give up the hope of accessing their pensions and return to the country in which they were born. Even as their unclaimed deductions forestall a pension crisis in the United States, unauthorized migrants experience their own crisis of care in an impossible transborder world.

NOTES

1. The U.S. government entered into a binational agreement with Mexico to import temporary workers, called "braceros," to work in the agricultural and railroad industries during the Bracero program, which lasted between 1942 and 1964. Braceros worked mostly in the American Southwest and helped build the modern agribusiness industry. One controversial aspect of the program is that workers' contracts bound them to their employers. The fact that temporary laborers became "illegal" if they skipped out on their contracts handed employers limitless power and effectively quashed complaints about squalid housing and unjust and unsafe labor conditions. The United States imported about 4.6 million Mexican men during this twenty-four-year period (Ngai 2004).
2. Strategies of erasure not only confront migrants with the immediate problem of proving their earnings and therefore their need for social assistance to the state but also frequently jeopardize migrants' chance at legalization through federal "amnesties." Legalization programs often predicate the ability to adjust one's legal status on duration of residence, such as the IRCA and the Senate bill passed in 2013. Like both the Senate bill and IRCA's Seasonal Agricultural Worker program, they additionally require applicants to demonstrate their record of employment. Strategies of erasure thus not only deprive migrants of social assistance but also lessen their chance of adjusting their legal status.
3. Because employers' workers' compensation insurance premiums are based not only on an employer's rate of accidents but also on the size of an employer's workforce, paying workers "off the books" additionally reduces a company's workers' compensation insurance premiums.
4. Applicants must have ten years of work history in the United States to qualify for assistance from the Social Security Administration, such as Supplemental Security Income (SSI)—a modest stipend from the federal government to assist the elderly with low retirements—or permanent disability (SSDI). Thus workers who once held a tenuous legal status are often ineligible, as they often fall victim to strategies of erasure that diminish their wage and benefit histories.
5. When unauthorized employees work under their own names but use invented SSNs, the SSA reports a "mismatch" between the two forms of identification presented. The funds deposited under that name are then placed in a "No-Match Earnings Suspense File" and are eventually diverted to fund the retirements of U.S. citizens and legal permanent residents.
6. Similarly, a team of Harvard Medical School researchers found that the foreign-born population generated a cumulative surplus of $115 billion for the Medicare trust fund between 2002 and 2009, even as the American-born population incurred a $28 billion deficit (Zallman et al. 2013). Nevertheless, it remains unclear how much of this subsidy

derives solely from the younger average age of the migrant population and how much results from the unclaimed contributions of unauthorized migrants.

7. Much scholarship on the SAW program focuses on its relatively lax requirements, as it allowed applicants to substitute a letter from a labor supervisor for official documentation of employment (see, for example, Martin 1994). This exception was necessary to include farmworkers who lacked check stubs or official contracts because they had been employed under the table, as Ofelia had been. As don Santiago's case suggests, the SAW program thus placed labor supervisors in a position to make a business off of furnishing fraudulent letters for migrants, turning a profit from their workers' need for legal status. However, a sizeable minority of migrants such as don Luis and don Santiago did not participate in the paper racket and were ineligible for the SAW program due to injuries. Their stories are less frequently presented in the scholarship on SAW.

REFERENCES

Booker, Salih, and William Minter. 2001. "Global Apartheid." *The Nation* 273(2): 11–17.

Bourgois, Philippe, and Jeffrey Schonberg. 2009. *Righteous Dopefiend*. Berkeley: University of California Press.

Burawoy, Michael. 1976. "The Functions and Reproduction of Migrant Labor: Comparative Material from Southern Africa and the United States." *American Journal of Sociology* 81(5): 1050–87.

Coutin, Susan Bibler. 2000. *Legalizing Moves: Salvadoran Immigrants' Struggle for US Residency*. Ann Arbor: University of Michigan Press.

Heyman, Josiah McC. 1998. "State Effects on Labor Exploitation: The INS and Undocumented Immigrants at the Mexico-United States Border." *Critique of Anthropology* 18(2): 157–80.

———. 2001. "Class and Classification at the U.S.-Mexico Border." *Human Organization* 60(2): 128–40.

Horton, Sarah. 2015. "Identity Loan: The Moral Economy of Migrant Document Exchange in California's Central Valley." *American Ethnologist* 42(1): 55–67.

———. 2016. *They Leave Their Kidneys in the Fields: Illness, Injury, and "Illegality" Among California's Farmworkers*. Berkeley: University of California Press.

Martin, Philip L. 1994. "Good Intentions Gone Awry: IRCA and US Agriculture." *Annals of the Academy of Social Science* 534:44–57.

Massey, Douglas, S. Jorge Durand, and Nolan J. Malone. 2002. *Beyond Smoke and Mirrors: Mexican Immigration in an Era of Economic Integration*. New York: Russell Sage Foundation.

Meissner, Doris. 2004. "U.S. Temporary Worker Programs: Lessons Learned." Migration Policy Institute, March 1. http://www.migrationpolicy.org/article/us-temporary-worker-programs-lessons-learned.

Menjívar, Cecilia. 2006. "Liminal Legality: Salvadoran and Guatemalan Immigrants' Lives in the United States." *American Journal of Sociology* 111(4): 999–1037.

NCFH (National Center for Farmworker Health, Inc.). 2012. "National Center for Farmworker Health Fact Sheets: Demographics." http://www.ncfh.org/uploads/3/8/6/8/38685499/naws_ncfh_factsheet_demographics_final_revised.pdf.

Ngai, Mae. 2004. *Impossible Subjects: Illegal Aliens and the Making of Modern America.* Princeton, NJ: Princeton University Press.

Parreñas, Rhacel. 2006. "Migrant Filipina Domestic Workers and the International Division of Reproductive Labor." In *Global Dimensions of Gender and Care Work*, edited by Mary Zimmerman, Jacquelyn S. Litt, and Christine E. Bose, 48–65. Stanford, CA: Stanford University Press.

Rouse, Roger. 1992. "Making Sense of Settlement: Class Transformation, Cultural Struggle, and Transnationalism Among Mexican Migrants in the United States." *Annals of the New York Academy of Sciences* 65(1): 25–52.

Schumacher-Matos, Edward. 2010. "How Illegal Immigrants Are Helping Social Security." *The Washington Post*, September 3. http://www.washingtonpost.com/wp-dyn/content/article/2010/09/02/AR2010090202673.html.

Sharma, Nandita. 2006. *Home Economics: Nationalism and the Making of "Migrant Workers" in Canada.* Toronto: University of Toronto Press.

———. 2007. "Global Apartheid and Nation-Statehood: Instituting Border Regimes." In *Nationalism and Global Solidarities: Alternative Projections to Neoliberal Globalization*, edited by James Goodman and Paul James, 71–90. New York: Routledge.

Spener, David. 2009. *Clandestine Crossings: Migrants and Coyotes on the Texas-Mexico Border.* Ithaca, NY: Cornell University Press.

Walter, Nicholas, Philippe Bourgois, and H. Margarita Loinaz. 2004. "Masculinity and Undocumented Labor Migration: Injured Latino Day Laborers in San Francisco." *Social Science and Medicine* 59(6): 1159–68.

Zallman, Leah, Steffie Woolhandler, David Himmelstein, David Bor, and Danny McCormick. 2013. "Immigrants Contributed an Estimated $115.2 Billion More to the Medicare Trust Fund Than They Took Out in 2002–2009." *Health Affairs* 32(6): 1153–60.

17

PORTRAITS OF FOOD INSECURITY IN COLONIAS IN THE U.S.-MEXICO BORDER REGION

Ethnographic Insights on Everyday Life Challenges and Strategies to Access Food

GUILLERMINA GINA NÚÑEZ-MCHIRI,
DIANA RIVIERA, AND CORINA MARRUFO

HUNGER AND FOOD insecurity within colonias are topics rarely associated with issues of "homeland security." The colonias can be defined as neighborhoods or communities located near large urban centers while being based in rural areas along the U.S.-Mexico border region that provide an alternative form of affordable housing and home ownership (Núñez 2008). Our research site is located in the El Paso del Norte border region. The main threats in these communities continue to be associated with their environment as communities situated and defined by their proximity to the U.S.-Mexico border (these communities are also discussed in chapters 1 and 15). Nationally, federal enforcement of immigration policies and practices of surveillance make rural communities residents more visible in their movements. Over the past fifteen years since September 11, 2001, the U.S.-Mexico border region has experienced the increased presence of homeland security forces through the deployment of the Army National Guard and robust Border Patrol enforcement aimed at monitoring and controlling the border to curb unauthorized immigration (Dunn 1996, 2009). Regionally, rural unincorporated communities known as colonias contend with their local environments impacted by sketchy patches of infrastructures, such as unpaved roads, lack of sidewalks and public lighting, and numerous truncated development efforts. The health of a community is tied to its availability of economic and social resources and its ability to access these as individuals and households (also see chapter 9), and collectively as members of a community through civic participation and collaboration.

Hunger, food insecurity, and poverty in the U.S.-Mexico region are significant areas of concern for the well-being and security of its regional population, though not as attractive and politically charged as the rhetoric surrounding contemporary immigration and border enforcement, debates to draw attention to these issues remain unsought. In 2006, the U.S. Department of Agriculture (USDA) introduced new language to refer to various levels of food security and insecurity. Food insecurity is a household-level economic and social condition of limited or uncertain access to adequate food. Hunger is an individual-level physiological condition that may result from food insecurity. Hunger refers to a potential consequence of food insecurity that "because of prolonged, involuntary lack of food, results in discomfort, illness, weakness, or pain that goes beyond the usual uneasy sensation." In a more recent report, *Household Food Security in the United States in 2014*, Coleman-Jensen et al. (2015) indicate that 14 percent of U.S. households, or 17.4 million people, are "food insecure" and lack access to adequate food and nutrition due to cost, proximity, and/or other resources.

Approximately 6.9 percent of people in the United States are "very food insecure," which means 6.9 million people lack money and other resources for food at a level that causes a reduction in food intake or eating patterns of one or more household members during the year. Children represent 20.9 percent, or 15.5 million people, of those who experience food insecurity. In New Mexico, 30 percent of children experience food insecurity while 27.4 percent of children in Texas experience food insecurity, compared to a national child food insecurity rate of 21.4 percent. Around 22.4 percent of Hispanic/Latino families experience food insecurity compared to 11 percent of white households. Coleman-Jensen et al. (2015) also found that Hispanic/Latino communities have one-third of the number of supermarkets usually found in white neighborhoods and also struggle with high rates of obesity, unemployment, and depressed economies.

The social phenomenon of colonias is couched within the complex history, politics, economy, and environment of the U.S.-Mexico border. Their geographic particularities, mainly their location outside of large urban centers, influence the quality and quantity of food available in these communities. As Sharkey, Dean, and Johnson (2011) have indicated, food insecurity in colonias will vary by household and community characteristics with households with children being among the most, 61.8 percent, food insecure.

The size of a colonia influences the absence or presence of markets available to supply residents with a diverse offering of fresh fruits and vegetables. Colonias such as Sunland Park, New Mexico, and Anthony in southern New Mexico and west Texas, are incorporated and have access to amenities such as supermarkets and public services provided by governmental and nonprofit entities, while other colonias are tucked away closer to rural agricultural fields and dairies and have sparse populations of thirty to forty households. For colonia residents located in more remote settings, access to food is possible by commuting anywhere from five to ten miles up to thirty to forty-five miles one-way to a nearby city to access well-stocked supermarkets. Although food insecurity and hunger have distinctive definitions, they occur simultaneously and coexist ubiquitously within the contexts of unincorporated communities, known as colonias, throughout the U.S.-Mexico border or as Vélez-Ibáñez suggests in this volume, the Southwest North American (SWNA) region.

A political ecology framework for examining the everyday life of colonias is useful in allowing researchers to examine human-environmental relationships that combine local economics and ecologies with global dynamics (Greenberg and Park 1994; Biersack 2006; Little 2007). Through a political ecology framework, Núñez (2006b, 2012; Núñez-Mchiri 2009) has previously examined the regional particularities of colonias in southern Mexico and west Texas impacted by environmental threats such as flash flooding and other related challenges associated with the absence of urban planning and physical infrastructure, mainly access to water and sewage services. In this chapter, we discuss women's efforts to navigate and negotiate food insecurity in colonias as neighborhoods and communities, with a focus on the political ecology of the body (Hayes-Conroy and Hayes-Conroy 2013; Carney 2014). The political ecology of the body allows for the ethnographic analysis of affective and emotional dimensions generated from a close-range view of emerging micro-phenomena. Through this approach, we contribute toward a feminist political ecological analysis of women's negotiations of hunger and food insecurity in their everyday lives and bodily interactions in their microenvironments (Rocheleau, Thomas-Slayter, and Wangari 1996; Biersack 2006). Through our ethnographic encounters in women's homes and in community spaces, we have observed and documented the locations in which women experience their conflicts and their strategies for overcoming these while figuring out where to get food and how to stretch their resources to feed their families.

This work also contributes to a postcolonial intersectionality that examines Mexican-origin women on the border beyond issues of gender, class, civil status (single, widow, married, civil union/domestic partnership), and sexual orientation (Collins 1990; Dill and Kohlman 2012) to include race as a critical factor shaping access to resources (Mollet and Faria 2013). Additional factors impacting women in colonias that truncate their efforts to seek and access food include age, (im)mobility caused by their unauthorized immigration status, lack of geographic knowledge, (dis)abilities, access to childcare services, and lack of transportation. Thus, these multiple backgrounds and identities influence how our informants see themselves, what they know, whom they know, and their ability to mobilize to seek solutions to their hunger and their food insecurity to ultimately find ways to take food to their families' table (Page-Reeves 2014).

We zoom out to provide a brief historical context of colonias and then zoom back in and angle our lens to capture and present portraits of women who experience food insecurity in colonias. Through the use of portraitures in particular, we examine the lived experiences of women who are at the forefront of negotiating hunger and food insecurity at the household and community levels (Lawrence-Lightfoot and Davis 1997; Lawrence-Lightfoot 2005). Through the collectivity of our work, we set out to "see" and document what food insecurity looks like by harnessing our individual experiences gathering thick descriptions (Geertz 1973) of multiple examples of women's personal negotiationsof hunger and food insecurity in the colonias of the U.S.-Mexico border region. Herein, we present portraits of women's experiences that describe how they make do by using narratives that extend further than simple statistics on poverty. Portraiture calls for joining social science, art, and the humanities via the integration of "empirical description with aesthetic expression" (Lawrence-Lightfoot and Davis 1997, 3). These portraits are assembled based on our work in colonias, with two particular goals. The first goal is to "capture the richness, complexity, and dimensionality of human experience (and assets) in social and cultural context, conveying the perspectives of the people who are negotiating those experiences" (3). The other is to document and present the "goodness" and the "expression [of the participants'] strengths" within their lived experiences (3, 141). While there is a "high distribution of sadness" and pain (Vélez-Ibáñez 1996, 2004) in colonias, we argue that there are also solution-driven individuals and families who generate strength and resiliency by challenging hunger and food insecurity in their own subaltern ways. Portraits effectively allow for the portrayal of stories that contain not only stress and insecurity but also harmonious affective and emotional characteristics that positively describe people's sense of resolve, honor, and integrity within a qualitative image of food insecurity.

We offer these contemporary portraits while being keenly aware of the need to address hunger and poverty in colonias without further promoting stereotypes and ahistorical analyses of U.S.-Mexico border regional communities (Hill 2003). Not everyone who lives in colonias is poor and food insecure. Colonias house a variety of people from various economic and professional backgrounds, including retirees, U.S. veterans, farmworkers, dairy workers, and entrepreneurs. The women we write about in this chapter are not stuck in time and are continuously struggling to overcome vicious cycles of poverty and entrapment while raising their families to the best of their abilities (Núñez and Heyman 2007). A key theme expressed by the women in this chapter involves feelings of being "alone in their own little world" (Riviera 2014). This phenomenological expression of alienation speaks to the stress, loneliness, depression, and social stigmas described in the women's experiences with poverty and hunger. We argue that the negotiation of hunger and food insecurity is by all means gendered, as men occupy traditional roles of "providers" and as such are often absent from the day-to-day decision-making processes involving the planning, preparation, and delivery of what a family will eat on any given day. Women and mothers, in particular, tend to carry the responsibility of feeding their children in colonia households while trying to figure out how to access, prepare, and harness food by making it "stretch out" until they are able to get food again.

FRONTERIZA ETHNOGRAPHY AND PORTRAITS OF FOOD INSECURITY IN COLONIAS

This chapter brings together the ethnographic research efforts of three Chicana/Latina ethnographers who provide a critical analysis of women's narratives and experiences from colonias in southern New Mexico and in El Paso, Texas, between 2014 and 2015. This work acknowledges our contribution to doing *fronteriza* ethnography and contributing to studies of Mexican-origin women on the U.S.-Mexico border region. Our research reflects deep involvement in food insecurity as it relates to our positionality as Chicana/Latina fronteriza ethnographers and practitioners as applied social scientists and community engaged scholars (Anzaldúa 1987; Murchison 2010). As researchers of gendered borderlands (Zavella and Segura 2007, 2008), we are aware of the need for us to acknowledge and manage our own insider and outsider identities as Chicanas/Latinas, as children of immigrants, working in communities where Spanish is widely spoken by first-generation immigrants and English is preferred by residents who were born in the United States, particularly in New Mexico and Texas, who have grown up in colonias throughout their lives (Zavella 1993). Ethnographic research in the form of participant observation, household interviews, and narrative analysis, in particular, has facilitated our ability to zoom into the micro-interactions that take place in private spaces within the household and in public spaces such as at food pantries where the distribution of food baskets take place.

The qualitative data gathered through ethnographic research is also complemented by applied efforts of working in local community settings as volunteers and interlocutors in local efforts aimed at addressing food insecurity and hunger in colonias. Through our praxis and engagement, we have found that among the most vulnerable individuals and families impacted by poverty and food insecurity are single mothers with children, older adults who have limited physical mobility, people who do not have access to transportation, and recent immigrants who are living in social isolation and have not yet established social networks and safety nets that could otherwise help them successfully access information, navigate, and access resources.

As a child of migrant farmworkers, Núñez grew up crossing the U.S.-Mexico border while navigating various environments while seeking to make sense of migration, negotiating power relationships in new places, as well as seeking to fulfill a deep need to feel rooted (Núñez 2006a). As farmworkers, food insecurity came with the stresses caused by the intermittent employment and income associated with the seasonal harvesting of food. As part of her research, Núñez has conducted surveys and participant observation research in more than seventy-five households in five colonias in New Mexico. Riviera's upbringing as a child of a single immigrant mother also gave her the empathy and sensitivity to get up-close and personal with her informants through a phenomenological lens, being able to exchange stories and experiences as single mothers living day-to-day with food insecurity in colonias. Marrufo has grown up as a child of immigrants and as a young woman scholar rooted in a colonia in El Paso, Texas. During her undergraduate education, she conducted service learning in colonias, where she interacted with her neighbors and with service providers at a faith-based food pantry. It was in this community space that Marrufo learned about food insecurity and hunger on a firsthand basis by interacting with, and getting to know the stories and circumstances of, the people seeking monthly food donations. It was her commitment to learn from her community and to serve colonia populations that motivated her to pursue a graduate degree in social work. Through this collaborative research effort, we bring our personal experiences and professional training to the analysis of hunger and food insecurity. This work is also reflective of the "funds of knowledge" and strategies employed by the women we interviewed as well as by our own families, who have taught us to negotiate food insecurity in the El Paso del Norte border region.

A BRIEF HISTORICAL CONTEXT OF COLONIAS

Colonias, as has been stated can be defined as neighborhoods or communities located near large urban centers while being based in rural areas along the U.S.-Mexico border region that provide an alternative form of affordable housing and home ownership (Núñez 2008). To qualify for government funding, colonias are federally defined by the U.S. Department of Housing and Urban Development as a community that is in the states of Arizona, California, New Mexico, or Texas, within 150 miles of the U.S.-Mexico border and that lacks adequate sewage systems and safe housing; the colonia must have existed before November 28, 1989. Colonias are especially present in Texas, and most colonia research is focused here (e.g., Simmons, 1997; Richardson 1999; Ward 1999; Coronado 2003; Dolhinow 2006; Esparza and Donelson 2010). Our research is based in the less studied El Paso del Norte border region, both Doña Ana County, New Mexico, and El Paso County, Texas.

The colonia phenomenon has yet to receive the attention it deserves partly because it does not conform to preexisting categories of "rural" and "urban" research settings. Anthropologists have long focused mainly on indigenous peoples and rural peasant communities (especially in the global South), including those working in political ecology (e.g., Sheridan 1996; Cruz Torres 2004; Biersack and Greenberg 2006; Escobar 2008). In contrast, urban anthropologists and sociologists have focused on urban migrants—how they fare there as well as how life in the city is shaped by them (e.g., Foster and Kemper 1979; Low 1999; Zenner 2002; Núñez and Klamminger 2010). Yet colonias are liminal and in-between places on the U.S.-Mexico border, insufficiently addressed in academic scholarship. The rise of colonias is linked to at least five decades of economic growth and inward migration to the U.S.-Mexico border region (Ganster and Lorey 2008). This process relates to rapid expansion in manufacturing (maquiladoras), services, and agricultural sectors that draw migrants from across Mexico in the hope of higher wages and thus creates an integrated and asymmetrical regional phenomena.

As much as colonias are defined in policy language in deficit-based terms, conditions in these communities are remarkably different. In Doña Ana County, New Mexico, for example, environmental and social conditions are likely to vary from the northern part of the county to the central and southern parts of the county. For instance, in northern Doña Ana County, near the village of Hatch, immigrant rights have taken precedence over farmworker rights issues mainly because these colonias are located beyond a Border Patrol checkpoint; in central Doña Ana County, in colonias such as Vado, Mesquite, La Mesa, and Berino, residents confront environmental and water issues; and in southern Doña Ana County, colonias such as Chaparral, Sunland Park, and Anthony are similar in terms of their semi-urban geographies, more social and physical infrastructure, and greater population densities, and therefore, access to transportation is a bigger priority than the need for infrastructure (Veronica Carmona, community organizer, personal communication). Industry-specific factors further influence the geography and the quality of life in colonias. In southern New Mexico, agriculture and dairies have created a demand for labor, while not necessarily providing housing and other amenities for workers. The colonias of Vado and Del Cerro are some of the colonias built by dairy and pecan farm owners to help house their workers (Stanford 2014). Hence, farmworkers are responsible for finding affordable housing near the workplace. The seasonality of agricultural work means laborers lack a consistent income to establish credit histories that, in turn, facilitate renting or buying homes, purchasing goods, and buying food on credit (Coronado 2003). Other colonias in West Texas are linked to urban service sector employment in retail, trucking, and construction, which make it necessary for male residents, in particular, to commute in and out of their communities in their search for employment. The continuous absence of males in colonias creates conflicts between gender relations in the home and the demands of everyday life. Dolhinow (2006) documents the struggles women in colonias go through on a daily basis to change their positions in domestic power relations, as men take on roles as providers and disciplinarians while women take on roles as mothers and caretakers of their families. Zavella's (2011) analysis of quotidian struggles challenges ethnographers to capture human ingenuity, creativity, and resiliency among Mexican-origin populations in the United States. Page-Reeves and her colleagues (2014) invite us to understand the dynamics of food insecurity centered around gendered nuances.

PORTRAITS OF WOMEN IN COLONIAS NEGOTIATING FOOD INSECURITY

Throughout their struggles, some of the women interviewed in this work are more successful at exercising their agency by building on their social capital, and thus they experience gradual changes and improvements over time (Bourdieu 1986). As we will detail in the subsequent portraitures, these women's food-procurement strategies reflect what Dean and Sharkey (2011, 1455) refer to as "collective social functioning" built upon the social, cultural, and historical commonalities of a particular community. These collective efforts reflect Bourdieu's notion of social capital as social actors create or employ strategies to access a social group's assets. Portes (1998) describes three effects of social capital: it allows for greater social control, provides family support, and provides other benefits outside of families. We include in our analysis an affective component that is often omitted in discussions of social capital that speaks to the quality of these interactions between members of a community, which involve kindness, compassion, and support between family, neighbors, nonprofit organizations, agencies, and members of faith communities.

The nonprofit sector is critical in supporting networks that help bolster the colonia residents' efforts to navigate hunger and food insecurity through community-building efforts. Various nonprofit organizations have worked, with mostly good intentions, to lessen the needs and scarcity that impact these communities. In spite of their limitations, it is important to acknowledge that the nonprofit sector has been able to contribute in many ways to develop and support the leadership efforts of women to help develop successful projects for their communities' well-being. Among the nonprofit organizations that have emerged in southern New Mexico and west Texas to promote the health and well-being of colonias are AYUDA in San Elizario, Texas; Vecinos Unidos in Chaparral; Anthony Youth Farm in Anthony; La Semilla Food Center in Anthony and Chaparral, New Mexico; Tres Manos from La Mesa; and Familias Triunfadoras in the lower valley of El Paso County, Texas.

As noted earlier, food poverty or insecurity in the U.S. context refers to the inability of households to obtain sufficient food to meet the nutritional needs of all members of a household for a healthy and active life (Messer 2004; Dean and Sharkey 2011). Riviera's (2014) research with single mothers in colonias identified three major factors that impact their daily access to food, leading to food insecurity in colonias: (1) lack of economic resources, (2) lack of access to personal transportation, and (3) lack of a steady income. The following describes Riviera interviews with two single-mother heads of household, by the names of Casilda and Esperanza, in Anthony, Texas, who had to rely on their neighbors for help with bringing food to their tables (Page-Reeves 2014).

CASILDA'S PORTRAIT

Casilda had big brown eyes and a friendly round face. Her most notable features were her hands, which captured Riviera's attention every time she tapped them on the table. She had long thin fingers that seemed to be extended by her fingernails. They were always well manicured, and by the sound of the tapping, they matched her strong spirit. She was about six months pregnant at the time of her interviews and carried the girth of a healthy pregnancy. For Casilda, food insecurity was marked by the inability to obtain gainful employment, followed by the denial of public assistance. As Casilda recalls: "I was in need of food and was denied public assistance. So being who I am, of course, I started asking a family here and there if they . . . you know. . . . if they had extra food—could we have it? They're like, of course." When Casilda's food and financial resources had been depleted, she relied on her neighbors, family, and friends who could share with her whatever food they had to spare to feed her family. The majority of those contributions consisted of canned food items and any other food that was already cooked or left over that her friends and neighbors could part with.

ESPERANZA'S PORTRAIT

Esperanza's physical appearance belied her age; she was in her mid-forties. She wore her life's struggles like war wounds. Her skin was dark brown and leathery in texture; it reflected the time that she had shared with the sun. Esperanza walked with a limp due to her near-fatal epileptic seizure, and when her balance was unreliable, she used a cane. Her hair was dark brown, thick, and shoulder length. It showed no sign of delicateness and it was her most profound feature. Her eyes represented the uniformity of her other features; they were dark brown in color, but they reflected her inner optimism.

Esperanza had access to family and friends who were occasionally willing to help her and her daughters with food; however, she made her own attempts to combat food insecurity, which consisted mostly of bartering her cleaning services in exchange for food at the local church, negotiating the payment of a nominal household bill, requesting assistance at local food pantries, and sometimes accepting help from acquaintances, neighbors, and relatives. Esperanza recalls: "After accumulating hours helping at the church, I approach the Father and say: 'Will you help me, Father? Will you help me with groceries?'" Besides bartering her labor for money to buy groceries, Esperanza, like Casilda, also relied on her neighbors for their leftover food. Esperanza ends her day successfully through her hustle: "I find myself very happy along with my daughters, that at least they have food."

Esperanza's food security also depended on her ability to prepare and store food. During her interview with Esperanza, Riviera was taken to the kitchen. Esperanza had not had access to natural gas service in several years; she cooked on an electric griddle. She opened the refrigerator to show Riviera what she had to eat. She picked up a gallon of milk, nearly empty. There were a few ears of corn and a few other items. There was a cardboard box half-filled with *mole* (a chile-chocolate-based sauce) that had been donated to her by her neighbor. Esperanza shared her culinary plans to prepare her daughter's favorite dish, chicken *mole*. "It makes me happy to see their smiles when they come home from school and see that I have *mole* for them" said Esperanza. The previous day, Riviera filled two five-gallon water containers for Esperanza and her daughters because the family had run out of water. During the tour of her kitchen, Esperanza showed Riviera the containers and thankfully said, "The three of us were drinking water, and what thirst we had because you can see how hot it is in this trailer . . . I remember how thirsty we were."

Esperanza's and Casilda's narratives revealed markers associated with food insecurity. They shared experiences where decisions regarding access to food had to be considered as a result of not having other means to provide for their households. Both of these women reached out to others and sought a transfer of resources by tapping into the "collective social functioning" that is common in rural poverty-stricken regions with food insecurity challenges (Walker et al. 2007; Dean and Sharkey 2011, 1455). Esperanza's food scarcity was associated with her inability to be legally employed given her unauthorized immigration status in the United States. Her social network consisted of a safety net of neighbors and friends who could contribute to her food-procurement strategies. Casilda's pregnancy made it difficult for her to hold on to a full-time job; thus, she relied on her neighbor's support by asking for leftover food to help feed herself and her children.

LUZ'S PORTRAIT

When Luz and her family first arrived to the colonia of Sparks in El Paso County, Texas, she lived in a mobile home (trailer) with her sister-in-law until they had enough money to buy a small mobile home of their own. Shortly after losing his job, Luz's husband returned to Ciudad Juárez to seek employment in construction. He worked on his sister's house in exchange for payment. Luz remembered not having food or money to help feed her family:

> When my husband lost his job, he went to help his sister build her home in Juárez. So my husband went to work there, while I stayed with his sister in Sparks. My husband thought that his sister was giving me money for food, and one time when he got to El Paso, he saw I had no food and then he decided to come back instead. I remember I thought it was awful to have to be asking my other sister-in-law for milk and food all the time and so often; she was the one who helped us more, but she also had two little girls that also needed to eat. I would worry the most about the milk because I had a one-year-old daughter. We struggled with the little we had from my husband's unemployment (benefits), that is, when I had to ask my sister-in-law for milk for my daughters. She was the only person I knew and trusted to ask for help. There were not a lot of people here; we were only a few, and we all lived so far from each other.

Addressing hunger and food insecurity in our research in colonias made us quite aware of the social stigmas and shame associated with the discourses of hunger and poverty. As Goffman (1963) indicates, "The term *stigma* is used to refer to an attribute that is deeply discrediting, but it should be seen that a language of relationships, not attributes is really needed." As such, the bonds and interactions that researchers and service providers working in colonias make with residents must be made with awareness, respect, and care. Trust and relationship building help to secure future interactions and research in these communities. Negative experiences with nonprofit organizations and "outsiders" are likely to make people hesitant to disclose their experiences with hunger, though participants were well aware of their need to build relationships with others as a way of expanding their social networks and social capital to help mitigate their precarious situations. Many of the women we interviewed interacted with their neighbors and other women activists working in colonias. Dolhinow (2006) indicates that women's domestic responsibilities lead and prepare women to become activists. However, several of the women we interviewed had a tendency to not be too involved, to avoid bringing attention to their economic circumstance and their immigration status.

Previous negative interactions with residents and activists involved in nonprofit organizations have the potential to shut down future interactions between colonia residents and outsiders. For example, Marrufo volunteered and conducted service learning participant observations with nonprofit organizations and a faith-based organization to help organize and distribute food in colonias through a food pantry. There is one food bank in El Paso, El Pasoans Fighting Hunger. This food bank receives the majority of its donations from Feeding America and distributes food to its partner agencies, which includes food pantries, shelters, soup kitchens, and meal programs. The food bank, pantries, and other emergency food providers provide a viable alternative for residents undergoing economic difficulties leading to food insecurity and hunger. Although food banks serve as a safety net for food insecure households, the quality of food further contributes to the issue of food insecurity as the demand for nutritious meals proposed by the USDA is not being met. As Stanford indicates: "Residents often show up early on the day of the food distribution, waiting in long lines in a community center or at an empty parking lot. For residents seeking aid, missing the distribution can result in losing out on food needed for subsequent weeks. Those who arrive early, usually get the best selection of limited quantity fruits and vegetables" (2014, 118). The act of standing in line waiting to have food distributed also gives visibility to the number of residents in need of food rations; while also creating opportunities for people to socialize and interact positively and negatively with others. It is not uncommon for residents to observe and comment on who is and who is not deserving of being in line for a food donation. During her time volunteering at a food pantry in a colonia in Texas, Marrufo observed an interaction that caused her to question the need to explore alternative ways of distributing food without shaming the residents who need this service. Marrufo witnessed a woman who was called out, turned away, and publicly shamed while waiting for her food basket. Marrufo later interviewed the woman in line at the pantry, who recalled:

> They (a volunteer) called me to come get a food basket, and when I got to the food pantry, I had one of the women working or volunteering there ask me, "What are you doing here? You don't qualify for a *despensa* [food basket] because you don't even live in this colonia." I told her someone called me and told me they had food baskets to give out to residents from colonias nearby and that is why I came. I had never been treated this way before.

The volunteer in this situation knew the woman had received a food basket at a different location in the past. She did not know other volunteers had called on residents from nearby communities to show up to this particular food pantry to receive aid. By questioning the woman in public, the volunteer at the food pantry humiliated the woman in front of others. Word of this exchange got around to other residents, volunteers, and to the nonprofit organization's leadership, causing people to become hesitant to seek food in the subsequent months. The volunteer at the food pantry had inadvertently compromised the relationships already established between the nonprofit organization and families in need. In the end, the volunteer was relieved of her duties at this particular food pantry while volunteers resumed services and trust-building efforts.

A PORTRAIT OF LASTING MEMORIES OF FOOD INSECURITY

DORA'S EXPERIENCES WITH HUNGER AND LINGERING MEMORIES

Dora is a heavyset woman. She is creative and resourceful in trying to make ends meet to feed her family. She lives in a mobile home that has expanded over the years through added rooms built by her husband and son. She's an older woman who never learned to drive and depended on her husband for transportation. Dora reflected on her family's history of hunger and food insecurity and the lasting impacts on her children. Dora immigrated to a colonia in New Mexico after her husband found a home for them to move into in the 1980s. She recalled how her family was affected by her husband's migration patterns as a seasonal farmworker living in the United States while she and their children lived in Mexico. He would visit her during brief periods of time in Chihuahua, Mexico, and provided little financial support to raise and feed their six children. With sadness and anger in her voice, she recalled: "I suffered a lot with my children during all of those years we lived in Ciudad Juárez. When we lived in Juárez, I was able to use the bus to go to the supermarket and buy food for my family; now if I can't find a ride to the store I can't buy food. How can I buy food if I cannot even drive here?" Dora reflected on having to figure out life in New Mexico, recognizing that her family's food preferences and expectations had changed over time. She recalled:

> My children lived on soups and beans when we lived in Ciudad Juárez; now they can't stand the sight or smell of *fideo* soups. My husband does not like potatoes; what do you think about that? He doesn't like potatoes . . . hmmph. If he only knew how much hunger we have suffered. When my children came to this country, it took them at least a year to get over their hunger. When we first got here, one of my sons would make

> sandwiches [*tortas*] this big and would still not get full [with her hands one foot apart, she gestured the size of a well-stacked sandwich]. Now my kids call me to see what's for lunch. If I say I only have soup or beans for lunch, they don't drop by to eat.

In hearing his spouse recall spouts of hunger and food insecurity while living in Mexico, Dora's husband indicated that his children were still having a challenging time filling their hunger since they migrated to a colonia in New Mexico. He noted that "his children now have a strong preference for large quantities of meat since they came to the U.S." As cited by Dickinson (2014), Fitchen (1988) observes how individuals follow mainstream practices to meet their subjective needs and their food needs. As such, these behaviors guide their food preferences, which also have an impact on their health, as some of these food items are low in nutrition and are energy dense. By adopting these mainstream behaviors, individuals try to demonstrate well-being and the ability to live like the majority of Americans. Dickinson (2014) expands on the implications that this has on households receiving Supplemental Nutrition Assistance Program (SNAP) benefits who engage in these behaviors and are not able to make ends meet with the minimal assistance they receive. She observes how certain skills and knowledge are necessary to achieve a well-balanced diet that entails consuming the appropriate sides of vegetables, protein, grains, and fruit rather than serving themselves large proportions of meat (Fitchen 1988; Dickinson 2014). Although skills and knowledge of nutrition are important in making food choices, many of the colonia residents are disadvantaged due to the absence of supermarkets; as many colonias are close to agricultural fields and yet are in fact food deserts.

PORTRAITS OF FOOD INSECURITY AND INTERPERSONAL CONFLICT IN COLONIAS

A final area that captures food insecurity in colonias relates to interpersonal conflict experiences in relation to how residents of these local communities respond to hunger and their efforts to satiate their basic needs. Wilmot and Hocker (2014) define interpersonal conflict "as an expressed struggle between at least two interdependent parties who perceive incompatible goals, scarce resources, and interference from others in achieving their goals" (13). The importance of voice in our research is about recognizing the human existence of previously hidden populations engaged in local power struggles over resources, in particular water, food, electricity, and waste disposal services, and not only ascertaining an accurate head count of people living with food insecurity. As important as that is, it perpetuates the invisibility of the interpersonal conflicts that exist. We showcase the need of these colonia residents to go beyond their households in search of resources. Such inquiry helps to clarify people's feelings, perceptions, and plans when faced with diverse political, economic, and ecological issues. Here, there is no substitute for detailed ethnographic work in the community.

LUZ'S CONFLICT

The identities of colonia families, many of which are in mixed-citizenship-status households, influence how families see themselves in a broader national landscape. Whether residents seek public aid and resources in the United States is tied to plans they have to become U.S. residents and U.S. citizens in the future. Many residents openly discuss not wanting to live off the government or to have any debts pending in case they seek to become U.S. citizens in the future. As Luz indicated:

> When I first got here I was not well informed. I was afraid to seek help because I did not have papers although my daughters were U.S. citizens, but I was not. I was afraid to seek help. I did not want this to be used against me in the case I want to become a U.S. resident or a U.S. citizen in the future. There was not much help here in my community. I don't want them [Homeland Security officials] to think that I came here to exploit the system by asking for free food and services, so that is why I didn't ask for help. Two years after we moved here, we began to see those people who offered help by giving food out once a month, and yes, we eventually got their help.

Luz avoided getting any services or applying for any benefits during her first two years in the United States. She later decided to seek the help of *ayudas* (assistance) for her two youngest children primarily because her husband was in and out of work in his construction job. Luz's internal struggle is evident in her narrative. Luz experienced food insecurity in light of her future goal to become a U.S. resident and perhaps a future U.S. citizen. Luz's conflict is closely connected to her identity as an unauthorized immigrant living in the United States and her role as a mother of U.S.-citizen children who experienced hunger because of the father's intermittent employment opportunities. Luz's portrait highlights the stress and the determination women face as purveyors of human needs and conflict resolutionists through a critical analysis of their environment, their social-economic and political status, and their altered perceptions (Wilmot and Hocker 2014).

HAYDEE'S CONFLICT

Another woman, Haydee, from the colonia of Sparks notes the importance of buying on credit as a coping strategy. When she first arrived to El Paso, she was not familiar with the city and did not know how to drive. Her husband used the family vehicle to travel to and from work. Her experience of food insecurity was one that intersected with her language and transportation barriers. Born and raised in Ciudad Juárez, Haydee had never learned to speak English. She notes: "I had to ask for rides, wait for my husband to take me or learn how to use public transportation. I learned to drive after my second child was born. When we first got here, we went without any welfare assistance." Haydee said she and her family qualified for food stamps, but because she qualified for very little, they opted to go without them. They would buy only basic staples they could afford. She notes, "If during the week I ran out of food or other items I had to wait for the weekend to arrive for my husband to get paid." She explained that in some instances when her need was urgent and she ran out of food, she would go walking to a small store to buy on credit. Haydee recalls: "At first they would sell food on credit, and then they cut everyone off. They put a sign that read 'Hoy no fio, mañana tal vez' (Today, I don't sell on credit, tomorrow, maybe so), so you can imagine that after reading that sign, the available credit was no longer available to us at all. On weekends, we would go to the store and buy everything I could so we wouldn't go without. If we ran out of food, we would eat whatever we had."

Luz's and Haydee's interpersonal conflicts with food scarcity were tied to issues of mobility and future opportunities for them to become U.S. residents and U.S. citizens. In Luz's case, her perception of her immigration status and the taboo of receiving food assistance caused her conflicts. Changing her view of her perceived interconnection meant changing her food insecurity circumstances, albeit not permanently. Haydee's interpersonal conflict was developed through her reality of food acquisition through credit. Her perception was that the only way to eat was through the use of store credit. Once that convenience ended, she resolved her conflict by changing her perceptions of the need to buy a variety of food with another one: to eat what they had available to them at home (a limited variety). Colonia residents continuously face geographical and personal impediments to food access. When the colonia of Sparks in El Paso, Texas, was in its developing stage, the nearest supermarket was a thirty- to forty-minute drive away. Haydee and Luz did not have their own cars to drive to the supermarket, and the lack of public transportation in the community further contributed to their food insecurity. The absence of grocery stores in colonias is a significant element contributing to residents' food insecurity. In the past ten years, nonprofit organizations such as La Semilla in southern New Mexico have been working with residents to transfer the agricultural experiences and funds of knowledge of colonia residents into local gardening efforts. These efforts are intergenerational and often involve technical training and knowledge sharing among neighbors and people who specialize in agriculture through agricultural sciences degrees and sustainable gardening efforts. Although these efforts to reengage people with their local environments are noteworthy in helping to address food insecurity and hunger in colonias, they require investment and commitments for long-term community buy-in and sustainability that merits future research and attention.

The ecology of the body helps us explore the affective responses of these women's experiences with hunger and food insecurity as outcomes of their phenomena (Hayes-Conroy and Hayes-Conroy 2013). These embodied responses are feelings described as emotional currency; the result of encountering and resolving food insecurity. Emotional currency is the unintentional exchange of the food insecurity experience for the agentive outcome. The embodiment of food insecurity can be observed through the experiences presented above.

As with monetary currency, experiences vary yet are interconnected to the biopolitics of food insecurity (Carney 2014). Esperanza's feelings of validation were propelled by the *mole* that was donated by her neighbor. Casilda's feelings of determination were the result of her inability to obtain gainful employment due to pregnancy. Luz's feelings of shame were instigated by her food pantry experience in contradiction to the food-citizenship rapport building favored in colonias. Dora and her family migrated to the United States, and the transformation of the food-scape induced feelings of uncertainty in meeting her family's food preferences and expectations. Haydee's lack of personal transportation and unpredictability of buying food on credit interrupted her quest for food acquisition, thus generating feelings of quell. These examples of food insecurity in colonias are significant as they present various portraits of food insecurity throughout various stages of women's life trajectories. As researchers, practitioners, and transplanted residents of these spaces, it is equally important to draw attention to the feelings that are produced through the bodies of women responsible for meeting their family's nourishment, despite their own embodied hunger (Page-Reeves et al. 2014). We must recognize that these embodied feelings are what inform our work and our claims for social justice.

PERSPECTIVES OF FOOD INSECURITY—HEALTH DISPARITIES AND FOOD STRETCHING

Among some low-income households in colonias, access to food is not a problem, when supermarkets are relatively close. However, many cannot afford nutritious foods to help manage and ameliorate their health conditions. Luz, for example, describes how she had to change her diet due to her diabetes. She reflected on the lack of options, for many low-income households, to incorporate healthier foods. Dora and her husband eventually qualified for monthly food baskets provided by a nonprofit-based organization located outside of Las Cruces, New Mexico. Although they received these food items, including cans of fruit juice and cereals, she felt frustrated that the food would go to waste since she and her spouse could not consume them because of their high sugar content. Dora was concerned about having an excess of certain foods she considered harmful to consume because of her advanced age and her deteriorating health conditions. Dora elaborated on the complications associated with her diabetes and the depression she felt from being emotionally and physically isolated in her own home. The lack of supermarkets and public transportation in her colonia have kept Dora physically bound to her home, primarily because she does not know how to drive a vehicle and she has to rely on her husband as the primary means of transportation. Occasionally, she has also relied on her next-door neighbor or on her niece for rides to the store or to the clinic. She recalled with nostalgia the freedom and physical mobility she had while living in the border city of Ciudad Juárez, where she could walk up to a street corner and take a bus to the supermarket to buy and eat the food she preferred to eat. Now, if she cannot get a ride to a supermarket, she has no other way of accessing food.

Here again, the value of ethnographic work is accentuated. Ethnography enables microanalysis of human-environmental relationships modified by such things as economic competition, ecological events (e.g., flash flooding), or premeditated political decisions to segregate people (e.g., immigrants). It leads to a new understanding of poverty in two ways: people with scarce resources are "rendered human" again as competent and moral social actors, and description of their lived experiences in relation to larger political-economic constraints helps to make sense of seemingly irrational choices people who live on the margins sometimes make (Goode 2009; Núñez and Klamminger 2010). For example, the single mothers Riviera interviewed in her 2014 study indicated they felt they lived in their "own little worlds" while seeking to mediate and negotiate their poverty and food insecurity in their everyday lives. The "little worlds" of female-headed households are usually limited to their household and contacts with a few neighbors in the absence of extended family members, leading to feelings of loneliness and isolation.

Through her interviews and service-learning interactions with women in the colonia of Sparks in El Paso, Texas, Marrufo inquired about strategies women used to "stretch out" their resources to make sure they had enough food to eat. Luz recalled:

> I am always looking for specials to save money. I have also changed how I see our diet. When we first got here, I was focused more on getting full and giving my daughters food that would fill them up. Now, I am focusing more on nutrition and trying to get more fruits and vegetables into our diets. I have diabetes now, and I have learned that what affects my health will affect my entire family. I saw my doctor, and he suggested I eat healthy foods, less-processed foods, and more vegetables.

Luz reflected on her diet and what had changed since immigrating to the United States. She discussed how she had traditionally bought food that helped "fill her and her daughters up," such as potatoes, soups, beans, sandwiches, and cereal. She also discussed shopping on both sides of the border when possible as a strategy for stretching out her food as long as possible. Over time, Luz indicated that her shopping behavior had shifted after becoming more mindful of her food choices. She noted: "I buy more vegetables now, like nopales [cactus pads] versus buying bread, cookies, and tortillas. Now I buy more fruits and vegetables than before. Adding nopales to my diet has helped me a lot with my diabetes." Luz said her doctor suggested she try eating more organic foods with less chemicals and less processing. She recalls eating flavored oatmeal and thinking this was a healthy option for her, but this would make her blood sugar levels rise. Luz recalled: "The doctor told me it was the type of oatmeal I was buying that was rising my blood sugar. Now, I try to buy food at lower prices that is also of good quality. Sometimes this food is more expensive, but it is better for my health so I prefer to buy it even if it is a little more expensive." Luz's awareness of how certain foods impact her health, have significantly influenced her awareness of how foods influence her body.

Among the strategies described for "stretching out" their food, Luz discussed adding more vegetables to increase the bulk and nutrients in her food. She noted: "I can help make my food last by adding other things to our food, like root vegetables, meat, and cabbage so I can make the food more plentiful. When I cook a dish, I add vegetables like potatoes and other things so I can make a meal more complete." Luz recalls: "Before I had no money to buy groceries so we had to put up with hunger. When I did not have a credit card to pay for groceries, I just had to do without. Now, they built a big store not too far from our community, and now I have a credit card I can use when I am struggling to buy food and I don't have the money." Luz and her family have now established roots in her community and over time have developed a line of credit to buy at a large supermarket.

MAKING ENDS MEET BY SELLING FOOD TO OTHERS

Hunger and food insecurity are negotiated at the personal, household, and community levels. The search for food and the need to provide for self and families points to colonia residents' efforts to find ways to curtail their household needs through innovative and creative enterprises. Eric Wolf's (1966) contributions to the concept of "funds of knowledge" are fitting in the anthropological scholarship surrounding colonias. The term was coined "to define resources and knowledge that households manipulate to make ends meet in the household economy" (Hogg 2011, 667).

Carlos G. Vélez-Ibáñez's (1988, 1996, 2004) work has featured funds of knowledge and bonds of mutual trust processes. The political ecology framework is ideal for considering funds of knowledge, as colonia residents are continuously engaged in social and economic relationships where math, science, and entrepreneurial skills are used to contribute to the production and maintenance of household goods. The intricacies of accessing information, resources, and services are shared among colonia families to seek self-sufficiency.

The participants in these studies, and particularly in this chapter, have built on their lived experiences, personal strategies, ingenuity, and social networks to increase their access to food by enacting their own strategies, techniques, and exchange of funds of knowledge. In the examples of Casilda and Esperanza, we can examine the women's agency in exercising their self-sufficiency to make ends meet. In the case of Esperanza, we learned about her strategies to employ her own body within her local community to barter her cleaning services in exchange for groceries or a payment to help pay for her utility bill.

Mobility, or lack thereof, has been a key argument in examining the food insecurity and hunger in colonias on the U.S.-Mexico border. Women mobilize their resources, their networks, and their bodies to exchange their labor for food. The low population densities that characterize colonias contribute to the scarcity of food-vending facilities, mainly supermarkets. Although not having access to supermarkets is a major challenge for residents, this void also creates a number of opportunities for small businesses to occupy a significant niche in colonias. Necessity in these communities creates opportunities for innovative responses to address food insecurity at various levels, primarily at the level of microenterprise, as small businesses can be operated within people's homes.

As resourceful agents of social change, women in colonias engage in multiple strategies to secure food, and some even engage in income-generating activities as microentrepreneurs. In the colonias of northern Doña Ana County, New Mexico, for example, women dry chile, make and sell canned salsas, and make *chile ristras* (braids of red chile) to harness dry chile to use throughout the year for household consumption and to sell to neighbors and to tourists driving by. Other entrepreneurs take advantage of the brand loyalty New Mexicans and others have to Hatch chiles and travel to northern New Mexico and up to Colorado to sell famous New Mexican chiles. The chile ristras that adorn so many homefronts and businesses throughout New Mexico and the Southwest are a key example of traditional knowledge and strategies employed to offset food insecurity, as dried red chiles can be rehydrated in warm water and processed into a red chile paste to be used in a variety of dishes, including enchiladas and red chile stews known as asado. Green chiles can be dehydrated in the sun as well, though they are usually roasted and frozen to be used throughout the rest of the year.

FIGURE 17.1. Red chile *ristras* (braided red chile), often assembled in people's homes, are found hanging inside of people's kitchens and in patios in the colonias of northern Doña Ana County and sold at the Hatch Chile Festival every Labor Day weekend. Photo by author.

During household interviews and participant observation in the colonias of Doña Ana County, New Mexico, Núñez observed women who sold homemade food items such as tamales, burritos, and *gorditas* (stuffed corn cakes filled with ground beef), as well as treats appealing mostly to children such as donuts, nachos, candies, and frozen treats (Núñez 2006b). Other women put up makeshift restaurants and sold prepared food to their neighbors on weekends. As supermarkets are scarce in colonias, so are fast-food establishments and restaurants; women cook, bake, and sell specialty foods for additional income. On weekends, women entrepreneurs are likely to make "specialty" foods such as menudo (a red chile stew made with hominy and cow tripe), flautas (rolled tacos), and asado (pork in a New Mexican red chile sauce). Dishes were sold by the plate, bowl, or the pot-full for a flat rate. Some women specialized in making bread (both white and wheat), homemade donuts, and the New Mexican sweet cookies known as *biscochos*. Wheat bread was sold to colonia residents who have diabetes and those who prefer to consume complex carbohydrates instead of products made with white flour. Overall, the lack of supermarkets and restaurants has led residents to find innovative ways to make food to meet their families' needs and their neighbors' preferences. Foods made to sell out of people's home kitchens in colonias are usually dense in calories and rarely include a variety of fresh fruits and vegetables as part of their preparation or consumption, which ultimately has other health implications for residents.

CONCLUSION

Ethnography, with its multifaceted techniques, methodological flexibility, and emphasis on researcher sensitivity and reflexivity, is ideally placed to lead in food insecurity studies (Madden 2010; Murchison 2010). As Chicana/Latina ethnographers, we have navigated our insider/outsider roles to address the intersectional issues of hunger and food insecurity in colonias (Zavella 1993). We have found that discussions of hunger are usually laden with examples of sadness, shame, and social stigma, which can have a lasting impact on the decision-making processes of people and on their subsequent generations. By employing a number of strategies to gain access to food through familial and social networks, food pantries, and entrepreneurship, women in colonias, particularly women with children, have negotiated strategies to deal with limited food choices in their rural unincorporated communities.

Political ecology is a field focused on promoting socioeconomic justice and understanding for the disadvantaged (Biersack and Greenberg 2006; Robbins 2012). Their location as communities outside of urban landscapes in the SWNA region means colonia residents have a different set of economic and environmental challenges to contend with that impact their food choices and their access to diverse food options. Building trust with vulnerable residents, particularly immigrant women, single mothers, and older adults, allowed us to document how hunger and food insecurity were addressed in everyday life circumstances as people navigated their multiple ecologies, particularly their bodies, their households, and communities. The multiple stressors and strategies involved in the women's procurement of food are particularly significant, as the lessons learned are relevant to the training of social service providers, students, and other stakeholders within the nongovernmental and governmental sectors working or volunteering in colonias as communities that are often hidden and out of sight in the border region's landscape.

Communities such as colonias are particularly vulnerable to external pressures, such as economic recessions; environmental challenges, such as flooding and drought events; and anti-terrorism initiatives after September 11, 2001. Political ecologists need to work with local communities to understand and address these processes and their differentiated impacts on households and individuals. The ways in which people negotiate, resist, and seek help from others helps mitigate such shocks in a world where they are often stigmatized for being "poor," "female," and "brown." The use of ethnographic research methods forms part of a wider political and ethical engagement by political ecologists working in hidden and hard-to-reach communities who struggle to feed their families while trying to make ends meet.

The use of portraiture is paramount to providing qualitative images made up of narratives, in order to access the struggles within the crevices inherent in colonias. These portraitures showcase women's life circumstances and their ways of confronting food insecurity and hunger while employing efforts to remediate their situations while seeking solutions to help feed themselves and their children. As such, these portraitures are not meant to present stagnant representations of poverty; rather, these snapshots provide insights into the strategies of resistance and perseverance that characterize life in the SWNA region.

As we learned from Riviera's ethnographic research, some women relied on their neighbors and social networks as a safety net to mediate hunger on any given day, while others sought support from leaders in their faith communities. Some colonia residents have sought to develop lines of credit but struggled to pay for their bills when they lacked a steady income. Colonia residents who do not have the legal authorization to live and work in the United States are less likely to seek and qualify for public assistance and must rely on other sources of support that comes from friends, family, and neighbors who are empathetic and compassionate. Relying on public services such as monthly food pantries brings forward a number of stigmatizing factors that make residents' hunger and poverty visible and shameful.

Through her ethnographic and applied efforts to address food insecurity and hunger in colonias, Marrufo provided insights into colonia residents' struggle with accessing food due to limited mobility, lack of transportation, health conditions, and the fluidity of credit offered by local grocers. Women's willingness to rise above circumstances that are seemingly impossible is a testament to the strength that is generated through the human need to find solutions to their everyday challenges. She also brings forth the importance of respect, compassion, and empathy and the need for sensitivity among volunteers working in food pantries to avoid shaming and further stigmatizing people in need. Generous as they are, food pantries collect and distribute atypical food items meant to satiate the "one type fits all" consumer, excluding those with diagnosed dietary health conditions.

Núñez's commitment to colonias studies and mentorship invites researchers to see and experience life in colonias through various angles and lenses. Individuals and families alike who recognize the lack of food services and businesses in colonias have developed strategies to help ameliorate and address their food needs through the aid of the social and familial networks as well as through emerging entrepreneurship opportunities in the form of small businesses based in homes and through weekend pop-up dining halls and food stalls that provide residents with meals on weekends and during special events. These are innovative ways women find solutions to the scarcity of food-vending business, while also generating income to contribute financially to their households, while serving up cultural familiarity through food. Agency and resourcefulness are features of Núñez's work as she covers the entrepreneurial spirit that emanates from need.

Collectively through a Chicana/Latina feminist approach, we have applied a political-ecological framework and have zoomed into a political ecology of the body to document the micro-phenomena that take place in the quotidian struggles to secure food in colonias. We challenge researchers to expand the boundaries of U.S.-Mexico border scholarship grounded in issues of national security. We present these portraits as qualitative images of food insecurity and perseverance to life in the U.S.-Mexico borderlands.

REFERENCES

Anzaldúa, Gloria. 1987. *La Frontera/Borderlands: The New Mestiza*. San Francisco: Aunt Lute Books.

Biersack, Aletta. 2006. "Reimaging Political Ecology: Culture/Power/History/Nature." In *Reimagining Political Ecology*, edited by Aletta Biersack and James B. Greenberg, 5–83. Durham, NC: Duke University Press.

Biersack, Aletta, and James B. Greenberg, eds. 2006. *Reimagining Political Ecology*. Durham, NC: Duke University Press.

Bourdieu, Pierre. 1986. "The Forms of Capital." In *Handbook of Theory and Research for the Sociology of Education*, edited by J. G. Richardson, 241–58. New York: Greenwood Press.

Carney, Megan A. 2014. "The Biopolitics of 'Food Insecurity': Towards a Critical Political Ecology of the Body in Studies of Women's Transnational Migration." *Journal of Political Ecology* 21:1–18.

Coleman-Jensen Alisha, Matthew P. Rabbitt, Christian Gregory, and Anita Singh. 2015. *Household Food Security in the United States in 2014*. ERR-194, U.S. Department of Agriculture, Economic Research Service.

Collins, Patricia H. 1990. *Black Feminist Thought: Knowledge, Consciousness, and the Politics of Empowerment*. Boston: Unwin Hyman.

Coronado, Irasema. 2003. "*La vida en las colonias de la frontera*. Life in Colonias on the Border." *Latino Studies* 1:193–97.

Cruz-Torres, María Luz. 2004. *Lives of Dust and Water: An Anthropology of Change and Resistance in Northwestern Mexico*. Tucson: University of Arizona Press.

Dean, Wesley R., and Joseph R. Sharkey. 2011. "Food Insecurity, Social Capital and Perceived Personal Disparity in a Predominantly Rural Region of Texas: An Individual-Level Analysis." *Social Science & Medicine* 72(9): 1454–62.

Dickinson, Maggie. 2014. "Women, Welfare, and Food Insecurity." In *Women Redefining the Experience of Food Insecurity: Life Off the Edge of the Table*, edited by Janet Page-Reeves, 65–85. Lanham, MD: Lexington Books.

Dill, Bonnie Thornton, and Marla H. Kohlman. 2012. "Intersectionality: A Transformative Paradigm in Feminist Theory and Social Justice." In *Handbook of Feminist Research: Theory and Praxis*, edited by Sharlene Nagy Hesse-Biber, 154–73. 2nd ed. Los Angeles: Sage.

Dolhinow, Rebecca. 2006. "Mexican Women's Activism in New Mexico Colonias." In *Women and Change at the U.S.-Mexico Border: Mobility, Labor, and Activism*, edited by Doreen J. Mattingly and Ellen R. Hansen, 125–41. Tucson: University of Arizona Press.

Dunn, Timothy J. 1996. *The Militarization of the U.S.-Mexico Border, 1978–1992: Low-Intensity Conflict Doctrine Comes Home*. Austin: University of Texas Press.

———. 2009. *Blockading the Border and Human Rights: The El Paso Operation That Remade Immigration Enforcement*. Austin: University of Texas Press.

Escobar, Arturo. 2008. *Territories of Difference: Place, Movements, Life, Redes*. Durham, NC: Duke University Press.

Esparza, Adrian X., and Angela J. Donelson. 2010. *The Colonias Reader: Economy, Housing and Public Health in U.S.-Mexico Border Colonias*. Tucson: University of Arizona Press.

Fitchen, Janet M. 1988. "Hunger, Malnutrition, and Poverty in the Contemporary United States: Some Observations on Their Social and Cultural Context." *Food and Foodways* 2(1): 309–33.

Foster, George M., and Robert V. Kemper. 1979. "Anthropological Fieldwork in Cities." In *Urban Life*, edited by George Gmelch and Walter P. Zenner, 131–45. 4th ed. Long Grove, IL: Waveland.

Ganster, Paul, and David E. Lorey. 2008. *The U.S.-Mexican Border into the Twenty-First Century*. Lanham, MD: Rowman & Littlefield.

Geertz, Clifford. 1973. "Thick Description: Toward an Interpretive Theory of Culture." In *The Interpretation of Cultures: Selected Essays*, edited by Clifford Geertz, 3–30. New York: Basic Books.

Goffman, Erving. 1963. *Stigma: Notes on the Management of Spoiled Identity*. Englewood Cliffs, NJ: Prentice-Hall.

Goode, Judith. 2009. "How Urban Ethnography Counters Myths About the Poor." In *Urban Life*, edited by George Gmelch, Robert V. Kemper, and Walter P. Zenner, 185–201. 5th ed. Long Grove, IL: Waveland.

Greenberg, James B., and Thomas K. Park. 1994. "Political Ecology." *Journal of Political Ecology* 1:1–12.

Hayes-Conroy, Jessica, and Allison Hayes-Conroy. 2013. "Veggies and Visceralities: A Political Ecology of Food and Feeling." *Emotion, Space and Society* 6:81–90.

Hill, Sarah. 2003. "Metaphoric Enrichment and Material Poverty: The Making of 'Colonias.'" In *Ethnography at the Border*, edited by Pablo Vila, 141–67. Minneapolis: University of Minnesota Press.

Hogg, Linda. 2011. "Funds of Knowledge: An Investigation of Coherence Within the Literature." *Teaching and Teacher Education* 27:666–77.

Lawrence-Lightfoot, Sara. 2005. "Reflections on Portraiture: A Dialogue Between Art and Science." *Qualitative Inquiry* 11(3): 3–15.

Lawrence-Lightfoot, Sara, and Jessica H. Davis. 1997. *The Art and Science of Portraiture*. San Francisco: Jossey-Bass.

Little, Paul. 2007. "Political Ecology as Ethnography: A Theoretical and Methodological Guide." *Horizontes Antropológicos* 3. http://socialsciences.scielo.org/.

Low, Setha M. 1999. "Spatializing Culture: The Social Production and Social Construction of Public Space." In *On the Plaza: The Politics of Public Space and Culture*. Austin: University of Texas Press.

Madden, Raymond. 2010. *Being Ethnographic: A Guide to the Theory and Practice of Ethnography*. Los Angeles: Sage.

Messer, Ellen. 2004. "Hunger and Human Rights: Old and New Roles for Anthropologists." In *Human Rights: The Scholar Activist*, edited by Carole Nagengast and Carlos G. Vélez-Ibáñez, 43–63. Oklahoma City: Society for Applied Anthropology.

Mollet, Sharlene, and Caroline Faria. 2013. "Messing with Gender in Feminist Political Ecology." *Geoforum* 45:116–25.

Murchison, Julian M. 2010. *Ethnography Essentials: Designing, Conducting, and Presenting Your Research*. San Francisco: Jossey-Bass.

Núñez, Guillermina G. 2006a. "In Search of the Next Harvest." In *Homelands: Women's Journeys Across Race, Place, and Time*, edited by Patricia J. Tumang and Jenesha de Rivera, 1–24. Emeryville, CA: Seal.

———. 2006b. "The Political Ecology of Colonias in the Hatch Valley: Towards an Applied Social Science of the U.S.-Mexico Border." PhD dissertation, Department of Anthropology, University of California, Riverside.

———. 2008. "Colonias." In *The Borderlands: An Encyclopedia of Culture and Politics on the U.S.-Mexico Divide*, edited by Andrew G. Wood, 57–58. Westport, CT: Greenwood Press.

———. 2012. "Housing, Colonias and Social Justice in the US Mexico Border Region." In *Social Justice in the U.S.-Mexico Border Region*, edited by Mark Lusk, Kathleen Staudt, and Eva Moya, 109–25. Dordrecht: Springer.

Núñez, Guillermina G., and Josiah McC. Heyman. 2007. "Entrapment Processes and Immigrant Communities in a Time of Heightened Border Vigilance." *Human Organization* 66:354–65.

Núñez, Guillermina G., and Georg M. Klamminger. 2010. "Centering the Margins: The Transformation of Community in Colonias on the U.S.-Mexico Border." In *The Paso del Norte Metropolitan Region*, edited by Kathleen Staudt, César M. Fuente, and Julia E. Monárrez Fragoso, 147–72. New York: Palgrave Macmillan.

Núñez-Mchiri, Guillermina G. 2009. "The Political Ecology of the Colonias on the U.S.-Mexico Border: Human Environmental Challenges and Community Responses in Southern New Mexico." *Southern Rural Sociology* 24:67–91.

Page-Reeves, Janet. 2014. *Women Redefining the Experience of Food Insecurity: Life Off the Edge of the Table*. Lanham, MD: Lexington Books.

Page-Reeves, Janet, Amy Anixter Scott, Maurice Moffett, Veronica Apodaca, and Vanessa Apodaca. 2014. "'Is Always That Sense of Wanting . . . Never Really Being Satisfied': Women's Quotidian Struggles with Food Insecurity in a Hispanic Community in New Mexico." *Journal of Hunger & Environmental Nutrition* 9(2): 183–209.

Portes, Alejandro. 1998. "Social Capital: Its Origins and Applications in Modern Sociology." *Annual Review of Sociology* 24(1): 1–24.

Richardson, Chad. 1999. *Batos, Bolillos, Pochos, and Pelados*. Austin: University of Texas Press.

Riviera, Diana. 2014. "The Southwest Borderlands as the Silenced Center and the Voice of Single-Mothers." PhD disseration, Nova Southeastern University.

Robbins, Paul. 2012. *Political Ecology*. 2nd ed. Oxford: Wiley-Blackwell.

Rocheleau, Diane, Barbara Thomas-Slayter, and Esther Wangari, eds. 1996. *Feminist Political Ecology*. London: Routledge.

Sharkey, Joseph R., Wesley R. Dean, and Cassandra M. Johnson. 2011. "Association of Household and Community Characteristics with Adult and Child Food Insecurity Among Mexican-Origin Households in Colonias Along the Texas-Mexico Border." *International Journal for Equity in Health* 10(1): 19–32.

Sheridan, Thomas E. 1996. *Where the Dove Calls*. Tucson: University of Arizona Press.

Simmons, Nancy. 1997. "Memories and Miracles: Housing the Rural Poor Along the United States–Mexico Border: A Comparative Discussion of Colonia Formation in El Paso County, Texas and Doña Ana County, New Mexico." *New Mexico Law Review* 27:33–75.

Stanford, Lois. 2014. "Negotiating Food Insecurity Along the U.S.-Mexico Border: Social Strategies, Practice, and Networks Among Mexican Immigrant Women." In *Women Redefining the Experience of Food Insecurity: Life Off the Edge of the Table*, edited by Jane Page-Reeves, 105–24. Lanham, MD: Lexington Books.

Vélez-Ibáñez, Carlos, G. 1988. "Networks of Exchange Among Mexicans in the U.S. and Mexico: Local Level Mediating Responses to National and International Transformations." *Urban Anthropology* 17(1): 27–51.

———. 1996. *Border Visions: Mexican Cultures of the Southwest*. Tucson: University of Arizona Press.

———. 2004. "Regions of Refuge in the United States: Issues, Problems, and Concerns for the Future of Mexican-Origin Populations in the United States." *Human Organization* 63(1): 1–20.

Walker, Jennifer L., David H. Holben, Mary L. Kropf, John P. Holcomb, and Heidi Anderson. 2007. "Household Food Insecurity Is Inversely Associated with Social Capital and

Health in Females from Special Supplemental Nutrition Program for Women, Infants, and Children Households in Appalachian Ohio." *Journal of American Dietetic Association* 107(11): 1989–93.

Ward, Peter M. 1999. *Colonias and Public Policy in Texas and Mexico*. Austin: University of Texas Press.

Wilmot, William, and Joyce L. Hocker. 2014. *Interpersonal Conflict*. New York: McGraw-Hill.

Wolf, Eric R. 1966. *Peasants*. Englewood Cliffs, NJ: Prentice-Hall.

Zavella, Patricia. 1993. "Feminist Insider Dilemmas: Constructing Ethnic Identity with 'Chicana' Informants." *Frontiers: A Journal of Women Studies* 13(3): 53–76.

———. 2011. *I'm Neither Here Nor There: Mexicans' Quotidian Struggles with Migration and Poverty*. Durham, NC: Duke University Press.

Zavella, Patricia, and Denise A. Segura, eds. 2007. *Women and Migration in the U.S.-Mexico Borderlands: A Reader*. Durham, NC: Duke University Press.

———. 2008. "Introduction: Gendered Borderlands." *Gender and Society* 22(5): 537–44.

Zenner, Walter P. 2002. "Beyond Urban and Rural: Communities in the 21st Century." In *Urban Life*, edited by George Gmelch and Walter P. Zenner, 53–60. Long Grove, IL: Waveland.

18

TRANSBORDER ECONOMIC, ECOLOGICAL, AND HEALTH PROCESSES

A Commentary

JUDITH FREIDENBERG

HOW MANY WAYS are there to imagine a boundary, a line that separates? Many, because in separating, the choice of line demarcation reveals elements of the persons, ideas, goods, and services that it separates. In *Ethnic Groups and Boundaries*, Frederik Barth argued that an ethnic group was defined more by what it is not than for what it is; that is, by excluding those defined as "others," we define the group we feel we are included in. These processes of inclusion and exclusion, as Barth tells us, persist regardless of whether there is movement across the groups. If "cultural differences can persist despite inter-ethnic contact and interdependence" (1969, 10), Barth tells us, they need to be explained. This is precisely what this section of this timely contribution by Vélez-Ibáñez and Heyman actually attempts in its regional approach to borders. While a transborder region contains a geopolitical border, it is also a space of interconnectivity in three important ways. First, by focusing on linking and hybridity, rather than country of birth alone, the section contributes to the understanding of how space colors personal experience. Second, by delimiting the question of the permanence of differences despite mobility—the back and forth movement of persons, goods, services, ideas—in the geographical space occupied by northern Mexican states and southern U.S. states, the ethnographic cases in part 4 help us understand transborder processes and their impact on framing constructs of Mexico and the United States as interdependent nation-states. Third, by using lived experience to understand boundaries, the section helps us think about borders between nations as well as borders within nations. Assuming that in separation there is connection, I will briefly discuss the four anthropological case studies in the section with special attention to how actual practices of target populations regarding access to vital resources erect boundaries within and across populations and to how the maintenance of such boundaries bear on human rights. Who controls what, over whom, where, and when become vital information to the political economy of space. The chapters that comprise part 4 deal with breaches in human rights—restricted access to basic human needs such as water, retirement benefits, health, and food.

A major commodity in a desert is water. Radonic and Sheridan's chapter centers on how access to water framed human interaction throughout the history of the Sonoran Desert since the peopling of the Americas and examines similarities and differences in the regional political ecology of water. The processes were markedly similar in both sides of the border as population and capital increased and as water technology facilitated the growth of agricultural businesses in the twentieth century and accelerated urbanization in the twenty-first century. Yet, litigation to ensure access rights in the changed political ecology of water had markedly different results on the two sides of the border: while tribal governments in Arizona managed to play a stakeholder role in the water market, through a diversification of its water portfolio, the Yaqui in Mexico still struggle to implement water rights regulations that were allocated almost a century ago, and they are caught between the federal- and state-level courts regarding the building of an aqueduct that would divert water to the city of Hermosillo without their authorization. Using a historical and comparative approach, this case study adeptly illustrates the process of politicization of group boundaries when access to valuable resources is at stake.

While policies are meant to provide normative procedures to organize social interaction, their legal implementation affects people's lives differently. In fact, the construction of borders (whether walls or policies) often impact the well-being of people who literally look into each other's backyards. Obtaining legal documentation to work incites corruption in both the workers and their employers, but as Horton's collection of life histories vividly shows, such practices result in Social Security benefits insufficient to allow elderly farmworkers to stop working, since they cannot make ends meet and retire, i.e., leave the workforce, regardless of their legal status. Their marginality triples by the time they reach old age, having worked in a low-pay occupation, under temporary work contracts, and for what Horton calls "strategies of erasure," that is, tactics by which employers and the state have profited by making workers appear to disappear. Since access to benefits such as Social Security, pensions, Medicare, and Medicaid, among others, was made inaccessible to unauthorized workers, their wage contributions to the state have become appropriated by their employers and/or the government, who know too well that benefit deductions will remain unclaimed at least until, or if, legal status is normalized.

Staudt carefully details the process of long-term research on the deleterious impact of a polluted environment on the health of residents in U.S. territory yet ten miles from Mexico. Staudt laments the lack of attention to context-based research designs, the bias toward statistically significant results, and the dearth of scholarly publications intent on demonstrating the policy impacts of research. A steel plant and faith-based nongovernmental organizations are among the organizations that the residents interact with. The joint space occupied by a colonia (a rural or semi-rural informal settlement of Mexicans, attracted by work in cities or in agriculture, alongside the U.S.-Mexico border, with unmet social and health needs) and an industrial disposal plant exemplifies the contradictions of globalization: the plant imports steel waste from Ciudad Juárez in Mexico, a hub of the maquiladora industry, and the colonia houses people born in Mexico. Because the plant sits in residential space housing low-income persons, it illustrates what has been called environmental racism that calls for policies in environmental justice. As a result of community organizing to denounce extremely high levels of pollution, and the perceived links to cancer, the plant was ordered to commission a study, yet, Staudt argues, most environmental research does not lead to establishing causal connections but rather to webs of causality (highway pollution, income, smoking, etc.), some pointing to the beneficial effects of migration and closeness to a more accessible health care system. In turn, residents, attracted to the U.S. side by higher wages, tend to normalize environmental hazards in a business-centered society.

Núñez-Mchiri, Riviera, and Marrufo focus on food insecurity in colonias, showing its interrelatedness to other unaddressed needs, such as poverty, and presenting ethnographic evidence on the role of social networks that mitigate its deleterious impacts. They aptly deconstruct demographic categories such as poverty into interrelated and changing situations, such as the unpredictability of employment related to the agricultural cycle and the availability and composition of social networks, to highlight women's agency. In addition to tapping into networks, the women employ subsistence strategies such as micro-entrepreneurship, selling raw, cooked, and canned food to residents in a food-vending desert area.

Together, these case studies illustrate how diminished access to resources results in unaddressed human needs that impact a collective sense of self. Thus, control over water resources affect tribal identity; lack of access to government benefits severely impairs the elderly's actual and perceived senses of well-being; a state of civic alienation contributes to normalizing deleterious effects of polluted environments on health status; and lack of food predictability among colonia residents leads to overutilization of social networks in lieu of using government subsidies. Using place-based analytical approaches to regions such as the Sonoran Desert, small shack enclaves, or colonias, these case studies demonstrate the inadequacy of focusing on geopolitical borders to understand the human condition in zones of exacerbated human mobility. Together, the case studies show how issues tackled separately—water, government benefits, health, food—are intimately connected as basic human needs. They also show how it is not only the presence of resources but also what contributes or prevents access to them that becomes central in understanding the dynamics of space. Access to resources and indigenous knowledge that allow households to meet human needs result in strategies that attest to human creativity.

I suggest that it is access to valued scarce resources that prompts the erection of human differences that get solidified into borders, which divide and limit and which engender vulnerabilities and marginalize some. Borders, in short, are metaphors for power differences that result in mechanisms invisible to policy documents that stratify populations along an inclusion-exclusion continuum. Too often we focus our analytical gaze on the victims of exclusion to the detriment of the perpetrators, failing to understand the structures of inequality and the strategies employed to perpetuate them over time. Let's diminish our focus on national and ethnic populations and focus on what the dynamics of an interconnected space does to human experience. There are several ways we can switch from specific populations to the structural context they are a part of: uncovering context through the experience of people, as Carlos Vélez-Ibáñez does in *Border Visions* (1996); focusing on the increasing militarization of the physical border to understand government and ideology (Fassin 2011); providing ethnographic and historical depth to the understanding of those who live at the border and bringing the state back into focus (Heyman and Campbell 2004); and rethinking the metaphors associated with borders and considering the metaphor of bridge—as simultaneously partition and connector which "are meant to be crossed and they are built to span obstacles. They are connectors of the diverse and the disparate, as well as of history and meaning, people and places" (Álvarez 2012, 38). The understanding of bridges as borders calls for the combined perspectives of ethnography, history, and political economy to understand personal experiences of the state.

My research on Prince George's County, Maryland, is a case study of the sociopolitical transformation of the region and the nation-state through the lived experience of immigrants (Freidenberg 2016). By balancing the immigrant life history narratives with the historical and media record, I attempt to show that spaces, like human beings, are imbued of a history and permeated by ideologies that influence the articulation for newcomers. These qualities of spaces become internalized. This is so because borders, whether territorial or symbolic, can transform difference into inequality with reference to access to resources. This process occurs in time and is thus rarely contemplated in the formulation of public policies. International crossings are monitored to the detriment of internal territorial borders, or borders between social classes, for example. In addition, territorial mobility includes the crossing of multiple borders: between countries, between states, between counties, between neighborhoods. A border crosser incorporates characteristics of the space that is left behind with the space arrived at. As space becomes internalized, so are norms and cultural expectations normative of the new social space. The contemporary reduction of border to a political category of sovereignty obscures the existence of symbolic borders of difference that are historically conditioned. A third meaning of border relates to internalized difference as constructed by the media and the institutions of the larger society. The term Latin@, for example, is often associated with threat (Chavez 2013). Finally there is a border of inequality inherent in public policies that classify residents of the territorial spaces on the basis of prefabricated categories of inclusion and exclusion with labels such as citizen, immigrant, and temporary visa holder. As people move across space, for whatever reason, these social constructions of borders and difference travel with them.

Anthropologists have become erudite documenters of difference. Mary Douglas (1966) noted that difference is construed as danger as if the discrepant were incompatible with the normative. Because unmistakably few spaces are homogeneous, it behooves us to discern similarity in difference. Waiting in a long line to enter the United States recently, I reflected on the meaning of the ubiquitous signs reading Customs Control and Border Security. Why should I understand that stamping my passport protects the nation? From whom?

I suggest that human mobility occurs in spaces. Spaces map social differentiation and whether, when, how, and why differences become transformed into social inequality. As social constructs of difference, borders influence the crossers' articulation of individual and collective identities, since human practices occur in space, whether experienced or imagined. It is through the kinds of meticulous and nuanced understanding of social reality, such as presented in the case studies here, that we can figure out alternatives, such as spaces of difference without inequality, thinking of social differences without reference to the nation-state and weighing symbolic versus physical borders. Whether visible or not, spaces—borders included—bear the imprint of mankind and thus can be transformed.

REFERENCES

Álvarez, Robert R. 2012. "Borders and Bridges: Exploring a New Conceptual Architecture for US-Mexico Border Studies." *Journal of Latin American and Caribbean Anthropology* 17(1): 24–40.

Barth, Frederik. 1969. *Ethnic Groups and Boundaries: The Social Organization of Cultural Difference*. New York: Little, Brown.

Chavez, Leo. 2013. *The Latino Threat: Constructing Immigrants, Citizens, and the Nation*. 2nd ed. Stanford, CA: University of Stanford Press.

Douglas, Mary. 1966. *Purity and Danger: An Analysis of the Concepts of Pollution and Taboo*. London: Routledge.

Fassin, Didier. 2011. "Policing Borders, Producing Boundaries: The Governmentality of Immigration in Dark Times." *Annual Review of Anthropology* 40:213–26.

Freidenberg, Judith Noemí. 2016. *Contemporary Conversations of Immigration in the United States: The View from Prince George's County, Maryland*. Lanham, MD: Lexington Books.

Heyman, Josiah, and Howard Campbell. 2004. "Recent Research on the US-Mexican Border." *Latin American Research Review* 39(3): 205–20.

Vélez-Ibáñez, Carlos G. 1996. *Border Visions: Mexican Cultures of the Southwest United States*. Tucson: University of Arizona Press.

CONCLUSION

CARLOS G. VÉLEZ-IBÁÑEZ

THE CONTRIBUTORS to this volume fully comprehend that the broad neoliberal forces of economy and their accompanying political and legal enforcements create deep contradictions and circumstances that distribute arcs of stratifications and inequality for large swaths of the populations of the Southwest North American (SWNA) region. Simultaneously we understand that human resistance, accommodation, opposition, and invention emerge in the form of political, social, and economic discontents of many sorts. These range from "slanting," i.e., using societal spaces and places flexibly sufficient to manipulate power holders, to confrontations such as the No Border Wall group described by Margaret Dorsey and Miguel Díaz-Barriga (chapter 3).

These too also form an arc of discontents that is distributed according to circumstances, historical epochs, and the availability of resources. These form the outline and content of the understandings that contribute to an engaged anthropology—one that, in Judith Freidenberg's words, "recovers the common humanity in both researchers and the populations we study" (personal communication).

Our mutual works complement each other by the thread of our commitment to the communities with whom we work and interact. These range from informing our broader anthropological visions with tightly argued foci of the manner in which grand neoliberal projects have guaranteed inequality, desperation, and disparity to their opposite. These include counterpoints of resistance, adoption, and innovation. These detail the incessant struggles for water rights by indigenous populations of the SWNA region in the face of debilitating political processes. Others inform us of the health and nutritional disparities in transborder colonias. Our commitment is to develop anthropological narratives that are read such that in the midst of the telling of the human struggles that these populations attempt to resolve not only their economic and social disparities but also their struggles to be seen as human are shown. This struggle is to regard these human beings not as a cheap commodity but rather as labor to be respected and protected—giving them the opportunity to be read as a subject worthy of basic human respect and not burdened by labels and categories. From our perspective they should not be blamed for crossing the killing fields of the desert but rather should be regarded as simply amazing. Our commitment is to provide narratives that detail the courage and bravery of often-maligned colonias on both sides of the region, which battle against disparities of environment, health, and education; neoliberal policies; neglect; and seemingly insurmountable obstacles and impediments. These narratives include details about the indefensible positions in which aged Mexicanos are made to suffer their final days in often-lonely and forced employment past their physical and emotional capacities to do so.

These narratives are also attentive to the sources of such circumstances. Freidenberg's commentary aptly stated it: "Borders, in short, are metaphors for power differences that result in mechanisms invisible to policy documents that stratify populations along an inclusion-exclusion continuum." We have tried to detail the necrocratic state and its skewed policies, contradictions of economy, institutionalized reborderings, constitutional misdirections, physical illness in the midst of available medical institutions, and food availability and shortcomings in the midst of plenty, as well as ecological dangers and damage with their attendant denials contradicted by available useful knowledge such as that provided in this volume. We ask from where emerge the powers of imposition, extraction, and production discipline of the region? Where are their concomitant structures of political authority and coercion that define entire populations as "cheap labor" or "illegals?" Where does the metanarrative of "individual achievement" originate that guarantees inequality and acute stratifications for great swaths of the region's people as described in the colonias and barrios and in regions of refuge detailed in many of the chapters in this volume?

From where do the powers spring that create the ecological malformations and degradations of land, water, flora, and fauna through the entire SWNA region? Thus, my father and I as a child shoveling river bottom sand onto his Model A Ford pickup from the Santa Cruz River was a fond memory but is now skewed by the river's present reality. The river flowed, depending on the season, for 184 miles beginning in the San Rafael Valley east of Patagonia, Arizona, running south into Sonora, Mexico, for several miles and then looping back into Arizona north along the Interstate 19 highway for 140 miles until it reaches the Gila River near Casa Grande, Arizona. Its journey in the present is quite an interrupted one since the water that does flow is mostly from treated sewage and chemically altered flow from the maquiladora plants that ring Nogales, Sonora, as it heads back north, where it is mostly sucked up by urban areas north of the border city all the way to Tucson as well as partially interrupted by the open-pit copper mines and then sucked up by the city itself as well as by ranches, industrial plants, and other human settlements (Southern Arizona Guide 2016). What trickles into the Gila then trickles into the Colorado then empties into the Sea of Cortez in quite diminished and contaminated form then unbalances the necessary freshwater to saltwater natural formula imperative for the gestation of shrimp larva at the mouth of the Colorado River itself. Such interruption at the mouth of the Colorado of natural shrimp then reduces the ability of local fishers, for example in Sinaloa, to take advantage of this resource to feed their families. Such fishers then try to grow more beans, corn, and legumes on *ejido* (Mexican cooperative rural land and community holdings) land for local and regional sale. To do so, however, they may entertain becoming mules to carry seventy-two kilos of marijuana for one of the drug cartels from Nogales to Tucson. Doing this twice a year allows them to buy the necessary seed, insecticides, and pesticides for increased crop production to offset the reduction of natural shrimp resources. They may also try to work on shrimp farms that emerged in the region because of the lack of the natural biomass and with all these activities solve the calculus of economic necessities for their families. But in a pinch, the entire family may move to Tijuana or Nogales to work in the maquiladoras, among the original sources for the interruption of a natural resource.[1]

Such serpentine connectivity is an important part of the theoretical underpinnings of this volume where at different levels of economic and political articulation, from the very local to the faraway, consequences are distributed ecologically, socially, and culturally. So, in the southern side of the SWNA region, at the level of the household, questions on a daily basis are raised about how come and why all of a sudden a child has to pay three times more for her books and fees in the Mexican "public" school. Or, why is a father, to pay for those increases away in Nogales, again crossing the border "at work" even though both parents work in the shrimp farms, fish for whatever is available, knock coconuts down, and sit around husking them for later copra, all while trying to prevent a neighbor from stealing the crop of beans ready to harvest by sitting up all night and in the morning being responsible for rounding up all the women of the ejido to form a *cuadrilla* to pick the tomatoes and lettuce for eventual export to Nogales and to the Los Angeles market?[2] And comparably in the northern region, as detailed in this volume, in the households, neighborhoods, colonias, and communities, equivalent questions are asked, but in dollars, in the same discursive manner.

Yet, in the midst of these affronts to humanity, there are the populations with whom we work who in spite of all these conditions unhesitatingly strive to create the basic social platforms for following generations to have a somewhat better chance and means to ensure their children's human development. Within such parameters, in our discussions lay the potential to not only confront the causes and sources of the worst affronts but also attempt to restructure the narratives involved with those that are historicized, contextualized, and materially cognizant of the manner in which an entire region was bifurcated. The narratives include discussion of how the present was made "supernormal" by the establishment of contending capitalist global and transborder structures against and across political boundaries simultaneously. Regional and transnational economic frames of reference must be embedded in our understandings to reveal the underlying contradictions of uninformed policies, analyses, and premises to an anthropology of this SWNA border region. This can be linked also to those worldwide caught in the asymmetry of constructed histories.

We think that we have contributed to this enhanced narrative by providing myriad examples by which border region specialists in anthropology have conceptualized, theorized, and developed useful methodological approaches that enhance our approaches to an anthropology of engagement that is contributory to unhinging narrow national boundaries as part of these broader narratives. For the most part, the chapters in the volume have embedded within them underlying "extended case studies" embossed by a critical structure induced by the presence of a two-thousand-mile borderline. Their contributions to anthropological theory are inestimable by bringing to bear a wide range of economic, ecological, social, political, legal, linguistic, cultural, and ideological cases, processes, and data. These are coupled together with critical and humanistic underpinnings and form broader anthropological visions and the manner in which to historicize, problematize, and expand our understandings of this highly complex region and its peoples in the midst of transnational and global processes. These are perhaps accompanied with a slight chip on all of our shoulders that has been learned and developed and will remain unconstrained until those visions are made more proximate to their more positive realities.

Likewise, the accompaniment of a sound heuristic such as the SWNA region construct in which historic attention is paid to the way in which empires and nations have availed themselves of extracting and using labor, minerals, water, flora, and fauna to create structures of economic and political power is necessary, especially along imposed borders from a political ecology perspective. Borders such as the two-thousand-mile-long impediment established two generations of grandmothers ago (160 years) seem to become permanent fixtures to our understandings of historical processes and become borders of the mind. Migrating populations become naturalized as foreign, or aliens, or noncitizens, or as strangers and, depending on their utility, are seen as a minor and sometimes major annoyance to be expelled, temporarily accepted, or welcomed if needed in the agricultural and post-industrial combines of the region, both in the north and the south. Such populations are reduced to a narrative of singular identity of utility of back and hands but not of mind. To include their minds is to admit their humanity and thus their moral treatment as social beings. Materialism aside for a moment, this volume for many of us represents a moral quest to render our best understandings of the rootedness of inequality, asymmetry, and extreme stratification of a region long used as the mercantile, industrial, and post-industrial capitalist ecological playground and now ensconced within an ever-expanding global stretch of the extraction of value and energies of places, persons, and natural resources. All have been and continue to enhance the increasing wealth of the few and make improbable the wealth of many more so that it becomes increasingly impossible to live in a transborder world. Theoretically, to reiterate Heyman's contentions in chapter 2 of this volume:

> These unequal relationships are, it merits emphasizing, not just silent and economic, but are painfully symbolized, such as racist views of Mexican-origin people as entirely illegal outsiders, the walled border as a perfect womb protecting against all dangers (Heyman 2012), and the squalor of Mexican border cities as "out of sight, out of mind" (that is, in another country).... To understand the border, we need to acknowledge the inequalities at its core, inequalities that involve relational flows and spatial divisions, via a broadly Marxist dialectics without doctrinaire predetermination.

Thus this volume represents a combination of moral commitment and disquiet as well as theoretical materialist positions informed by the realities of fieldwork, taking on the daily issues of making a living and refusing to accept the intellectual status quo of the ahistoricism and "naturalism" of border demarcations either imposed by national or imperial interventions, invasions, wars, or forced treaties that bifurcate human populations into the unwanted or despised, and these often rationalized by racialist or cultural generalities. We would hope that this volume has provided both direction and avenues for discourses that go beyond the reductionist national discussions permeating the globe.

TRANSBORDER EPILOGUE

The anthropological visions employed here sought to complement so many fine works accomplished by similarly envisioned anthropologists of the northern and southern regions, with the latter not represented because of the development of the original conference leading to this volume. Yet, what must be emphasized is that despite this weakness in this volume, it does recognize the fine works conducted by our Mexican counterparts from south of the northern region. Among many others are included anthropologists such as Arturo Lizzaraga Hernández (2004), whose pioneering work on Sinaloa adeptly narrated and analyzed the daily lives of Sinaloans in Phoenix,

Arizona, from a political ecology perspective. Mariángela Rodríguez (1998) is among the first Mexican anthropologists to conduct serious fieldwork in Los Angeles, antedated only by the very early work of Manuel Gamio. The fine works by the Mexican and American team of Jorge Durand and Douglas Massey (2001) stand out and are based on the enormously important Mexican Migration Project. And without doubt those who are exemplary among the new generation of Mexican social scientists are the Sinaloans' Arturo Santamaría (2001), Erika Cecilia Montoya (2012), and Montoya Zavala, O'Leary, and Woo Morales (2014); Blas Valenzuela Camacho et al. (2014), and Guillermo Ibarra and Ana Luz Ruelas (2014). All utilize Sinaloa as their ecological platform to unravel the interstitial and interconnectivities of economy and family in the regional connections between northern Sinaloa and Phoenix, Arizona. But institutionally the center for transborder research lies at the Colegio de la Frontera Norte, whose daily series of seminars, workshops, reports, and publications and its superb training and instruction of transborder scholars through the PhD program are exemplary. It has no equal in the production of the highest-quality research and amazing works ranging from economics to cultural studies, from health to ecology, and from politics to the social relations of neighborhoods, cities, regions, and the transborder region. Their webpage (https://www.colef.mx/?lang=en) is an amazingly consistent source documenting their many activities and accomplishments.

We would hope that our next iteration of this volume will incorporate our counterparts from the southern part of the SWNA region.

NOTES

1. These recapitulations are generated from my observations made over many years in different coastal towns of the Mexican state of Sinaloa and documented in Cruz-Torres (2004).
2. Cruz-Torres (2014). See among hundreds more the following: Nicholls (1998); Durand and Massey (2001); Gómez et al. (2001); Hernández (2004); Montoya (2012); Ibarra and Ruelas (2014); and Montoya Zavala, O'Leary, and Woo Morales (2014).

REFERENCES

Cruz-Torres, María Luz. 2004. *Lives of Dust and Water: An Anthropology of Change and Resistance in Northwestern Mexico*. Tucson: University of Arizona Press.

Durand, Jorge, and Douglas Massey. 2001. *Milagros en La Frontera: Retablos de migrantes mexicanos a Estados Unidos*. San Luis Potosí: El Colegio de San Luis.

Gómez, Arturo Santamaría, Nayamín Martínez Cossío, Alejandra Castañeda Gómez, and José Jaime Sáinz S. 2001. *Mexicanos en Estados Unidos: La nación, la política y el voto sin fronteras.* Mexico City: Universidad Autónoma de Sinaloa.

Hernández, Arturo Lizarraga. 2004. *Nos llevó la Ventolera: El proceso de la emigación rural al extranjero en Sinaloa.* Culiacán: Universidad Autónoma de Sinaloa.

Heyman, Josiah McC. 2012. "Constructing a 'Perfect' Wall: Race, Class, and Citizenship in US-Mexico Border Policing." In *Migration in the 21st Century: Political Economy and Ethnography*, edited by Pauline Gardiner Barber and Winnie Lem, 153–74. New York: Routledge.

Ibarra, Guillermo, and Ana Luz Ruelas. 2014. *Desde lo local a lo global: Ciencias sociales en Sinaloa.* Mexico City: Facultad de Estudios Inernacionales y Políticas Públicas, Universidad Autónoma de Sinaloa.

Montoya, Erika Cecilia. 2012. *Migrantes, empresarias, políticas, profesionistas y traficantes de drogas: Mujeres en la esfera pública y privada.* Mexico City: Facultad de Estudios Inernacionales y Políticas Públicas, Universidad Autónoma de Sinaloa.

Montoya Zavala, Erika Cecilia, Anna Ochoa O'Leary, and Ofelia Woo Morales. 2014. "'A Headache Every Day Since the New Law': Mexican Women in the Hair Salon Business and Anti-immigrant Policies in Arizona." *Migraciones Internacionales.* El Colegio de la Frontera Nortes 7(3): 133–64.

Rodríguez, Mariángela. 1998. *Mitos, identidad y rito chicanos y mexicanos en California.* Mexico City: CIESAS-Porruá.

Southern Arizona Guide. 2016. "Where Does the Santa Cruz River Start & End?" http://southernarizonaguide.com/where-does-the-santa-cruz-river-start-end.

Valenzuela Camacho, Blas. 2014. "Proceso migratorio hacia Phoenix, Arizona: Retos metodológicos y éticos de su estudio." In *Desde lo local a lo global: Ciencias sociales en Sinaloa*, edited by Guillermo Ibarra and Ana Luz Ruelas, 123–42. Culiacán: Universidad Autónoma de Sinaloa.

CONTRIBUTORS

Amado Alarcón, PhD in sociology, is a professor of sociology at Universitat Rovira i Virgili, Spain. His area of research relates migrations, labor markets, and language. In this area he has conducted research in two bilingual societies: Catalonia (Spain) and El Paso (United States). Alarcón is a visiting professor at the Center for Migration and Development, Princeton University, and a Fulbright Visiting Scholar at the Center for Inter-American and Border Studies, University of Texas at El Paso. He is the president of the Research Committee on Language & Society, International Sociological Association.

Robert R. Álvarez is a professor emeritus of ethnic studies, University of California, San Diego. His research has focused on immigrant communities on the U.S.-Mexico border and global agriculture, especially transborder and transnational markets, entrepreneurs, and the ethnic fruit trade. He has conducted research throughout Mexico, Panama, and along the Mexico-U.S. borderlands and participated in applied research and education in the U.S. Southwest, California, Micronesia, Hawaii, Belau, and the Northern Marianas. He is currently past president of the Society for Applied Anthropology.

Miguel Díaz-Barriga is a professor of anthropology at the University of Texas Rio Grande Valley and recently served as the Carol L. Zicklin Endowed Chair for the Honors Academy at Brooklyn College. He received his bachelor's degree in anthropology from the University of Chicago and his master's and doctorate degrees from Stanford University. His research has focused on concepts relating to Mexican-American politics and identity, Latin American social movements, and border studies. He is the recipient of grants and research awards including one from National

Science Foundation for the project "The Border Wall, Immigration, and Citizenship on the United States/Mexico Border." Díaz-Barriga served as the president of the Association of Latina and Latino Anthropologists of the American Anthropological Association (AAA) from 2010 to 2012. He is currently completing a book project with Margaret Dorsey titled *Militarization on the Edge: Necro-citizenship and the U.S.-Mexican Border Fence*.

Margaret E. Dorsey is an associate professor of anthropology and the founding curator of the Border Studies Archive at the University of Texas Rio Grande Valley. In 2014 and 2015, Dorsey was a visiting associate professor of anthropology at Brooklyn College (CUNY). In 2016 Dorsey co-curated an exhibit titled "Fencing in Democracy" at apexart (New York City). Dorsey resided in Santa Fe as an Ethel-Jane Westfeldt Bunting Fellow at the School for Advanced Research. She has won numerous grants (National Endowment of the Humanities, National Science Foundation) and is currently completing a book manuscript with Miguel Díaz-Barriga on border security titled *Militarization on the Edge: Necro-citizenship and the U.S.-Mexican Border Fence*. Her other book-length projects include *Linda Escobar and Tejano Conjunto Music* (video, 2013) and *Pachangas: Borderlands Music, U.S. Politics, and Transnational Marketing* (University of Texas Press, 2006).

Judith Freidenberg is a professor of anthropology at the University of Maryland at College Park, where she also directs the Anthropology of the Immigrant Life Course Research Program and the Certificate in Museum Scholarship and Material Culture. She is a co-editor of *Practicing Anthropology*. She was affiliated with the Instituto de Investigaciones Gino Germani, Facultad de Ciencias Sociales, Universidad de Buenos Aires as a visiting researcher during her sabbatical stay in Argentina in 2016. Her books include *Contemporary Conversations on Immigration in the United States: The View from Prince George's County, Maryland* (Lexington, forthcoming), *Growing Old in El Barrio* (New York University Press, 2000), *Memorias de Villa Clara* (Museo Histórico Regional, 2005), and *The Invention of the Jewish Gaucho: Villa Clara and the Construction of Argentine Identity* (University of Texas Press, 2009; translated into Spanish by Prometeo Editorial). She has edited books and journal issues and published numerous articles.

Ruth Gomberg-Muñoz is an assistant professor of anthropology at Loyola University Chicago. Her research explores how undocumented people and their family members navigate the political and socioeconomic landscape of the United States. Results from Gomberg-Muñoz's ethnographic research have been published in journals such as *American Ethnologist*, *American Anthropologist*, *Human Organization*, and the *Journal of Ethnic and Migration Studies* as well as in two books, *Labor and Legality: An Ethnography of a Mexican Immigrant Network* (Oxford, 2011) and *Becoming Legal: Immigration Law and Mixed Status Families* (Oxford, 2016).

James Greenberg is a professor of anthropology and a senior research anthropologist in the School of Anthropology at the University of Arizona. His areas of expertise lie in political ecology, economic anthropology, globalization, law and development, violence, urban anthropology, migration, and household livelihoods. His research looks at the political ecology of economic development and the history of its impacts. Specifically, he is interested in the anthropology of credit in this regard.

Josiah Heyman is a professor of anthropology, Endowed Professor of Border Trade Issues, and director of the Center for Interamerican and Border Studies at the University of Texas at El Paso. He is the editor of the influential book *States and Illegal Practices* (Berg, 1999) and author of *Life and Labor on the Border: Working People of Northeastern Sonora, Mexico, 1886–1986* (University of Arizona Press, 1991) and *Finding a Moral Heart for U.S. Immigration Policy: An Anthropological Perspective* (American Anthropological Association, 1998). He has published over one hundred scholarly articles and book chapters, and in 1999, he received the Curl Essay Prize of the Royal Anthropological Institute of Great Britain and Ireland for "Respect for Outsiders? Respect for Law? The Moral Evaluation of High-Scale Issues by U.S. Immigration Officers."

Jane H. Hill is a Regents' Professor of Anthropology and Linguistics (Emerita) at the University of Arizona. She is author or editor of seven books and nearly two hundred articles, chapters, and reviews on topics ranging across multiple questions on the structure and history of American Indian languages, as well as studies of language and racism. She has been awarded the Viking Fund Medal in Anthropology and the Franz Boas Prize of the American Anthropological Association, and she is a Fellow of the American Association for the Advancement of Science, the American Academy of Arts and Sciences, and the Linguistic Society of America.

Sarah Horton is an associate professor of anthropology at the University of Colorado, Denver. Dr. Horton is a medical anthropologist, and her research examines the ways that public policies leave their imprint on migrant farmworkers' health. She is the author of numerous articles published in *American Ethnologist*, *American Anthropologist*, *Medical Anthropology*, *Medical Anthropology Quarterly*, and *Social*

Science and Medicine. She has been conducting fieldwork in a migrant farmworking community in California's Central Valley for more than a decade. Her new book, *"They Leave Their Kidneys in the Fields": Injury, Illness, and "Illegality" Among US Farmworkers* (University of California Press, 2016), explores the social and political production of heat death among migrant farmworkers.

Alejandro Lugo is a professor and director of the School of Transborder Studies at Arizona State University. For twenty years (1995–2015), he taught at the University of Illinois at Urbana-Champaign in the Department of Anthropology and the Department of Latina/Latino Studies. While at Urbana, he also served as director of graduate studies in anthropology and as associate dean of the Graduate College. He has also taught at Bryn Mawr College in Pennsylvania and at the University of Texas at El Paso. He has published in such journals as *Cultural Anthropology* and *Cultural Dynamics* and most recently (2015) in *Religion and Society: Advances in Research*. His most recent book, *Fragmented Lives, Assembled Parts: Culture, Capitalism, and Conquest* (University of Texas Press, 2008) received the 2008 Southwest Book Award and the 2009 Association of Latina and Latino Anthropologists (ALLA) book award. He has been on the editorial boards of the journals *Aztlán* and *Reviews in Anthropology*, and he has served as an associate editor of the journal *Latino Studies*.

Luminița-Anda Mandache is a PhD candidate in sociocultural anthropology at the School of Anthropology at the University of Arizona. Her dissertation research focuses on the impacts of "alternative" economies in local development in a context of extreme poverty and violence in northeast Brazil.

Corina Marrufo graduated with a BA in psychology in 2015. She is currently a master's of social work student at the University of Texas at El Paso. She has been a member of the Society of Saint Vincent de Paul since 2013 and conducts home visits with low-income families and individuals. During her undergraduate career, she conducted service learning in a food pantry located in Horizon City, Texas.

Guillermina Gina Núñez-Mchiri is an associate professor of anthropology and interim director of women's and gender studies at the University of Texas at El Paso. She has a PhD in cultural anthropology from UC Riverside (2006), where she studied under the mentorship of Dr. Carlos G. Vélez-Ibáñez, Dr. Maria Cruz-Torres, and Dr. Michael Kearney. She conducts research on the U.S.-Mexico border, Latinas in STEM fields, and service learning and ethnography across the higher education curriculum.

Anna Ochoa O'Leary is an associate professor and head of the Mexican American Studies Department at the University of Arizona. She holds a doctorate in cultural anthropology from that institution. In 2006 she was awarded a Fulbright scholarship to research the project "Women at the Intersection: Immigration Enforcement and Transnational Migration on the U.S.-Mexico Border," in which migrant women's encounters with immigration enforcement agents was examined. She has published numerous research articles in both English and Spanish on migration and gender, has published a Chicano Studies textbook (Kendall Hunt, 2007), is a co-editor (with Colin Deeds and Scott Whiteford) of *Unchartered Terrain: New Directions in Border Research Method and Ethics* (University of Arizona Press, 2013), and has edited a two-volume reference work, *Undocumented Immigrants in the United States Today: An Encyclopedia of Their Experiences* (ABC-Clio/Greenwood Press, 2014).

Luis F. B. Plascencia is an independent scholar and received his PhD in social anthropology from the University of Texas at Austin in 2005. His book *Disenchanting Citizenship: Mexican Migrant and the Boundaries of Belonging* was published in 2012 (Rutgers University Press). His recent book chapters and journal articles include "Attrition Through Enforcement and the Elimination of a 'Dangerous Class'" in *Latino Politics and International Relations: The Case of Arizona's Immigration Law SB1070*, edited by Lisa Magaña and Eric Lee (Springer, 2013); "State-Sanctioned Coercion and Agricultural Contract Labor: Jamaican and Mexican Workers in Canada and the United States, 1909–2014" in *On Coerced Labour: Work Compulsion After Chattel Slavery*, edited by Marcel van der Linden and Magaly Rodríguez García (Brill, in press); and "The Military Gates to U.S. Citizenship: Latina/o 'Alien and Noncitizen Nationals' and Military Work," *Latino Studies* (2015).

Lucero Radonic is an assistant professor in the Department of Anthropology and the Environmental Science and Policy Program at Michigan State University. She focuses on human-environmental relationships, particularly the political ecology of water resources. Her research is directed toward developing a better collective understanding of water governance across rural and urban spaces by examining the interconnections between urbanization, water rights, and cultural politics in Latin America and the U.S. Southwest.

Diana Riviera received her PhD in conflict analysis and resolution from Nova Southeastern University in 2014, where she is also the associate director of Licensure and State Relations. Her research on the borderlands is centered on how single mothers navigate and negotiate this landscape while raising their children. Other research interests include identity, ethnic conflict, grit, food insecurity, life on the borderlands, and marginalization.

Thomas E. Sheridan is a research anthropologist at the Southwest Center and Professor of Anthropology at the School of Anthropology at the University of Arizona. He is the author or editor of fourteen books, including *Arizona: A History* (rev. ed., University of Arizona Press, 2012) and *Moquis and Kastiilam: Hopis, Spaniards, and the Trauma of History* (University of Arizona Press, 2015). His research interests include the relations between conservation and communities; the production of space; wilderness and working landscapes; common property theory; ranching, urbanization, and environmentalism; and the political ecology of the American West and northern Mexico.

Kathleen Staudt is a professor of political science and Endowed Professor of Western Hemispheric Trade Policy Studies at the University of Texas at El Paso (UTEP). She received her PhD from the University of Wisconsin in 1976. Among other books, she has edited and authored ten books about the U.S.-Mexico border, the latest of which is *Courage, Resistance, and Women in Ciudad Juárez: Challenges to Militarization* (University of Texas Press, 2015) with Zulma Y. Méndez. She founded UTEP's Center for Civic Engagement, led it for ten years, and is active in community organizations. Kathy recently completed a term on the Association for Borderlands Studies Board and is finishing a comparative borders book titled *Border Politics in a Global Era*.

Carlos G. Vélez-Ibáñez, after professorships and serving as dean at other universities, presently is the Regents' Professor and Founding Director Emeritus of the School of Transborder Studies and Motorola Presidential Professor of Neighborhood Revitalization at Arizona State University. He received a PhD in anthropology from the University of California at San Diego in 1975. His intellectual interests are broadly comparative, with a focus on political ecology and economy. His publications include eleven books in English and Spanish and numerous chapters and articles. His honors are numerous, including the Bronislaw Malinowski Medal; the Robert Textor Prize for Anticipatory Anthropology; Fellow, American Association for the Advancement of Science, 1999; Fellow, Center for Advanced Study in the Behavioral Sciences, Palo Alto, California, 1993–94; Fellow, American Anthropology Association; and Fellow, Society of Applied Anthropology. In 2015, he was named Corresponding Member of the Mexican Academy of Sciences.

INDEX